THE
MEAT AND
POTATOES
COOKBOOK

Other Cookbooks by
Maria Luisa Scott and Jack Denton Scott

The Complete Book of Pasta

Feast of France
(with Antoine Gilly)

Informal Dinners for Easy Entertaining

Mastering Microwave Cooking

The Best of the Pacific Cookbook

Cook Like a Peasant, Eat Like a King

The Chicken and the Egg Cookbook

The Complete Convection Oven Cookbook

The Great American Family Cookbook

The Complete Book of Pies

A World of Pasta

Rice: *More Than 250 Unexpected*
Ways to Cook the Perfect Food

The New Complete Book of Pasta
(A Classic Revisited)

Maria Luisa Scott & Jack Denton Scott

THE
MEAT AND
POTATOES
COOKBOOK

FARRAR, STRAUS & GIROUX · New York

Published simultaneously in Canada by Collins Publishers, Toronto
Printed in the United States of America
Designed by Jacqueline Schuman
First edition, 1988
Charts of Retail Cuts of Beef, Pork, Lamb, and Veal
courtesy of the National Live Stock and Meat Board
Library of Congress Cataloging-in-Publication Data
Scott, Maria Luisa.
The meat and potatoes cookbook / Maria Luisa Scott and Jack Denton
Scott.—1st ed.
p.   cm.
Includes index.
1. Cookery (Meat)   2. Cookery (Potatoes)   I. Scott, Jack Denton.
II. Title.
TX749.S33   1988
641.6′6—dc19   88-9741
BOMC offers recordings and compact discs, cassettes
and records. For information and catalog write to
BOMR, Camp Hill, PA 17012.

C O N T E N T S

Foreword xi

P A R T O N E
MEAT

1 Appetizers and First Courses *5*

2 Soups *25*

3 Beef *45*

4 Lamb *109*

5 Pork, Ham, and Sausage *151*

6 Veal *203*

7 Variety Meats *245*

P A R T T W O
POTATOES

8 Potato Salads *263*

9 Potato Specialties *273*

10 Classic Potato Dishes *287*

11 Potato Partners *321*

12 Baked Potatoes and Potato Pancakes *361*

Index 379

A C K N O W L E D G M E N T S

Our thanks and appreciation for
guidance and expertise go to
Thomas J. McDermott, vice president of Information Programs of
the National Live Stock and Meat Board, and Roger Berglund, Director
of Public Information of the National Cattlemen's Association.

F O R E W O R D

Someone has said, probably Joseph Conrad, who made several astute observations regarding cookbooks, that of all books cookbooks are the most difficult to write, since readers act upon the words that they read. We take this responsibility seriously.

That's why as a team we each test all the recipes in our books, believing that four eyes and hands are better than two. Also, at the beginning of our books, we believe in sharing information with our readers that may be helpful to them in understanding the authors' beliefs and background. Thus, the fact that our professions have fortunately sent us around the world a dozen times, collecting information for magazine articles, books, and novels (all the while also collecting recipes and talking with chefs, cooks, restaurant owners, friends, and acquaintances about food), is pertinent.

Our readers should also know how lucky we are to have had Antoine Gilly as a friend. Antoine owned the famous La Crémaillère restaurant in New York City, and later its successor, La Crémaillère à la Campagne, in Banksville, New York, near Greenwich, Connecticut; and in addition to cooking in some of France's most prestigious hotels and restaurants, Antoine Gilly was the chef for King George V of England, the Prince of Wales, and Prime Minister Lloyd George.

Our friendship with this talented man produced perhaps the longest cooking course on record. We learned and worked with Antoine in his kitchen in Wilton, Connecticut, in Banksville, and in our kitchen in Washington, Connecticut, for over ten years, not only smoothing out the rough spots in our techniques, but learning a philosophy that serves us well today.

We learned early to scorn fads, trends, and gimmicks. Today, too many in the food media (books, magazines, newspapers, television), to keep themselves in the limelight, think they must relentlessly present the public with new tastes and textures. These often include weird and outrageous offerings that are an insult to and an assault on good taste.

Perhaps the most important lesson we have learned over the years is that in all cooking each ingredient should harmonize with, but not be confused with, the others. Good cooks feel that the pleasure of eating is enhanced by preserving the characteristic taste of separate ingredients, more than by blending them, no matter how artistically. Their approach is straightforward.

The best cooks do not resort to artifice. Good, simple cooking is, in fact, often more difficult to achieve than the elaborate, which resorts to masking with sauces and fiddling with colors. We do not condemn sauces, wines, and spices. Used properly, so that they do not destroy or submerge the personality of the dish, they can be a decided asset. But keep the touch delicate. Nowhere in all of cookdom is simple, superb cooking more perfectly illustrated than in a piece of pink, juicy, perfectly cooked roast beef.

The old European saying that good cooking begins in the market is especially true of the preparation of meat, and the United States has the best meat in the world. With this book, and with the tried-and-true recipes we have gathered from Europe and elsewhere, we have attempted to help you preserve the identity of the world's finest food—American meat and potatoes.

MEAT

When Americans entertain at home or in restaurants, their favorite food has always been red meat—beef, lamb, pork, and veal. Regardless of fads, whether they involve Cajun, Creole, Mexican, or California cuisine, when the results are computed, simple, savory, classic red meat has always emerged the winner.

The consumption of red meat in the United States in 1987 totaled 133.7 pounds per person on average. Compare this to the total annual poultry consumption, which includes broilers, mature chickens, and turkeys, at just 78.8 pounds, and it's clear what America prefers.

When we sit down and cut into a tender steak, pink and juicy, we do not consider its nutritional rewards, although they are many. On the edge of a drool, we are anticipating its flavor.

All meat—beef, lamb, pork, and veal—has this special appeal. Why? Because it always tastes good, always satisfies our appetite. It is also so versatile that we never tire of it. In the following chapters this versatility and unfailing appeal are amply illustrated.

But perhaps it would be helpful to begin with a few facts about red meat and nutrition. First of all, only those with a decided cholesterol problem need to worry constantly about fat. Today we are breeding leaner cattle, and meat markets routinely trim off most exterior fat. We can also trim at home. Moreover, three ounces of cooked lean beef contain just 76 milligrams of cholesterol. In comparison, the same amount of roast chicken has 76 milligrams, pork 79 milligrams, shrimp 129 milligrams, and cheddar cheese 90 milligrams. The American Heart Association recommends no more than 300 milligrams of cholesterol daily. Three ounces of red meat thus adds up to no more than 25 percent of that allowance.

In addition, nutritionists identify red meat as nutrient dense. That simply means that red meat offers a high proportion of many essential nutrients and minerals. Three ounces of six of beef's leanest cuts supply men and women with 20 percent of the Recommended Dietary Allowance of niacin, 40 percent of zinc, 76 percent of vitamin B_{12}, 14 percent of riboflavin, and 27 percent of iron. Forty to 60 percent of that iron is heme iron, which is more readily absorbed by the body. Beef also provides 41 percent of the protein we need and that protein contains all eight of the body-building amino acids.

It is commonly assumed that red meat is high in calories. Yet compare these equal portions of meat and chicken. Three ounces of lean beef contain 198 calories; three ounces of baked chicken without skin contain 174 calories, while the same amount of fried chicken has 246 calories. Finally, red meat, especially beef, is said to be difficult to digest. In fact, beef is easier to digest than vegetables. Beef is 97 percent digestible compared to vegetables' 65 percent.*

But with all foods, always let moderation be your guide!

* The above data are from the *Official United States Department of Agriculture Handbook of the Composition of Foods* (United States Department of Agriculture, 1986).

1

Appetizers and First Courses

Appetizer Ham Logs

Basic Batter for Crêpes or Cannelloni

Chopped Beef, Ricotta, and Mozzarella Cannelloni

Meatballs and Peas Cannelloni

Ham and Asparagus Crêpes

Hungarian Goulash Crêpes

Canadian Bacon and Onion Quiche

Edward T. Thompson's Watercress Sausage

Kielbasa Snap-Ups

Greek Lamb Tidbits

Onions Stuffed with Lamb and Mushrooms

Ham-Stuffed Mushrooms

Lamb-Stuffed Mushrooms

Meatballs with Herbs

Sweet and Sour Lamb Meatballs

Pâté of Baby Beef Liver

Pâté of Veal

Salami and Black Olive Crostata

The French are given credit for originating, or at least popularizing, those very thin pancakes, "crêpes." They stuff them with various meats and vegetables, roll them, and serve them either as an appetizer or as a first course. We believe that the Italians originated the idea with their cannelloni, using the same procedure but, in our opinion, more interesting stuffing ingredients. We offer versions of both in this chapter, which also includes delectable quiches, lamb tidbits (the Greek way of tantalizing the appetite), stuffed mushrooms, meatballs, pâtés, and sausages.

Appetizer Ham Logs   MAKES ABOUT 24 APPETIZERS

2 cups ground, cooked ham
1 egg, beaten
¼ teaspoon freshly ground black pepper
Fine bread crumbs for dredging
½ cup prepared horseradish
1 tablespoon Düsseldorf mustard, or one of your choice
⅛ teaspoon celery salt
Vegetable oil for deep frying

1. In a bowl, combine and mix well the ham, egg, and pepper. Shape into 1-inch logs. Dredge with bread crumbs. Cover and refrigerate for 1 hour.
2. In a bowl, combine and blend well the horseradish, mustard, and celery salt. Cover and chill.
3. In a deep fryer or heavy saucepan, heat the cooking oil to 365°. Cook a few logs at a time, not crowding them in the fryer, until golden (about 2 or 3 minutes). Remove with a slotted spoon and drain on paper towels. Serve while still hot with the horseradish-mustard sauce.

Basic Batter for Crêpes or Cannelloni

TO MAKE
APPROXIMATELY
24 SIX-INCH CRÊPES

1 cup medium cream

1 cup water (other liquids, such as club soda, broth, or tomato juice, can be substituted to give the crêpe flavor)

4 eggs

1 teaspoon salt

2 cups sifted all-purpose white flour (measure after sifting)

3½ tablespoons melted unsalted butter

1. Combine all ingredients, except the melted butter, in an electric blender container. Blend at high speed, covered, for 1½ minutes. Scrape flour sticking to the sides down into the batter. Add the melted butter, cover and blend for another half minute. It is important that this batter rest (right in the blender jar) in the refrigerator for 3 hours before using. This gives the flour time to expand in the liquids, a process that produces light and tender crêpes. The batter should be the consistency of medium cream, and should coat a spoon. If too heavy, it not only makes thick crêpes but spreads too slowly in the pan, so that lumps appear in the center. If necessary, the batter can be thinned by stirring in small amounts of milk. After you remove the crêpe batter from the refrigerator, blend it again. A true crêpe is parchment-thin. Thus you must be careful about the amount of batter you pour into the pan. We use a spouted glass jigger marked in ounces and pour in just under 1 ounce for a 5-inch crêpe; just barely over an ounce for a 6-inch crêpe. In tablespoons this would be 1½ tablespoons for a 5-inch and just under 2 tablespoons for a 6-inch crêpe. A small ladle is handy, but after cooking a few crêpes, you'll easily work out the precise amount of batter.

2. Brush the crêpe pan lightly with oil. Place it over high heat, testing it with a drop of cold water. When the water droplet evaporates instantly, the pan is ready. Reduce heat to medium. Place the blender jar with batter in a convenient place, a long spoon beside it to stir the batter frequently. Pour the measured batter into

the still-hot pan; quickly tip the pan in several directions to completely cover the bottom with a thin coating of batter. If there is excess batter, pour it back into the blender jar. Place the pan on medium heat (if holes appear in the crêpe, spoon a small amount of batter just to cover) and when the crêpe begins to look dry, is bubbling from the center and browning slightly around the edges, loosen those edges with a spatula and flip it over. The entire cooking operation takes a total of 1 minute for both sides, more for the first side than for the second. With practice you'll get the timing.

3. The first is a test. You can discard it. You'll note that the side cooked first will be golden brown, more attractive than the spotty second side. That's as it should be. The second side is the inside, the portion that is filled and doesn't show. Stack the cooked crêpes on top of one another; this keeps them moist and in shape.

Chopped Beef, Ricotta, and Mozzarella Cannelloni   SERVES 6

2 tablespoons olive oil
1 medium-sized onion, minced
1 pound ground chuck or round steak
1 garlic clove, minced
2 tablespoons minced parsley
Salt and freshly ground black pepper to taste
1½ pounds fresh ricotta (put in a strainer over a bowl to drain)
1 egg yolk
1½ cups grated Parmesan cheese
1 teaspoon sugar
12 six-inch crêpes (p. 7)
12 slices of mozzarella, cut into pieces 4 inches long, ½ inch
    wide, ¼ inch thick
3 cups tomato sauce (homemade or commercial)

1. In a frying pan, over medium heat, heat the oil. Cook the onion until soft. Add the beef, garlic, and parsley, and stir until the beef loses its pink color. Sprinkle with salt and pepper. Remove the beef

from the pan with a slotted spoon and put in a strainer over a bowl to drain off fat and liquid.

2. In a bowl, mix the drained ricotta with the egg yolk, ½ cup Parmesan, and the sugar.

3. Lay out the crêpes. In the center of each, put one slice of the mozzarella, a heaping tablespoon of the ricotta mixture, a table-spoonful of the beef, then a tablespoon of tomato sauce. Roll the crêpes and lay them seam side down (so the mozzarella will be on top), side by side, in a shallow, buttered baking dish. Spoon 2 or 3 tablespoons of tomato sauce over the crêpes and sprinkle with the remaining cheese. Cook in a preheated 375° oven 20 minutes, or until bubbling. A long, narrow spatula is helpful in serving.

Meatballs and Peas Cannelloni

SERVES 6

1 pound chopped chuck or round steak
1 medium-sized onion, minced
1 garlic clove, minced
1 tablespoon minced parsley
3 tablespoons fine bread crumbs
¼ cup dry red wine
3 eggs
1½ cups grated Asiago or Parmesan cheese
Salt and freshly ground black pepper to taste
3 tablespoons olive oil
1 package frozen tiny green peas, slightly undercooked, with 1
  teaspoon sugar added to the water, then drained
2 cups tomato sauce (homemade or commercial)
12 six-inch crêpes (p. 7)

1. Combine and blend well, but lightly, the beef, onion, garlic, parsley, bread crumbs, wine, 1 beaten egg, ⅓ cup cheese, salt, and pepper. Roll into balls about ½ inch in diameter.

2. Heat the olive oil in a frying pan over medium heat, add the balls, and brown evenly. Drain on paper towels.

3. Beat the remaining 2 eggs with ⅓ cup of the cheese. Put the peas and meatballs in a saucepan and, over low heat, stir in the egg-and-cheese mixture and cook a few seconds until the eggs set. Remove from heat, taste for seasoning. Stir in enough tomato sauce to make mixture moist but not soupy.

4. Spoon 2 heaping tablespoons of the mixture onto the lower third of each crêpe. Roll crêpes and lay seam side down, side by side, in a shallow, buttered baking dish. Spoon remaining sauce over the crêpes. Sprinkle with remaining cheese and put in a pre-heated 375° oven 15 minutes, or until heated through and bubbling. A long, narrow spatula is helpful in serving.

Ham and Asparagus Crêpes   SERVES 6

3 tablespoons unsalted butter
3 tablespoons flour
2 cups milk, warmed
Freshly ground black pepper to taste
¼ teaspoon nutmeg
½ cup heavy cream
2 ounces Madeira
1½ cups grated Parmesan cheese
24 slim asparagus stalks (scrape stems and cook in boiling water
    until just tender)
12 thin slices of cooked ham (prosciutto, Virginia, or boiled ham)
12 six-inch crêpes (p. 7)

1. In a saucepan, over medium-low heat, melt the butter. Stir in the flour and cook, stirring, into a smooth paste. Add the milk, a small amount at a time, and simmer, stirring constantly, until it becomes a smooth, medium-thick sauce. Season with pepper. Add the nutmeg. Stir in the cream, Madeira, and half the cheese. Continue cooking, stirring, until the cheese has melted and the sauce thickened. Taste for seasoning.

2. Roll 2 asparagus stalks in a slice of ham. Place on the lower

third of each crêpe. Spoon 1 tablespoon sauce over the ham and roll the crêpe. Lay, seam side down, side by side, in a shallow, buttered baking dish. Spoon sauce over the crêpes, then sprinkle with the remaining cheese.

3. Bake in a preheated 375° oven 15 minutes, or until heated through and golden. A long, narrow spatula is helpful in serving.

Hungarian Goulash Crêpes   SERVES 6

3 tablespoons unsalted butter
1 tablespoon olive oil
1 large onion, finely chopped
1 garlic clove, minced
1½ pounds tenderloin or other tender cut of beef, cut into
   ¼-inch cubes
Salt and freshly ground black pepper to taste
½ teaspoon Hungarian paprika
2 tablespoons flour
1 cup beef broth
½ cup tomato juice
1 cup sour cream
12 six-inch crêpes (p. 7)

1. In a heavy saucepan, over medium heat, heat the butter and oil. Add the onion and garlic, and cook until soft. Do not brown. Add the beef and cook 3 minutes, stirring often. Sprinkle with salt, pepper, paprika, and flour, and blend. Add the beef broth and tomato juice, cover, and cook over low heat until the beef is very tender (about 30 minutes). If liquid cooks off, add a very small amount of hot broth or water to keep a little liquid in the bottom of the pan. Add the sour cream and mix well.

2. Remove the beef and onion with a spoon along with some of the sauce (it should not be soupy, just moist) and place 2 heaping tablespoons on the lower third of each crêpe. Roll crêpes, and place, seam side down, side by side, in a shallow, buttered baking dish.

Spoon the sour-cream sauce over the crêpes and cook in a pre-heated 375° oven 15 minutes, or until heated through. A long, narrow spatula is helpful in serving.

Canadian Bacon and Onion Quiche SERVES 6

5 tablespoons unsalted butter
10 slices Canadian bacon, cut ¼ inch thick
2 cups thinly sliced onions
Salt and freshly ground black pepper to taste
9-inch pastry shell (p. 216), partially baked
½ cup grated Gruyère cheese
¼ cup grated Asiago or Parmesan cheese
2 whole eggs
2 egg yolks
2 cups medium cream
1 ounce dry sherry

1. In a saucepan, over medium heat, melt 2 tablespoons butter. Add the Canadian bacon and cook 15 seconds on each side. Remove, drain, and cut into ½-inch dice.
2. Add the remaining butter to the saucepan, lower heat to medium-low. Add the onions and cook, covered, until soft. Do not brown. If the onion liquid cooks off before the onions are soft, add a small amount of hot water, then cook that off. Sprinkle on salt (remember that the Canadian bacon will supply some salt) and pepper.
3. Distribute the bacon pieces over the bottom of the pastry shell, then the onions over the bacon, and sprinkle the cheeses over the onions. Carefully add a mixture of the eggs, cream, and sherry beaten together.
4. Bake in a preheated 350° oven 30 minutes, or until puffy and golden, and a knife inserted slightly off center comes out clean. Do not overcook. If the top starts getting too brown before the custard is set, cover lightly with aluminum foil.

Edward T. Thompson's Watercress Sausage

MAKES ABOUT
6 POUNDS

When he was editor in chief of *Reader's Digest*, our friend Ed Thompson was known as a fearless and talented editor. He brings those same qualities to his cooking. His creations are always unique—like this sausage, which he rolls into little balls, browns in butter, then spears with toothpicks and offers with drinks. He sometimes varies the recipe by using lean lamb instead of pork.

> 5½ pounds pork shoulder, skinned and boned
> 1 pound pure white pork fat
> 1 tablespoon salt
> 1 tablespoon black pepper (freshly ground is best)
> 1 tablespoon whole caraway seeds
> ½ cup crumbled sage leaves
> 2 cups minced broadleaf parsley
> 2 cups chopped scallions (tops finely chopped, bulbs coarsely
>   chopped)
> 2 cups finely chopped watercress leaves
> 2 teaspoons dill
> 2 teaspoons dried sweet marjoram
> 1 teaspoon dried rosemary
> 2 teaspoons dried oregano
> 2 teaspoons dried tarragon

1. Grind the pork and fat to hamburger consistency. In a large mixing bowl, mix the meat and fat with your hands so they are evenly blended. Add all the other ingredients and blend thoroughly with your hands.

2. In a small frying pan, fry a patty of the mixture to test the seasoning, adjusting if necessary.

3. Shape the sausage into small balls as an appetizer, or into patties the size of your choice, wrap in foil, and freeze.

Note: It is not necessary to thaw these sausage patties before cooking, so they're an excellent last-minute meal. We often have them for supper with mashed potatoes and a little lemoned broccoli.

Kielbasa Snap-Ups

SERVES 8

Sausage may be the most satisfying of appetizers. It's the poor sausage that doesn't have personality to spare. These tiny sandwiches will be snapped up so fast you'll wish you had prepared more.

2 pounds smoked kielbasa sausage
1 loaf party-size rye bread (we like Pepperidge Farm)
Kosciusko mustard

1. This sausage is precooked. Regardless, we broil it for 5 minutes, then remove the skin and slice it into rounds.
2. Toast one side of the rye bread slices.
3. Spread untoasted side well with mustard. Cut the slices into halves.
4. Place one sausage round on top of each slice of mustard-spread bread.
5. Slide the sausage-on-bread rounds under the broiler for 2 minutes. Serve hot.

Greek Lamb Tidbits

SERVES 6 TO 8

2 pounds lean lamb from the leg, trimmed and cut into small
   cubes
Salt and freshly ground black pepper
Juice of 3 lemons (at room temperature)
2 teaspoons dried oregano

1. Skewer the cubes of lamb, dividing them into 6 to 8 equal portions. Sprinkle with salt and pepper.
2. Cook over charcoal (or under a broiler), turning frequently, so the meat browns evenly. Do not overcook; the lamb should be pink and juicy inside (about 8 minutes, depending on the size of the cubes).
3. Pour a mixture of the lemon juice and oregano onto a wide, flat plate. Roll the lamb on the skewers in the mixture and broil for 20 seconds on each side.

Onions Stuffed with Lamb and Mushrooms   SERVES 6

6 whole white onions, 3 inches in diameter, peeled, root ends
    scored
2 tablespoons olive oil
1 garlic clove, minced
4 medium-sized mushrooms, finely chopped
1½ cups cooked ground lamb
1 egg, beaten
1 tablespoon tomato puree
2 tablespoons dry white wine
Salt and freshly ground black pepper to taste
⅛ teaspoon nutmeg
½ cup fine bread crumbs
Cream (optional)
1 cup beef broth
1 bay leaf
½ cup grated Asiago or Parmesan cheese

1. In a large saucepan, cook the onions in boiling, salted water for 10 minutes. Drain and cool. With a spoon, carefully scoop out a depression in each onion, leaving a shell about ¼ inch thick. Chop ⅓ of the scooped-out onion.

2. In a frying pan, over medium heat, heat the olive oil. Add the chopped onion and garlic, and cook 5 minutes, or until the onion is soft. Do not brown. Add the mushrooms and cook 2 minutes. Remove from the heat, cool slightly, and stir in the lamb, egg, tomato puree, wine, salt, pepper, and nutmeg, mixing well. Stir in the bread crumbs and, if mixture seems dry, stir in just enough cream to moisten it slightly.

3. Divide the stuffing into 6 portions and mound in the onion shells. Arrange the stuffed onions in a flameproof casserole, large enough to hold them snugly but not touching. Pour the broth around the onions, add the bay leaf, bring to a boil on top of the stove, cover and cook in a preheated 375° oven 20 minutes, or until the onion shells are tender. Remove, sprinkle tops with cheese, and place under the broiler until golden brown.

Ham-Stuffed Mushrooms

SERVES 4

12 large, firm mushrooms
2 tablespoons unsalted butter, melted
3 tablespoons unsalted butter
3 shallots, minced
½ cup soft bread crumbs
1½ cups chopped cooked ham
½ cup finely crumbled Feta cheese
1 tablespoon brandy
Salt and freshly ground black pepper to taste

1. Remove the stems from the mushrooms and mince them. Rub the outsides of the mushroom caps with the melted butter. Lightly salt the insides, and invert on paper towels.
2. Heat half the remaining butter in a saucepan over medium heat. Add the shallots and cook 2 minutes, or until soft. Do not brown. Add the minced mushroom stems. Cook 1 minute. Add remaining ingredients and blend well.
3. Heap the stuffing into the mushroom caps and dot with the remaining butter.
4. Arrange in a shallow baking dish and cook in a preheated 375° oven 15 minutes, or until golden brown and the mushrooms are crisp-tender.

Lamb-Stuffed Mushrooms

TO FILL 36 MUSHROOMS

36 large mushrooms, washed and dried
¼ cup unsalted butter, melted
Juice of 1 lemon
6 tablespoons unsalted butter
1 pound lean ground lamb
2 tablespoons minced parsley
2 tablespoons minced onion
Salt and freshly ground black pepper to taste
¼ cup grated Parmesan cheese

¼ cup grated Swiss cheese
¾ cup fine bread crumbs
½ cup dry sherry

1. Cut the stems off the mushrooms and chop them finely. Dip the outside of the caps in the melted butter. Sprinkle the insides with lemon juice.
2. In a frying pan, heat 4 tablespoons butter. Add the lamb, mushroom stems, parsley, and onion, cooking until the lamb is still fairly pink. Sprinkle with salt and pepper.
3. In a bowl, combine and blend well (but lightly) the lamb mixture, grated cheese, ½ cup bread crumbs, and sherry.
4. Shake the lemon juice from the mushroom caps and divide the lamb mixture evenly among them. Sprinkle lightly with the remaining bread crumbs and dot with the remaining butter. Bake in a preheated 375° oven 15 to 20 minutes. Serve hot.

Meatballs with Herbs   SERVES 8 TO 10

1 pound ground lean beef, top or bottom round
½ pound ground lean pork
1 medium-sized onion, finely chopped
1 teaspoon salt
½ teaspoon freshly ground black pepper
1 cup finely chopped mixed fresh herbs, such as dill, parsley,
   tarragon, thyme, oregano, marjoram, chives
4 tablespoons (½ stick) unsalted butter
2 tablespoons olive oil
2 tablespoons flour
1½ cups beef broth
¾ cup sour cream

1. In a large bowl, combine and blend well (your hands are good for this) the beef, pork, onion, salt, and pepper. Make bite-sized meatballs.

2. Spread the herbs on waxed paper and roll the meatballs in the herb mixture.

3. Heat the butter and oil in a frying pan over low heat. Add the meatballs and cook, covered, turning occasionally, for 20 minutes, or until cooked through. Remove from pan and keep warm.

4. Stir the flour into the pan, mixing well. Slowly stir in the beef broth, cooking and stirring until it becomes a smooth, medium-thick sauce. Add the sour cream and blend well without boiling. Taste for seasoning. Return the meatballs to the pan; mix well with the sauce. Heat through without boiling and serve with toothpicks.

Sweet and Sour Lamb Meatballs   TO MAKE 30 TO 40 MEATBALLS

1½ pounds lean ground lamb
½ cup fine bread crumbs
1 egg, beaten
¼ cup beef broth
Salt and freshly ground black pepper to taste
⅔ cup sweet-and-sour sauce (found in jars in specialty food stores)
½ can (8½ ounces) crushed pineapple with juice
¼ cup chopped scallions
¼ cup diced green pepper
2 tablespoons grated carrot
1½ tablespoons white vinegar
1½ tablespoons soy sauce

1. In a bowl, combine and blend well, but lightly, the lamb, bread crumbs, egg, beef broth, salt, and black pepper. Shape into balls about ¾ inch in diameter. Place the meatballs on a baking sheet with sides. Broil 4 inches from the heat 7 to 10 minutes, shaking pan gently to cook and brown evenly. Remove from oven and drain on paper towels.

2. In a saucepan, combine and blend the sweet-and-sour sauce, pineapple and juice, scallions, green pepper, carrot, vinegar, and

soy sauce. Simmer about 20 minutes. Add the meatballs and stir gently, spooning sauce over them until they are well coated and heated through.

Pâté of Baby Beef Liver

FILLS SIX 5⅔-INCH × 3¼-INCH × 2-INCH LOAF PANS

1 pound unsalted fatback with streaks of lean (labeled in some stores Pork for Beans), blanched in simmering water for 10 minutes, drained, dried, cooled (rind removed and discarded)
3 pounds baby beef liver, trimmed
2 large onions, chopped, cooked in 3 tablespoons butter until soft (do not brown)
5 tablespoons unsalted butter
5 tablespoons flour
1 pint heavy cream
1 teaspoon salt, or to taste
½ teaspoon freshly ground black pepper, or to taste
4 large eggs, beaten
1 tablespoon salt
1½ teaspoons freshly ground black pepper
1½ teaspoons ground allspice
⅛ teaspoon dried thyme
⅛ teaspoon dried tarragon
½ teaspoon seasoned salt
¼ teaspoon ground nutmeg
2 garlic cloves, pushed through a garlic press
6 ounces brandy

1. Cut up and put the fatback and liver through a meat grinder, using the fine blade. Mix well with the cooked onions. Puree mixture in a food processor (or blender) until it is blended well. Transfer to a large bowl.
2. In a saucepan, over medium heat, melt the butter; stir in the flour, blending into a smooth, golden paste. Lower heat and stir in

the cream, a small amount at a time, stirring until it becomes a smooth, thick sauce. Season with salt and pepper.

3. Beat the cream sauce into the bowl with the fatback and liver. Mix together the beaten eggs and the remaining ingredients and blend thoroughly with the liver and cream mixture. Lightly butter six small loaf tins, and fill each three-quarters full.

4. Place the tins in a pan of hot water, with the water coming midway up the sides of the pâté tin. Cover pâté with foil. Cook in a preheated 350° oven on center rack 45 minutes, or until a knife or skewer inserted into the center of the pâté comes out clean.

5. Let pâté cool briefly. Cover with waxed paper or plastic wrap; place pâté in its loaf pan on a plate with a depression to catch the drippings, arrange a weight on top of the pâté, and refrigerate, preferably overnight. The weight should be distributed evenly, pressing the liver loaf into the firm, compressed, classic pâté shape. We use a wooden block (for the small ones), with a regular building brick on top.

6. Serve the pâté as an appetizer or as a first course at dinner.
Note: The pâté is rich. We find that it is better to have a small pâté, freshly cooked and eagerly eaten, than a large one partially leftover in the refrigerator. This pâté can also be cooked in a Pyrex or metal loaf pan, if you are serving a large number of people. It can be frozen, uncooked, in the foil tins but defrost it before cooking.

Pâté of Veal   SERVES 10

This dish is a favorite in Burgundy, when the grapes have been harvested and wine and food are in order for the celebration. It makes a delicious appetizer served with toast and cornichons, small sour tarragon pickles. It is also an elegant first course.

1 pound veal leg, cut into ¼-inch strips
3 pounds boned veal (the lean portions of veal shank are excellent), cut into small chunks.

¾ pound lean pork from loin or shoulder, cut up into small
   chunks
½ pound slice of ham (with its fat), cut up into small chunks
½ pound pork fatback, with streaks of lean (labeled in some
   stores as Pork for Beans), blanched in simmering water for 5
   minutes (rind removed and discarded), cut up
2 tablespoons butter
2 medium-sized onions, chopped
2 garlic cloves, chopped
1 tablespoon salt
¼ teaspoon thyme
¾ teaspoon quatre épices (see p. 22)
¼ cup flour
¼ cup brandy
1 cup dry white wine
3 eggs

1. Butter a 9 × 5 × 4-inch loaf pan or terrine. Set aside the strips
of lean veal. Put the veal chunks, lean pork, ham, and fatback
through the fine blade of a meat grinder, or use a food processor,
grinding in small batches and not overprocessing. Place the ground
meats in a large bowl.
2. In a saucepan, over medium heat, melt the butter and cook the
onions and garlic 3 minutes, or until soft. Do not brown. Stir the
onions and garlic into the ground meats, add the salt, thyme, and
quatre épices.
3. Place the flour in another bowl. Add the brandy and wine in
small amounts, mixing constantly and adding only enough liquid
to form a smooth paste. Beat the eggs into this flour mixture. Stir
the beaten egg mixture and the remaining brandy and wine into
the ground meat. Blend well (your hands work best). Cover and
marinate 4 hours or, even better, overnight in the refrigerator.
4. When you are ready to cook the pâté, spread a ½-inch layer
of the ground-meat mixture on the bottom of the buttered terrine
or loaf pan. Arrange three rows of lean veal strips over this layer

of meat, the full length of the pan. Repeat layers, alternating force-meat and strips of veal, ending with a layer of forcemeat.

5. Cover snugly with a sheet of foil. Place in a *bain marie* (a shallow pan of hot water, with the water coming halfway up the sides of the loaf pan). Cook on the center rack in a preheated 325° oven for 2 hours. The pâté is cooked when a skewer or a thin knife blade pushed into its center comes out clean.

6. Cool. Leave foil on. Place a weight on top (an ordinary building brick works well) and refrigerate overnight.

The pâté keeps for a week in the refrigerator.

QUATRE ÉPICES   2 TABLESPOONS

> 1 tablespoon freshly ground black pepper
> 1 teaspoon ground cloves
> 1 teaspoon grated nutmeg
> 1 teaspoon ground cinnamon

Combine all the ingredients in a jar and shake well to mix thoroughly.

Salami and Black Olive Crostata   SERVES 6

> 1 nine-inch pastry shell, partially baked (p. 216)
> 8 thin slices of salami, cut into ½-inch squares
> 12 large black olives (the plump, purplish ones, not the wrinkled ones), pitted and halved
> 2 whole eggs
> 3 egg yolks
> 1½ cups medium cream, or half-and-half
> ½ teaspoon salt
> ¼ teaspoon freshly ground black pepper
> 1 tablespoon flour

1 large, ripe tomato, peeled, seeded, chopped, drained in a strainer
½ cup grated Fontina cheese
½ cup grated Asiago or Parmesan cheese

1. Cover the bottom of the pastry shell with the salami. Scatter the olives over the salami.

2. In a bowl, combine and lightly beat together the eggs, egg yolks, cream, salt, pepper, and flour. Stir in the tomato, the Fontina cheese, and one half of the Asiago cheese. Spoon over the salami and olives. Sprinkle the remaining Asiago on top.

3. Bake in a preheated 350° oven 30 minutes, or until set, puffed, and golden, and a knife inserted just off center comes out clean. Do not overcook. If the top starts browning before the custard is set, cover lightly with aluminum foil. Serve immediately.

2

Soups

Alsatian Soup
Beef (or Oxtail) Soup
Beef, Barley, and Mushroom Soup
Beef Stock
Borscht
Dutch Meat and Potato Soup
German Lentil Soup
Ham, Leek, and Succotash Soup with Croutons
Hungarian Lamb Soup
Chilled Potato Beet Soup
Soup Parmentier
Potato and Cheese Soup
Potato Corn Chowder
Pork Meatball and Swiss Chard Soup
Sausage and Pasta Soup
Scotch Broth
Veal Ragout Soup
Vernon Jarratt's Golden Soup
Vichyssoise
White Stock

Soup may be our oldest food. Archaeologists uncovered evidence of a carbonized hippopotamus tooth in a cooking pot which they dug up in the Faiyum basin in Egypt, dated 6000 B.C. The word for all soups probably evolved from the German *sop*, the bread over which broth, pottage, or hot liquid was poured. Every nation has its own word: *chupe, soop, sopa, sope, soepe, suppa, soppe, soep, suppe, soppa, sopreo, soupe, zuppa, zup*. Some of the best soups stem from meat and potatoes.

Alsatian Soup   SERVES 6

   ¼ pound salt pork, blanched in boiling water 5 minutes, drained, dried, and cut into ¼-inch cubes
   ½ pound lean pork, cut into ½-inch cubes
   3 medium-sized slender carrots, scraped, cut into bite-sized pieces
   6 small white onions, peeled, root ends scored
   2 celery stalks, scraped and cut into bite-sized pieces
   1 parsnip, scraped, cut into bite-sized pieces
   1 bay leaf
   1 veal bone, cracked
   6 cups chicken broth
   2 medium-sized potatoes, cut into ½-inch cubes
   1 small, firm cabbage (about 1 pound), core removed, finely shredded
   3 small leeks (white part only), thoroughly washed, each cut into bite-sized slices
   ½ pound garlic sausage, cut into bite-sized slices
   Salt and freshly ground black pepper to taste

1. In a large soup pot, over medium heat, cook the salt pork until it has rendered its fat and is golden. Remove with a slotted spoon and drain on paper towels. Reserve. If there is excessive fat, pour off all but 3 tablespoons. Add the pork and cook 2 minutes, stirring. Remove with a slotted spoon and reserve with the salt pork. Add

the carrots, onions, celery, and parsnip, and cook 2 minutes, stirring. Remove vegetables and reserve.

2. Return the pork and salt pork to the soup pot. Add the bay leaf, the veal bone, and the chicken broth. Bring to a boil. Lower heat and simmer, covered, 45 minutes. Add the reserved vegetables and cook 15 minutes.

3. Add the potatoes, cabbage, leeks, and sausage, and cook 45 minutes, or until the pork and vegetables are tender.

4. Taste for seasoning before adding salt and pepper.

5. Serve, dividing the vegetables among 6 soup bowls.

If the soup seems too thick for your taste, add more hot broth.

Beef (or Oxtail) Soup   SERVES 6

STEP 1

> *5 tablespoons unsalted butter*
> *1 tablespoon olive oil*
> *2 pounds soup beef on the bone cut into 2-inch pieces,*
> * or 2 pounds oxtail, cut into 2-inch pieces*
> *2 medium-sized onions, sliced*
> *2 medium-sized carrots, sliced*
> *2 celery stalks, sliced*
> *1 garlic clove, peeled*
> *1 cup tomato juice*
> *8 cups beef broth*
> *1 bouquet garni (2 parsley sprigs, 1 bay leaf, ½ teaspoon dried*
> * thyme, and a handful of celery leaves tied in cheesecloth)*
> *½ teaspoon crushed black peppercorns*
> *Salt to taste*
> *2 tablespoons flour*

1. In a large soup pot, heat 3 tablespoons butter and the oil, and brown the beef. Transfer it to a bowl. Add the onions, carrots, celery, and garlic, and cook until soft and golden. Do not brown.

2. Return the beef to the pot with any liquid that has accumulated

in the bowl. Pour in the tomato juice and beef broth. Add the bouquet garni and peppercorns. Simmer, partially covered, for 3 hours, or until the beef is tender, skimming off the top as necessary. Remove the beef from the bone, dice the meat, and set aside.

3. Strain the broth into a large bowl, discarding the vegetables. Let settle and skim off the fat. Taste for seasoning and add salt if necessary. The beef broth may supply enough salt.

4. In a frying pan, over medium heat, melt the remaining 2 table-spoons butter. Stir in the flour and cook, stirring, until golden. Gradually stir in 2 cups of broth and blend well. Return the broth to the soup pot and add the flour mixture, blending well.

STEP 2

> ½ *cup Madeira*
> ½ *cup finely diced cooked carrots*
> ½ *cup finely diced cooked celery*
> ½ *cup finely diced cooked turnips*
> *Reserved diced beef*

Add the Madeira to the soup pot; bring to a boil. Add the cooked vegetables and meat. Heat through and serve.

Beef, Barley, and Mushroom Soup   SERVES 6

> *2 pounds shin beef on the bone*
> *1 large onion*
> *2 cloves*
> *2 leeks, well washed, sliced*
> *1 celery stalk, sliced*
> *1 medium-sized carrot, sliced*
> *2 teaspoons salt*
> ½ *teaspoon freshly ground black pepper*
> *3 quarts water*
> *1 cup barley*
> ½ *pound small mushrooms, thinly sliced*

3 tablespoons unsalted butter
1 tablespoon fresh lemon juice
Chopped parsley

1. Place the beef, onion studded with cloves, leeks, celery, carrot, salt, pepper, and water in a soup pot and bring to a boil. Lower heat and cook, partially covered, for 2 hours, or until the beef is tender, skimming the top as necessary.
2. Remove the beef, cool and dice it. Set aside. Discard the bone.
3. Strain the stock, return it to the pot, and over medium-high heat, uncovered, reduce to half its volume. Add the barley and cook ½ hour, or until tender.
4. Cook the mushrooms in the butter and lemon juice 2 minutes. Add the mushrooms (and the liquid they cooked in) and the meat to the soup pot. Simmer 10 minutes. Taste for seasoning. Serve sprinkled with parsley.

Beef Stock   MAKES ABOUT 2 QUARTS

A good beef stock is useful to have on hand for soups and sauces. It freezes well.

4 pounds beef, shank or shin, cut into 2- or 3-inch pieces
5 quarts cold water
2 large beef bones with marrow
1 tablespoon salt
8 peppercorns
6 medium-sized white onions, 3 studded with 1 whole clove
2 large leeks, well washed, each cut into 3 pieces
2 celery stalks (including leaves), scraped and each cut into 3
    pieces
3 carrots, scraped and each cut into 3 pieces
4 parsley sprigs
2 small bay leaves

1. Place the beef and bones in a large soup pot. Add the water (it

should cover the beef by 2 inches; if not, add more). Bring to a boil. Reduce heat until the water barely simmers. Skim the foam from the surface as it forms. Stir in all the other ingredients.

2. Cook at a bare simmer, partially covered, stirring occasionally and skimming the top when necessary, about 5 hours.

3. At the end of that period, taste stock for strength and seasoning. If desired stronger, continue to cook until it suits your taste.

4. Strain through 2 or 3 layers of cheesecloth set in a strainer.

5. Place stock in refrigerator overnight. Remove the solidified fat. Ladle out the stock, leaving the sediment in the bottom to be discarded.

6. Freeze the stock in pint or half-pint containers.

Note: The meat can be cut up and used for hash or for a hearty soup for supper.

Borscht   SERVES 6 TO 8

4 tablespoons (½ stick) unsalted butter
3 large beets, scraped and grated
1 small carrot, scraped and grated
1 medium-sized onion, chopped
1 garlic clove, minced
2 celery stalks (with leaves), scraped (chop the leaves and thinly slice the stalks)
2 tablespoons white vinegar
1 teaspoon sugar
3 medium-sized, firm, ripe tomatoes, peeled, seeded, and finely chopped
2 medium-sized potatoes, peeled and cut into ¾-inch cubes
2 cups finely shredded cabbage (do not use core)
2 quarts beef broth
1 pound boiled beef, cut into ¾-inch cubes
Salt and freshly ground black pepper to taste
Sour cream
2 tablespoons chopped fresh dill or parsley

1. In a large saucepan or soup pot, over medium heat, melt the butter. Add the beets, carrot, onion, garlic, celery (and leaves), vinegar, sugar, and half the tomatoes. Cover and cook 15 minutes. Add the potatoes and cabbage and cook 10 minutes, or until the potatoes are just tender.

2. Add the broth, beef, and remaining tomatoes, and cook 10 to 15 minutes to heat through and until the potatoes are cooked. Taste for seasoning; then add salt and pepper.

3. Ladle into bowls and float a dollop of sour cream on top. Sprinkle with dill or parsley.

Dutch Meat and Potato Soup   SERVES 6

2 tablespoons unsalted butter
1 tablespoon olive oil
1 pound lean beef chuck, cut into ½-inch cubes
2 large onions, coarsely chopped
1 teaspoon caraway seeds
½ teaspoon thyme
1 garlic clove, minced
1 teaspoon sweet Hungarian paprika
2 tablespoons flour
3 tablespoons red wine vinegar
7 cups beef broth
3 medium-sized potatoes, peeled and cut into ½-inch cubes
Salt to taste
2 tablespoons chopped fresh chives

1. Heat the butter and oil over medium-high heat in a large saucepan or soup pot. Add the beef and onion, and cook, stirring occasionally, until the onion is golden.

2. Lower heat to medium-low. Add the caraway, thyme, and garlic. Sprinkle in the paprika and flour, and cook, stirring, until they are well blended. Stir in the vinegar.

3. Gradually stir in 2 cups of the broth. Pour in the remaining

broth, bring to a boil, lower heat, and simmer, uncovered, 45 minutes, or until the beef is almost tender. Add the potatoes and cook 30 minutes, or until the beef and potatoes are tender. Taste for seasoning before adding salt.

4. Sprinkle with chopped chives.

German Lentil Soup   SERVES 6 TO 8

1 cup dried lentils, picked over
2 tablespoons unsalted butter
5 slices lean, thick-sliced bacon, diced
1 medium-sized onion, thinly sliced
1 medium-sized carrot, scraped and thinly sliced
1 celery stalk, scraped and thinly sliced
1 ham bone or smoked ham hock
6 cups beef broth
2 medium-sized potatoes, peeled and cut into ½-inch cubes
1 bay leaf
⅛ teaspoon dried marjoram
Salt and freshly ground black pepper to taste
2 knockwurst, skinned and cut into ¼-inch-thick slices
1 cup medium cream

1. Rinse the lentils in several changes of water. Cover with water and soak 5 hours. Do not discard the water.
2. Over medium heat, melt the butter in a pot large enough to hold all the ingredients. Add the bacon and onion, and cook until the onion is soft. Add the carrot, celery, ham bone, lentils (with the water they soaked in), and beef broth. Cover the pot and simmer 1 hour. Add the potatoes, bay leaf, and marjoram. Simmer, covered, 30 minutes, or until the potatoes and lentils can be mashed against the side of the pot. Taste and season with salt and pepper.
3. Add the knockwurst slices and simmer, uncovered, 10 minutes. Stir in the cream and heat just to a boil. Discard the bay leaf.
Note: If preferred, the soup can be pureed in a blender or a food

processor, but instead of dicing the bacon, cut it into large pieces so they can be removed before pureeing, along with the ham bone and bay leaf. After pureeing, add the sausage slices and cream, and heat.

Ham, Leek, and Succotash Soup with Croutons

SERVES 6 TO 8

3 tablespoons unsalted butter
6 small leeks (using all the white part and some of the light-green part), thoroughly washed, cut into 1-inch pieces
2 medium-sized carrots, scraped and cut into 1-inch-long, thin strips
6 cups chicken broth
2 cups 1-inch-long, thin strips of cooked ham
1 ten-ounce package frozen baby lima beans, defrosted
1 ten-ounce package frozen corn kernels, defrosted
Salt and freshly ground black pepper to taste
Croutons (see below)

1. In a large saucepan or soup pot, heat the butter. Stir in the leeks and carrots, and cook until soft, stirring from time to time. Do not brown.
2. Stir in the broth, ham, lima beans, and corn. Cook, uncovered, stirring once or twice, for 15 minutes, or until the limas and corn are tender. Taste for seasoning before adding salt and pepper.
3. Serve with the croutons floating on top.
If the soup is too thick, add more chicken broth.

CROUTONS

3 tablespoons unsalted butter
4 slices white bread (crusts removed), cut into ½-inch cubes

In a large frying pan, heat the butter. Add the bread cubes and cook, stirring and shaking the pan, until golden brown. Drain on paper towels.

Hungarian Lamb Soup

SERVES 6

1 pound lean lamb, cut into ½-inch cubes

6 cups White Stock (p. 43)

3 medium-sized, ripe tomatoes (peeled, seeded), finely chopped

1 green pepper (seeds and white ribs removed and discarded),
  finely chopped

1 medium-sized carrot, scraped and finely chopped

1 medium-sized onion, finely chopped

1 medium-sized potato, peeled and cut into ½-inch cubes

2 tablespoons unsalted butter

2 tablespoons flour

2 egg yolks

½ cup sour cream

1 tablespoon strained, fresh lemon juice

Salt and freshly ground black pepper to taste

2 tablespoons chopped parsley

1. In a soup pot, over medium heat, cook the lamb in the stock until the lamb is almost tender.

2. Add the tomatoes, green pepper, carrot, onion, and potato, and cook, partially covered, until the vegetables are tender-crisp.

3. In a saucepan, over medium heat, melt the butter and stir in the flour, blending into a smooth paste. Gradually add 1 cup of the broth the lamb cooked in and cook, stirring, into a smooth, thick sauce. Stir this back into the soup pot.

4. Reduce heat and add a mixture of the egg yolks, sour cream, and lemon juice, and blend well. Do not boil, but heat through. Taste for seasoning and add salt and pepper if necessary. Sprinkle each serving with parsley.

Chilled Potato Beet Soup

SERVES 4 TO 6

2 cups mashed potatoes

2 cups cooked, chopped beets

4 scallions (white part only), chopped
Salt and freshly ground black pepper to taste
3 tablespoons fresh lemon juice
2 cups beef broth, approximately
½ cup sour cream
2 tablespoons minced fresh dill

1. In the container of an electric blender, combine the potatoes, beets, scallions, salt, pepper, and lemon juice. Cover and blend at high speed. With the motor running, add 1½ cups of the broth. Taste for seasoning. If the soup is too thick, add more broth.
2. Serve chilled, with a large dollop of sour cream and a sprinkling of dill.

Soup Parmentier

SERVES 6 TO 8

Antoine-Auguste Parmentier introduced potatoes to Paris and all of France. Many potato dishes bear his name.

4 medium-sized leeks (white part only)
4 tablespoons (½ stick) unsalted butter
1 medium-sized onion, coarsely chopped
1 carrot, scraped and coarsely chopped
1 celery stalk, scraped and coarsely chopped
4 medium-sized potatoes (slightly more than 1 pound), peeled
   and sliced
4 cups White Stock (p. 43)
Salt and freshly ground black pepper to taste
¾ cup light cream
¾ cup heavy cream
Mace

1. Wash the leeks well under running water. Cut into halves lengthwise, then into ¼- to ½-inch-thick slices.
2. In a pan that will accommodate all ingredients, over medium heat, heat 2 tablespoons butter. Add the leeks, onion, carrot, and

celery, and cook until the vegetables are somewhat soft. Do not brown. Add the potatoes, stock, salt, if needed (the stock may supply enough salt), and pepper. Cover and simmer 30 minutes, or until the vegetables can be mashed against the side of the pan.

3. Push the soup through a strainer, pressing as much of the vegetables through as possible, or use a blender.

4. Return the soup to the pan and stir in the light cream. Bring to a simmer, and stir in the remaining butter and the heavy cream. Taste for seasoning. If too thick for your taste, add a small amount of hot milk. Serve hot, with a light sprinkling of mace.

Potato and Cheese Soup SERVES 6 TO 8

3 tablespoons unsalted butter
1 medium-sized onion, diced
1 garlic clove, minced
2 medium-sized leeks (white part only), thoroughly washed and diced
4 medium-sized potatoes (slightly more than 1 pound), peeled and diced
2 cups White Stock (p. 43)
2 cups medium cream
1 cup milk
2 cups grated Gruyère cheese
Salt to taste
½ cup peeled, seeded, finely chopped, well-drained ripe tomatoes
2 tablespoons chopped fresh basil

1. In a large pan, over medium heat, melt the butter and cook the onion, garlic, and leeks, stirring, for 3 minutes. Do not brown. Add the potatoes and stock, and cook, covered, 20 minutes, or until the potatoes can be mashed against the side of the pan. Cool slightly and pour into a blender container or food processor to puree.

2. Return the soup to the pan, add the cream and milk. Heat to

a simmer. Add the cheese, and over low heat, cook, stirring, until the cheese has melted. Taste for seasoning before adding salt.

3. Serve with the fresh tomato and a sprinkling of basil on top.

Potato Corn Chowder

SERVES 6 TO 8

4 ounces pork fatback (labeled in some stores as Pork for Beans*), blanched in boiling water for 5 minutes, drained, cut into ¼-inch cubes (rind removed and discarded)*
1 medium-sized onion, finely chopped
1 large celery stalk (with leaves), scraped and finely chopped
2 tablespoons flour
2 cups water
3 medium-sized potatoes (about 1 pound), peeled and cut into ½-inch cubes
2 cups corn kernels (fresh or frozen)
Salt and freshly ground black pepper to taste
1 cup White Stock (p. 43)
3 cups milk
½ cup heavy cream
3 tablespoons unsalted butter

1. In a large pan, over medium heat, cook the fatback until crisp and golden. Remove with a slotted spoon, leaving the fat in the pan. Drain the golden cubes on paper towels and reserve.

2. Pour off all but 3 tablespoons of fat (if the fatback has not rendered that amount, add butter). Add the onion and celery, and cook until the onion is soft. Do not brown. Stir in the flour, blending well. Slowly stir in 1 cup water. Add the potatoes and the remaining water, and cook, covered, 15 minutes, or until the potatoes are almost tender. Add the corn, salt, pepper, stock, and milk, and simmer, uncovered, 10 minutes, or until the potatoes and corn are just tender. Taste for seasoning.

3. Just before serving, stir in the cream and butter. Serve with the crisp fatback sprinkled on top.

Pork Meatball and Swiss Chard Soup   SERVES 6

2 pounds meaty pork bones
¼ pound salt pork, cut into ¼-inch cubes
1 large onion, finely chopped
1 garlic clove, minced
3 quarts water
1 bay leaf
2 teaspoons salt
¼ teaspoon freshly ground black pepper
Swiss Chard (see below)
Meatballs (see below)

1. Place the bones in a soup pot and cover with cold water. Bring to a boil and drain. Rinse with cold running water; drain and set aside.
2. In the soup pot, over medium heat, cook the salt pork until it has rendered its fat and is golden and crisp. Remove the salt pork with a slotted spoon and drain on paper towels. Set aside. Pour off all but 3 tablespoons of the fat.
3. Add the onion and garlic, and cook 5 minutes, or until soft. Do not brown.
4. Add the pork bones, water, bay leaf, salt, and pepper to the soup kettle, and cook 1 to 1½ hours, partially covered, skimming the top as necessary. Reduce liquid by at least one half.
5. Add the prepared Swiss chard and simmer 10 minutes.
6. Stir in the meatballs and continue to simmer, partially covered, 20 to 25 minutes. Taste for seasoning.
7. Remove and discard the bones.
8. Serve, dividing the meatballs equally, and sprinkle top with the crispy salt-pork cubes.

SWISS CHARD

1 pound Swiss chard
2 tablespoons unsalted butter
Salt and freshly ground black pepper to taste

1. Cut the tougher stems from the Swiss chard leaves and coarsely chop the stems. Chop, less coarsely, the leaves.
2. In a saucepan, heat the butter. Add the stems and cook 4 minutes, or until somewhat soft. Add the leaves and cook 3 minutes. Sprinkle with salt and pepper. Set aside.

MEATBALLS

½ pound lean ground pork
½ cup fine bread crumbs
1 egg, beaten
2 tablespoons heavy cream
1 tablespoon minced onion
1 tablespoon minced fresh parsley
1 teaspoon caraway seeds, toasted, crushed
Salt and freshly ground black pepper to taste

1. In a bowl, combine and blend well, but lightly, all the ingredients.
2. Form into ½-inch balls. Set aside.

Sausage and Pasta Soup   SERVES 6 TO 8

The Italians have magical ways with sausages. Here's one of their best.

1 pound pea beans, picked over, soaked in cold water 5 hours,
  and drained
3 quarts chicken broth
2 tablespoons olive oil
3 hot Italian sausages, pricked in several places
3 sweet Italian sausages, pricked in several places
3 small potatoes, peeled and diced
1 large carrot, scraped and chopped
2 small white onions, peeled and chopped
2 small celery stalks, scraped and chopped
4 medium-sized ripe tomatoes, peeled, seeded, and diced
Salt and freshly ground black pepper to taste
2 cups al dente-cooked orzo (soup pasta shaped like rice)

1. Place the beans in a large pot and cover with 2 quarts chicken broth. Bring to a boil over high heat, then lower to medium heat and simmer 1 hour.

2. In another pot, heat the oil and cook the sausages over medium-high heat, browning them evenly. Pour off all but 2 tablespoons of the fat. Add the potatoes, carrot, onions, celery, tomatoes, salt, and pepper. Cover the pot, lower the heat, and simmer, stirring, for 15 minutes.

3. Remove the sausages and cut them into ¼-inch-thick rounds. Return the sausage slices to the pot, pour in the remaining chicken broth, and simmer, uncovered, 20 minutes.

4. Add the contents of this pot to the bean pot. Stir in the cooked pasta and simmer, uncovered, 5 minutes.

Scotch Broth SERVES 6 TO 8

The Scots aren't really stingy; they're just smart. When they bone a leg of lamb, they save the bone and the stewing pieces (the less lean, less perfect chunks of the leg of lamb). Ask your butcher to do the same. This soup uses the bone and about 2 pounds of lamb.

> Bone from leg of lamb
> 2 pounds lamb pieces, in largish cubes
> Leaves from 3 ribs of celery, chopped
> 3 large onions, coarsely chopped
> 1 bay leaf
> 4 cloves
> 3 quarts cold water
> 2 teaspoons salt
> ¼ teaspoon freshly ground black pepper
> 4 medium-size carrots, scraped and diced
> 3 celery stalks, scraped and diced
> 4 small scallions (white part only), chopped
> ¾ cup barley
> 3 tablespoons chopped parsley

1. In a deep pot, place the lamb bone, the pieces of lamb, the celery leaves, onions, bay leaf, cloves, water, salt, and pepper. Bring to a boil over medium heat. Lower heat and simmer, covered, for 1½ hours, or until the lamb is fork-tender, occasionally skimming the foam that rises to the top of the pot.

2. Remove the lamb bone and meat. Cool.

3. Strain the liquid in the soup pot, return it to the pot, and add the carrots, celery, scallions, and barley. Simmer over medium heat 30 minutes, or until the vegetables and barley are cooked.

4. Dice the cooled lamb meat, and any meat adhering to the bone, and add it to the soup pot. Stir well and taste for seasoning. Serve very hot, sprinkled with parsley.

Veal Ragout Soup
SERVES 4 TO 6

2 tablespoons unsalted butter
1 pound ground veal
Salt and freshly ground black pepper to taste
4 tablespoons chopped fresh parsley
1 parsnip, scraped and cut into thin strips
2 medium-sized carrots, scraped and cut into thin strips
2 celery stalks, scraped and cut into thin strips
2 tablespoons flour
5 cups White Stock (p. 43)
1 teaspoon fresh lemon juice, strained
2 egg yolks beaten with ½ cup sour cream

1. In a large saucepan or soup pot, melt the butter over medium heat. Add the veal, sprinkle with salt and pepper, and stir until it loses its pink color and is golden brown. Stir in half the parsley, the parsnip, carrots, and celery. Cook, stirring, until tender. Sprinkle on the flour, mix well, and slowly stir in 1 cup stock. Add the remaining stock, stirring until well blended. Bring to a boil, lower heat, and simmer, uncovered, 10 minutes. Stir in the lemon juice. Taste for seasoning.

2. Pour the egg yolk and sour-cream mixture into a soup tureen. Ladle the very hot soup into it, stirring after each ladleful has been added. Sprinkle with the remaining parsley.

Vernon Jarratt's Golden Soup
SERVES 4 TO 6

Vernon Jarratt is the creator of George's, one of Rome's most famous restaurants.

> 6 tablespoons unsalted butter
> 1 medium-sized onion, peeled and chopped
> 2 large potatoes, peeled and diced
> 1-pound can tomatoes, drained and put through a food mill or
>   blender
> 4 cups good beef stock
> Salt and freshly ground black pepper to taste
> ½ cup grated Parmesan cheese
> Croutons

1. In a large pan, melt 3 tablespoons butter over medium heat and cook the onion until slightly golden. Add the potatoes and cook, stirring, 3 minutes. Stir in the tomatoes and cook 10 minutes. Pour in the stock, bring to a boil, lower to a simmer, cover, and cook 25 minutes, until the potatoes are tender. Season with salt and pepper.
2. Just before serving, stir in the remaining butter and half the cheese.
3. Serve hot, sprinkled with the remaining cheese and the croutons.

Vichyssoise
SERVES 6 TO 8

This classic leek-and-potato soup is traditionally served cold.

> 2 tablespoons unsalted butter
> 4 medium-sized leeks (white part only), thoroughly washed,
>   drained, and chopped

2 medium-sized white onions, chopped
4 medium-sized potatoes (slightly more than 1 pound), peeled
   and thinly sliced
4 cups White Stock (p. 43)
¼ teaspoon nutmeg
1½ teaspoons salt, or to taste
1½ cups medium cream
2 tablespoons chopped watercress leaves (no stems)

1. In a large pan, over medium heat, melt the butter and cook the leeks and onions 5 minutes. Do not brown. Add the potatoes and stock. Cook, covered, for 15 minutes, or until the potatoes can be mashed against the side of the pot. Cool slightly.
2. Pour into a blender container or food processor and process into a velvety-smooth puree. Add the nutmeg and salt, and process 2 or 3 seconds. Taste for seasoning. Chill.
3. Just before serving, stir in the cream.
Serve chilled (but not icy cold), garnished with the watercress.
Note: This may also be served hot.

White Stock

MAKES 2 QUARTS

1 veal knuckle
2 pounds veal, trimmings or from the shoulder
2 pounds veal bones
4 quarts cold water
2 celery stalks (with leaves), sliced
2 leeks (white part only), sliced
2 onions
4 cloves (studded into the onions)
2 carrots, sliced
1 tablespoon salt
1 bay leaf
6 peppercorns

1. Cook the knuckle, veal, and bones in boiling water 5 minutes. Drain and rinse.

2. Place in a large soup pot, add the water, and, over high heat, bring to a boil. Lower heat and simmer, skimming off the top as the foam collects. Add the remaining ingredients and cook partially covered for 3 hours, skimming the top as the foam builds up. Strain the stock through cheesecloth or a fine strainer into a large bowl.

3. Set in the refrigerator overnight, and in the morning remove any fat that has collected on top. Carefully ladle out the stock and discard the sediment in the bottom of the bowl.

3

Beef

Beef and Italian Sausage Patties
Blue Cheese–Stuffed Burgers
First-Alert Chili con Carne
German Caraway Meat Eggs
Hamburger Steaks
Fillet of Beef Haché Antoine Gilly
Meat Patties with Lemon Cream Sauce
Katherine Spadaccino's Foggia Beef Roll
Swedish Meatballs
Turkish Meatballs
Beef Bourguignonne
Beef with Braised Celery Hearts
Beef en Daube
Beef Soufflé
Plaka Beef Stew
Carbonnades à la Flamande
Beef Stroganoff in Patty Shells
Cold Beef Salad
Corned Beef Hash
Curried Steak
Émincé de Filet de Boeuf Sauce
Bordelaise
Miroton of Boiled Beef
Short Ribs of Beef with Caper Lemon
Sauce
Sirloin with Cider
Steak and Kidney Pie with Oysters
Steak Strips with Sour Cream
Beef Brisket with Balsamic Vinegar
Sauce and Vegetables
Quick Oven Stew
Beef à la Mode
Boeuf à la Ficelle

Boiled Beef with Horseradish-Walnut
Sauce
Braciola
Caterer's Rib of Beef
Coffee-Braised Round Roast of Beef
Braised Rump of Beef Florentine
Glazed Brisket of Corned Beef
Corned Beef Brisket with Herbed
Vegetables
Fillet à la Antoine Gilly
Pot-au-Feu
Roast Beef Rump with Creamy Caper
Sauce
Deviled Short Ribs of Beef Gilly
Royal Standing Rib
Sauerbraten
Steak Teriyaki
Beef Fillet with Olives Tuscany
Beefsteak Pommarola
Bistecca alla Fiorentina
Braised Andalusian Steak
Rick Canali's Fillet of Beef Michelangelo
Antoine Gilly's Filets Mignons
Pan-Broiled Fillets of Beef
Minute Steaks with Herb Butter
Portuguese Beef (or Veal) Birds
Rumstecks Carbonnade à la Flamande
Steak Candeur
Steaks with Red Wine Butter Sauce
Sirloin Steak Lyonnaise
Steak au Poivre
Steak Diane
Strip Steak with Gorgonzola "Sauce"
Tournedos Rossini

There is no doubt that Julia Child is America's leading lady of food. With her writing and television programs she has brought common sense and class to tables all over the country.

Between takes of one TV show, *Dinner at Julia's*, she was asked what her favorite entrée was. "Beef!" she exclaimed. "I'm a red-meat eater. I feel I need red meat to keep my blood circulating, my color good, and my energy up."

Most of us agree. In fact, it requires 107,000 cattle every day to satisfy our taste for beef. In *A Tramp Abroad*, Mark Twain wrote of a homesick traveler in Europe: "Imagine an angel suddenly swooping down and setting before him a mighty porterhouse steak an inch-and-a-half thick, hot and sputtering from the griddle; dusted with fragrant pepper; enriched with melting bits of butter; the precious juices of the meat trickling out and joining the gravy." Few of us require such a description to whet our appetites for beef.

And few of us need any help in broiling a steak or fixing a hamburger. But beef is among the most versatile of all foods. Our aim is to expand your horizons, with such recipies as Fillet of Beef Haché, Foggia Beef Roll, Steak and Kidney Pie, Short Ribs with Lemon Caper Sauce, Braised Rump, a simple way to roast a standing rib without checking it even once, Pan-Broiled Fillets, Minute Steaks with Herb Butter.

At the beginning of each meat chapter is an illustrated chart showing cuts of meat and suggested cooking methods. Keep in mind that the tender cuts of beef come from the rib and loin sections, which make up about one-fourth of the carcass. Cuts from these sections—porterhouse, T-bone, sirloin, tenderloin, rib—are the most prized. The remaining carcass offers chuck, shoulder, round, flank; pot roasts, arm, blade, round, rump, chuck, briskets; then stew meat, brisket, neck, shank, flank, heel of round. (This is just a quick rundown; the charts are more specific.)

Beef

· RETAIL CUTS ·
WHERE THEY COME FROM
HOW TO COOK THEM

ROUND
SIRLOIN
SHORT LOIN
RIB
FLANK
SHORT PLATE
BRISKET
CHUCK
FORE SHANK

ROUND

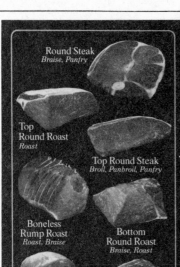

Round Steak
Braise, Panfry

Top Round Roast
Roast

Top Round Steak
Broil, Panbroil, Panfry

Boneless Rump Roast
Roast, Braise

Bottom Round Roast
Braise, Roast

Tip Roast, Cap Off
Roast, Braise

Eye Round Roast
Braise, Roast

Tip Steak
Broil, Panbroil, Panfry

SIRLOIN

Sirloin Steak, Flat Bone
Broil, Panbroil, Panfry

Sirloin Steak, Round Bone
Broil, Panbroil, Panfry

Top Sirloin Steak
Broil, Panbroil Panfry

FORE SHANK & BRISKET

Shank Cross Cut
Braise, Cook in Liquid

Brisket, Whole
Braise, Cook in Liquid

Corned Brisket, Point Half
Braise, Cook in Liquid

Brisket, Flat Half
Braise

CHUCK

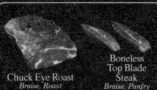
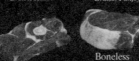

Chuck Eye Roast
Braise, Roast

Boneless Top Blade Steak
Braise, Panfry

Arm Pot Roast
Braise

Boneless Shoulder Pot Roast
Braise

Mock Tender
Braise

Cross Rib Pot Roast
Braise

Under Blade Pot Roast
Braise, Roast

Blade Roast
Braise

7-Bone Pot Roast
Braise

Short Ribs
Braise, Cook in Liquid

Flanken-Style Ribs
Braise, Cook in Liquid

SHORT LOIN

T-Bone Steak
Broil, Panbroil, Panfry

Boneless Top Loin Steak
Broil, Panbroil, Panfry

Porterhouse Steak
Broil, Panbroil, Panfry

Tenderloin Roast
Roast, Broil

Tenderloin Steak
Broil, Panbroil, Panfry

RIB

Rib Roast, Large End
Roast

Rib Roast, Small End
Roast

Rib Steak, Small End
Broil, Panbroil, Panfry

Rib Eye Roast
Roast

Rib Eye Steak
Broil, Panbroil, Panfry

Back Ribs
Braise, Cook in Liquid, Roast

FLANK & SHORT PLATE

Flank Steak
Broil, Braise, Panfry

Flank Steak Rolls
Braise, Broil, Panbroil, Panfry

Skirt Steak
Braise, Broil, Panbroil, Panfry

OTHER CUTS

Ground Beef
Broil, Panfry, Panbroil, Roast (Bake)

Cubed Steak
Panfry, Braise

Beef for Stew
Braise, Cook in Liquid

Cubes for Kabobs
Broil, Braise

Beef and Italian Sausage Patties

SERVES 6

1 pound ground beef, top or bottom round
1 pound sweet Italian sausage, casings removed
1 garlic clove, minced
4 tablespoons chopped fresh parsley
4 slices of white bread, soaked in milk, with milk squeezed out
2 eggs, beaten
Salt and freshly ground black pepper to taste
Olive oil
Fine bread crumbs for dredging

1. In a large bowl, combine and blend well, but lightly (your hands are good for this), the beef, sausage, garlic, parsley, bread, eggs, salt, and pepper.
2. Shape into small patties no larger than 2 inches in diameter.
3. In a deep frying pan, heat about ¼ inch of oil over medium-high heat. Dredge the patties with bread crumbs and brown evenly in the hot oil. Drain on paper towels and serve with or without a sauce (a tomato sauce is a good choice).
Serve with Swiss Potato Balls (p. 283).

Blue Cheese–Stuffed Burgers

SERVES 4

½ teaspoon salt
¼ teaspoon freshly ground black pepper
1½ pounds lean ground round steak
1½ ounces cream cheese
3 tablespoons crumbled blue cheese
1 tablespoon minced onion
1 teaspoon prepared horseradish, well drained

1. Sprinkle the salt and pepper over the ground beef; mix lightly but well. Divide the meat into 8 equal portions and form into 4-inch patties.
2. Combine cream cheese, blue cheese, onion, and horseradish.

Place one-quarter of the mixture in the center of 4 of the patties. Top with remaining patties. Press edges together securely to seal. Place on a grill over ash-covered coals (embers) so the burgers are 5 to 6 inches from coals. Broil 5 to 6 minutes on one side, turn and broil 5 to 6 minutes, or to doneness desired.

We like these burgers with Stuffed Potato "Chops" (p. 281).

Note: The burgers can be cooked under the broiler of a conventional oven or pan-cooked with a little butter.

First-Alert Chili con Carne   SERVES 8

Chili is one of beef's best ambassadors. There are as many recipes for it as there are for fried chicken. The best come from Texas and the Southwest, as this one did, passed on by a friend from San Antonio, where Mexican women, cooking for the U.S. Army, first created chili. This is a reasonably hot chili; it won't burn, but it will make you sit up and take notice.

> 4 tablespoons (¼ cup) olive oil
> 4 large onions, chopped
> 1 medium-sized fresh red pepper, seeded, cored, chopped
> 4 garlic cloves, minced
> 2 large celery stalks, scraped and coarsely chopped
> 4 pounds ground beef chuck (if a trifle fatty, so much the better)
> 1 teaspoon oregano
> ½ teaspoon ground red pepper
> 1 teaspoon ground cumin
> 1 teaspoon paprika
> 1 tablespoon chili powder
> 1 teaspoon celery seeds
> 1½ teaspoons salt
> 1 pound, 12-ounce can Italian plum tomatoes, put through a
>   food processor or blender to break up into a smooth, lumpless
>   consistency
> 2 sixteen-ounce cans red kidney beans (with liquid)

1. In a frying pan, heat half the oil over medium-high heat and cook the onions, fresh red pepper, garlic, and celery 5 minutes, stirring.

2. In a large, heavy pot, heat the remaining oil and brown the meat, stirring to break up the lumps and to produce a smooth, uniform mixture.

3. Stir in the cooked onions, fresh red pepper, garlic, and celery. Add the oregano, ground red pepper, cumin, paprika, chili powder, celery seeds, salt, and tomatoes, blending all well.

4. Simmer 1 hour, uncovered, stirring occasionally so the mixture doesn't stick to the bottom and scorch.

5. Add the kidney beans and their liquid, blend and simmer 30 minutes, stirring occasionally. Taste for seasoning, adding salt if needed.

Note: This can be varied by substituting cubed beef for the ground beef and pinto beans for the kidney beans.

German Caraway Meat Eggs   SERVES 6

1½ pounds lean pork, ground
1 pound lean beef chuck, ground
½ cup fine bread crumbs
1½ teaspoons salt
½ teaspoon freshly ground black pepper
¼ teaspoon Bell's seasoning
1 tablespoon minced fresh parsley
½ cup milk
2 large eggs, beaten
6 tablespoons (¾ stick) unsalted butter
2 tablespoons olive oil
1 medium-sized onion, minced
6 large mushrooms, cut into ¼-inch slices
2 cups beef broth
1½ cups sour cream

3 tablespoons flour
2 teaspoons crushed caraway seeds

1. In a large bowl, combine and blend well, but lightly (your hands are good for this), the pork, beef, bread crumbs, salt, pepper, Bell's seasoning, parsley, milk, and eggs. Shape into medium-sized eggs.
2. In a deep, heavy-bottomed saucepan, heat 4 tablespoons of butter and the oil. Brown the meat eggs evenly, a few at a time (do not crowd them in the pan). As they brown transfer to a dish or bowl. Pour any fat from the pan.
3. Add the remaining butter to the pan. Add the onion and cook 2 minutes, or until soft. Do not brown. Add the mushrooms and cook 1 minute. Pour in the beef broth, add the meat eggs, cover, and simmer over low heat 45 minutes.
4. In a bowl, blend the sour cream, flour, and caraway seeds. Stir this mixture into the pan with the meat eggs. Lower heat and simmer, stirring gently, until the sauce just starts to bubble and thickens. Do not boil. Taste for seasoning. Serve with the sauce spooned over.
This dish takes kindly to the unique Athenian Potato Soufflé (p. 274).

Hamburger Steaks   SERVES 6

2 pounds ground lean beef, top or bottom round
1 medium-sized onion, finely chopped
1 whole egg and 2 egg yolks, lightly beaten
Salt and freshly ground black pepper to taste
7 tablespoons unsalted butter
2 ounces brandy

1. In a large bowl, combine and blend well the beef, onion, egg, egg yolks, salt, and pepper.
2. Mold the meat mixture into six ½-inch-thick "steaks."
3. In a large frying pan, heat 4 tablespoons butter over medium-high heat. Add the beef and brown on both sides. The inside should

be pink, or however one prefers beef cooked. Transfer to a hot serving dish.

4. Add the remaining butter and the brandy to the frying pan, and cook until most of the brandy has evaporated.

Spoon over the steaks and serve with Shirley Capp's au Gratin Potatoes (p. 329).

Fillet of Beef Haché Antoine Gilly   SERVES 4

Naturally a chef of Antoine Gilly's talent would have his own recipe for ground beef. This may seem like a cavalier way to treat fillet, but the result is impressive.

8 tablespoons (1 stick) unsalted butter
½ cup chopped shallots
2 tablespoons cognac
½ cup cold water
1 teaspoon salt, or to taste
½ teaspoon freshly ground black pepper
1 tablespoon Worcestershire sauce
1 tablespoon Dijon mustard
2 pounds lean beef fillet, put through the medium blade of a
   food chopper
½ cup white bread crumbs
Sauce Fleurette (see below)

1. In a saucepan, over medium-high heat, melt half the butter. Stir in the shallots and cook 3 minutes. Do not brown. Add the cognac, water, salt, pepper, and Worcestershire, blending; simmer 2 minutes. Transfer to a mixing bowl.

2. Add to the bowl the mustard, beef, bread crumbs, and the remaining 4 tablespoons of butter, which should be soft. Blend well.

3. Shape into 4 patties, 1½ inches thick, and place in the refrigerator 2 hours.

4. In a frying pan, over medium-high heat, sauté (according to

your taste, rare or medium) in a small amount of butter.

Serve with Sauce Fleurette, which Antoine borrowed from one of his mentors, the famed Alexandre Dumaine.

SAUCE FLEURETTE

> *½ cup finely chopped watercress leaves (no stems)*
> *1 tablespoon finely chopped parsley*
> *8 tablespoons (1 stick) unsalted butter, softened*
> *1 tablespoon fresh lemon juice*
> *Salt and freshly ground white pepper to taste*
> *1 tablespoon heavy cream*

Place all ingredients in a bowl and blend thoroughly with a whisk until very smooth. This sauce is notable for its piquant flavor and lightness.

We like the haché with a simple potato dish, Tiny New Potatoes alla Ralph Guidetti (p. 358).

Meat Patties with Lemon Cream Sauce   SERVES 4 TO 6

> *4 cups ½-inch cubes cooked beef (or pork or veal), ground with*
> *   2 slices prosciutto (or a good-quality cooked ham)*
> *⅓ cup grated Asiago or Parmesan cheese*
> *4 slices white bread soaked in beef broth (with the broth*
> *   squeezed out)*
> *2 eggs, beaten*
> *½ teaspoon allspice*
> *2 tablespoons minced broadleaf parsley*
> *Salt and freshly ground black pepper to taste*
> *2 tablespoons unsalted butter*
> *2 tablespoons olive oil*
> *Fine bread crumbs for dredging*
> *Lemon Cream Sauce (see below)*

1. In a large bowl, combine and mix well, but lightly (your hands are good for this), the meat, cheese, bread, eggs, allspice, parsley, salt, and pepper.

2. Shape into patties no larger than 2 inches in diameter.

3. In a deep frying pan, heat the butter and oil. Dredge the patties with the bread crumbs and brown evenly in the fat, about 1 minute on each side. Add more oil and butter if needed. Serve with Lemon Cream Sauce.

LEMON CREAM SAUCE   MAKES ABOUT 2 CUPS

> *2 tablespoons unsalted butter*
> *2 tablespoons flour*
> *1½ cups milk*
> *½ cup heavy cream*
> *¼ teaspoon nutmeg*
> **Salt and freshly ground black pepper to taste**
> *1½ tablespoons fresh lemon juice*

1. In a saucepan, over medium heat, melt the butter. Stir in the flour and blend into a smooth paste. Gradually add the milk and stir into a smooth, medium-thick sauce.

2. Stir in the cream, nutmeg, salt, pepper, and lemon juice. Heat to a simmer, stirring. Do not boil.

Serve with double-fried French Fries (p. 293).

Katherine Spadaccino's Foggia Beef Roll   SERVES 8 TO 10

Katherine was a close friend and relative who lived in Danbury, Connecticut, and influenced much of the community (at least the Italian part) with her superb cooking techniques.

> *3 pounds ground top round*
> *1 cup fine bread crumbs*
> *1 large onion, finely chopped*
> *1 garlic clove, minced*
> *4 fresh mint leaves, finely chopped (or ½ teaspoon dried)*
> *½ cup finely chopped parsley*
> *3 eggs, lightly beaten*
> *1 cup coarsely grated Asiago or Parmesan cheese*
> *Salt and freshly ground black pepper to taste*

Olive oil

3 four-inch-long sweet Italian sausages, broiled

4 hard-boiled eggs, shelled, and white ends cut off so the yolks show

2 half-inch-thick slices of Provolone cut into ½-inch strips

3 cups tomato sauce

1 teaspoon sugar

¼ teaspoon cinnamon

½ teaspoon dried oregano

½ pound small fresh mushrooms, halved

1. In a large bowl, combine and mix well (your hands are good for this) the ground meat, bread crumbs, onion, garlic, mint, parsley, raw eggs, ½ cup of the grated cheese, salt, and pepper.

2. Lay, overlapping, two 2-foot-long sheets of wax paper on a flat work surface. Smear the paper with olive oil. Place all but ½ cup of the mixture on the paper and pat it into a squarish rectangle ½ to ¾ inch thick.

3. Lengthwise, on the rectangle, arrange the sausages and the hard-boiled eggs, end to end in a straight line, so that when the roll is sliced each piece will have a slice of sausage and a slice of egg showing. Arrange the Provolone strips on the meat mixture between and around the sausage and eggs. Sprinkle on the remaining grated cheese.

4. Pick up a long end of the wax paper and, using it as a guide, lift the meat and roll it (lengthwise, as you would a dessert roll) into a firm cylinder, sealing the filling inside. Seal the ends. If any of the filling is showing, patch the roll with the meat you reserved.

5. Slide the roll off the wax paper and into an oiled, shallow baking dish. Bake, uncovered, in a preheated 450° oven 15 minutes, or until it is firm and slightly brown.

6. Mix 2 tablespoons of the fat from the pan with the tomato sauce. Heat the sauce and pour it over the roll. Sprinkle a mixture of the sugar, cinnamon, and oregano over the sauce. Lower oven heat to 350° and bake 35 minutes, occasionally basting the roll. Sprinkle the mushrooms around the roll and bake 10 minutes.

7. Transfer to a serving dish and let set for 15 minutes, to become firm and slightly cooler for easier slicing.

Spoon the sauce from the pan lightly over each slice of beef roll and serve with an appropriate dish of Italian Shoestring Potatoes and Vermicelli (p. 357).

Swedish Meatballs   SERVES 6

¾ cup zwieback crumbs, or bread crumbs
1 cup medium cream, or half-and-half
8 tablespoons (1 stick) unsalted butter
1 large onion, minced
1 pound lean chuck beef
½ pound lean pork
½ pound veal
1 medium-sized potato, boiled and mashed
1 teaspoon salt
½ teaspoon freshly ground black pepper
¼ teaspoon nutmeg
2 egg yolks, beaten
1 tablespoon olive oil
2 cups beef broth
2 tablespoons flour

1. Soak the crumbs in the cream or half-and-half.
2. In a large, deep frying pan, over medium heat, melt 3 table-spoons butter and cook the onion 2 minutes, or until soft. Do not brown.
3. Grind the beef, pork, and veal together 3 times. In a large bowl, combine and mix well, but lightly, the meat, crumbs, onion, potato, salt, pepper, nutmeg, and egg yolks. Shape into balls 1 to 1½ inches in diameter.
4. In the frying pan in which the onions cooked, heat 3 tablespoons butter and the oil. In a single layer (if necessary cook a few at a time), brown the balls evenly, shaking the pan as they are cooking.

When all are brown, return to the pan, pour in the broth, cover tightly, and simmer 15 minutes, or until cooked through so that the centers are no longer pink.

5. Remove with a slotted spoon and keep warm. Thicken the broth in the pan by stirring in kneaded butter (made with the remaining butter kneaded with the flour), cooking the sauce until it has thickened. Taste for seasoning. Serve the meatballs in the sauce.

Potatoes with Anchovy Butter and Spinach (p. 345) make this a delicious duet.

Turkish Meatballs   SERVES 4

5 tablespoons unsalted butter
1 large onion, minced
1 large garlic clove, minced
1 pound twice-ground beef round
2 slices white bread soaked in milk, with the milk squeezed out
4 mint leaves, minced, or ½ teaspoon dried
3 tablespoons minced parsley
½ teaspoon ground cumin
⅛ teaspoon cinnamon
1 egg, beaten
Salt and freshly ground black pepper to taste
Flour for dredging
1 tablespoon olive oil
2 green peppers (seeded and white ribs removed), cut into 1-inch strips
4 medium-sized, ripe, firm tomatoes, peeled, seeded, and cut into cubes

1. In a small frying pan, over medium heat, melt 2 tablespoons butter. Add the onion and garlic, and cook until the onion is soft. Do not brown.

2. In a large bowl, combine and mix well the onion, garlic, beef, bread, mint, parsley, cumin, cinnamon, egg, salt, and pepper. Mois-

ten your hands with water and shape into small, egg-shaped "balls,"using about a heaping teaspoon for each.

3. Lightly dredge the balls with flour.

4. In a large, deep frying pan, heat the remaining butter and the oil, and evenly brown the meat. Add more butter if needed. Transfer the balls to a warm bowl.

5. Add the peppers to the frying pan the meatballs cooked in and cook 2 to 3 minutes, or until they start to get soft. Add the tomatoes and cook over medium heat, uncovered, for 20 minutes, or until most of the liquid has cooked off. Return the meatballs and any liquid in the bowl to the pan and simmer 15 minutes. Taste for seasoning.

Pommes de Terre Amandine (p. 344) make this an international menu.

Beef Bourguignonne SERVES 6

This recipe is unusual in that no browning of the beef is required.

2 pounds beef rump, cut into 1½-inch cubes
2 garlic cloves, minced
2 teaspoons salt
2 tablespoons flour
2 medium-sized onions, sliced
½ cup tomato puree
½ teaspoon freshly ground black pepper
1 bay leaf
½ teaspoon thyme
1 cup dry red wine
1 tablespoon cognac
18 very small onions, peeled and root ends scored
4 medium-sized carrots, scraped, cut into 1-inch pieces
18 medium-sized mushrooms, halved
3 tablespoons chopped parsley
1 cup croutons (p. 33)
6 medium-sized boiled potatoes

1. In a casserole, toss the beef with a mixture of the garlic and salt and coat with flour. Add the sliced onions, tomato puree, and pepper. Cover and cook in a preheated 325° oven for 1 hour.

2. Add the bay leaf, thyme, and a mixture of the wine and cognac (heated to a boil), cover, and cook 30 minutes. Add the whole onions and carrots, cover, and cook 15 minutes. Add the mushrooms and cook 15 minutes, or until the meat is tender. Taste for seasoning. Discard bay leaf.

Serve sprinkled with the parsley and garnished with the croutons and potatoes.

Beef with Braised Celery Hearts   SERVES 6

2 tablespoons unsalted butter
3 tablespoons olive oil
3 pounds lean chuck beef, cut into 1-inch cubes
2 teaspoons minced fatback
1 medium-sized onion, peeled and chopped
1 large celery stalk, scraped and chopped
2 garlic cloves, minced
Salt and freshly ground black pepper to taste
1/8 teaspoon thyme
1/2 cup Marsala
1/2 cup tomato puree
3 cups beef broth

1. In a flameproof casserole, heat the butter and oil. Add the beef and brown evenly over high heat.

2. Lower heat to medium, add the fatback, onion, celery, and garlic, and cook 3 minutes, or until the onion is soft. Do not brown. Sprinkle with salt, pepper, and thyme.

3. Pour in the Marsala; shake pot to distribute it. Cook off about half the wine. Stir together the tomato puree and beef broth, then pour in enough of the mixture to barely cover the beef. Cover the pot, bring to a boil on top of the stove, then place in a preheated

325° oven for 2½ hours (adding more broth mixture, if needed), or until the beef is tender. Taste for seasoning.

4. While the beef is cooking, prepare the celery.

BRAISED CELERY

    3 large, crisp, firm bunches of celery
    1 cup beef broth
    4 tablespoons (½ stick) unsalted butter
    Salt and freshly ground black pepper to taste

1. Remove the tougher outside stalks from the bunches of celery. Cut off the tops so you have three 4- to 5-inch-long hearts. Do not separate the stalks forming the hearts. Scrape the outside stalks with a vegetable scraper.

2. Cut the hearts in half lengthwise. Wash and drain, then tie the halves together with a cord so you again have three intact hearts.

3. Pour the beef broth into a pot and place over medium heat. Add the tied celery hearts and simmer, covered, until crisp-tender. Turn as they cook. Drain well. Remove the cord.

4. In a frying pan, over medium-high heat, melt the butter. Arrange the celery halves in a single layer in the pan and cook until golden, turning once. Do not brown. Season with salt and pepper.

5. When ready to serve, transfer the beef with its sauce to a hot serving dish and arrange the celery heart halves on top.

Pommes de Terre Cocotte (p. 299) are a simple, tasty accompaniment.

Beef en Daube   SERVES 6 TO 8

To cook beef "en daube" is to braise it in stock and wine and season it with herbs. It is a slow, airtight method of cooking, resulting in very tender, flavorful meat.

    3 tablespoons butter
    2 tablespoons olive oil
    3 pounds chuck, blade or hip steak, cut into pieces 1½ × 1 ×
       ½ inches

Salt and freshly ground black pepper to taste
3 ounces brandy
2 tablespoons tomato puree
3 tablespoons flour
2 cups beef stock (or canned broth)
Bouquet garni (1 bay leaf, ¼ teaspoon thyme, and a parsley
  sprig wrapped in cheesecloth)
1 tablespoon currant jelly
2 garlic cloves, minced
2 cups dry red wine, approximately
16 medium-sized mushrooms, quartered
16 pitted black olives (the plump, purplish ones), chopped
2 medium-sized, ripe, firm tomatoes, skinned and cut into 6 to 8
  equally thick slices
½ cup grated Parmesan cheese (or a cheese of your choice)

1. Heat the butter and oil in a flameproof casserole over medium heat. Brown beef evenly. Sprinkle with salt and pepper. Add more butter and oil, if needed. If too much fat remains in the pot after browning, pour off all but 3 tablespoons. Pour in the brandy and shake the pot to distribute it (be careful, as it might ignite). Remove meat from the pot.

2. Lower heat, add the tomato puree and flour to the pot, and mix well. Add the beef stock, a small amount at a time, stirring constantly, until the sauce is smooth. Add the bouquet garni, jelly, and garlic. Return the meat to the pot and pour in enough wine to barely cover the meat. Cover pot with aluminum foil, then its own cover. Bring to a boil on top of the stove. Place in a preheated 300° oven for 1½ hours, or until the beef is fork-tender. If liquid cooks off, add small amounts of hot stock.

3. When the beef is just tender, add the mushrooms and olives, and cook, covered, for 10 minutes. Remove and discard the bouquet garni. Taste for seasoning.

4. Arrange the slices of tomato on top of the meat, sprinkle on the cheese, and put under the broiler until the cheese is golden.

Duchesse Potatoes (p. 290) are an excellent accompaniment.

Beef Soufflé

5 medium-large Idaho potatoes (about 2 pounds), peeled, quartered, and cooked in boiling salted water until tender; drained,
dried over heat, and put through a ricer into a large bowl

5 tablespoons soft butter

½ cup warm milk, approximately

Salt and freshly ground black pepper to taste

¼ teaspoon nutmeg

1 cup grated Gruyère cheese

5 egg yolks, beaten

5 egg whites, stiffly beaten

2 cups Brown Sauce (see below)

3 cups cooked beef (braised, boiled, or roasted) in ½-inch
cubes, mixed with enough of the Brown Sauce to barely coat

1. Blend the potatoes with the butter and add just enough milk to
bind them. Add and blend well the salt, pepper, nutmeg, cheese,
and egg yolks. Fold in the egg whites. Spoon half the mixture into
the bottom of an 8-inch, buttered baking dish.

2. Line the sides of the dish with the potato mixture about ½ inch
thick. Arrange the beef over the bottom layer of potatoes. Cover
with the remaining potato mixture. Cook in a preheated 375° oven
45 minutes, or until puffed and golden on top.

Pass the remaining Brown Sauce at the table.

BROWN SAUCE   MAKES ABOUT 2 CUPS

3 tablespoons unsalted butter

1 tablespoon minced shallots or white onion

3 tablespoons flour

2 cups beef broth

Salt and freshly ground black pepper to taste

¼ teaspoon dried thyme

1 tablespoon minced fresh parsley

1. In a saucepan over medium-low heat, melt the butter. Add the
shallots or onion and cook 1 minute, or until soft. Do not brown.

2. Stir in the flour, blending well, and cook, stirring, into a smooth thick paste.

3. Gradually add the beef broth and cook, stirring, into a smooth, medium-thick sauce. Season with salt and pepper and stir in the thyme and parsley.

Plaka Beef Stew   SERVES 4 TO 6

The Plaka is the old section of Athens, full of *tavernas*, throbbing *bouzouki* music, and good food, including this stew.

> *2 pounds chuck beef, cut into 1-inch cubes*
> *Flour for dredging*
> *3 tablespoons unsalted butter*
> *2 tablespoons olive oil*
> *Salt and freshly ground black pepper to taste*
> *1 cup beef broth*
> *½ cup dry white wine*
> *1 tablespoon tomato paste*
> *1 large garlic clove, minced*
> *1 large onion, chopped*
> *1 celery stalk, scraped and chopped*
> *2 whole cloves and 1 bay leaf, tied together in cheesecloth*
> *½ teaspoon cinnamon*
> *½ teaspoon oregano*
> *1 teaspoon sugar*
> *3 tablespoons chopped parsley*

1. Dredge the beef very lightly in the flour, shaking off any excess.

2. In a flameproof casserole, heat the butter and oil. Add the beef cubes and brown evenly, adding more butter and oil if needed. Sprinkle with salt and pepper.

3. Stir in the broth and wine, then add all other ingredients except the parsley.

4. Bring to a boil on top of the stove. Place in a preheated 325°

oven, covered, for 2½ hours, or until the meat is tender. If the sauce should become too thick before the beef is tender, add a small amount of hot broth.

5. Remove and discard the bay leaf and cloves. Serve sprinkled with the parsley.

Perfect with plaka: Czechoslovakian Potato Pudding (p. 336).

Carbonnades à la Flamande

SERVES 4 TO 6

(Beef Braised in Beer, Belgian style)

2 tablespoons unsalted butter
2 tablespoons olive oil
2 pounds bottom or top round of beef, cut into 1½-inch cubes
Salt and freshly ground black pepper to taste
3 slices lean bacon, coarsely chopped
3 medium-sized onions, coarsely chopped
1 garlic clove, minced
2 tablespoons flour
1 cup rich beef broth
2 cups beer
1 bay leaf
¼ teaspoon dried thyme

1. In a frying pan, over medium heat, heat the butter and oil. Add the beef and brown evenly, sprinkling with salt and pepper (add more butter and oil if needed). Transfer the meat to a flameproof casserole.

2. Pour off any fat from the frying pan, add the bacon, and cook over medium heat 3 minutes. If more than 3 tablespoons of fat have been rendered, pour off all but that amount. If less, add a little butter. Stir in the onions and garlic and cook 4 minutes, or until soft. Do not brown. Blend in the flour, then gradually add the broth and beer, stirring constantly, scraping up the browned-on bits from the bottom, until the sauce is well blended and starts to thicken. Pour into the casserole over the meat. Add the bay leaf and thyme.

3. Bring to a boil on top of the stove. Transfer to a 325° preheated oven and cook, covered, for 2 hours, or until tender. Taste for seasoning. Discard bay leaf.

Serve with Potatoes Chantilly (p. 304).

Beef Stroganoff in Patty Shells

SERVES 6

6 frozen patty shells (we like Pepperidge Farm)
4 tablespoons (½ stick) unsalted butter
2 medium-sized onions, finely chopped
½ pound fresh, firm mushrooms, thinly sliced
1½ pounds fillet of beef tips or sirloin, cut into strips 1 × ¼
*   × ¼ inch*
½ cup beef broth
½ cup dry vermouth
¼ cup tomato juice
Salt and freshly ground black pepper to taste
1 tablespoon flour
¾ cup sour cream
Chopped parsley

1. Prepare patty shells according to package directions. Set aside and keep warm, or prepare in advance and heat just before serving.
2. In a large frying pan, heat the butter over medium heat. Add the onions and mushrooms, and cook 2 minutes, or until the onions are soft. Do not brown.
3. Turn heat to high, add the beef, and cook, stirring, until the beef is browned. Stir in the beef broth, vermouth, and tomato juice, sprinkling lightly with salt and pepper. Lower heat to medium and cook 30 minutes, or until the beef is tender.
4. Sprinkle flour lightly over contents of frying pan and cook, stirring, until thickened. Taste for seasoning.
5. Spoon into the warm patty shells. Top with a good dab of sour cream and a sprinkling of parsley.

Cold Beef Salad

4 cups cold boiled beef, all fat removed, cut into pieces ¾ × ½ × ¼ inch

½ cup Swiss or Gruyère cheese, cut into small cubes

1 small red Italian onion, thinly sliced, slices rinsed in cold water and well drained

2 scallions, white part only, thinly sliced

1 cup coarsely chopped celery heart (scrape celery before chopping)

12 thin, crisp green pepper strips

3 firm, ripe tomatoes, peeled and quartered

6 tablespoons virgin olive oil

2 tablespoons white wine vinegar

1 teaspoon Kosciusko mustard

Salt and freshly ground black pepper to taste

3 hard-boiled eggs, quartered

½ cup chopped fresh parsley

1. In a large bowl, combine the beef, cheese, onion, scallions, celery, green pepper, and tomatoes.
2. Pour a salad dressing made of the olive oil, vinegar, mustard, salt and pepper over the contents of the bowl and mix well but carefully. Taste for seasoning, adding anything more that your taste desires. Transfer to a serving bowl.
3. Garnish with the egg quarters and sprinkle on the parsley.
Serve with hot bread and Hot German Potato Salad (p. 266).

Corned Beef Hash

2 tablespoons unsalted butter

1 small onion, minced

1 celery stalk, scraped, finely chopped

2 cups chopped, cooked corned beef (about 1 pound)

3 medium-sized cold, boiled potatoes, chopped

¼ teaspoon nutmeg

Cream (just enough to moisten—about 2 tablespoonfuls)
Salt and freshly ground black pepper to taste
Parsley sprigs

1. In a frying pan, over medium heat, melt the butter. Add the onion and celery, and cook until soft. Do not brown.
2. Add the beef, potatoes, nutmeg, cream, salt, and pepper, and stir until well mixed. Spread evenly and cook over low heat until the bottom is browned and crusty. Loosen with a spatula and turn out onto a hot serving dish. Garnish with parsley.
Classically, this is offered topped with poached eggs.
Alternate method: Once mixed, the hash can be transferred to a buttered 9-inch baking dish and baked, uncovered, in a 425° oven until crusty on top, about 25 minutes.
Note: Chopped parsley or chopped green or red pepper (cooked with the onion and celery) can be added to the hash mixture, or, for a "Red Flannel Hash," add a cup of finely chopped cooked beets.

Curried Steak   SERVES 6

3 tablespoons peanut oil
3 medium-sized onions, sliced
1 garlic clove, minced
3 slices fresh ginger root
2 pounds sirloin steak, cut into slices $\frac{1}{8} \times 1 \times 2$ inches
Salt and freshly ground black pepper to taste
2 tablespoons curry powder
2 tablespoons soy sauce
2 cups chicken broth
3 tablespoons cornstarch mixed with $\frac{1}{4}$ cup water

1. In a large frying pan, over medium heat, heat the oil. Add the onions and cook until soft. Do not brown. Remove the onions with a slotted spoon; reserve.
2. Add the garlic and ginger root to the frying pan and cook 1

minute, or until the garlic is slightly golden. Do not brown. Discard the ginger root.

3. Add the beef to the pan, sprinkle lightly with salt (the soy sauce will add more salt) and pepper. Brown on both sides, adding more oil if needed.

4. Return the onions to the pan, stir in the curry powder, and mix well. Stir in the soy sauce and chicken broth. Cover and cook over medium heat 20 minutes, or until the beef is tender.

5. Slowly stir in the cornstarch mixture and cook, stirring, until the sauce has thickened. Taste for seasoning and serve immediately. Serve with Czechoslovakian Potato Pudding (p. 336).

Émincé de Filet de Boeuf Sauce Bordelaise   SERVES 4
(Tenderloin Tips with Marrow Sauce)

2 tablespoons olive oil
4 tablespoons (½ stick) unsalted butter
1½ pounds tenderloin tips, cut into strips 2 × 1½ × ¼ inch
Salt and freshly ground black pepper to taste
2 tablespoons chopped shallots
2 cups sliced fresh mushrooms
1½ cups Bordelaise Sauce (see below)
2 tablespoons chopped fresh parsley

1. In a heavy-bottomed skillet, heat the oil and half the butter. Add the beef, sprinkle lightly with salt and pepper, and cook 10 minutes over high heat, stirring to brown evenly. With a slotted spoon, transfer the beef to a deep saucepan. Keep warm.

2. Pour off any fat remaining in the skillet. Melt the rest of the butter in it, add the shallots, and cook over medium heat for 2 minutes, or until soft. Do not brown. Add the mushrooms and cook 3 minutes, stirring.

3. Stir in the Bordelaise Sauce and simmer 5 minutes. Pour the sauce over the beef and bring to a simmer. Taste for seasoning.

4. Transfer to a hot serving dish and sprinkle with parsley. Serve with Potato Fritters (p. 306).

3 shallots, minced
¾ cup good, full-bodied red wine
1/16 teaspoon cayenne pepper, or to taste
1 cup Brown Sauce (p. 62)
1 tablespoon brandy
3 tablespoons softened, unsalted butter
½ cup beef marrow, poached in simmering water for 2 minutes,
  well drained, diced and kept warm (optional)
Salt to taste

1. In a stainless saucepan, over medium-low heat, simmer the shallots until soft in the wine. Add the cayenne and cook, raising the heat, reducing the liquid to one-half its volume.
2. Stir in the Brown Sauce and reduce heat, bringing the sauce to a simmer. Stir in the brandy and remove from heat.
3. Just before serving, stir in the butter and the warm beef marrow. Taste for seasoning, adding salt.

Miroton of Boiled Beef   SERVES 6

Here's a delicious way to serve leftover boiled beef.

2 tablespoons unsalted butter
1 tablespoon olive oil
3 medium-sized onions, thinly sliced
3 tablespoons flour
3 cups warm beef broth
2 tablespoons red wine vinegar
2 tablespoons tomato puree
Salt and freshly ground black pepper to taste
12 slices boiled beef, cut ¼ inch thick
2 tablespoons chopped parsley

1. In a heavy-bottomed pot, heat the butter and oil. Add the onions and cook 3 minutes, or until the onions are soft. Do not brown.

2. Sprinkle on the flour and mix well. Slowly add the beef broth, stirring until well blended. Stir in the vinegar, tomato puree, salt, and pepper. Simmer for 5 minutes, or until the sauce has slightly thickened. Taste for seasoning.

3. Add the sliced beef, moving it around carefully in the sauce until well coated. Cover the pot and, over low heat, heat through. Sprinkle with parsley and serve with Potatoes Rösti (p. 312).

Short Ribs of Beef with Caper Lemon Sauce   SERVES 4 TO 6

5 pounds short ribs of beef, cut into 2- or 3-inch-long pieces
Salt and freshly ground black pepper
4 tablespoons (½ stick) unsalted butter, approximately
1 tablespoon olive oil
6 medium-sized white onions, thinly sliced
2 garlic cloves, finely chopped
1 large carrot, scraped and thinly sliced
1 bay leaf
2 whole cloves
3 cups beef broth
2 cups water
½ cup stale pumpernickel bread crumbs
1 tablespoon capers, rinsed, drained, and chopped
1 teaspoon grated lemon rind

1. Season the short ribs with salt and pepper.

2. In a large flameproof casserole, heat the butter and oil and brown the ribs evenly (add more butter and oil if needed). Remove the ribs and keep warm.

3. Add the onions and garlic to the casserole (and more butter if needed) and cook until the onions are soft. Do not brown. Add the carrot, bay leaf, cloves, broth, and water. Stir well, scraping up the browned-on bits from the bottom of the pan. Bring to a boil.

4. Return the ribs to the pot, cover, and cook in a preheated 375°

oven 1½ hours, or until they are fork-tender. Transfer them to a hot serving dish and keep warm.

5. Skim the fat from the pot and strain the liquid, pushing the vegetables through the strainer. Return the liquid to the pot. Add the bread crumbs, capers, and lemon rind, blending well. Simmer, uncovered, for 10 minutes, or until thickened, stirring occasionally. Spoon over the short ribs.

Serve with Wyoming Camp Potatoes (p. 360).

Sirloin with Cider   SERVES 6

4 tablespoons (½ stick) unsalted butter
2 tablespoons flour
2 cups beef broth
1 tablespoon tomato paste
2 tablespoons white wine vinegar
1 teaspoon molasses
⅛ teaspoon ground ginger
Salt and freshly ground black pepper to taste
2 tablespoons olive oil
3 pounds top sirloin beef, cut into pieces 1 inch square, ½ inch
   thick
4 medium-sized onions, thinly sliced
1 garlic clove, minced
2 cups sweet cider, approximately
1 bay leaf
¼ teaspoon dried marjoram
2 tablespoons chopped parsley

1. In a saucepan, over medium-low heat, melt 2 tablespoons butter. Add the flour and cook, stirring constantly, into a smooth, golden paste. Gradually add the broth, stirring into a smooth, medium-thick sauce. Stir in the tomato paste, vinegar, molasses, ginger, salt, and pepper. Set aside.

2. In a flameproof casserole, heat the oil and the remaining butter. Add the beef and brown evenly, adding more butter and oil if needed. Transfer to a bowl and reserve.

3. If fat remains in the pot, pour off all but 2 tablespoons. If not, add that amount of butter. Lower heat, add the onions and garlic, and cook, stirring, until the onion is soft. Do not brown. Return the meat to the pot. Add the prepared sauce, 1 cup of cider, the bay leaf, and the marjoram. Blend.

4. Cover and bring to a boil on top of the stove. Transfer to a preheated 350° oven for 1½ hours (adding more cider if sauce becomes too thick), or until the meat is fork-tender. Discard bay leaf. Taste for seasoning.

5. Transfer to a hot serving dish and sprinkle with parsley.

Excellent with Mashed Potatoes with Scallions (p. 316).

Steak and Kidney Pie with Oysters SERVES 4 TO 6

2 pounds round steak, cut into bite-sized pieces
Salt and freshly ground black pepper
Flour for dredging
6 tablespoons unsalted butter
1 tablespoon olive oil
1 large onion, coarsely chopped
2 cups beef broth
2 veal kidneys (remove outer membrane, hard core in center,
    and fat), cut into bite-sized pieces
1 pint oysters, drained
3 tablespoons chopped parsley
1 pastry crust (see below)
1 egg yolk beaten with 1 tablespoon water

1. Sprinkle the steak pieces with salt and pepper and lightly dredge with flour. In a flameproof casserole, heat 4 tablespoons butter and the oil and brown the beef evenly. Remove with a slotted spoon and reserve.

2. Add the onion to the casserole and cook 2 minutes, or until soft. Do not brown. Return the beef to the pan, pour in the broth, and bring to a boil, stirring to loosen browned-on bits from the bottom. Transfer to a preheated 350° oven and cook, covered, for 45 minutes.

3. Dredge the kidney pieces lightly with flour. In a frying pan, over medium heat, melt the remaining 2 tablespoons butter and lightly brown the kidney pieces. Transfer them and the butter they cooked in to the casserole and cook 10 minutes.

4. Stir the oysters and parsley into the casserole. Transfer to a deep pie dish. Cool slightly.

5. Roll the pastry to a ¼-inch thickness and cover the pie. Trim to slightly overlap the rim of the pie dish. Moisten the edges of the pastry and press against the pie plate. If desired, roll out the pastry you trimmed and cut into leaf shapes. Moisten undersides and arrange on the pastry. With a knife, cut 2 or 3 slits in the center of the pastry to allow steam to escape. Brush pastry with the egg-water mixture.

6. Bake in a preheated 425° oven for 30 minutes, or until the crust is golden brown.

PASTRY

> 1½ cups sifted flour
> 1 teaspoon salt
> ⅓ cup lard, or Crisco
> 3 tablespoons butter
> ¼ cup cold water

1. In a bowl, with a pastry blender (or cutting with two knives), mix the flour, salt, lard, and butter until they have the texture of coarse grain.

2. Add the water and mix with a fork just until the dough holds together. When you can gather the dough into a neat ball, stop working it. Put plastic wrap around it and refrigerate until ready to roll out.

Steak Strips with Sour Cream

6 top-round steaks, cut ½ inch thick and each weighing between
*   5 and 6 ounces, all fat and gristle removed*
5 tablespoons unsalted butter
2 tablespoons olive oil
3 medium-sized onions, chopped
3 tablespoons flour
1 teaspoon Hungarian paprika
2 cups beef broth
Salt and freshly ground black pepper to taste
1 teaspoon Worcestershire sauce
1½ cups sour cream
Fresh dill sprigs for garnish

1. Pound the steaks with a meat mallet until ¼ inch thick, or have your butcher do it.
2. In a large frying pan, heat 2 tablespoons butter and the oil. Brown the steaks evenly two or three at a time (do not crowd), depending on the size of the pan. Add more butter and oil if needed. As the steaks brown, transfer them to a cutting board and cut into strips approximately 1 inch wide and 3 inches long. Arrange them in a flameproof casserole large enough to handle the strips in 2 layers. Overlap, if necessary.
3. To the frying pan the steaks browned in, add the remaining butter and cook the onions until soft. Do not brown. Lower heat, stir in the flour and paprika, and mix well. Gradually add the beef broth, stirring into a smooth, medium-thick sauce. Stir in the salt, pepper, and Worcestershire.
4. Pour the sauce over the beef in the casserole, cover, and bring to a boil on top of the stove. Transfer to a preheated 325° oven and cook for 1 hour, or until the beef is tender. Add more hot broth if the sauce becomes too thick. Transfer the meat to a hot serving dish and keep warm.
5. Blend the sour cream with the sauce in the casserole. Bring to a simmer, stirring; do not boil. Taste for seasoning. Pour through

a strainer over the beef strips and garnish with the dill sprigs. Serve with Potato and Leek Casserole (p. 351).

Beef Brisket with Balsamic Vinegar Sauce and Vegetables

SERVES 6

3 tablespoons olive oil
1 large onion, cut into ¼-inch-thick slices
3½- to 4-pound brisket of beef
1 cup red wine
Bouquet garni (1 sprig parsley, handful of celery leaves, 1 bay
  leaf, 3 peppercorns, 2 whole cloves, 1 thyme sprig [or ¼ tea-
  spoon dried] tied in a cheesecloth bag)
Balsamic Vinegar Sauce (see below)
Vegetables (see below)
¼ cup finely chopped fresh parsley

1. In a flameproof casserole large enough to hold the beef fairly snugly, heat 1 tablespoon of the oil. Add the onion and cook until soft. Do not brown. With a slotted spoon, transfer to a large bowl.
2. Add the remaining oil to the pot, and over medium-high heat, brown the beef evenly. Transfer to the bowl with the onion. Pour off any fat remaining in the casserole. Pour in the wine, and over medium heat, simmer, scraping up the browned-on bits from the bottom of the pot.
3. Return the onion and beef to the pot, including any liquid that has accumulated in the bowl. Pour in enough water to just cover. Add the bouquet garni and bring to a boil, covered, on top of the stove.
4. Transfer to a preheated 325° oven and cook 3 hours, or until the beef is fork-tender.
5. Remove and discard the bouquet garni. Allow the meat to cool somewhat in its liquid. Refrigerate for several hours (or overnight).
6. To serve, slice the beef thinly. Arrange in the center of a large serving dish with slices overlapping. Spoon Vinegar Sauce over the beef (without overwhelming it). Arrange the vegetables around the beef and sprinkle with parsley.

BALSAMIC VINEGAR SAUCE

1½ cups olive oil
½ cup balsamic vinegar
  (or red wine vinegar)
1 teaspoon sugar
1 teaspoon Kosciusko mustard
Salt and freshly ground black pepper to taste

Combine all ingredients and blend well. Any remaining sauce will keep in the refrigerator for up to a week. Shake well before using.

VEGETABLES

¾ pound broccoli flowerets
12 small carrots, scraped
6 small leeks, using all but the last 2 inches of dark green, cut
  into 3-inch lengths, thoroughly washed under running water

1. Cook the vegetables in lightly salted boiling water until crisp-tender. Drain well.
2. Marinate the vegetables separately in several spoonfuls of the Vinegar Sauce at least 1 hour (do not overwhelm with sauce).

Quick Oven Stew

3 tablespoons butter
2 pounds lean beef chuck, cut into 1-inch cubes
12 small onions, root ends scored
12 small carrots, scraped
¼ cup flour
2 teaspoons salt
¼ teaspoon freshly ground black pepper
1 tablespoon prepared mustard
1 bay leaf
2 cups water
1 cup tomato juice
2 cups Mashed Potatoes with Scallions (p. 316)

1. In a frying pan, over medium heat, melt the butter and evenly

brown the beef. Transfer to a casserole. Add the vegetables.

2. Combine the flour, salt, pepper, mustard, bay leaf, water, and tomato juice in a large jar with a top and shake well to blend. Pour into the frying pan and simmer 10 minutes, stirring, scraping up the browned-on bits from the bottom of the pan. Pour over the meat and vegetables in the casserole.

3. Cook, covered, in a preheated 325° oven for 2 hours, or until the beef is tender. Discard bay leaf.

4. Arrange the potatoes around the edges of the stew. Increase oven heat to 400° and bake 15 minutes, or until the potatoes are golden brown.

Beef à la Mode   SERVES 4 TO 6

3-pound top or bottom round beef roast
Flour for dredging
3 tablespoons unsalted butter
1 tablespoon olive oil
Salt and freshly ground black pepper
8 ounces tomato sauce (homemade or commercial)
1/2 cup water
1/2 cup red wine
1 large celery stalk, quartered
1 large onion, quartered
1/2 teaspoon dried marjoram

1. Dredge the meat with flour, and in a flameproof casserole, just large enough to hold the beef snugly, heat the butter and oil and brown the meat evenly. Sprinkle with salt and pepper. Pour off any fat in the pan.

2. Add the tomato sauce, water, and wine. Add the celery, onion, and marjoram. Bring to a boil on top of the stove. Cover with aluminum foil, then the top of the pot.

3. Cook in a preheated 300° oven for 3 hours, or until the meat is fork-tender.

Serve with Potato Pancakes (p. 373).

Boeuf à la Ficelle

We continue to mention the name of Antoine Gilly. He learned this dish, "Beef Hung with a String," from Gaston Magrin, chef on the luxurious French ocean liner *Normandie*, a favorite mode of transportation for Antoine, who loved to eat well as he traveled to and from France.

4 quarts beef broth
12 medium-sized carrots, scraped and halved
6 medium-sized onions
6 cloves (1 studded into each onion)
6 celery stalks, scraped and halved
6 small leeks, white part only, well washed
2 garlic cloves, unpeeled
Salt to taste (the broth may supply enough salt)
12 peppercorns
4 pounds beef in a solid piece, chuck, rump, or sirloin
Sturdy butcher's twine
12 small new potatoes, shaped as eggs, boiled separately

1. Place the broth in a very large pot, adding the carrots, onions, celery, leeks, garlic, salt, and peppercorns. On high heat, bring to a boil, then reduce heat to medium and simmer 45 minutes, or until vegetables are tender.
2. Remove the vegetables, discarding the garlic cloves. Keep warm.
3. Tie the piece of beef around the center with butcher's twine and hang it from a crossbar (a large wooden spoon works well) in the pot of broth. Hang it so the meat is not touching the sides of the pot but is suspended in and surrounded by the beef broth.
4. Cover tightly with foil, and simmer over medium heat 20 minutes per pound (about 1½ hours).
5. The beef will emerge from the broth medium-rare (pink) and very tender. Place on a large, warm serving dish and surround with the vegetables and potatoes. Serve immediately. The beef should be sliced against the grain, 1 inch thick.

Boiled Beef with Horseradish-Walnut Sauce   SERVES 4 TO 6

1 pound short ribs
2 onions
3 cloves (studded into 1 onion)
1 celery stalk, cut into several pieces
1 large carrot, scraped and cut into several pieces
1 bay leaf
1 teaspoon peppercorns
1 teaspoon salt
3 quarts water
3-pound brisket of beef
Horseradish Sauce with Walnuts (see below)

1. In a soup pot, over medium-high heat, combine the short ribs, onions, celery, carrot, bay leaf, peppercorns, salt, and water. Bring to a boil, lower heat, and simmer 1 hour, skimming off the top as necessary.

2. Add the brisket (carefully, as the stock will be hot). If the liquid does not cover the beef, add enough boiling water to cover. Cook, partially covered, 3 hours, or until tender. (Vegetables, such as leeks, potatoes, cabbage, and carrots, can be added during the last half hour of cooking.)

Slice the beef, and arrange on a hot serving dish surrounded by vegetables if desired. Pass the sauce at the table.

Serve with Lemon Dill Potatoes (p. 340).

HORSERADISH SAUCE WITH WALNUTS   SERVES 6

Antoine Gilly liked to offer this sauce with boiled beef and cold roast beef. It is served cold.

1 cup sour cream
2 tablespoons heavy cream
⅓ cup grated fresh horseradish (or well-drained prepared)
4 ounces walnuts
1½ teaspoons sugar
Salt to taste

1. In a bowl, blend the sour cream, heavy cream, and horseradish.
2. Hand chop the walnuts; pieces should be fine but not pulverized as they would be in a processor or blender. They should add crunch to the sauce. Stir the walnuts, sugar, and salt into the cream sauce, blending well.

Braciola

SERVES 4 TO 6

This is a large stuffed, rolled round of beef.

TO PREPARE THE ROLL:

> *2-pound piece of round steak in one piece cut about ½ inch thick*
> *4 tablespoons (½ stick) unsalted butter*
> *½ cup chopped fresh parsley*
> *1 garlic clove, minced*
> *1 cup fresh bread crumbs, soaked in milk; with the milk squeezed out*
> *2 slices lean prosciutto, chopped (about ½ cup)*
> *4 slices Genoa salami, chopped (about ½ cup)*
> *3 tablespoons minced raisins*
> *3 tablespoons coarsely chopped pignoli, cooked in 2 tablespoons butter until golden*
> *½ cup grated Asiago or Parmesan cheese*
> *1 egg, beaten*
> *Salt and freshly ground black pepper to taste*

1. Have your butcher pound the beef to ¼-inch thickness, or do it yourself with a meat mallet, being careful not to perforate it anywhere.
2. Place on a flat surface. Spread a paste of the butter, parsley and garlic over the steak evenly.
3. In a bowl, combine and blend well with a fork the bread crumbs, prosciutto, salami, raisins, pignoli, cheese, and egg. Spread the mixture evenly over the butter paste on the beef. Sprinkle with salt and pepper.

4. Roll the beef up tightly, jelly-roll-fashion, starting from the smaller end, and tie securely with cord in several places so the filling will not escape during cooking. The roll will look like a large, fat sausage.

TO COOK THE ROLL:

>2 tablespoons butter
>2 tablespoons olive oil
>Salt and freshly ground black pepper to taste
>1 medium-sized onion, chopped
>¼ cup Marsala
>1 cup beef broth
>1 one-pound can Italian tomatoes, run through a food mill or blender
>2 tablespoons tomato paste

1. In a flameproof casserole just large enough to comfortably hold the roll, heat the butter and oil. Add the roll and brown evenly, sprinkling lightly with salt and pepper, turning it with two wooden spoons as it browns. Transfer to a plate and set aside.
2. Pour off all but about 1 tablespoon fat, if not absorbed by the meat, or add 1 tablespoon butter. Add the onion and cook 2 minutes, or until soft. Do not brown. Pour on the Marsala and cook, stirring up the browned-on bits from the bottom of the pot, until the wine has reduced by half.
3. Pour in the beef broth, tomatoes, and tomato paste, stirring to blend. Return the beef to the casserole. The liquid should not cover the meat but should come about halfway up the side of the roll. If more liquid is needed, add hot beef broth or water. Bring just to a boil on top of the stove. Transfer to a preheated 350° oven and cook, covered, for 1 hour, or until the beef is tender, basting several times or turning (with the wooden spoons).
4. Remove the beef, strain the sauce, return to the pot, and, over medium-high heat, cook until the sauce thickens.
5. To serve, spoon the sauce onto a hot, rimmed serving dish.

Remove the cord from the roll and cut the meat into 1-inch-thick slices. Arrange overlapping (if necessary) on the sauce and spoon sauce over the slices as they are served.

Serve with Potatoes Parma (p. 349).

Caterer's Rib of Beef

Contrary to what is generally believed, rib roasts are not all that easy to prepare. When we lived in Washington, Connecticut, we knew a talented cook and caterer, Dorothy Gayat, who turned out perfect rib roasts every time. She believed that they need little seasoning, that rare beef speaks for itself. Here's the rest of her secret.

3-rib beef roast (center cut)
Salt and freshly ground black pepper

1. Preheat the oven to 525°. Rub the roast well with salt and pepper.
2. On a rack, in an uncovered pan, cook the beef (the roast should be cooked 15 minutes per rib) for 45 minutes.
3. Turn the oven off and let the roast set for two hours. Most important! *Do not open the oven to take a peek* or the whole cooking technique will be thrown off.

Serve this with Mustard Sauce (see below) and Copenhagen Sugared Potatoes (p. 332).

Note: This procedure is only for those who prefer their beef rare.

MUSTARD SAUCE   MAKES ABOUT 1¼ CUPS

1 cup sour cream
¼ cup Dijon mustard
1 tablespoon minced fresh chives
1 teaspoon minced fresh tarragon
1 teaspoon balsamic vinegar

In a bowl, combine and blend well all ingredients.

Coffee-Braised Round Roast of Beef

SERVES 6

You don't have to be a coffee lover to get a lift from this unusually tasty roast.

4-pound top round roast of beef
2 garlic cloves, peeled and quartered
1 cup red wine vinegar
2 tablespoons olive oil
2 cups strong black coffee
2 cups water

1. With a sharp knife, cut slits in the roast, the number according to the number of pieces of garlic. Insert a piece of garlic into each slit.

2. Place the beef in a non-metallic bowl and pour the vinegar over it, cover with plastic wrap, and refrigerate for 24 hours, turning the meat in the vinegar a half dozen times.

3. Remove the meat from the bowl and dry it. In a flameproof casserole, heat the oil and evenly brown the meat. It should be well browned.

4. Pour the coffee over the meat and add 2 cups water. Cover, bring to a boil on top of the stove, place in a preheated 300° oven, and braise for 3 hours.

Serve the tender slices of beef with Potato Cones with Mushroom Sauce (p. 347).

Braised Rump of Beef Florentine

SERVES 4

Although Italy is not generally noted for its beef, Florence is an exception. The ancient city is famous for its steaks. Several restaurants serve fillets and strip sirloins nearly as good as those in the United States. This beef dish is braised in Chianti from the area around Florence, one of the most famous of Italy's wines. Although this is reminiscent of a German sauerbraten in the way it's prepared, the flavors are distinctly different.

3-pound rump roast of beef
1 cup red Chianti
3 tablespoons brandy
1/8 teaspoon nutmeg
2 bay leaves
2 garlic cloves, halved
1/2 teaspoon thyme
1 teaspoon salt
1/2 teaspoon freshly ground black pepper
Flour for dredging
3 tablespoons olive oil
2 cups beef broth

1. Place the beef in a large bowl and pour in the Chianti and brandy, turning the beef in it several times. Add the nutmeg, bay leaves, garlic, thyme, salt, and pepper.

2. Marinate at room temperature for 3 hours, turning the beef in the marinade several times.

3. Remove the beef from the bowl (reserving the marinade) and dry well with paper towels. Dredge with the flour.

4. In a large flameproof casserole, heat the olive oil and brown the beef evenly. Add the beef broth and the reserved marinade.

5. Bring to a boil on top of the stove, then place in a preheated 300° oven and cook, covered, for 3 hours, or until the beef is tender.

6. Remove the beef, reduce the braising liquid over high heat by two-thirds, and moisten the sliced beef with the light but authoritative sauce.

At the Albergo Excelsior, where we first enjoyed this dish, they delighted us by serving it with Gnocchi (p. 296).

Glazed Brisket of Corned Beef   SERVES 6

We tend to overlook the brisket, a deliciously different cut and treatment of beef.

4-pound corned beef brisket
1 medium-sized onion, peeled, halved
6 black peppercorns, crushed
1 bay leaf
⅓ cup Kosciusko mustard
⅓ cup balsamic vinegar
½ cup dark brown sugar, packed
1 tablespoon white wine Worcestershire sauce

1. Place the brisket in a heavy pot and cover with cold water. Soak for 5 hours. Drain.
2. Cover the beef with water again. Add the onion, peppercorns, and bay leaf. Cover and simmer over medium heat for 3 hours, or until the beef is tender. Drain and dry brisket.
3. In an enamel-lined saucepan, combine the mustard, balsamic vinegar, brown sugar, and white wine Worcestershire. Blend well and simmer 3 minutes, stirring.
4. Place the beef in a roasting pan, fat side up. Spread the sugar glaze over the beef. Bake, uncovered, in a preheated 350° oven 40 minutes.
We like this with Aunt Edie's Roasted Potatoes (p. 324).

Corned Beef Brisket with Herbed Vegetables

SERVES 4 (with enough beef left over for Corned Beef Hash, p. 66).

2½- to 3½-pound corned beef brisket
8 baby carrots, scraped
8 small new potatoes, scrubbed, left whole, with skins
½ pound fresh young string beans
16 pearl onions
3 tablespoons unsalted butter
1 teaspoon chopped fresh thyme, or ⅓ teaspoon dried
1 teaspoon chopped fresh tarragon, or ⅓ teaspoon dried
¼ teaspoon dry mustard
Salt and freshly ground black pepper to taste

1. Place corned beef in a Dutch oven and cover with cold water. Bring to a boil. Cover, reduce heat, and simmer 3 hours, or until meat is tender.

2. Cook the carrots, potatoes, string beans, and onions separately until crisp-tender, or tender according to taste.

3. Melt the butter in a saucepan; stir in the thyme, tarragon, and mustard. Sprinkle with salt and pepper. Add the vegetables and toss gently to coat them with the herbed butter.

4. Carve (across the grain) thin slices and serve surrounded with vegetables.

Fillet à la Antoine Gilly SERVES 4

Our mentor often prepared that star of the beef stage, the fillet, very simply.

3 tablespoons soft unsalted butter
1 large garlic clove, minced or put through a garlic press
1 teaspoon salt
Hot Hungarian paprika
3-pound fillet, trimmed, at room temperature

1. In a bowl, combine and blend well the butter, garlic, and salt. Coat the entire fillet evenly with the butter mixture and sprinkle very lightly with the paprika.

2. Place the fillet on a rack in a pan. Cook, uncovered, in a preheated 525° oven for 8 minutes; turn, cook for another 8 minutes.

3. Reduce oven heat to 350° and continue cooking 25 minutes. Test for doneness by making a small incision with a sharp knife in the thickest part to check for pinkness. (We like ours very pink.) Rest fillet for 10 minutes on a warm platter before slicing.

4. While the fillet rests, make the sauce (see note below).

Serve with a Burgundian Potato-Leek Pie (p. 328).

Note: Antoine also used a simple method for sauces to accompany his roasts. Either he would add a heaping tablespoon of currant jelly to the drippings, then blend well and serve hot, or he would thicken the drippings slightly with flour, then add a wineglass of good claret, blending the mixture well.

Pot-au-Feu
SERVES 6

(French Boiled Dinner)

> *3 pounds boneless rump of beef, in one solid piece*
> *2 pounds beef marrow bones*
> *1 tablespoon salt*
> *Bouquet garni (1 bay leaf, celery tops, parsley sprig, 6 pepper-corns tied in a cheesecloth)*
> *2 medium-sized onions*
> *2 cloves (one studded into each onion)*
> *3 garlic cloves, unpeeled*
> *3 quarts beef broth or water*
> *6 celery stalks, scraped and cut into halves*
> *3 small white turnips, scraped and cut into halves*
> *6 small potatoes, peeled*
> *6 small carrots, scraped*
> *6 leeks (white part only), thoroughly washed*
> *2 tablespoons chopped parsley*

1. Place the beef, bones, salt, bouquet garni, onions, garlic, and beef broth or water in a deep stockpot large enough to hold them comfortably (the water should come well above the contents of the pot). Bring to a boil; skim the foam from the top as it forms. Lower heat and simmer, partially covered, for 3 to 3½ hours, or until the beef is almost tender. Remove the marrow bones, and with a table knife remove the marrow and reserve. Discard the bones.
2. Remove the meat from the pot. Spoon off excess fat and strain the stock (discarding the onions, garlic, and bouquet garni). Return it, with the meat, to the pot. Add the celery, turnips, potatoes, carrots, and leeks, and cook 45 minutes, or until the beef and vegetables are tender. If the vegetables cook more quickly, remove them as they become tender, then return them to the pot just before

serving to heat through. Taste stock for seasoning.

3. Serve stock in soup bowls as a first course, with small cubes of the marrow, sprinkled with parsley.

4. Follow with sliced beef surrounded by the vegetables as the main course.

Hot Horseradish Sauce (see below) is excellent with the beef.

HOT HORSERADISH SAUCE   MAKES ABOUT 1½ CUPS

> *3 tablespoons butter*
> *3 tablespoons flour*
> *1½ cups beef stock*
> *½ cup heavy cream*
> *½ teaspoon sugar*
> *Salt and freshly ground black pepper to taste*
> *1 tablespoon fresh lemon juice*
> *¼ cup (or to taste) freshly grated horseradish (if not available,*
>   *use slightly more prepared horseradish squeezed dry)*

1. In a saucepan, over medium heat, melt the butter. Add flour. Stir into a smooth paste. Gradually add the beef stock, stirring into a smooth sauce. Add the cream, sugar, salt, and pepper.

2. Just before serving, stir in the lemon juice and horseradish, and taste for seasoning.

Roast Beef Rump with Creamy Caper Sauce   SERVES 6

> *3 tablespoons olive oil*
> *3-pound (approximately) rump roast of beef*
> *½ teaspoon rosemary*
> *¼ teaspoon thyme*
> *Salt and freshly ground black pepper*
> *Creamy Caper Sauce (see below)*

1. In a flameproof casserole, heat the olive oil and brown the beef evenly. Sprinkle on the rosemary, thyme, salt, and pepper.

2. Transfer to a preheated 450° oven and cook, uncovered, 15

minutes. Lower heat to 350° and, basting frequently, cook 35 minutes for rare beef. Remove from oven and let juices settle for 20 minutes before slicing. Serve with Creamy Caper Sauce and Potatoes Anna (p. 302).

CREAMY CAPER SAUCE

> *1½ cups whipped cream*
> *2 tablespoons prepared mustard*
> *2 tablespoons capers, rinsed and well drained*

Combine all ingredients in a bowl and blend well. Chill.

Deviled Short Ribs of Beef Gilly   SERVES 4

The meat closest to the bone has often been called the sweetest.

> *4 pounds short ribs of beef*
> *1 cup Dijon mustard*
> *1½ cups white bread crumbs*
> *½ cup olive oil*
> *1 tablespoon salt*
> *1 tablespoon freshly ground black pepper*

1. In a shallow roasting pan, cook the ribs, uncovered, in a preheated 350° oven for 1 hour.
2. While the ribs are roasting, in a bowl, blend the mustard, bread crumbs, oil, salt, and pepper into a spreadable paste.
3. Remove the meat from the oven after 1 hour and spread the paste evenly over the top side of the ribs. Roast 1 more hour at 350°.
4. Place the ribs under the lowest elevation of the broiler, cooking slowly 10 minutes. Move them to the broiler's highest position for 5 minutes, to form a crust. Watch carefully so the top doesn't burn. Remove the bones and carve the ribs into four portions.
Antoine Gilly served these with Sauce à la Diable (see below) and Straw Potatoes (p. 318).

½ cup chopped shallots
¼ cup Madeira
1 cup Brown Sauce (p. 62)
1 teaspoon salt
½ teaspoon freshly ground black pepper
2 tablespoons Worcestershire sauce
1 tablespoon Dijon mustard
1 tablespoon chopped fresh tarragon, or 1 teaspoon dried
2 tablespoons cognac
6 tablespoons unsalted butter, softened

1. Place the shallots and Madeira in a saucepan and simmer over medium heat 5 minutes.
2. Stir in the brown sauce, simmer 5 minutes. Add salt, pepper, Worcestershire, mustard, and tarragon. Simmer 2 minutes. Stir in the cognac.
3. Push through a fine strainer into a bowl. Mix the butter into the sauce slowly, just before serving, so the sauce will be smooth and the butter flavor at its best.

Royal Standing Rib   SERVES 6

With good reason the standing rib roast is known as the royalty of meats. Not only does it have a noble bearing, but all it needs is its own succulent personality.

4- to 5-pound standing rib roast, at room temperature
Kosher salt

1. Rub the roast well with the salt.
2. Preheat oven to 500°.
3. Place roast, uncovered, standing upright on its ribs, in a large, heavy roasting pan. Cook 15 minutes.
4. Reduce heat to 350° and cook the roast 15 minutes per pound (for rare), 20 minutes per pound (for medium), or 25 minutes per

pound (for, heaven forbid!, well done).

Serve with Potato Pudding for Roast Beef (p. 351).

Note: See another simply done rib roast, Caterer's Rib of Beef (p. 82).

Sauerbraten   SERVES 4 TO 6

Our friend Rita Reimanis often cooks this German specialty.

> *3- to 4-pound solid piece of lean chuck, top or bottom round*
>   *pot roast*
> *Salt*
> *2 cups red wine vinegar*
> *2 cups water*
> *½ lemon, thinly sliced*
> *1 large onion, thinly sliced*
> *1 large carrot, thinly sliced*
> *1 garlic clove, halved*
> *6 peppercorns*
> *2 bay leaves*
> *3 whole cloves*
> *Flour for dredging*
> *4 tablespoons (½ stick) unsalted butter*

1. Rub the beef with salt and place in a deep non-metal bowl. Combine the remaining ingredients, except the flour and butter, in a saucepan and heat just to a boil. Pour the hot marinade over the beef, cool, cover, and refrigerate 3 days, turning the meat once or twice a day.

2. Remove the meat (strain and reserve the marinade). Dry the meat well and dredge with flour. In a heavy flameproof casserole, over medium-high heat, melt the butter. Add the beef and brown evenly. Pour half the marinade over, bring to a boil on top of the stove, cover tightly, and cook in a preheated 350° oven for 2 hours, or until the meat is tender. If liquid cooks off, add more hot marinade to maintain about 2 cups of liquid.

3. Slice the beef and serve with one of the following sauces spooned over the slices.
Serve with German Potato Dumplings #1 or #2 (p. 295 or p. 296).

SAUCE #1

> *Beef marinade*
> *¾ cup gingersnaps, crumbled*
> *1½ teaspoons sugar*

Strain the liquid in the casserole and stir in the crumbled gingersnaps and the sugar. Simmer until the sauce thickens. Taste for seasoning.

SAUCE #2

> *Beef marinade*
> *2 tablespoons flour*
> *¼ cup water*
> *1 tablespoon chopped fresh dill or 1 teaspoon dried*

Strain the liquid in the casserole and stir in the flour mixed with the water. Simmer, stirring, until the sauce thickens. Stir in the dill. Taste for seasoning.

Steak Teriyaki

SERVES 6

Here's our version of a Japanese favorite.

> *3-pound piece top round steak, 2 inches thick*
> *1 large garlic clove, mashed*
> *1 tablespoon chopped fresh ginger*
> *1 tablespoon sugar*
> *2 tablespoons cider vinegar*
> *½ cup soy sauce*
> *¼ cup dry white wine*

1. Place the steak in a shallow dish (but deep enough to hold the marinade). In a bowl, blend remaining ingredients into a marinade.
2. Pour the marinade over the steak and marinate at room tem-

perature for 4 hours, turning frequently.

3. Place the steak on a rack in the broiler pan and broil in the high position for 20 minutes. Turn steak over and broil for 20 minutes, or to your taste (rare or medium).

Serve carved in thin slices, cut across the grain.

Serve with Potatoes Frigo (p. 350).

Beef Fillet with Olives Tuscany   SERVES 6 TO 8

Here's another beef dish from Florence, which is on the outskirts of Italy's noted olive country. Both olive oil and olives dominate this dish. Start this recipe a day ahead of cooking time.

3 tablespoons white wine Worcestershire sauce
2 garlic cloves, minced
1 teaspoon salt
½ teaspoon freshly ground black pepper
3-pound trimmed fillet of beef
Flour for dredging
4 tablespoons olive oil
1 cup pitted black and green olives, halved
1½ teaspoons Kosciusko mustard
1½ cups beef broth

1. In a small bowl, combine and blend well the Worcestershire sauce, garlic, salt, and pepper.

2. Rub the beef well with this blend and refrigerate 8 hours or overnight.

3. Dredge the beef with flour. In a flameproof casserole, heat the olive oil and brown the fillet evenly.

4. Remove beef; add olives, mustard, and beef broth to the pot, blending well. Return the beef to the pot, bring liquid to a boil, cover and cook in a preheated 300° oven 35 minutes for medium rare, spooning sauce over the beef several times. Test for doneness with a sharp knife.

Serve with Baked Potatoes with Avocado Sauce (p. 362).

Beefsteak Pommarola

(Steak with Fresh Tomato Sauce)

> 4 tablespoons olive oil
> 2 garlic cloves, each cut into 3 pieces
> 3 large, ripe tomatoes, peeled, seeded, and coarsely chopped, or
>   3 cups drained, canned tomatoes, chopped
> 2 teaspoons basil
> 1/8 teaspoon (or to taste) crushed hot red pepper flakes
> Salt to taste
> 3-pound sirloin, T-bone, or porterhouse steak, cut 1½ inches
>   thick

1. In a medium-sized saucepan, heat 2 tablespoons olive oil. Add garlic and cook until golden (about 2 minutes). Do not brown. When soft, press down with wooden spoon, but do not break up.
2. Add the tomatoes, basil, and red pepper flakes. Sprinkle in salt and cook over medium heat, uncovered, for 15 minutes, or until most of the liquid has evaporated. Taste for seasoning.
3. In a frying pan just large enough to comfortably hold the steak, heat the remaining olive oil. Brown the steak over high heat on both sides. Lower heat. Spoon on the tomato sauce and cook 8 to 10 minutes, or according to your taste. Rare or medium rare steaks are the most tender.
Serve with Potato-Broccoli Pudding (p. 346).

Bistecca alla Fiorentina

(Steak Florentine Style)

> ⅓ cup olive oil
> ⅓ cup wine vinegar, preferably balsamic
> 1 garlic clove, minced
> ½ teaspoon dried oregano
> 2 tablespoons chopped broadleaf parsley
> 3-pound, 1½-inch-thick porterhouse steak, well trimmed of all fat
> Salt to taste

1. Combine all ingredients, except the steak and salt, and blend well.

2. Place steak in a shallow dish, pour on half the marinade, turn the steak, and pour on the remainder of the marinade.

3. Marinate the steak at room temperature for 3 hours, turning in the marinade 4 times.

4. Preheat the broiler to high. Remove the steak from the marinade and dry with paper towels. Discard the marinade (or save it for the next day and use the same procedure for broiling pork chops).

5. Season on both sides with salt, and broil the steak 3 inches from the heat for 5 minutes. Turn the steak and broil for 5 minutes. Serve with Potato-Cauliflower Puree (p. 316).

Braised Andalusian Steak   SERVES 6

3-pound piece of bottom round steak, cut into 6 serving pieces
    and dried with paper towels
1 minced garlic clove
1 teaspoon salt
½ teaspoon freshly ground black pepper
⅛ teaspoon cayenne
¹⁄₁₆ teaspoon ground cloves
½ teaspoon thyme
4 tablespoons olive oil
1 large green pepper, seeds and ribs removed, coarsely chopped
⅔ cup small stuffed green olives, well drained
Bouquet garni (1 bay leaf, 2 sprigs parsley, several celery leaves,
    and 2 whole cloves tied in a cheesecloth)
2 large, ripe tomatoes, peeled and coarsely chopped
2 cups beef broth
6 medium-sized potatoes, peeled and halved
6 large, firm mushrooms, thickly sliced
3 tablespoons dry sherry

1. Rub the pieces of steak with a mixture of the garlic, salt, pepper, cayenne, cloves, and thyme.

2. In a large frying pan, heat the oil and brown the pieces of beef on both sides. Transfer them to a casserole large enough to hold them in one layer, or slightly overlapping.

3. To the frying pan, add the green pepper, olives, bouquet garni, tomatoes, and beef broth. Bring to a boil and pour over the steaks. The mixture should barely cover the meat. If it doesn't, add more hot broth or water.

4. Cover and braise in a preheated 350° oven for 1 hour. Add the potatoes and cook 30 minutes. Add the mushrooms and sherry, and cook 10 minutes, or until the beef and potatoes are tender. Taste for seasoning. Discard the bouquet garni.

Rick Canali's Fillet of Beef Michelangelo   SERVES 4

Trattorie, those small neighborhood family-owned restaurants in Italy, have become famous for their special dishes. Such places are rare indeed in the United States, but we discovered a gem in upstate New York: The Palms, in Elmira, which is run by owner-chefs, Bernice and Lou Canali and their son Rick. Although the Canalis' pastas are superb, they also serve unusually elegant meat dishes, among them this beef fillet created by Rick Canali. Says Rick, "When people celebrate, they nearly always go for red meat, often beef, and fillet is a favorite."

> *2 pounds trimmed beef fillet, cut into 8 one-inch-thick slices*
> *(about 4 to 5 ounces each)*
> *Canali Sauce (see below)*
> *2 garlic cloves, sliced into 24 slivers*
> *Coarsely ground black pepper*
> *Salt*
> *1 to 2 tablespoons extra virgin olive oil*
> *2 tablespoons unsalted butter*
> *2 tablespoons fresh Italian parsley, coarsely chopped*

1. Make 3 tiny slices with a sharp paring knife in each of the steaks. Insert the slivers of garlic. Rub the pepper on each side of the steak. Salt to taste. Set aside while you make the sauce.

2. Heat a large, heavy, tall-sided sauté pan. In the oil and butter, sauté the steaks over high heat 2 to 3 minutes on each side for rare. Transfer steaks to a large hot serving platter. Ladle the sauce sparingly over all. Sprinkle with parsley.

Serve with Green Mashed-Potato Pancakes (p. 376).

CANALI SAUCE

> 1 onion, very finely chopped
> 1 carrot, very finely chopped
> 1 celery stalk, very finely chopped
> 10 to 11 tablespoons (1¼ sticks) unsalted butter
> 1 cup good-grade Italian red wine
> ½ cup good meat stock
> 1 cup demiglaze, or brown beef gravy
> 2 tablespoons tomato paste
> 1 pound fresh mushrooms, thinly sliced
> ½ teaspoon dried thyme
> ½ teaspoon dried basil

1. In a heavy-bottomed saucepan, sauté the onion, carrot, and celery in 8 tablespoons butter over low heat until quite soft and golden. Add wine, stock, demiglaze, and tomato paste. Let simmer 15 minutes. Strain.

2. In a sauté pan, quickly cook the mushrooms in 2 or 3 tablespoons butter for 2 minutes. Add to the strained sauce. Return the sauce to the heat and add the herbs. Simmer about 15 minutes. Keep warm.

Antoine Gilly's Filets Mignons
SERVES 4

This classic dish is sometimes called Filet Mignon Marquis de Sade, but since Antoine Gilly produced it so beautifully, as far as we're concerned, it deserves his name.

½ cup beef broth

1 tablespoon tomato paste

1 black truffle (cut 4 thin slices from the center and chop the
remainder)

1 tablespoon olive oil

3 tablespoons unsalted butter

4 filets mignons, 1½ inches thick, about 6 ounces each

Salt and freshly ground black pepper to taste

4 half-inch-thick slices French bread, cut the same size as the filets, fried in butter until golden and crisp, drained on paper
towel, kept warm

½ cup fine dry Spanish sherry

½ cup heavy cream

1 tablespoon cornstarch

1. In a small saucepan, heat the beef broth and tomato paste,
stirring well to blend. Add the chopped truffle (do not stir in the
slices). Set aside off heat.

2. In a frying pan, heat the oil and 2 tablespoons butter, and cook
the filets 1½ minutes on each side, or to suit your taste preference.
Sprinkle with salt and pepper.

3. On warm individual plates, place a slice of bread. Top with a
filet. Keep warm.

4. To the pan in which the filets cooked, add sherry, and over high
heat, reduce by half, stirring, scraping up the browned-on bits from
the bottom of the pan. Blend in the beef broth and tomato-paste
mixture and the remaining butter.

5. In a small bowl, whip the cream with the cornstarch; the cream
should not be stiffly beaten.

6. Stir the cream-cornstarch mixture into the saucepan, blending
well over heat just until the sauce is hot and thickened. Taste for
seasoning, adding salt and pepper if needed.

7. Spoon a discreet amount of sauce over each filet on its toast
raft. Place a slice of truffle on top of each one and serve immediately.
Serve with Hashed Brown Potatoes with Vinegar (p. 297).

Pan-Broiled Fillets of Beef

SERVES 4

1½ tablespoons olive oil
1 large garlic clove, quartered
4 fillet steaks, 1½ inches thick
Salt and freshly ground pepper to taste
2 ounces brandy
3 tablespoons unsalted butter
3 tablespoons chopped fresh parsley

1. In a frying pan large enough to hold all the fillets, heat the oil. Add the garlic, then the fillets. Lavishly mill with pepper and lightly sprinkle with salt, on both sides, and sauté, turning very often (about 10 minutes), until evenly brown on both sides and juicy and red or pink inside (depending on your taste). Discard garlic.
2. Transfer to a hot serving dish and keep warm.
3. Pour the brandy into the frying pan (carefully, standing back, as the brandy could flare up) and cook on medium heat until half of it has evaporated. Add the butter, stirring until it has melted and is hot. Pour the sauce over the fillets and sprinkle on the parsley. Serve with Au Gratin Potatoes and Carrots (p. 322).

Minute Steaks with Herb Butter

SERVES 4

1½ to 2 pounds boneless beef, top sirloin, or top round, cut into
4 servings, pounded very thin with a meat mallet
Salt and freshly ground black pepper to taste
4 tablespoons (½ stick) unsalted butter
4 tablespoons olive oil
Herb Butter (see below)

1. Sprinkle each steak lightly with salt and pepper.
2. In a large frying pan (or use two pans), heat 1 tablespoon butter and 1 tablespoon oil for each steak. Add the steaks and over high heat cook quickly, about 2 minutes, turning.

Serve very hot, immediately, with a square of Herb Butter melting on each steak.

8 tablespoons (1 stick) soft unsalted butter
2 tablespoons finely chopped parsley
2 teaspoons finely chopped fresh tarragon, or ⅔ teaspoon dried
2 tablespoons finely chopped chives
Salt to taste

1. Combine all ingredients, blending well with a fork.
2. Chill. When firm enough to handle, reshape into a stick as it was before the butter was softened. Refrigerate and cut into squares as needed. This will freeze well.

Pommes de Terre Marguerite (p. 300) convert a simple minute-steak dinner into elegant fare.

Portuguese Beef (or Veal) Birds   SERVES 6

12 thin slices top sirloin, boneless beef, or top round (or veal),
*   weighing about 2 pounds*
2-inch cube of fatback, cut up
4 tablespoons (½ stick) unsalted butter
2 garlic cloves, quartered
3 tablespoons chopped parsley
⅛ teaspoon leaf sage
8 tablespoons fine bread crumbs
8 tablespoons grated Asiago or Parmesan cheese
Salt and freshly ground black pepper to taste
Flour for dredging
3 tablespoons olive oil
4 ounces Madeira
2 cups beef broth
1 medium-sized onion, finely chopped
2 medium-sized carrots, scraped, cut into short, narrow strips
2 celery stalks, scraped, cut into short, narrow strips

1. Pound the slices of meat until very thin without perforating them, forming 4-inch squares (more or less).

2. In a blender or processor (or chop by hand), combine and blend into a paste the fatback, butter, garlic, parsley, and sage. Divide the paste among the 12 beef squares and spread over the meat. Sprinkle them with equal amounts of bread crumbs and cheese (2 teaspoons of each for each square) and season with salt and pepper. Roll into cylinders and tie with cord, or skewer with toothpicks. Dredge lightly with flour.

3. In a frying pan (or use two) large enough to hold the rolls in a single layer, heat the oil over medium heat. Add the rolls and brown evenly. Transfer to a warm dish. Pour excess fat from the pan. Stir in the Madeira, scraping the bottom of the pan to loosen the browned-on bits, and reduce the wine by two-thirds. Pour in the broth. Return the rolls to the pan and cook, uncovered, 15 minutes, or until almost tender. Add the onion, carrots, and celery strips, and cook 10 minutes, or until the meat and vegetables are tender. Serve with the vegetable strips.

Make it international by serving it with a Swiss Potato Torte (p. 283).

Rumstecks Carbonnade à la Flamande
(Rump Steaks Cooked in Beer)

SERVES 4

3 tablespoons unsalted butter
4 medium-sized onions, sliced
Salt and freshly ground black pepper to taste
4 rump steaks, each 1 inch thick (about ½ pound each)
Flour for dredging
3 tablespoons olive oil
3 ounces brandy
1 cup beef broth
2 cups dark beer
1 teaspoon brown sugar
2 garlic cloves, minced
Bouquet garni (1 sprig parsley, 1 bay leaf, ¼ teaspoon thyme,
    and some celery leaves tied in a cheesecloth)

1. Over medium heat, in a flameproof casserole, heat the butter. Add the onions and cook until golden. Sprinkle lightly with salt and pepper. Do not brown. Set casserole aside.

2. Dredge the steaks lightly with flour, shaking off any excess.

3. In a frying pan, heat the oil and brown the steaks on both sides, sprinkling lightly with salt and pepper. Pour the brandy over the steaks and, standing back, flambé the brandy.

4. Push half the onions aside in the casserole, arrange the steaks in a single layer over the remaining onions, then cover with the other half of the onions, so that the meat is sandwiched between onions.

5. Gradually add the broth and beer to the frying pan, stirring and scraping up the browned-on bits from the bottom of the pan. Stir in the sugar and garlic. Pour into the casserole (the liquid should cover the steak and onions. If not, add more broth) and add the bouquet garni. Bring to a boil on top of the stove, cover tightly, and cook in a preheated 325° oven for 2 hours, or until tender.

6. Spoon fat from top before serving. Taste for seasoning. Remove and discard the bouquet garni.

Delicious served with Rissolé Potatoes (p. 317).

Steak Candeur

SERVES 4

The French consider this a "candid" dish—simple but very flavorful.

> 1½ pounds boneless beef sirloin, cut into 4 serving pieces
> Flour for dredging
> 3 tablespoons unsalted butter
> 2 teaspoons spicy mustard
> 1 teaspoon Worcestershire sauce
> 3 tablespoons chopped chives
> 2 tablespoons brandy
> ½ cup beef broth

1. Pound steaks to about ¼-inch thickness. Dredge them with flour.

2. In a large frying pan, over medium heat, melt 2 tablespoons

butter and brown the steaks for 2 minutes on each side. Transfer to a hot dish and keep warm.

3. Spread both sides of the steaks with mustard and sprinkle with Worcestershire.

4. In a small frying pan, melt the remaining butter and cook the chives 1 minute, stirring constantly. Add brandy and broth, and cook, stirring, over high heat until reduced by half.

5. Return the steaks and any liquid that has collected in the dish to the large frying pan and heat through, turning 2 minutes. Spoon the hot brandy-chive sauce over just before serving.

Serve with Potatoes Nanette (p. 310).

Steaks with Red Wine Butter Sauce SERVES 4

4 shallots (or very small white onions), minced
1 small garlic clove, minced
1 bay leaf
1 cup dry red wine
8 tablespoons (1 stick) unsalted butter
Salt and freshly ground black pepper to taste
2 or 3 additional tablespoons butter (optional)
2 tablespoons olive oil
4 one-inch-thick shell steaks
3 tablespoons chopped fresh parsley

1. In an enamel-lined or stainless pan, combine the shallots (or onions), garlic, bay leaf, and wine, and cook, uncovered, until reduced to one-quarter of the original volume. Discard bay leaf.

2. In another saucepan, melt one stick of butter and slowly stir it into the seasoned wine. Season with salt and pepper. Stir in the additional butter if sauce seems too thin. Taste for seasoning.

3. Over high heat, coat the bottom of a frying pan, large enough to hold the steaks comfortably in one layer without touching, with the olive oil. Add the steaks, season with salt and pepper, and cook 5 minutes, turning almost constantly. (Using tongs will prevent the

loss of juice.) Lower heat and cook steaks, turning once, 2 to 3 minutes on each side, or to doneness desired. At 2 or 3 minutes they should be rare.

4. Heat the wine-butter sauce over low heat. Do not boil. Stir in the parsley. Spoon enough on the steaks to barely coat them.

Offer any remaining sauce at the table, and serve with Creamed Potatoes au Gratin (p. 334), a simple French classic.

Sirloin Steak Lyonnaise
(Sirloin Steak with Onions)

SERVES 4

5 tablespoons unsalted butter
2 tablespoons olive oil
3 medium-sized white onions, thinly sliced
Salt and freshly ground black pepper to taste
1 teaspoon red wine vinegar, preferably balsamic
1 tablespoon meat glaze, or Bovril
2 ounces dry vermouth
1½ to 2 pounds of 1-inch-thick boneless sirloin steak, cut into 4
    portions, slightly flattened
2 tablespoons chopped parsley

1. In a frying pan, heat 2 tablespoons butter and 1 tablespoon oil. Add the onions and cook 6 minutes, or until golden, stirring occasionally. Do not brown. Season with salt and pepper. Add the vinegar, meat glaze, and vermouth. Lower heat and simmer 4 minutes. Set aside and keep warm.

2. In another frying pan (large enough to hold all the steaks comfortably, or use two pans), heat the remaining butter and oil. Add the steaks, season with salt and pepper, and cook, turning frequently, until evenly browned and cooked to doneness desired— 4 to 5 minutes for rare, 7 to 8 for medium.

3. Transfer the steaks to a hot serving dish. Spoon on the onions and any liquid from the pan. Sprinkle with parsley.

Serve with Potatoes Macaire (p. 310).

Steak au Poivre

(Steak with Crushed Peppercorns)

> *2 tablespoons very coarsely ground black pepper, or crushed*
> *   peppercorns*
> *4 boneless shell steaks, 1 inch thick, about 6 ounces each*
> *2 tablespoons olive oil*
> *2 tablespoons unsalted butter*
> *Salt to taste*
> *4 shallots, minced*
> *½ cup beef broth*
> *2 tablespoons brandy*
> *3 tablespoons soft butter*

1. Press the pepper into both sides of the steaks and let set at room temperature 30 minutes.
2. In a large frying pan, heat the oil and 1 tablespoon butter. Cook the steaks over medium-high heat 4 minutes on each side, depending on how rare you like them. Season with salt and transfer to a hot serving dish. Keep warm.
3. Add the remaining tablespoon of butter to the frying pan and, over medium heat, cook the shallots 1 minute. Pour in the broth and cook, stirring, to scrape up the browned-on bits from the bottom of the pan. Reduce by about one-third.
4. Pour in the brandy and cook 1 minute. Remove from the heat and stir in the softened butter until it has melted and is well blended. Spoon over the steaks on their serving dish.
Serve with Polish Potato Puffs (p. 299).

Steak Diane

We first had this delight in Copenhagen, Denmark, at the small classic hotel the Terminus. It was prepared in a chafing dish at our table. We also like doing it this way for guests. But use your own system. Strip sirloins are often used, but we prefer tender fillets.

8 tablespoons (1 stick) unsalted butter
4 fillet steaks, each 1 inch thick, trimmed
Salt and freshly ground black pepper to taste
1 garlic clove, minced
2 shallots, minced
1 tablespoon minced fresh chives
1 tablespoon minced broadleaf parsley
1 tablespoon Worcestershire sauce

1. In a large frying pan, over medium-high heat, melt 4 tablespoons butter. Season the fillets with salt and pepper, and cook for 1½ minutes on each side, or according to taste, browning well.

2. Transfer the fillets to a hot dish and keep warm. In the same pan, over medium heat, melt the remaining butter, stir in the garlic, shallots, chives, parsley, and Worcestershire, simmering and stirring 3 to 5 minutes, without browning, blending well. Return the steaks to the pan, spooning the sauce over them. Serve piping hot on warm plates.

Serve with Cottage Fried Potatoes (p. 332).

Strip Steak with Gorgonzola "Sauce"   SERVES 4

We first had this in Italy's Po Valley, where Gorgonzola, a creamy-yellow cheese shot through with blue-green, is made. They told us that this marvelous cheese, which we prefer to Roquefort, was originally called Stracchino, because Stracco means tired, and the milk used in making Gorgonzola comes from tired cows (after they have been herded for long distances through the Italian Alps). The steak, being Italian, was somewhat tough (tired steer?), but the sauce was different and delicious.

2 tablespoons olive oil
6 tablespoons (¾ stick) unsalted butter
4 shell steaks, trimmed (about 8 ounces after trimming)
Salt and freshly ground black pepper to taste
½ cup crumbled Gorgonzola

1. In a large frying pan, heat the oil and 1 tablespoon butter. Add the steaks and cook 6 to 7 minutes on each side (this will produce a medium steak—cook more or less time to suit your taste). Season with pepper and very lightly with salt, bearing in mind that the cheese is salty.

2. Transfer the steaks to a hot serving dish and keep warm.

3. Pour off any fat left in the frying pan. Add the remaining butter and, over medium heat, melt the butter. Add the cheese, blending it very well with the butter.

4. Spoon equal amounts of the cheese "sauce" over the steaks and serve.

Serve with Basil-Baked New Potatoes en Papillote (p. 365).

Tournedos Rossini

SERVES 6

The tournedo is cut on the bias from the small end of the fillet. Here it's served with foie gras on artichoke bottoms.

6 fresh or canned artichoke bottoms
8 tablespoons (1 stick) unsalted butter
1 tablespoon olive oil
6 fillet steaks, 1½ inches thick
Salt and freshly ground black pepper to taste
¼ cup dry vermouth, or Madeira
½ cup Brown Sauce (p. 62)
½ cup beef broth
6 slices pâté de foie gras, ¼ inch thick
6 thin slices black truffles

1. Cook the artichoke bottoms lightly on both sides in 2 tablespoons butter. Do not brown. Set aside and keep warm. (A 250° oven is good for this.)

2. In a large frying pan, heat 2 tablespoons butter and the olive oil over medium-high heat. Evenly brown the steaks, cooking them about 1½ to 2 minutes on each side. Add more butter if needed.

The beef should be well browned on the outside and pink inside. Season with salt and pepper. Transfer to a hot dish and keep warm (in that 250° oven).

3. Add the vermouth or Madeira to the frying pan and, over medium heat, cook to reduce by half, stirring, scraping up the browned-on bits from the bottom of the pan. Add the Brown Sauce and beef broth, cooking, stirring, until thickened. Off heat, stir in 2 tablespoons butter.

4. In another pan heat the foie gras and truffles slightly in 2 tablespoons melted butter, being careful not to break up the foie gras.

5. Arrange the artichoke bottoms on a hot serving dish. Place a steak on top of each. Place a slice of foie gras on each steak. Spoon on the sauce and top with a slice of truffle.

Serve with Château Potatoes (p. 290).

Variations: Replace the artichoke bottoms with a slice of ½-inch-thick French bread, the same size as the steak, that has been browned and crisped in butter. Replace the truffle with flat mushroom caps that have been lightly browned in butter 30 seconds.

4

Lamb

Greek Lamb Sausages without Casings
Kibbeh
Eastern European Stuffed Cabbage
Lamb Loaf with Apple Slices
Lamb Sausage with Greek Lemon Sauce
Meat Loaf à la Turca
Moussaka with Zucchini
Pakistani Lamb Patties
Athenian Lamb with Chestnuts
Abbacchio Chianti Style
Curry of Lamb with Baked Bananas
Armenian Shish Kebab
Hungarian Lamb and Pork
Hungarian Lamb Stew
Irish Stew
Lamb and Lamb-Kidney Pie
Lamb Cubes with Okra
Lamb with Couscous
Lancashire Hot Pot
Piraeus Lamb Stew
Lamb Paprikash

Navarin of Lamb
Asia Minor Tongue and Potato Salad
Shepherd's Pie
Lamb Chops in Tomato Sauce
Baked Lamb Chops with Mushrooms
   and Sour Cream
Noisettes d'Agneau à l'Estragon
Lamb Steak Véronique
Lamb Shanks in Red Wine
Arabian Lamb Shanks
Etienne Merle's Jarret d'Agneau Braisée
Double Racks of Lamb
Etienne Merle's Rack of Lamb Persillé
Lamb Shanks with Acorn Squash
Abbacchio alla Romana
Gigot Rôti Boulangère
Lemon-Zested Glazed Lamb Roast
Leg of Lamb Greek Style
Madeline Altman's Parsleyed Leg of Lamb
Stuffed Leg of Lamb Cooked with Port
   Wine

It's a puzzle: although many Americans came here from Europe, where lamb is very popular, or from the Middle East, where it is the number-one meat, lamb until very recently was far from being commonly eaten. Perhaps one reason is that when Americans do serve lamb, they usually overcook it. Lamb is a tender, juicy meat that doesn't respond to being hardened and dried out from long cooking (except in stews), but it's unbeatable if offered pink and juicy.

We think that lamb is impressive. Etienne Merle's Rack of Lamb Persillé, a dramatic, delicious dish, always carved at the table, is a celebration. So are noisettes, tender morsels of boned loin meat, in 3-ounce pieces, one inch thick, served two to a diner. But there's much more to lamb than roast leg, racks, tenderloin morsels, and savory stews. We offer the classic shish kebab, lamb curry with baked bananas, lamb and lamb-kidney pie, the famous French Navarin, the *gigot*, braised lamb shanks, shepherd's pie, lamb steak Véronique and "abbachio," lamb Roman style. If you're not already partial to lamb, we hope the following pages will help you discover its merits.

Greek Lamb Sausages without Casings

SERVES 4 TO 6

6 slices white bread, crusts removed
Milk to soak bread in
1½ pounds lean ground lamb (from the leg)
2 eggs, beaten
1 teaspoon salt
Freshly ground black pepper to taste
⅛ teaspoon cinnamon
½ teaspoon ground cumin
1 small garlic clove, put through a garlic press
2 tablespoons olive oil

1. In a bowl, cover the bread with milk and soak just until the bread is well moistened. Squeeze the milk from the bread.
2. In a large bowl, combine the bread and all other ingredients

Lamb

· RETAIL CUTS ·
WHERE THEY COME FROM
HOW TO COOK THEM

LEG
RIB
SHOULDER
LOIN
FORESHANK & BREAST

Rib Roast
Roast

Rib Chop
Broil, Panbroil, Panfry, Roast

Frenched Rib Chop
Broil, Panbroil, Panfry

Crown Roast
Roast

RIB

Whole Leg
Roast

Short Cut Leg, Sirloin Off
Roast

Shank Portion Roast
Roast

Center Leg Roast
Roast

Center Slice
Broil, Panbroil, Panfry

American-Style Roast
Roast

Frenched-Style Roast
Roast

Boneless Leg Roast
Roast, Broil if butterflied

Hind Shank
Braise, Cook in Liquid

Sirloin Chop
Broil, Panbroil, Panfry, Braise

Boneless Sirloin Roast
Roast

LEG

Loin Roast
Roast

Loin Chop
Broil, Panbroil, Panfry

Double Loin Chop
Broil, Panbroil, Panfry

LOIN

Shank
Braise, Cook in Liquid

Spareribs
Braise, Broil, Roast

Boneless Rolled Breast
Roast, Braise

Riblets
Braise, Cook in Liquid, Broil

FORESHANK & BREAST

Square-Cut Shoulder, Whole
Roast, Braise

Pre-Sliced Shoulder
Roast, Braise

Boneless Shoulder Roast
Roast, Braise

Neck Slice
Braise, Cook in Liquid

Blade Chop
Braise, Broil, Panbroil, Panfry

Arm Chop
Braise, Broil, Panbroil, Panfry

SHOULDER

Lamb for Stew
Braise, Cook in Liquid

Cubes for Kabobs
Broil, Braise

Ground Lamb
Broil, Panbroil, Roast (Bake)

OTHER CUTS

except the olive oil. With a fork, mix well but lightly, lifting the mixture so it doesn't become packed.

3. Make a small patty, brown on both sides in a little oil, and taste for seasoning, adding salt and pepper if needed.

4. Shape the lamb mixture into cylinders 1 × 2 or 3 inches, as desired.

5. In a frying pan, over medium heat, heat the oil and cook the "sausages" until well browned, adding more oil if needed. Drain on paper towels.

A moist potato dish, Potato and Leek Casserole (p. 351), is an excellent accompaniment.

Kibbeh

SERVES 6

This is the Middle Eastern equivalent of hamburger, meat loaf, meatballs, you name it. It's the favorite ground-meat dish everywhere in that part of the world.

½ cup bulgur (cracked wheat)
½ cup hot chicken broth
1½ pounds lean lamb, ground twice
2 small white onions, minced
½ cup tomato sauce
1 teaspoon salt
¼ teaspoon freshly ground black pepper
½ teaspoon ground cumin
¼ teaspoon cinnamon
½ cup chopped fresh broadleaf parsley
½ cup pignoli, cooked in 2 tablespoons butter until golden and crisp
4 tablespoons (½ stick) unsalted butter, melted

1. In a bowl mix the bulgur with the broth. Let stand 1 hour. Drain and spoon the bulgur through cheesecloth, squeezing out all liquid.

2. In a bowl combine the bulgur, lamb, onions, tomato sauce, salt, pepper, cumin, cinnamon, parsley, and pignoli. Knead with your

hands (moistening them with water from time to time) until the meat is smooth and well blended.

3. Grease a 9 × 10-inch pan and evenly spread the meat and wheat mixture. Score with a knife into a large diamond-shaped design. Pour the melted butter over and cook, uncovered, in a preheated 400° oven 40 minutes, or until the top is crisp and golden brown.

4. To serve, cut in diamond-shaped wedges. Serve with Potatoes with Ricotta Cheese (p. 353).

Eastern European Stuffed Cabbage   SERVES 4 TO 6

1 large head of cabbage (about 3 pounds)
2 slices of bacon, minced
2 medium-sized onions, finely chopped
1 garlic clove, minced
1½ pounds ground lamb
2 boiled potatoes, grated
1 tablespoon paprika
1½ teaspoons salt
½ teaspoon freshly ground black pepper
⅛ teaspoon dried thyme
1 egg, beaten
3 cups sauerkraut, drained
1½ cups beef broth
2 tablespoons tomato paste
3 tablespoons chopped parsley
Yogurt (optional)

1. Remove (and discard) any bruised outside leaves from the cabbage. Cut out as much of the center core as possible. Place the cabbage in a large, deep pot, cover with boiling water, and simmer 10 minutes, or until the leaves can be easily separated. Remove the cabbage, drain, and cool. Carefully separate all the largest leaves intact and drain them on paper towels. Cut the tough spine out of large leaves and cut the leaves through to produce two smaller

leaves from each large one. If the inner leaves are difficult to remove, put the cabbage back into the boiling water to cook a few minutes.

2. In a frying pan, over medium heat, cook the bacon 2 minutes. Add the onions and garlic, and cook 5 minutes, or until soft. Do not brown.

3. Add the chopped meat, potatoes, paprika, salt, pepper, and thyme, blending well, and cook, stirring, 3 minutes. Taste for seasoning. Remove from heat and cool slightly. Stir in the egg.

4. Arrange the cabbage leaves on a work surface. Spoon a tablespoon of the mixture (or whatever amount each will hold) onto each leaf. Tuck in the sides and roll tightly into sausage-like bundles. If necessary, toothpicks can be used to secure the rolls.

5. Line the bottom of a flameproof casserole with the sauerkraut. Place the stuffed cabbage on top, "seam side" down. Blend the broth with the tomato paste and pour over the cabbage rolls. Cover the pot, bring to a simmer on top of the stove, transfer to a preheated 350° oven, and cook 1 hour.

6. Spoon the sauerkraut onto a large, hot serving dish, arrange the cabbage rolls on top, and spoon the sauce from the casserole over the cabbage. Sprinkle on the parsley and, if desired, serve with a bowl of yogurt.

Lamb Loaf with Apple Slices   SERVES 6

2 pounds lean ground lamb
½ cup fine bread crumbs
2 eggs, beaten
1½ teaspoons salt
¼ teaspoon freshly ground black pepper
3 tablespoons chopped chives
3 tablespoons chopped parsley
2 medium-sized, firm apples (we use Ida Red), skinned and
*   cored, with three ½-inch slices cut from the center of each*
½ cup of currant jelly, melted
2 tablespoons fresh lemon juice

1. In a bowl, combine and blend well, but lightly, the lamb, bread crumbs, eggs, salt, pepper, chives, and parsley. Form into a loaf.
2. Place on a rack in a shallow roasting pan and bake in a preheated 350° oven 45 minutes, or until cooked through and firm.
3. Arrange the apple slices over the lamb, overlapping if necessary. Blend the currant jelly and lemon juice together and pour over the apple slices. Cook 15 minutes, or until the apple slices are tender but not applesauce.
Serve with Belgian Potatoes (p. 326).

Lamb Sausage with Greek Lemon Sauce   SERVES 4

½ cup fresh bread crumbs
1 tablespoon dry red wine
1 tablespoon soy sauce
1 pound ground lean lamb
2 shallots, minced
1 tablespoon minced fresh mint
1 tablespoon minced broadleaf parsley
Grated peel of ½ lemon
1 egg, beaten
½ teaspoon freshly ground pepper
2 tablespoons unsalted butter
Greek Lemon Sauce (see below)

1. In a large bowl, blend the bread crumbs with the wine and soy sauce, and set aside for 5 minutes.
2. Add all other ingredients (except the butter and sauce) to the bread crumb bowl, thoroughly blending with your hands. Form into 4 equal-sized patties.
3. Over medium-high heat, melt the butter in a frying pan and evenly brown the patties. Serve each lamb patty topped with a generous spoonful of Greek Lemon Sauce.
Serve with Curried Potatoes and Peas (p. 334).

1 tablespoon cornstarch
⅓ cup fresh lemon juice, strained
2 egg yolks
1½ cups hot chicken broth

1. In a small bowl, dissolve the cornstarch in the lemon juice.
2. In another bowl, beat the egg yolks and blend in the cornstarch and lemon juice mixture.
3. Slowly whisk in the hot chicken broth.
4. Pour into a saucepan and heat over medium-low heat, stirring, until slightly thickened. Do not boil.

Meat Loaf à la Turca   SERVES 6
(Turkish Meat Loaf)

1 pound lean ground lamb
½ pound lean ground pork
½ pound ground veal
2 eggs, beaten
2 thin slices white bread soaked in milk, with most of the liquid squeezed out
1 tablespoon olive oil
1 medium-sized onion, minced
1 garlic clove, minced
2 tablespoons pignoli, lightly browned in 1 tablespoon olive oil
1 teaspoon ground allspice
2 tablespoons chopped fresh dill, or 2 teaspoons dried
1½ teaspoons freshly ground black pepper
3 or 4 slices bacon

1. In a bowl, combine and blend well, but lightly, all the ingredients (except the bacon).
2. Form into a loaf. Set in a lightly greased pan. Arrange the bacon

slices on top and bake, uncovered, in a preheated 350° oven for 1 hour, or until thoroughly cooked, basting from time to time with drippings from the bacon.

We like this with a "saucy" potato, Creamed Potatoes with Fresh Peas (p. 333).

Moussaka with Zucchini

SERVES 4 TO 6

3 zucchini, each about 6 inches long and 2½ inches in diameter
Salt and freshly ground black pepper
Flour for dredging
½ cup olive oil, or more
2 medium-sized onions, chopped
1 large garlic clove, minced
1½ pounds ground lean lamb
½ teaspoon cinnamon
¼ cup dry red wine
2 medium-sized, firm, ripe tomatoes, peeled, seeded, and
    chopped
½ cup tomato puree, or 2 tablespoons tomato paste
3 tablespoons chopped fresh broadleaf parsley
¾ cup grated Kefaloteri, Asiago, or Parmesan cheese
2½ tablespoons butter
2½ tablespoons flour
1½ cups milk
Pinch of nutmeg
2 eggs, beaten

1. Cut the zucchini lengthwise into ½-inch-thick slices. Sprinkle lightly with salt and pepper and dredge lightly with flour. Heat 3 tablespoons oil in a large frying pan and cook the zucchini slices over medium-high heat a few at a time until golden on both sides, adding more oil as needed. As the slices cook, drain them on paper towels.

2. Empty the frying pan and wipe out with paper towels. Pour in

3 tablespoons olive oil, and over medium heat, cook the onions and garlic until soft. Do not brown. Stir in the ground meat, breaking it up with a fork as it cooks, until it is well browned. Season with salt and pepper. Stir in the cinnamon. Add the wine, tomatoes, and tomato puree (or paste) and simmer 15 minutes, or until all the liquid has evaporated. Stir in the parsley.

3. Butter an 8-inch-square baking dish (about 3 inches deep). Arrange half the zucchini in a layer on the bottom. Sprinkle with 3 tablespoons cheese. Spoon all the meat mixture over the zucchini. Sprinkle with 3 tablespoons cheese. Arrange the remaining zucchini over the meat; sprinkle with half the remaining cheese.

4. In a saucepan, over medium heat, melt the butter, stir in the flour, and cook, stirring, into a smooth paste. Gradually add the milk and cook, stirring, into a thick smooth sauce. Add the nutmeg. Season to taste with salt and pepper. Stir some of the sauce into the beaten eggs. Return the sauce-and-egg mixture to the saucepan, stirring in quickly and thoroughly, but not allowing the sauce to boil. Spoon the sauce over the top layer of zucchini and sprinkle with the remaining cheese. Bake in a preheated 350° oven 30 minutes, or until the top is puffed and golden.

We like this with Accordion Potatoes (p. 322).

Pakistani Lamb Patties SERVES 6 TO 8

> 4 tablespoons olive oil
> 1 medium-sized onion, finely chopped
> 1 garlic clove, minced
> 3 slices of white bread, crusts removed, soaked in beef broth,
>   with broth squeezed out
> 2½ pounds ground lean lamb
> 2 eggs, beaten
> 2 tablespoons pignoli, cooked in 1 tablespoon olive oil until
>   golden, drained on paper towel
> 1 tablespoon minced broadleaf parsley
> 1 teaspoon ground coriander

½ teaspoon ground cumin
Salt to taste
⅛ teaspoon crushed red pepper, or to taste
2 tablespoons butter
Yogurt

1. In a frying pan, heat 2 tablespoons oil. Add the onion and garlic, and cook until the onion is soft. Do not brown.
2. In a large bowl, combine and blend well, but lightly, the onion, garlic, bread, lamb, eggs, pignoli, parsley, coriander, cumin, salt, and red pepper. The mixture should be light and fluffy. Form into patties about 2½ inches in diameter.
3. In a frying pan, heat the remaining oil and the butter, and brown the patties, cooking about 4 minutes on each side, so the inside is still pink, if desired.
4. Serve with a bowl of "curds" (yogurt).
Serve with Lleela's Madras Potato, Onion, and Tomato Mix (p. 340).

Athenian Lamb with Chestnuts   SERVES 4 TO 6

2 pounds chestnuts
4 tablespoons (½ stick) unsalted butter
1 tablespoon olive oil
2 pounds lean lamb (the leg is good), cut into 1-inch cubes
Salt and freshly ground black pepper to taste
1 medium-sized onion, coarsely chopped
1 celery stalk, scraped, coarsely chopped
1 tablespoon flour
1½ cups beef broth
1 teaspoon sugar

1. Cut a small cross into the flat side of each chestnut. Place on a baking sheet and cook in a preheated 400° oven until the shells crack (about 10 minutes). Remove the shells and inside skins. Set the nuts aside.

2. In a flameproof casserole, heat the butter and oil. Add the lamb, sprinkle with salt and pepper, and brown evenly. Transfer with a slotted spoon to a bowl and reserve. Add the onion and celery to the pot (adding more butter if needed), and cook 2 minutes, or until the onion is soft. Do not brown.

3. Return the lamb and any juices accumulated in the bowl to the pot. Sprinkle with flour and cook 1 minute, stirring, or until slightly browned.

4. Stir in the broth and bring to a boil. Lower heat and simmer 20 minutes, covered, stirring occasionally. Add the chestnuts, transfer to a preheated 350° oven, and cook, tightly covered, 45 minutes to 1 hour, until the lamb and chestnuts are tender. If liquid cooks off before this, add spoonfuls of hot broth or water. Taste for seasoning.

5. Just before serving, stir in the sugar.

Serve with Peruvian Potatoes (p. 343).

Abbacchio Chianti Style   SERVES 6

The Italians can't seem to make up their minds about whether they prefer veal or lamb. Consequently, they offer tempting versions of both meats.

3 tablespoons olive oil
3 garlic cloves
3 medium-sized onions, chopped
3 pounds lean lamb, from the leg, cut into 1½-inch cubes
Salt and freshly ground black pepper
⅛ teaspoon dried oregano
⅛ teaspoon dried rosemary
1½ cups red Chianti
1 one-pound, twelve-ounce can Italian-style tomatoes, drained and crushed (your hands are good for this)
2 tablespoons chopped broadleaf parsley
3 celery stalks, scraped, cut into 1-inch pieces
3 medium-sized potatoes, peeled, cut into 1-inch cubes

1. In a heavy pot, heat the oil. Cook the garlic until golden brown. Discard the garlic. Stir in the onions and cook 3 minutes. Do not brown. Push the onions aside and add the lamb cubes, a few at a time, sprinkling with salt and pepper. Brown evenly, adding more oil if needed. As the pieces brown, set them aside while you cook the others.

2. After all the lamb has been browned, return it to the pot and stir in the oregano, rosemary, Chianti, tomatoes, parsley, and celery. Reduce the heat and simmer, covered, for 35 minutes, stirring occasionally.

3. Add the potatoes and cook, uncovered, 15 minutes, or until the sauce has thickened and the lamb and potatoes are fork-tender. Taste for seasoning.

Curry of Lamb with Baked Bananas SERVES 6 TO 8

3 tablespoons unsalted butter
2 tablespoons olive oil
3 pounds lean, trimmed lamb, cut into 1½-inch cubes
 (the leg is good for this)
Salt
3 medium-sized onions, chopped
2 garlic cloves, minced
1 large, firm apple, peeled, cored, and chopped
2 tablespoons flour
2 tablespoons curry powder, commercial or homemade
 (see below)
½ cup dry white wine
2 firm, medium-sized tomatoes, peeled, seeded, and chopped
2 cups chicken broth, approximately
½ cup warm heavy cream

1. In a large, flameproof casserole, heat 2 tablespoons butter and 1 tablespoon oil. Season the lamb with salt, add to the pot, and evenly brown (brown just enough pieces at a time so as not to crowd them in the pot, adding more butter and oil as needed). As

the lamb browns, transfer it to a bowl.

2. Lower heat. Add the onions and garlic to the pan, using more butter and oil if necessary, and cook until the onions are soft. Add the apple and sprinkle on the flour and curry powder, stirring to blend well.

3. Stir in the wine and tomatoes. Return the lamb to the pan, mixing it with the other ingredients. Pour on enough of the chicken broth to not quite cover the lamb. Bring to a boil on top of the stove, cover, transfer to a preheated 350° oven, and cook 1 hour, or until the lamb is fork-tender. Taste for seasoning.

4. Just before serving, stir in the cream.

A natural with this is Lleela's Potatoes with Yogurt (p. 341).

CURRY POWDER

MAKES SLIGHTLY MORE
THAN 2 TABLESPOONFULS

2 teaspoons ground coriander
2 teaspoons ground cumin
1/2 teaspoon ground ginger
1 teaspoon turmeric
1/16 teaspoon ground red pepper, or to taste
1/4 teaspoon ground black pepper
1 teaspoon ground cardamom

Combine all ingredients and blend well.

BAKED BANANAS

One of the best accompaniments for a curry is also one of the simplest. We don't recall where we learned this one (probably the Canary Islands, where plenty of bananas are a way of life), but we've been enjoying it for years.

1 fat, ripe, but not overripe, banana per person

1. Preheat the oven to 400°.
2. Bake the bananas in their skins for 20 minutes.
3. Cool slightly before removing the skin. In fact, each diner should be served an unpeeled baked banana, having been forewarned that the skin shouldn't be removed when it is too hot.

Armenian Shish Kebab

SERVES 6

This way of preparing lamb may be the oldest method of cooking. Centuries ago, tribal warriors speared pieces of lamb, probably our first domestic animal (along with the goat), with their swords and held them over embers. Even today nomads broil these kebabs over desert campfires. Africans, Asians, and others also cook kebabs and call them by other names. The best recipes, however, were refined in the Middle East, where they never use the American system of alternating chunks of vegetables with the lamb. That system produces either undercooked vegetables or overcooked lamb.

1 leg of lamb, trimmed of fat and gristle, cut into 1½-inch cubes
4 garlic cloves, halved
1 bay leaf
½ teaspoon ground coriander
½ teaspoon ground cumin
1½ teaspoons oregano
1½ teaspoons salt
1 teaspoon freshly ground black pepper
1 cup dry red wine
¼ cup olive oil
Juice of 1 lemon

1. Place all ingredients in a bowl, blending well to coat the lamb cubes. Cover the bowl and refrigerate at least 6 hours. Overnight is even better.
2. Arrange the lamb on skewers, spearing each piece through the center. Broil over a low fire (or with medium heat in an electric or gas broiler), preferably charcoal, about 5 minutes on each side, or until evenly browned and tender.
Caution: Do not overcook. Lamb is always best pink and juicy. Overcooked shish kebab is dry and tough, with much of its flavor left on the coals.
Skip the cliché of broiled tomatoes and peppers, and offer a surprise, Fried Potatoes au Gratin (p. 335).

Hungarian Lamb and Pork

4 tablespoons (½ stick) unsalted butter

2 tablespoons olive oil

1½ pounds lean lamb from leg or shoulder, cut into 1½-inch cubes

1½ pounds lean pork, cut into 1-inch cubes

Salt and freshly ground black pepper

1 medium-sized onion, sliced

4 slender carrots, scraped and cut into 1-inch pieces

1 small Savoy cabbage, about 1½ pounds, trimmed and shredded

½ cup dry white wine

2 cups chicken broth

Bouquet garni (made of 1 bay leaf, 1 sprig fresh parsley, 1 garlic clove, and ½ teaspoon of dried marjoram tied in cheesecloth)

2 tablespoons chopped parsley

1. In a frying pan, heat 2 tablespoons butter and the oil, and evenly brown the lamb and pork a few pieces at a time, sprinkling lightly with salt and pepper. As the pieces brown, transfer them with a slotted spoon to a flameproof casserole. Lower heat.

2. If all the fat in the frying pan has been absorbed by the meat, add the remaining butter. Heat, add the onion, carrots, and cabbage. Cook 2 minutes, or until the onion is transparent. With a slotted spoon, transfer to the casserole.

3. Pour off any fat from the frying pan, add the wine and broth, and simmer 1 minute, scraping up the browned-on bits from the bottom of the pan. Add to the casserole along with the bouquet garni. Cover, bring to a boil on top of the stove, then cook in a preheated 325° oven for 1 hour. Remove cover and cook ½ hour, or until the lamb and pork are tender. Taste for seasoning. Remove and discard the bouquet garni. Transfer to a hot serving dish; sprinkle with parsley.

Serve with Potato-Turnip Bake (p. 353).

Hungarian Lamb Stew

3 tablespoons unsalted butter

2 tablespoons olive oil

3 pounds lean lamb, leg or shoulder, cut into 1½-inch squares,
½ inch thick

2 medium-sized onions, thinly sliced

1 garlic clove, minced

½ pound green beans, cut into 1-inch pieces

1 large, firm green pepper, seeds and white ribs removed, cut
into ½-inch-wide strips, 1 inch long

1 small eggplant (about 3 inches × 4 inches), peeled and cut
into ½-inch cubes

3 firm, medium-sized, ripe tomatoes, cut into ¼-inch-thick slices

Salt and freshly ground black pepper

Paprika

1 cup beef broth

1. In a deep, flameproof casserole, heat 2 tablespoons butter and the oil, and brown the lamb evenly, in a single layer (do not crowd). As the pieces brown, remove and reserve in a bowl.

2. Add the remaining butter to the casserole and cook the onions and garlic until soft. Do not brown. Remove with a slotted spoon and set aside. Pour all fat from the casserole.

3. Arrange a layer of the lamb on the bottom of the casserole to cover it. Place green beans, pepper slices, eggplant, and onions over the lamb, then the tomato slices (overlapping the slices if necessary). Season each layer lightly with salt and pepper and very lightly with paprika, but do not sprinkle the tomatoes with paprika. Pour in the broth and any liquid that collected in the bowl used for the lamb.

4. Cover, bring to a boil on top of the stove, then place in a preheated 325° oven for 30 minutes. Remove cover and bake until the lamb is tender and most of the liquid has cooked off. Taste for seasoning.

Irish Stew

Many of us believe that lamb is the best of all stew meats, more tender and flavorful even than beef. It sends its flavor and aroma into every vegetable that it touches. Each country has its favorite lamb stew, but probably the most famous is the Irish farmer's. Irish lamb and Irish potatoes seem to have a flavor all their own.

3 pounds boned lamb shoulder, cut into 1-inch cubes
1 pound thick, lean slab bacon, cut into 1-inch cubes
4 large potatoes, peeled and cut into 1½-inch cubes
8 medium-sized yellow onions, cut into ¼-inch slices
1½ teaspoons salt
½ teaspoon freshly ground black pepper
½ teaspoon rosemary
2 cups water

1. Place all ingredients in a large pot. Cover and bring to a boil over high heat.
2. Reduce heat to low and simmer 1½ hours, or until the lamb, bacon, and potatoes are tender, shaking the pot from time to time to prevent the contents from sticking to the bottom. (If the liquid should cook off, add small amounts of hot water.)
3. Taste for seasoning. Skim off fat.

Lamb and Lamb-Kidney Pie

7 tablespoons unsalted butter
5 shallots, chopped (about ⅓ cup)
¼ teaspoon dried thyme
¼ teaspoon dried oregano
¼ teaspoon dried rosemary
2½ pounds lean lamb (from the leg), cut into 1-inch cubes
Flour for dredging
2 tablespoons olive oil
Salt and freshly ground black pepper

6 lamb kidneys (membranes, hard core in center, and fat re-
  moved and discarded), cut into ½-inch-thick slices
2½ cups beef broth
½ cup Madeira
¼ pound small, firm mushrooms, cut into halves
¼ cup heavy cream
Pastry to cover pie (p. 73)

1. In a deep, heavy pot, heat 2 tablespoons butter. Add the shallots and cook until soft. Do not brown. Stir in the herbs. Remove pot from heat; set aside.

2. Dredge lamb with flour. In a frying pan, heat 3 tablespoons butter and the olive oil. Brown the lamb evenly, a few pieces at a time. Sprinkle with salt and pepper. Transfer the lamb to the pot with the shallots.

3. Add 2 tablespoons butter to the frying pan. Dredge the kidneys with flour, and over high heat, brown them (do not cook through). Sprinkle with salt and pepper. Transfer to a bowl; set aside.

4. Pour any fat from the frying pan, stir in 1 cup broth, and simmer 1 minute, scraping up the browned-on bits from the bottom of the pan. Pour into the pot with the shallots and lamb. Pour in the remaining broth and the wine. Cover and simmer 45 minutes, or until the lamb is almost tender and the sauce is somewhat thickened. Taste for seasoning.

5. Stir in the kidneys, mushrooms, and cream. Transfer everything to a shallow 2-quart baking dish, or one in which the contents will come to within ½ inch of the top (a shallow, rectangular Pyrex one works well). Place a custard cup, inverted, in the center to support the pastry. Roll out the pastry to a ¼-inch thickness, so it is ¾ inch larger all around than the rim of the baking dish (whether it is round or rectangular). Moisten edges with water and mold to the sides of the dish. Cut 2 small air holes in the top and prick with a fork in 2 or 3 places.

6. Place the baking dish on a baking sheet in a preheated 450° oven for 15 minutes. Lower oven temperature to 350° and continue baking for ½ hour, or until the crust is golden brown.

Lamb Cubes with Okra

4 tablespoons olive oil
3 pounds lean lamb, from leg or shoulder, cut into 1-inch cubes
Salt and freshly ground black pepper
1 medium-sized onion, sliced
1 garlic clove, minced
¼ teaspoon dried oregano
1 cup tomato juice
1 cup beef broth
¼ cup fresh lemon juice
1 teaspoon grated lemon rind
1 pound okra, fresh or frozen (if fresh, blanch 5 minutes in boil-
*   ing water; if frozen, defrost but do not cook)*
2 tablespoons chopped broadleaf parsley

1. In a flameproof casserole, heat 3 tablespoons olive oil. Brown the lamb evenly and sprinkle with salt and pepper. As the pieces brown, transfer them to a bowl and reserve. Lower heat, add the remaining oil if necessary, then the onion and garlic, and cook until the onion is soft. Remove the onion and garlic with a slotted spoon and pour off any oil left in the pot.
2. Return the lamb, onion, and garlic to the pot; add the oregano. Blend the tomato juice and broth, and barely cover the meat. Heat on top of the stove to a boil. Cover and transfer to a preheated 325° oven and cook 45 minutes, or until the lamb is almost tender.
3. Add the lemon juice and rind and the okra to the lamb. Return to the oven and cook, covered, for 15 minutes, or until the lamb is fork-tender. Taste for seasoning. Transfer to a hot serving dish and sprinkle with the parsley.
An excellent accompaniment, with some of the lamb sauce spooned over, is German Potato Dumplings #1 or #2 (p. 295 or p. 296).

Lamb with Couscous

The North Africans didn't invent couscous, a wheat grain resembling rice but with a nuttier flavor, but they made it popular. We discovered this recipe in Tangier.

3 tablespoons olive oil
2½ pounds lean lamb from the leg, cut into 1½- to 2-inch cubes
2 medium-sized white onions, chopped
Salt and freshly ground black pepper
7 cups chicken broth
1 bay leaf
½ teaspoon ground cumin
¼ teaspoon ground ginger
½ cup dry chick-peas, soaked in water 5 hours, drained, covered
   with fresh water, cooked over medium heat until slightly under-
   done, and drained
2½ cups couscous
½ cup raisins, plumped in a small amount of port wine and
   drained
½ cup pignoli (pine nuts), cooked in butter until golden and
   crisp

1. In a heavy pot, heat the oil and brown the lamb cubes evenly. Add more oil if needed. Add the onions and cook them 2 minutes, sprinkling lamb and onions with salt and pepper.

2. Pour in the chicken broth, add the bay leaf, cumin, and ginger, and bring to a boil. Reduce the heat, stir in the chick-peas, and simmer 30 minutes, or until the lamb is tender.

3. Stir in the couscous and raisins, cover, and bring to a boil. Remove from the heat and set aside for 10 minutes. Fluff the couscous with a fork. Discard bay leaf, and stir in the pignoli just before serving. Taste for seasoning.

Lancashire Hot Pot   SERVES 6

We first tasted this dish in the home of English friends. We weren't aware of its contents, except for the lamb, and each forkful offered a culinary surprise, especially the shellfish. Despite the length of cooking time, the oysters were surprisingly tasty and gave the entire dish a uniquely delicate flavor.

Butter to coat the casserole
7 medium-sized Idaho potatoes (slightly more than 2 pounds),
  peeled, cut into ¼-inch-thick slices
1½ pounds of ½-inch-thick slices of lamb, cut from the leg, the
  pieces not much larger than the potato slices
Salt and freshly ground black pepper
4 small white onions, thinly sliced
4 lamb kidneys, cored, membrane removed, soaked in salted
  water 20 minutes, rinsed well in cold water, and thinly sliced
24 oysters
1½ cups beef broth
3 tablespoons melted butter

1. Generously butter a 2-quart casserole. Layer it with half the potatoes and all the lamb. Sprinkle lightly with salt and pepper.
2. Arrange a layer of half the onions, then a layer of all the kidneys. Sprinkle lightly with salt and pepper. Arrange the oysters in a single layer, then the remaining onions, ending with a layer of the remaining potatoes. Sprinkle with salt and pepper.
3. Pour in the beef broth. Drizzle the melted butter over the potatoes. Cook, covered, in a preheated 350° oven 1½ hours. Remove cover and cook 20 minutes longer, or until the potatoes are crisply brown.

Piraeus Lamb Stew   SERVES 6

In Tourkolimano Harbor, Piraeus, not far from Athens, the favored food is fish, but they are also proud of this stew. In Europe, and especially in Greece, apricots are popular with many meat dishes, with good reason: they add a unique piquancy.

4 tablespoons olive oil
2 pounds lean lamb cubes, cut from the leg

Salt and freshly ground black pepper to taste
12 small onions, root ends scored to keep them intact
¼ cup fresh lemon juice
2 cups beef broth
¼ teaspoon cinnamon, or to taste
⅓ cup white raisins
8 dried apricots, halved

1. In a large pot, heat the oil and brown the lamb cubes evenly, sprinkling them with salt and pepper. This should take from 8 to 10 minutes. Add more oil if needed.
2. Stir in the onions, cooking for 4 minutes.
3. Add the lemon juice and beef broth. Cover, lower heat, and simmer 45 minutes.
4. Stir in the cinnamon, raisins, and apricots. Cover the pot and simmer another 45 minutes, stirring occasionally, until the lamb is fork-tender.

We like to serve this with an American touch, State of Maine Potato Pancakes (p. 377), with the meat sauce spooned over them.

Lamb Paprikash   SERVES 4 TO 6

2-inch cube of salt pork, poached in boiling water 5 minutes,
    drained and dried, and cut into ¼- to ½-inch cubes
2 pounds lean boned lamb shoulder, cut into 1½-inch cubes
3 medium-sized onions, sliced
1 garlic clove, minced
1 tablespoon Hungarian paprika
1 tablespoon tomato paste
1 cup chicken broth
Salt to taste
2 large green peppers (seeds and white ribs removed and dis-
    carded), cut into ½-inch strips
⅛ teaspoon cayenne, or to taste
1½ cups sour cream

1. In a flameproof casserole, over medium heat, cook the salt pork cubes until they have rendered their fat and are golden brown and crisp. Remove with a slotted spoon, drain on paper towels, and reserve.

2. Pour off all but 3 tablespoons of fat from the casserole. Add the lamb and brown evenly. Add the onions and garlic, and cook until soft. Do not brown. Stir in the paprika, tomato paste, broth, and salt. Bring to a boil on top of the stove. Transfer to a preheated 325° oven and cook, covered, for 1 hour, or until the lamb is almost tender. Add the pepper strips and cayenne, and cook until the lamb is tender and the liquid has evaporated.

3. Stir in the sour cream and salt pork cubes. Heat thoroughly without boiling.

Crunchy little potato balls, Pommes de Terre à la Parisienne (p. 299), add elegance to this dish.

Navarin of Lamb SERVES 6 TO 8

This savory French lamb stew is especially favored in Burgundy.

> 3 tablespoons unsalted butter
> 2 tablespoons olive oil
> 3 pounds lean lamb (leg or shoulder), cut into 1-inch cubes
> Salt and freshly ground black pepper to taste
> 1 teaspoon brown sugar
> 2 ounces dry sherry
> 3 tablespoons flour
> 2 garlic cloves, minced
> ½ cup tomato puree
> ½ cup dry white wine
> 2 cups beef broth
> ⅛ teaspoon thyme
> 1 bay leaf
> 1 medium-sized onion
> 1 clove (studded on the onion)
> 16 tiny onions, root ends scored

4 slender carrots, scraped and cut into ½-inch pieces
1 small turnip, peeled and diced
1 cup lima beans, cooked in salted water until crisp-tender
2 tablespoons chopped parsley

1. In a flameproof casserole large enough to hold all ingredients, heat the butter and oil. Add the lamb, a few pieces at a time, and brown evenly. Sprinkle with salt and pepper.
2. Pour off any excess fat. Sprinkle in the sugar and sherry. Shake the pan to distribute. Sprinkle with the flour and stir. Add the garlic, tomato puree, white wine, enough beef broth to barely cover the lamb, the thyme, bay leaf, and the onion with the clove. Cover and bring to a boil on top of the stove. Transfer to a preheated 350° oven and cook 30 minutes.
3. Add the tiny whole onions, carrots, and turnip to the casserole, and cook, covered, for another 30 minutes, or until the lamb and vegetables are fork-tender. Taste for seasoning. Add the limas and cook 10 minutes.
4. Remove and discard the bay leaf and the onion with the clove.
5. Transfer to a hot serving bowl and sprinkle with the parsley. Serve with Potatoes Dauphine (p. 303).

Asia Minor Tongue and Potato Salad SERVES 6

7 medium-sized new potatoes (slightly more than 2 pounds)
Salad Dressing (see below)
1 garlic clove, minced
6 scallions (white part only), coarsely chopped
2 cups cooked lamb tongue, cut into small cubes
6 small gherkins, coarsely chopped
2 tablespoons chopped fresh parsley

1. Cook the potatoes in their skins in boiling water until just tender. Do not overcook. Drain and dry in the pan over low heat. While the potatoes are still warm, peel and cut them into ¼-inch-thick slices. Spoon on half of the Salad Dressing and blend gently.

2. Mix in the garlic, scallions, tongue, and gherkins. Taste, then add more dressing if desired. Chill before serving and garnish with the parsley.

Eat this with Middle Eastern flat bread (pita bread) that has been split, buttered, and toasted.

SALAD DRESSING

   ¼ cup dry white wine
   3 tablespoons fresh lemon juice
   ⅔ cup olive oil
   ¼ teaspoon sugar
   ¼ teaspoon paprika
   Salt to taste
   ½ teaspoon ground cumin

Prepare the salad dressing and set aside at least 3 hours for flavors to ripen.

Shepherd's Pie

SERVES 4

Here's a classic and economical dish that always pleases.

   3 tablespoons unsalted butter
   1 medium-sized white onion, minced
   2 tablespoons flour
   1½ cups beef broth
   4 cups cooked lamb, cut into small cubes
   2 tablespoons finely chopped parsley
   Salt and freshly ground black pepper to taste
   ⅛ teaspoon mace
   1 teaspoon Worcestershire sauce
   3 cups mashed potatoes (mashed with cream and butter, but of
       a firm consistency)
   ¼ cup grated sharp cheese

1. In a saucepan or frying pan, heat 2 tablespoons butter. Add the onion and cook until soft. Do not brown. Stir in the flour, mixing well. Gradually add the beef broth, stirring into a smooth, thickened sauce.

2. Stir in the lamb, parsley, salt, pepper, mace, and Worcestershire sauce.

3. Butter a 2-quart baking dish. Spoon in the meat mixture, then evenly cover it with the mashed potatoes. Dot with the remaining butter and sprinkle on the cheese.

4. Bake, uncovered, in a preheated 400° oven 15 minutes, or until heated through and the top is golden brown and crusty.

Note: Beef or veal may be substituted for the lamb.

Lamb Chops in Tomato Sauce SERVES 4

Although there are many recipes for lamb chops, we maintain that the simple French method of "pan broiling" is the best. Two-inch-thick center-cut loin chops, generously sprinkled with salt and freshly milled pepper, are placed in a frying pan with just a dollop of olive oil (do not use butter). Over medium-high heat, they are turned often and cooked quickly according to taste—very pink, pink (our favorite), or less pink (but never well done).

But that is for the royalty of lamb chops. For lesser cuts, such as shoulder chops, try this Middle Eastern method.

1 tablespoon unsalted butter
1 tablespoon olive oil
4 shoulder lamb chops, ¾ inch thick
1 large onion, sliced
4 garlic cloves, peeled, left whole
3 medium-sized ripe tomatoes, skinned, seeded, and chopped,
    or a 1-pound can of tomatoes, drained and chopped
Salt and freshly ground black pepper to taste
2 tablespoons chopped fresh basil, or 2 teaspoons dried
3 tablespoons chopped fresh parsley
¼ teaspoon ground cinnamon, or to taste
Chicken broth or water

1. In a large frying pan, heat the butter and oil, and brown the

chops evenly. Transfer to a pan large enough to hold them snugly in a single layer.

2. In the original pan, cook the onion and garlic (if the butter and oil have been absorbed by the chops, add 1 tablespoon oil) until golden. Do not brown. Add the tomatoes, salt, pepper, basil, parsley, and cinnamon, and blend well. Simmer 5 minutes. Add ½ cup broth or water and cook 5 minutes.

3. Pour the tomato sauce over the lamb chops and simmer, uncovered, for 40 minutes, or until the chops are tender and the sauce has thickened. If the sauce thickens before the chops are tender, add small amounts of hot broth or water. If the chops are tender before the sauce thickens, raise the heat and cook until thickened. Taste for seasoning.

4. Serve chops with sauce spooned on top and a garlic clove on top of that sauce. After this amount of cooking, the garlic will be sweet and delicious.

Simple Cottage Fried Potatoes (p. 332) give the menu balance.

Baked Lamb Chops with Mushrooms and Sour Cream

SERVES 4

8 rib lamb chops, ¾ inch thick
Flour for dredging
Salt and freshly ground black pepper to taste
5 tablespoons unsalted butter
1 tablespoon olive oil
1½ cups chicken broth
⅓ cup dry sherry
6 large firm mushrooms, cut into ¼-inch-thick slices
1 cup sour cream

1. Dredge the chops lightly with flour and sprinkle with salt and pepper.

2. In a large frying pan, heat 3 tablespoons butter and the olive oil, and brown the chops evenly on both sides. Transfer to a flame-

proof casserole just large enough to hold them snugly in a single layer. (Set the frying pan aside to cook the mushrooms in later.) Pour the broth and sherry into the casserole. Bring to a boil on top of the stove. Transfer to a preheated 350° oven and cook, covered, for 30 minutes. Remove cover and cook 15 minutes, or until the chops are fork-tender. Transfer the chops to a hot serving dish and keep warm.

3. Heat the remaining butter in the frying pan and cook the mushrooms for 3 minutes. Stir them and the sour cream into the casserole in which the lamb chops cooked. Heat thoroughly on top of the stove, but do not boil. Taste for seasoning, and spoon over the chops.

For a well-balanced menu, we serve Shirley Capp's Potatoes, Beans, and Bacon (p. 330) with the chops.

Noisettes d'Agneau à l'Estragon   SERVES 4

Noisettes are tender morsels of boned loin meat cut in 3-ounce pieces, 1 inch thick. Serve two noisettes per person.

8 noisettes of lamb
Salt and freshly ground black pepper to taste
8 tablespoons (1 stick) unsalted butter
2 tablespoons chopped shallots
½ cup coarsely chopped fresh tarragon
¼ cup Madeira
¼ cup beef broth
16 whole fresh tarragon leaves (unblemished)
8 croutons, heart-shaped, pan-fried in butter until golden on
    both sides, drained on paper towels

1. Season the noisettes with salt and pepper.
2. In a frying pan, over medium-high heat, melt half the butter and cook the noisettes 2 minutes on each side, then another 2 minutes on each side. Remove. Keep warm.
3. Drain the fat from the pan. Over medium-high heat, melt the remaining butter; cook the shallots 2 minutes, and stir in the

chopped tarragon, Madeira, and beef broth. Reduce heat and simmer, stirring, 5 minutes. Strain this sauce.

4. Dip the tarragon leaves in hot water for 30 seconds, drain, dry, and place 2 leaves on each noisette, which has been arranged on the croutons. Spoon sauce lightly over the juicy pink noisettes and tarragon-leaf garnish.

Serve with a simple offering of Pommes de Terre Noisette, small potato balls (p. 299).

Lamb Steak Véronique   SERVES 4
(Lamb Steak with Grapes)

Olive oil
4 lamb steaks, or shoulder chops, cut ¾ inch thick
Salt and freshly ground black pepper to taste
¼ teaspoon nutmeg
½ cup dry vermouth
1 cup light cream, or half-and-half
2 egg yolks
½ bay leaf
1 chicken-bouillon cube
½ to 1 cup sliced green seedless grapes, or an 8-ounce can of
*   white grapes, halved*

1. In a large frying pan, heat enough oil to lightly coat the bottom of the pan. Over medium-high heat, brown the lamb. Turn the lamb, reduce the heat to medium-low, sprinkle with salt, pepper, and nutmeg, and cook until desired degree of doneness (about 5 minutes on each side for medium). Transfer the lamb to a hot serving dish and keep warm.

2. Pour all the fat from the frying pan. Pour in the vermouth and stir, scraping up the browned-on bits from the bottom of the pan. Turn heat to low, pour in a mixture of the cream and egg yolks, the bay leaf, and bouillon cube. Cook over low heat, stirring constantly, until the sauce thickens. Do not boil or overcook, as the egg yolks will curdle.

3. Remove and discard the bay leaf, stir in the grapes and serve over the lamb.

Potatoes Lyonnaise (p. 308) add a nice touch to the dish.

Lamb Shanks in Red Wine SERVES 4

Shanks are one of the bargains in lamb, meaty and flavorful. All you need is a unique recipe.

4 strips bacon, chopped
4 lamb shanks
1 medium-sized carrot, scraped and chopped
1 celery stalk, scraped and chopped
1 medium-sized onion, chopped
1 garlic clove, minced
Salt and freshly ground black pepper to taste
2 tablespoons flour
1 cup beef broth
1 cup dry red wine
1 bay leaf
¼ teaspoon rosemary
12 small white onions, root ends scored
16 small, firm, fresh mushrooms

1. In a flameproof casserole that will hold the shanks comfortably in a single layer, cook the bacon over medium heat 3 minutes, or until golden. Don't let it get too brown. Remove the bacon with a slotted spoon, drain on paper towels, and reserve.
2. Add the shanks to the casserole and brown evenly. Remove and reserve.
3. Pour all but 3 tablespoons of fat from the pan (if the bacon has not rendered that amount, add butter). Add the carrot, celery, chopped onion, and garlic. Season with salt and pepper, and cook until soft, but do not brown. Stir in the flour, blending it with the vegetables.
4. Slowly add the broth and wine, stirring constantly to blend well.

5. Return the shanks and bacon to the pan. Add the bay leaf and rosemary. Bring to a boil on top of the stove. Transfer to a preheated 325° oven and cook, covered, for 1½ hours, or until almost tender. Add the small onions, cook 15 minutes; add the mushrooms and cook, covered, 10 minutes, or until the lamb shanks and onions are tender. Taste for seasoning. Discard bay leaf.

Serve with classic Potatoes Dauphinoise (p. 304).

Arabian Lamb Shanks SERVES 4

3 tablespoons olive oil
4 lamb shanks
2 large onions, cut into ½-inch slices
1 garlic clove, minced
1 teaspoon allspice
½ teaspoon mace
Salt and freshly ground black pepper to taste
1-pound, 12-ounce can of tomatoes, broken up (your hands are
  good for this)
1 cup beef broth
3 tablespoons chopped fresh parsley

1. In a flameproof casserole just large enough to hold the shanks in one layer, heat the oil. Add the shanks and brown them evenly.
2. Arrange the onions over the shanks; sprinkle on the garlic, allspice, mace, salt, and pepper. Spoon on the tomatoes. Pour the beef broth around the edge of the dish. Bring to a boil on top of the stove, cover, and cook in a preheated 350° oven 1 hour, or until tender. Taste for seasoning.
3. Serve right from the casserole, or transfer the shanks to a rimmed serving dish and spoon the sauce around them. Sprinkle with parsley.

Serve with Potatoes with Three Cheeses (p. 277).

Etienne Merle's Jarret d'Agneau Braisée

SERVES 4

(Etienne Merle's Braised Lamb Shanks)

For information about this famous chef, see his recipe for rack of lamb (p. 142) and his remarks on braising, below.

2 tablespoons olive oil
4 lamb shanks
Salt and freshly ground black pepper to taste
2 cups beef broth
2 large carrots, coarsely chopped
2 medium-sized onions, coarsely chopped
2 celery stalks (with leaves), coarsely chopped
2 bay leaves
Thyme
Rosemary
2 garlic cloves, minced
2 cups dry white wine

1. In a frying pan, heat the oil and brown the lamb shanks evenly, sprinkling lightly with salt and pepper.

2. Remove the shanks and deglaze the pan with the beef broth.

3. Cover the bottom of a large, deep pot with the carrots, onions, and celery. Add the bay leaves, and lightly sprinkle on thyme, rosemary, and garlic.

4. Arrange the browned lamb shanks on top. Add the liquid (beef broth) from the braising pan, then the white wine. The vegetables should be barely covered.

5. Cover the pot, bring to a boil on top of the stove, then place in a preheated 300° oven for 3 hours, or until tender.

Note on Braising: As people try to avoid fats, braising will come to be, again, a popular cooking method. Braising permits less expensive, less tender pieces of meat to be used, because it tenderizes a lot of collagen (turns into gelatin), it permits multiple taste combinations with a variety of vegetables and seasonings, its scheduling in cooking can be easily integrated into anyone's busy schedule, and the meat can be held for a sizable amount of time after it finishes cooking. Various sizes of meat can be used.

Serve with Inca Spicy Potatoes with Cheese and Tomato (p. 338).

Double Racks of Lamb   SERVES 4

2 two-pound racks of lamb, with chine bone cracked
2½ tablespoons fresh herbs (½ tablespoon each fresh tarragon,
*   chives, shallots, parsley, and rosemary—if dried herbs are*
*   used, use ⅓ that amount), mixed with 3 tablespoons olive oil*
Salt and freshly ground black pepper

1. Have your butcher french the lamb, or do it yourself by trimming the fat from the ends of the chop bones, cutting down about 1 or 1½ inches between the bones toward the base, and cutting out the rectangle of fat and meat.

2. Rub the lamb well with a mixture of the herbs and olive oil, and sprinkle with salt and pepper. Let stand at room temperature about 2 hours. Wrap aluminum foil around the ends of the bones to prevent burning.

3. Cook in a shallow roasting pan, fat side up, in a preheated 450° oven for 15 minutes. Lower oven heat to 350° and cook 20 minutes, or to the doneness desired. Paper frills can replace the aluminum foil for an attractive presentation.

With this simple but succulent offering, we like Paprika Creamed Potatoes (p. 342).

Etienne Merle's Rack of Lamb Persillé   SERVES 2

In the Finger Lakes region of upstate New York, on a hill not far from Ithaca College and Cornell University, is a neat yellow farmhouse that has been converted into one of the finest restaurants in New York State: L'Auberge du Cochon Rouge, The Inn of the Red Pig.

The chef-owner is Etienne Merle, a fifth-generation master French chef, who is also president of the Groupe Américain of the Académie Nationale de Cuisine, an epicurean society of professional chefs and gastronomes. Merle is one of the most talented, in our opinion, as is consistently evinced by his work in his unique restaurant, which has become a mecca for epicures. The rack of lamb he serves there may be Etienne's most famous dish. In fact, for many, rack of lamb properly prepared is the most appealing of the red meats.

1½-pound rack (7 to 8 ribs) of baby lamb
Salt
3 tablespoons unsalted butter
2 garlic cloves, minced
2 tablespoons finely chopped curly parsley
2 tablespoons fresh bread crumbs

1. Have your butcher prepare the rack, the rib end of the loin, bones stripped, which form a natural rack to keep meat off the pan. (Etienne likes just enough fat left on the top section of the rack to "provide natural basting and flavor enhancement.")
2. Very lightly sprinkle the lamb with salt. Place in a pan and sear under high broiler for 3 minutes. (Searing adds color and flavor; it does not seal in the juices.)
3. Heat oven to 500°. When oven is very hot, cook the lamb, uncovered, fat side up, for 25 minutes. (This lamb will be a juicy medium-rare.)
4. While lamb is cooking, in a saucepan, over medium-high heat, melt the butter and sauté the garlic 2 minutes. Stir in parsley, blending; then blend in the bread crumbs, which will bind the mixture.
5. Remove the lamb from the oven. Evenly spread the *persillé* over the top of the lamb. Place in the oven for 3 minutes. Remove and carve the rack at the table.
Serve with Potatoes à la Parisienne (p. 299).

Lamb Shanks with Acorn Squash

SERVES 4

4 lamb shanks
Flour for dredging
Salt and freshly ground black pepper to taste
1 medium-sized acorn squash
2 tablespoons olive oil
¾ cup chicken broth
1 garlic clove, minced
¼ teaspoon dried rosemary
¼ teaspoon dried marjoram
2 medium-sized celery stalks, scraped and cut into 1-inch pieces

1. Dredge the shanks lightly with flour. Sprinkle with salt and pepper.
2. Quarter the squash lengthwise. Remove the seeds and fibers and peel. Cut into ¾-inch strips, lengthwise. Set aside.
3. In a flameproof casserole, heat the oil and evenly brown the shanks. If needed, add more oil. Pour off any oil remaining in the casserole. Add the broth, garlic, rosemary, and marjoram. Bring to a boil on top of the stove. Transfer to a preheated 350° oven and cook, covered, 1½ hours, or until the lamb is just about tender. Add the squash and celery, and cook 15 minutes longer, or until the vegetables and lamb are tender. If the liquid in the pot cooks off before the lamb and vegetables are tender, add a small amount of hot broth or water.
Serve with Sticky Potatoes (p. 355).

Abbacchio alla Romana

SERVES 4

(Lamb Roman Style)

This simple roast lamb is one of the favorite dishes of Rome. The Romans insist on milk-fed baby lamb, so small that a leg will barely feed four.

3-pound leg of lamb (or the smallest you can obtain)
12 fresh rosemary leaves

Salt and freshly ground black pepper
3 tablespoons olive oil
⅓ cup dry white wine

1. With a sharp knife, make 12 small incisions in the leg of lamb and push a rosemary leaf into each. Rub the lamb well with salt and pepper.
2. In a flameproof casserole, heat the olive oil and evenly brown the leg of lamb.
3. Cook for 45 minutes, uncovered, in a preheated 450° oven. At midpoint in the cooking, pour in the white wine and occasionally baste the lamb. Lamb should be pink, tender, and juicy.

Serve with Franconia Potatoes (p. 292), which are cooked with the lamb according to the recipe's directions.

Gigot Rôti Boulangère   SERVES 4

French chefs are fond of saying, "Heaven sends good meats; the Devil sends cooks," meaning that much good meat is ruined by indifferent or uninformed cooks. Nowhere in cookery is this more evident than in preparing a roast leg of lamb. The French call it simply "gigot," if it is roasted plain (4 garlic slivers are inserted, it's seasoned with salt and pepper, and cooked, uncovered, in a preheated 450° oven 15 minutes per pound). All roast lamb should be served pink. Here's a French favorite.

4-pound leg of lamb
1 large garlic clove, peeled and cut into 4 slivers
8 tablespoons (1 stick) unsalted butter
6 medium-sized onions, sliced
4 medium-sized potatoes, peeled and sliced the size of silver
  dollars
Salt and freshly ground black pepper to taste
¼ cup dry white wine
¼ cup chicken broth

1. Make 4 evenly spaced slits in the leg of lamb and insert a sliver of garlic in each.

2. In a saucepan, over medium-high heat, melt half the butter and cook the onions 5 minutes. Toss the onions with the potato slices and place in a casserole large enough to hold the leg of lamb.

3. Sprinkle lightly with salt and pepper and pour in the wine and chicken broth. Reserve.

4. In a flameproof casserole, over medium-high heat, melt the remaining butter and evenly brown the lamb. Cook the lamb, uncovered, in a preheated 450° oven 10 minutes on each side.

5. Remove the lamb from its casserole and place on top of the vegetables in the other casserole. Cover tightly with aluminum foil, reduce the oven heat to 400°, and bake an additional 35 minutes.

Lemon-Zested Glazed Lamb Roast SERVES 4 TO 6

1 tablespoon olive oil
1 tablespoon unsalted butter
6 shallots, chopped
1½ cups fresh white bread crumbs
⅓ cup chopped raisins
Grated rind of 2 lemons
⅓ teaspoon dried rosemary
⅓ teaspoon dried thyme
Salt and freshly ground black pepper to taste
Juice of 1 small orange
4- to 5-pound leg of lamb, boned
½ cup light-brown sugar, packed
Juice of 1 lemon
½ cup dry red wine
1 cup beef broth

1. In a frying pan, heat the olive oil and butter. Add the shallots and cook 3 minutes, or until soft. Do not brown. In a bowl, combine the shallots (and the fat they cooked in), the bread crumbs, raisins,

lemon rind, rosemary, thyme, salt, and pepper. Mix in enough orange juice to moisten the stuffing, blending well.

2. Arrange the stuffing on the spread-out boned lamb. Roll tightly into a leg shape, tying securely with cord to prevent stuffing from coming out. Place in a roasting pan that has been lightly coated with olive oil.

3. In a small saucepan, combine the brown sugar and lemon juice. Blend and cook over low heat, stirring, for 1 minute, or until the sugar has dissolved and the mixture has thickened. Spread the sugar mixture evenly over the lamb.

4. Cook, uncovered, in a preheated 375° oven for 1¼ hours, basting occasionally. This should be medium rare. If you prefer the lamb well done, cook approximately 30 minutes more. Transfer the lamb to a serving dish and keep warm in a 200° oven.

5. Stir the wine and beef broth into the lamb roasting pan, scraping up the browned-on bits from the bottom, and cook, stirring, over medium-high heat, until the sauce has reduced in volume and slightly thickened.

6. Serve the lamb with a dollop of sauce on each stuffing-centered slice.

Potatoes Lyonnaise (p. 308) are an excellent accompaniment.

Leg of Lamb Greek Style   SERVES 6

5-pound leg of lamb
4 tablespoons olive oil
Salt and freshly ground black pepper
4 tablespoons (½ stick) butter, melted
1½ cups warm tomato juice
1 small cinnamon stick, broken into several pieces

1. Rub the lamb well with the olive oil and sprinkle with salt and pepper. Place in a roasting pan on a rack and cook, uncovered, in a preheated 425° oven 20 minutes, basting twice with a mixture of the butter and tomato juice.

2. Reduce the oven heat to 325°. Pour the remaining tomato-juice mixture over the lamb. Drop the pieces of cinnamon in the pan. Cook, covered, 50 minutes, or to doneness desired, basting occasionally.

Serve the sliced lamb with a Potato-Carrot Pudding (p. 346).

Madeline Altman's Parsleyed Leg of Lamb SERVES 6

This was a favorite of Maria Luisa's older sister.

5- to 6-pound leg of lamb
Salt and freshly ground black pepper
2 garlic cloves, halved
2 medium-sized onions, chopped
2 medium-sized carrots, scraped and sliced
½ cup dry white wine
½ cup chicken broth
¼ cup Dijon mustard
1½ cups fresh bread crumbs
¾ cup of chopped broadleaf parsley
1 garlic clove, crushed
¼ cup melted unsalted butter

1. Rub the surface of the lamb with salt and pepper. The day before roasting, make 4 slits and insert half a garlic clove in each. Refrigerate overnight.

2. Lamb should reach room temperature before cooking. Place the lamb in a flameproof casserole without a rack. Sprinkle the onions and carrots around the meat. Pour in the wine and broth, and bring to a boil on top of the stove. Transfer to a preheated 325° oven and cook, uncovered, 1¼ hours for medium rare. It should be not quite done.

3. Remove the lamb from oven. Cool 15 minutes. Coat it with mustard; firmly pat on a mixture of the bread crumbs, parsley, and garlic, and sprinkle on the melted butter. Raise the oven temperature to 400°, return the lamb to the oven, and cook 20 minutes,

or until the top is crisp and golden. Transfer to a serving dish and let stand 20 minutes. Slice and serve with Potatoes Delmonico (p. 305).

Stuffed Leg of Lamb Cooked with Port Wine   SERVES 6

5-pound leg of lamb, boned
1¼ cups port wine
2 tablespoons olive oil
Salt and freshly ground black pepper
½ cup bread crumbs
2 bunches of scallions (use all but the last inch of the dark-green
*   end), trimmed and cut into ½-inch pieces*
2 hard-boiled eggs, coarsely chopped
2 tablespoons chopped fresh parsley
1 teaspoon dried rosemary
2 garlic cloves, minced
½ teaspoon salt
¼ teaspoon freshly ground black pepper
Juice and grated rind of one lemon

1. Spread the leg of lamb out, skin side down. Blend ¼ cup wine with the olive oil and brush the lamb well with the mixture. Sprinkle with salt and pepper.
2. In a bowl, combine and blend well with a fork the bread crumbs, scallions, eggs, parsley, rosemary, garlic, salt, pepper, lemon juice and rind, and distribute evenly over the lamb.
3. Roll and tie the lamb securely with trussing cord so the stuffing will not work its way out. Transfer the lamb to a roasting pan just large enough to hold it comfortably. Pour the remaining wine over the lamb.
4. Cook, uncovered, in a preheated 450° oven 20 minutes. Lower oven temperature to 325° and cook about 1 hour, or according to taste, basting occasionally as it cooks. Let the lamb stand 20 minutes before slicing.
Serve with Polish Potatoes for Game Dishes (p. 343).

5

Pork, Ham, and Sausage

American Country Sausage
Chorizo
Fricadelles Flamande
George Herz's Bacon-Pork Sausage
Abruzzi Potato and Sausage Pie
Irish Sausage and Potato Coddle
Italian Fennel Pork Sausage
Italian Sausage alla Pizzaiola
Italian Sausage Loaf
Porkburgers
Pork-Stuffed Peppers
Sausages in Potato Blankets
Bigos
Sausage in Red Wine, Burgundy Style
Barbara and Richard Perry's Pork Stew
Pork and Apple Pie
Portuguese Pork with Clams
Broiled Dijon Pork Chops
Helen Renné's Pork Chops Mahón
Herbed Pork Chops
Stuffed Loin Pork Chops
Pork Medallions Jagd-Schloss Fuschl
Knockwurst, Pork Chops, and Sauerkraut
Loin Pork Chops with Onion Sauce
Palermo Pork Chops with Glazed
Orange Slices
Pork Chops alla Doris Limoncelli
Pork Chops and Sausage à la Boulangère
Jim Anelli's Porchetti
Carré de Porc Fumé à la Mandarin

Crown Roast of Pork
Lithuanian Pork Roast
Mørbrad
Poached Pork Loin with Horseradish
Applesauce
Pork Loin en Leche
Pork Tenderloin with Mushroom Dill
Sauce
Pork Tenderloin Slices with Prunes
Slavic Pork Roast Glazed with Applesauce
Roast Pork Loin with Braised Red
Cabbage
Shoulder of Pork with Peppers
Barbecued Spareribs
Braised Pork Ribs Cacciatore
Pork Hocks with Winekraut
Roast Suckling Pig
Ham à la King
Ham-Cornmeal Soufflé
Ground Ham and Pork Loaf with Mustard
Sauce
Ham or Pork Croquettes
Ham Slices Oporto
Jack Daniel's–Glazed Ham
Lake Charles Ham Jambalaya
Leftover Ham with Saupiquet Sauce
Pennsylvania Dutch Ham
Sheehans' Vermont Smoked Ham
Potato and Ham Cakes
Scalloped Potatoes with Ham

Sometimes statistics tell a vivid story. With pork and ham the numbers are indeed impressive. Fifteen billion pounds of pork—worth nine billion dollars—are consumed yearly in this country. No other red meat has such a loyal following, and today's pork is bred to be much leaner than it used to be.

The value of boneless pork is worth considering. For example, a bone-in pork chop may cost $2.49 a pound, yet only about 60 percent of that chop is edible, raising the price to $4.15 a pound. A boneless chop may cost $3.29 a pound, but the whole chop is edible, saving the consumer 86 cents a pound.

Among the tastiest and most popular of pork is sausage, in all its varieties. We offer several of our favorite recipes, including American Country Sausage, which has long glorified the pancake as a breakfast treat, and a spectacular Italian sausage loaf. We also provide recipes for pork loin, one of the most elegant of all meats, as well as Portuguese Pork with Clams and Palermo Pork Chops with Glazed Orange Slices. Finally, there are French pork meatballs, Fricadelles Flamande, Jambalaya, Potato and Ham Croquettes, and a zesty Ham à la King.

American Country Sausage

MAKES 12 TO 16 PATTIES

With this sausage (in fact, with all sausage) careful and complete mixing and blending are important for even seasoning.

> 4 pounds ground pork, butt or shoulder, with fat
> 5 teaspoons salt
> 4 teaspoons ground sage
> 3 teaspoons coarsely ground black pepper
> 1 teaspoon ground nutmeg
> ½ teaspoon ground red pepper
> ¼ teaspoon ground ginger
> 1 tablespoon sugar
> ½ cup cold water

Pork

· RETAIL CUTS ·
WHERE THEY COME FROM
HOW TO COOK THEM

LEG
SIDE
LOIN
ARM SHOULDER
BLADE SHOULDER

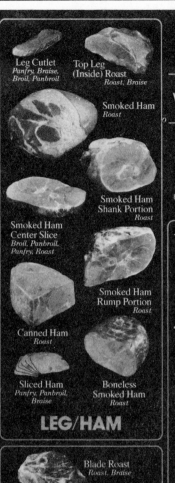

LEG/HAM

Leg Cutlet
Panfry, Braise, Broil, Panbroil

Top Leg (Inside) Roast
Roast, Braise

Smoked Ham
Roast

Smoked Ham Shank Portion
Roast

Smoked Ham Center Slice
Broil, Panbroil, Panfry, Roast

Smoked Ham Rump Portion
Roast

Canned Ham
Roast

Sliced Ham
Panfry, Panbroil, Braise

Boneless Smoked Ham
Roast

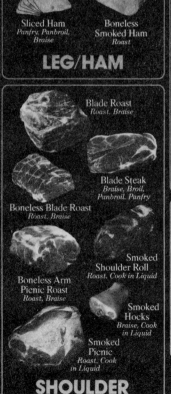

SHOULDER

Blade Roast
Roast, Braise

Blade Steak
Braise, Broil, Panbroil, Panfry

Boneless Blade Roast
Roast, Braise

Boneless Arm Picnic Roast
Roast, Braise

Smoked Shoulder Roll
Roast, Cook in Liquid

Smoked Hocks
Braise, Cook in Liquid

Smoked Picnic
Roast, Cook in Liquid

LOIN

Blade Chop
Braise, Broil, Panbroil, Panfry

Rib Chop
Broil, Panbroil, Panfry, Braise

Top Loin Chop
Broil, Panbroil, Panfry, Braise

Loin Chop
Broil, Panbroil, Panfry, Braise

Sirloin Chop
Braise

Butterfly Chop
Broil, Panbroil, Panfry, Braise

Sirloin Cutlet
Braise, Broil, Panbroil, Panfry

Back Ribs
Roast, Broil, Braise, Cook in Liquid

Country-Style Ribs
Roast, Braise, Broil, Cook in Liquid

Tenderloin
Roast, Braise, (Slices: Panfry, Braise)

Center Rib Roast
Roast

Top Loin Roast (Double)
Roast

Blade Roast
Roast, Braise

Boneless Blade Roast
Roast, Braise

Sirloin Roast
Roast

Center Loin Roast
Roast

Smoked Loin Chop
Roast, Broil, Panbroil, Panfry

Crown Roast
Roast

Boneless Sirloin Roast
Roast

Canadian-Style Bacon
Roast, Broil, Panbroil, Panfry

SIDE

Spareribs
Roast, Broil, Cook in Liquid, Braise

Sliced Bacon
Panfry, Broil, Roast (Bake)

OTHER CUTS

Cubed Steak
Braise, Panbroil, Panfry

Pork Pieces
Braise, Cook in Liquid

Cubes for Kabobs
Broil, Braise

Ground Pork
Broil, Panbroil, Panfry, Roast (Bake)

Sausage Links
Braise, Panfry, Roast

1. In a large bowl, combine and blend well all ingredients except the water (your hands are good for this).

2. To make bulk sausage (to form into patties) that will fry without crumbling, add the cold water gradually, kneading with the hands until the meat becomes slightly sticky and doughlike.

For a unique supper, try the homemade sausage patties with State of Maine Potato Pancakes (p. 377).

Chorizo
(Spanish Spicy Sausage)

MAKES ABOUT 14
SAUSAGES (3 POUNDS)

There's a tendency these days to serve food so spicy and hot that few know what they're eating. These Spanish sausages should be spicy enough for anyone. We find that they are good for picking up bland bean, chick-pea, and rice dishes, and we also serve them, sliced, as an hors d'oeuvre.

2 pounds pork butt (with fat), cubed
1 pound beef chuck, cubed
1 teaspoon Hungarian paprika
1 teaspoon ground cumin
1 tablespoon dried oregano
1 tablespoon salt
2 teaspoons freshly ground black pepper
2 teaspoons ground cayenne pepper, or to taste
1 medium-sized onion, minced
1 bell pepper, cored, seeded, and minced
4 garlic cloves, minced
¼ cup dry red wine
2 tablespoons brandy
Olive oil

1. Grind the pork and beef finely.

2. Place in a large bowl, add all remaining ingredients except for olive oil, and blend thoroughly with your hands.

3. Either place in casings or form into patties. If in casings, prick,

and poach for 3 minutes in a small amount of simmering water. Drain well and fry in olive oil. Patties should be browned. (We find putting the meat in casings and twisting them into 6-inch links best.) If you don't choose to serve these spicy sausages with the usual bean or rice dishes, try them with Vernon Jarrett's Ciapotta (p. 275).

Fricadelles Flamande   SERVES 6

This recipe for pork meatballs with vegetables came to us from the chef at the Hôtel Napoléon in Nice.

8 tablespoons (1 stick) unsalted butter
½ cup chopped shallots
2 garlic cloves, chopped
1 tablespoon salt
½ teaspoon freshly ground black pepper
⅛ teaspoon nutmeg
2 pounds trimmed, lean pork loin (no fat), put through the medium blade of meat chopper
3 egg yolks, beaten
1½ cups white bread crumbs
3 egg whites, stiffly beaten
4 tablespoons olive oil
24 small white onions, root ends scored
12 potatoes, trimmed to the size and shape of eggs
½ cup dry white wine
2 cups chicken broth
½ cup chopped parsley

1. In a saucepan, over medium-high heat, melt half the butter and cook the shallots 3 minutes. Add garlic and cook 2 minutes.
2. In a large bowl, combine the shallots and garlic and their butter, the salt, pepper, nutmeg, ground pork, egg yolks, bread crumbs, and the stiffly beaten egg whites, blending all well but lightly.
3. Shape the mixture into 12 balls, more egg-shaped than round.

In a frying pan, heat the olive oil and brown the meatballs, turning often so they brown evenly.

4. In another frying pan, over medium-high heat, melt the remaining butter and cook the onions until golden brown. Place the meatballs in a flameproof casserole, surrounding them with the onions and potatoes. Pour in the wine and chicken broth; there should be enough to just cover the ingredients.

5. Bring to a boil on top of the stove, cover and place in a preheated 400° oven for 40 minutes, or until the potatoes are tender. This dish should be cooked 30 minutes covered and 10 minutes uncovered. Place on a warm serving dish and sprinkle with parsley.

George Herz's Bacon-Pork Sausage   SERVES 4 TO 6

A friend of German heritage believes that the two tastiest pork products are bacon and sausage, and he frequently treats his breakfast guests to this combination. The French call a similar dish Boulettes de Bretagne.

> 9 slices lean bacon, finely chopped (a food processor does a
>   neat job)
> 1½ pounds ground lean pork
> 1½ teaspoons thyme
> 2 teaspoons finely grated lemon peel
> ½ teaspoon freshly ground black pepper
> 1 teaspoon salt
> ⅓ teaspoon nutmeg
> 2 tablespoons butter

1. Place all ingredients, except butter, in a large bowl, and thoroughly blend with your hands.

2. Make individual patties, ½ inch thick.

3. Melt butter in a frying pan over medium-high heat and brown the patties 6 minutes on each side, or until cooked through.

We like these at dinner with Potatoes Frigo (p. 350).

Abruzzi Potato and Sausage Pie

SERVES 6

*6 large Idaho potatoes (about 3 pounds), cooked in boiling water
in their skins until tender, drained, dried over heat, peeled,
and riced*
4 large sweet Italian sausages, casings removed
3 large hot Italian sausages, casings removed
Salt to taste
6 tablespoons unsalted butter
1 cup grated Asiago or Parmesan cheese
¼ teaspoon nutmeg
¾ cup medium cream, or half-and-half, heated

1. While the potatoes are cooking, in a frying pan, over medium heat, cook the sausage meat without any fat, stirring and breaking up with a fork, separating the meat as it cooks. Cook 15 minutes. Spoon into a strainer over a bowl to drain.

2. In a warm bowl, combine the potatoes with salt, butter, ¾ cup cheese, nutmeg, and enough cream to make a smooth mixture. It should be rather firm, not too soft. Whip the potatoes until fluffy. Taste for seasoning. Blend in the sausage.

3. Spoon into a shallow, buttered casserole, smoothing the top. Sprinkle the remaining cheese over the surface. Place, uncovered, in an oven preheated to 350° for 25 minutes, or until the top is crusty brown.

Irish Sausage and Potato Coddle

SERVES 4 TO 6

½ pound thick-sliced bacon, cut into 2-inch pieces
1 pound pork sausage links
2 large onions, sliced
*4 large potatoes (about 2 pounds), peeled and sliced medium-
thick*
Salt and freshly ground black pepper to taste
¼ cup chopped parsley
2 cups water

1. In a frying pan, cook the bacon pieces until golden, then drain on paper towels. Prick the sausages in several places and brown evenly in the bacon fat. Drain on paper towels and cut into ¼-inch-thick slices.

2. In a casserole, alternate layers of the bacon, sausages, onions, and potatoes, seasoning the onions and potatoes lightly with salt and pepper. Sprinkle all layers with parsley.

3. Pour off all but 2 tablespoons fat from the bacon-sausage frying pan. Add the water and bring to a boil. Pour over the potato casserole, cover, and bake in a preheated 350° oven 45 minutes. Remove the cover and cook 15 minutes, or until the top layer is browned and the potatoes are tender.

Italian Fennel Pork Sausage   ABOUT 6 POUNDS

2 Boston pork butts, skinned, boned, and cut into small chunks (including fat), weighing 6 pounds after trimming
1½ tablespoons salt
2 teaspoons black pepper
½ teaspoon crushed red pepper
5 tablespoons minced broadleaf parsley
½ cup grated Asiago cheese
4 tablespoons crushed fennel seeds, crisped in a pan in a pre-heated 325° oven for 10 minutes
3 garlic cloves, minced

1. In a large bowl, combine all ingredients and thoroughly blend with your hands. Cover the bowl with plastic wrap and refrigerate overnight for flavors to meld.

2. Put seasoned pork chunks through medium plate of a food chopper. Place in a large bowl and mix thoroughly to evenly distribute seasonings. Fry a sample patty in melted butter to test for proper seasoning.

3. All sausages can be prepared as patties (the easiest and many think the most flavorful method of preparation), or run through a

sausage-stuffer into hog casings, then frozen. All food choppers or grinders come with sausage-stuffing instructions.
Serve with Potatoes with Pizzaiola Sauce (p. 352).

Italian Sausage alla Pizzaiola SERVES 6

3 tablespoons olive oil
12 links sweet Italian sausages
2 large garlic cloves, cut into halves
4 cups of canned Italian plum tomatoes, placed in a bowl and
  broken up (your hands are good for this)
Salt and freshly ground black pepper to taste
½ teaspoon oregano
¼ teaspoon crushed red pepper flakes
½ teaspoon sugar
2 tablespoons chopped broadleaf parsley

1. In a deep pot, heat the oil and evenly brown the sausages with the garlic, turning and cooking about 20 minutes. When the garlic becomes golden, remove and discard it.
2. Pour all fat from the pot except 1 tablespoon. If the sausages were very lean and did not produce any fat, add 1 tablespoon oil to the pot. Pour the tomatoes into the pot and stir, scraping up the browned-on bits from the bottom of the pot.
3. Return the sausages to the pot and season with salt and pepper. Stir in the oregano, red pepper, and sugar, and simmer, uncovered, for 20 minutes, or until the sauce thickens and the sausages are cooked. Transfer to a hot serving dish and sprinkle with parsley. Serve with Potatoes Parma (p. 349).

Italian Sausage Loaf SERVES 6

Here's a tasty dish we had in a restaurant in Palermo, where the waiter obligingly rattled off the recipe from memory.

2 pounds ground Italian fennel sausage meat, no casings
   (p. 158)
2 tablespoons chopped raisins
¼ cup grated Asiago or Parmesan cheese
2 tablespoons tomato paste
2 eggs, beaten
1 cup fine bread crumbs
Salt and freshly ground black pepper to taste (the sausage
   could supply enough)

1. Place all ingredients in a large bowl and blend thoroughly but lightly with your hands.
2. Butter a 9 × 5 × 3-inch loaf pan and fill it with the sausage mixture, smoothing the top.
3. Set in a pan of hot water, with the water coming halfway up the loaf pan.
4. Bake, uncovered, in a preheated 350° oven 1½ hours, or until the loaf is crusty-brown on top. Allow to set for a few minutes before slicing.

We like it with mashed potatoes, Purée de Pommes de Terre (p. 313).

Porkburgers   SERVES 4 TO 6

Many people think that ground pork is superior to ground beef. We are among them.

2 pounds ground lean pork (shoulder is good)
½ teaspoon marjoram
1 teaspoon Worcestershire sauce, or to taste
Dash Tabasco sauce
Salt and freshly ground black pepper to taste
1 egg, beaten
1 cup fine bread crumbs
4 tablespoons (½ stick) unsalted butter
2 medium-sized onions, sliced and cooked in 3 tablespoons but-
   ter until golden, seasoned with salt and pepper, and kept hot

1. In a bowl, combine and blend well, but lightly, the pork, marjoram, Worcestershire sauce, Tabasco sauce, salt, and pepper, and form into 4 to 6 patties about ½ inch thick. Dip into the egg, then dredge with bread crumbs.

2. In a frying pan, melt the butter over medium-high heat and evenly brown the porkburgers. Lower heat and cook 20 minutes, or until cooked through, turning often.

3. Top with the hot, cooked onion slices.

Watercress Potato Soufflé (p. 359) makes this a meal to remember.

Note: Plain lean ground pork treated exactly as we do hamburgers is also remarkably tasty, but do not serve rare.

Pork-Stuffed Peppers   SERVES 6

3 large, firm, fresh green peppers
¼ cup dried currants
¼ cup Madeira mixed with ¼ cup water
2 tablespoons unsalted butter
2 tablespoons olive oil
1½ pounds lean ground pork
1 medium-sized onion, chopped
1 small carrot, scraped and chopped
1 celery stalk, scraped and chopped
Salt and freshly ground black pepper to taste
½ cup fine bread crumbs
3 tablespoons chopped walnuts
½ cup plain yogurt, approximately

1. Cut the peppers into halves lengthwise. Remove the stem ends, seeds, and white ribs, and discard. Cook in boiling salted water for 5 minutes. Invert and drain well.

2. Plump the currants in the Madeira and water for 10 to 15 minutes. Drain well and reserve.

3. In a frying pan, heat the butter and oil. Add the pork, onion, carrot, and celery, and cook about 15 minutes, or until the pork is

cooked through and no longer pink. Season with salt and pepper. With a slotted spoon, transfer the pork mixture to a bowl and add the bread crumbs, walnuts, currants, and yogurt. If mixture seems dry, add more yogurt. It should be slightly moist but not soupy.

4. Divide the mixture equally and mound it in the pepper halves. Place in a baking dish large enough to hold them comfortably. Pour in about ¼ inch water and bake in a preheated 350° oven for 30 minutes, or until the pepper is tender and the filling is heated through.

Serve with Caramelized Potatoes (p. 331).

Sausages in Potato Blankets   SERVES 4

This is an excellent supper or luncheon dish with a salad.

8 standard-size (about ¾ × 3 inches) breakfast sausages, or
    8 sausage patties shaped into cylinders the same size
1 small onion, minced
3 tablespoons soft, unsalted butter
Salt and freshly ground black pepper to taste
1 tablespoon minced fresh parsley
6 cups mashed potatoes
Flour for dredging
1 large egg beaten with 1 tablespoon milk
1½ cups fine bread crumbs
1 tablespoon crushed celery seed
Vegetable oil for deep frying

1. In a frying pan, cook the sausages thoroughly. Drain on paper towels. Pour off all but 1 tablespoon of the fat and cook the onion in the same pan until soft. Do not brown.

2. Combine and mix well the onion, butter, salt, pepper, parsley, and mashed potatoes. Cool.

3. Divide the potato mixture into 8 equal parts. Use each part to completely encase one sausage. Dredge the "blankets" with flour. Dip into the egg-milk mixture. Dredge with the bread crumbs mixed

with the celery seed and deep-fry in the oil until golden. Drain on paper towels.

We like to use American Country Sausage (p. 152) for this recipe.

Bigos

Sometimes called a Polish hunter's stew, bigos often includes venison as well as pork. We were taught how to prepare this dish by Steve Derry, a talented photographer and Jack's wartime companion, who learned it from his Polish mother, who learned it from hers. Sometimes bigos is teamed with fresh sauerkraut, but Derry uses just cabbage. The Poles enjoy this even more three days after it has been cooked; so do we.

5 tablespoons unsalted butter
2½ pounds lean pork (we like it cut from fresh ham), cut in 1-inch cubes
Salt and freshly ground black pepper
1 large celery stalk, scraped and chopped
1 large onion, chopped
2 medium-sized tart green apples (we use Granny Smith), peeled, cored, and coarsely chopped
6 medium-sized mushrooms, coarsely chopped
4 cups finely shredded Savoy cabbage
1 teaspoon caraway seeds
Bouquet garni (6 parsley sprigs, 1 bay leaf, and 3 cloves tied in cheesecloth)
2 ripe tomatoes, peeled, seeded, and coarsely chopped
1 tablespoon tomato paste
1 cup dry white wine
2 cups chicken broth
1 pound kielbasa, skinned, cut into 1-inch rounds
2 tablespoons chopped fresh dill

1. In a heavy, flameproof casserole, over medium heat, melt 4 tablespoons butter and evenly brown the pork, seasoning with salt and pepper. Transfer to a bowl with a slotted spoon.

2. Melt the remaining butter in the casserole, add the celery, onion, apples, and mushrooms, stirring and cooking just until soft, about 5 minutes.

3. Stir in the cabbage, caraway seeds, bouquet garni, tomatoes, tomato paste, wine, and 1 cup of the broth. Simmer, covered, for 10 minutes.

4. Stir in the browned pork with its juices and the kielbasa slices. Place, covered, in a preheated 325° oven for 1½ hours, or until the pork is tender.

5. If the liquid cooks off before the meat is tender, add small amounts of hot broth. If there is too much liquid, remove cover for last half hour of cooking, to allow the surplus liquid to cook off.

6. Discard the bouquet garni and sprinkle with dill before serving. Enhance this recipe with Potatoes with Three Cheeses (p. 277).

Sausage in Red Wine, Burgundy Style SERVES 6

12 French garlic sausages, or 6 sweet and 6 hot Italian sausages
2 tablespoons unsalted butter
1 tablespoon olive oil
3 garlic cloves, peeled and crushed, but each in one piece
2 cups dry red wine
2 tablespoons chopped parsley

1. Prick the sausages with a fork or the point of a knife in several places. In a frying pan, heat the butter and oil. Add the garlic and sausages, and brown the sausages evenly over medium heat. Remove and discard the garlic when it becomes golden. Do not let it brown. Pour off any fat. Pour in the wine and heat to a boil, stirring up any browned-on bits from the bottom of the pan.

2. Transfer the sausages to a shallow casserole that will just hold them comfortably. Pour in the hot wine and cook in a preheated 350° oven 45 minutes, or until cooked through. (If using smoked sausages, cut cooking time down to 30 minutes.) Sprinkle with parsley and serve.

A hot Potato-Broccoli Salad (p. 269) adds a nice touch to this dish.

Barbara and Richard Perry's Pork Stew

SERVES 6 TO 8

Those who are professionally involved in selling meat often are excellent sources of recipes. This simple and savory suggestion comes from Barbara, the wife of Richard Perry, meat manager of Minier's Market in the picturesque village of Big Flats, New York.

3 tablespoons unsalted butter
1 tablespoon olive oil
3 pounds lean pork, cut into 1-inch cubes
3 large onions, thinly sliced
2 tablespoons Hungarian paprika
13¾-ounce can condensed beef broth
1 cup water
1 bay leaf
1 teaspoon caraway seeds, crushed
Salt to taste
6 to 8 medium-sized carrots, scraped and cut into ½-inch slices
¾ pound fresh baby string beans

1. In a flameproof casserole, heat the butter and oil. Add the pork and brown evenly over medium heat, adding more butter and oil if needed.
2. Remove the pork; add the onions to the pot and cook over medium heat until soft. Do not brown. Stir in the paprika, blending well. Cook 1 minute.
3. Return the pork to the pot, adding the beef broth and enough water to barely cover the meat. Add the bay leaf, caraway seeds, and salt.
4. Bring to a boil on top of the stove. Cover and cook in a preheated 350° oven 1½ hours.
5. Add the carrots and cook 15 minutes, then stir in the string beans and cook 5 minutes. Discard the bay leaf.

The Perrys serve this with Polish Potato Dumplings (p. 298).

Pork and Apple Pie

2 pounds lean pork, cut into 1-inch cubes
*¼ cup flour, seasoned with 1 teaspoon salt and 1 teaspoon
    paprika*
2 tablespoons unsalted butter
2 tablespoons olive oil
2 medium-sized onions, thinly sliced
1½ cups beef broth
½ cup Madeira
1½ teaspoons sugar
1 teaspoon mace
*3 medium-sized tart green apples (we use Granny Smith),
    peeled, cored, and sliced*
Rich Salty Pastry (see below)
1 egg beaten with 1 tablespoon water (optional)

1. Dredge the pork with the seasoned flour.
2. In a flameproof casserole, heat the butter and oil and brown the meat evenly, adding more butter and oil if needed. As the pork browns, transfer it to a bowl with a slotted spoon.
3. If there is more than 1 tablespoon of fat in the casserole, pour off all but that amount. If the fat has been absorbed by the pork, add 1 tablespoon butter. Add the onions and cook until soft. Do not brown. Sprinkle any remaining seasoned flour over the onions and stir to blend well.
4. Stir in the broth, Madeira, sugar, and mace, and cook, stirring, until slightly thickened. Return the pork to the casserole; cover and cook in a preheated 325° oven for 1 hour (if the liquid cooks off, add small amounts of hot broth), or until the pork is fork-tender. Taste for seasoning.
5. In a deep pie dish or baking dish, arrange alternate layers of apple slices and pork cubes. Cover with the sauce. Cool slightly. Roll the pastry to about ⅛ inch thick, 1 inch larger than the rim of the baking dish. Cut half-inch-strips from the edge of the pastry. Moisten the rim of the dish and lay the strips on it, pressing against

the dish. Moisten the pastry rim and cover the pie with the remaining pastry, pressing it down onto the pastry rim. Trim and flute. Cut several slashes to allow steam to escape. Brush the egg and water mixture over the top and bake in a preheated 400° oven 30 minutes, or until the crust is golden brown.

RICH SALTY PASTRY

> *2 cups sifted all-purpose flour*
> *1 teaspoon baking powder*
> *1 teaspoon salt*
> *¾ cup unsalted butter*
> *1 egg, beaten*
> *1 or 2 tablespoons cream (optional)*

1. In a bowl blend the flour, baking powder, salt, and butter with a pastry blender until it has the consistency of cornmeal.
2. Add the egg and blend with a fork until the dough can be gathered into a ball. If it crumbles, add just enough cream to hold it together.
3. Seal in plastic wrap and refrigerate at least 1 hour before rolling out.

Portuguese Pork with Clams   SERVES 6

In Lisbon they surprise everyone (except the citizens) with this unlikely combination.

> *3-pound boned pork loin, cut into 1-inch cubes*
> *2 cups dry white wine*
> *1½ teaspoons salt*
> *1 teaspoon freshly ground black pepper*
> *½ teaspoon dried thyme*
> *3 tablespoons olive oil*
> *Salt and freshly ground black pepper to taste*
> *¼ teaspoon cayenne pepper, or to taste*
> *18 littleneck clams, well scrubbed*
> *2 tablespoons chopped parsley*

1. In a large bowl, combine the pork cubes, wine, salt, pepper, and thyme. Mix well and marinate for 3 hours, stirring from time to time.

2. Drain and reserve the marinade. Dry the pork cubes well. In a flameproof casserole, heat the oil and brown the pork evenly, lightly sprinkling with salt and pepper. Add more oil if needed. When all the meat is browned, pour off any fat in the casserole.

3. Stir the cayenne into 1 cup of the marinade and pour over the pork. Bring to a boil on top of the stove, cover top with aluminum foil, then the cover of the casserole, and cook in a preheated 350° oven 50 minutes, or until the pork is fork-tender. If the liquid cooks off before the pork is tender, add small amounts of the marinade, heated.

4. Add the clams, cover, and cook 10 minutes, or until the clams open. Sprinkle with parsley before serving from the casserole.

Offer Potatoes à la Maître d'Hôtel (p. 308) as a double surprise.

Broiled Dijon Pork Chops   SERVES 4

4 loin pork chops, 1¼ inches thick
3 tablespoons balsamic vinegar, or red wine vinegar
4 tablespoons olive oil
1 tablespoon Dijon mustard
¼ teaspoon chopped fresh chives
⅛ teaspoon dried tarragon

1. Place the chops on a rack in a broiler pan (or on a charcoal grill) so the meat's surface is 4 to 5 inches from heat. Broil at medium temperature 10 minutes; turn and broil another 10 minutes.

2. Brush the chops with a mixture of the vinegar, olive oil, mustard, chives, and tarragon, and broil 5 minutes. Turn, brush the second side with the mustard mixture, and continue, turning every 5 minutes and brushing with the mixture, until the chops are tender.

Potato-Broccoli Pudding (p. 346) makes this menu unique.

Helen Renné's Pork Chops Mahón

SERVES 4

Mayonnaise, that tangy sauce of olive oil, eggs, and lemon (supposedly first used in Mahón, capital of the Balearic Island of Minorca), weds tastefully with many meats, including pork. No other seasoning is required to produce juicy, flavorful chops.

> 5 tablespoons mayonnaise (one with all-natural ingredients, such as Cain's, is best)
> 4 loin pork chops, 1 inch thick
> 2 cups fine bread crumbs

1. Spread the mayonnaise on a large, flat plate and dredge the chops well on both sides, completely coating them.
2. Dredge with the bread crumbs, encasing the chops completely.
3. Place in a shallow roasting pan. Cook in a preheated 400° oven, uncovered, 45 minutes, or until tender.
Serve with Potatoes with Salt Pork (p. 354).

Herbed Pork Chops

SERVES 4

> 1 teaspoon dried rosemary
> ½ teaspoon ground sage
> 1 garlic clove, chopped
> Salt and freshly ground black pepper to taste
> 4 loin pork chops, about 1 inch thick
> 2 tablespoons olive oil
> ¾ cup water
> ¾ cup dry white vermouth

1. Mix the rosemary, sage, garlic, salt, and pepper. Rub the mixture into the chops.
2. In a frying pan, heat the olive oil and sauté the chops for 5 minutes, turning once. Add the water and cover. Lower heat and simmer until all the water has been absorbed, about 20 minutes. Remove the cover and brown the chops on both sides.

3. Add the vermouth and cook until most of it has evaporated and the chops are tender (about 10 minutes), turning them occasionally. Serve with German Sour-Cream Pancakes (p. 374).

Stuffed Loin Pork Chops

SERVES 2 WITH VERY HEARTY APPETITES; WE OFTEN SHARE ONE

4 tablespoons (½ stick) unsalted butter
2 tablespoons chopped onion
2 tablespoons chopped celery
4 chicken livers, trimmed and chopped
1½ cups small dry bread cubes (not crumbs)
Salt and freshly ground black pepper to taste
½ teaspoon Bell's seasoning
1 teaspoon finely chopped raisins
1 teaspoon finely chopped parsley
2 tablespoons grated Asiago cheese
1 cup chicken broth
2 loin pork chops, 1½ inches thick
Flour for dredging
Bread crumbs for dredging
1 egg
2 tablespoons olive oil

1. In a frying pan, over medium heat, melt the butter and cook onion and celery 5 minutes; add chicken livers and cook 3 minutes. In a bowl, mix the onion, celery, livers, the butter they cooked in, the bread cubes, salt, pepper, Bell's seasoning, raisins, parsley, cheese, and 3 tablespoons chicken broth to moisten. Blend thoroughly.
2. With a sharp knife, cut through the center of the chops horizontally to the bone. Use fingers to open up a substantial pocket, being careful not to break through the back of the chops. The purpose is to form an envelope to hold the stuffing.
3. Spread the flour and bread crumbs, separated, on a large sheet of wax paper. Beat the egg in a shallow dish large enough to hold

one chop at a time. Stuff the chops, pushing the stuffing into the very end of the pocket. The chops will become very fat and bulky. Dredge the stuffed chops carefully in flour, sealing the stuffing-filled pocket with flour. Dip in the beaten egg (both sides of the chop), then dredge in bread crumbs, sealing in the stuffing.

4. In a frying a pan, heat the olive oil and add the chops, browning evenly on both sides. Transfer the chops to a casserole. Heat the remaining chicken broth and pour around the chops. Place, covered, in a preheated 350° oven for 40 minutes, or until the chops are tender.

We like a few slender French Fries (p. 293) with these enormous chops.

Pork Medallions Jagd-Schloss Fuschl   SERVES 4

We discovered this delicious pork presentation when we stayed at the elegant Jagd-Schloss Fuschl, an ancient hunting castle a few miles from Salzburg, Austria. The Germans and Austrians have a respect for pork that borders on reverence.

2 tablespoons unsalted butter
2 tablespoons olive oil
4 loin pork chops, 1½ inches thick (boned, pounded on both
    sides with a meat mallet, re-formed with the hands, then tied
    into rounds or medallions)
Salt and freshly ground black pepper
6 shallots, minced
1 garlic clove, minced
¼ cup gin
1 cup Brown Sauce (p. 62), or brown gravy
3 tablespoons heavy cream
2 tablespoons minced broadleaf parsley

1. In a large frying pan, heat 1 tablespoon butter and the olive oil. Sauté the pork medallions over medium-high heat, sprinkling lightly with salt and pepper, browning evenly, 12 minutes on each side.

Remove the pork, discard the strings, place the pork on a warm serving dish and keep warm in a 200° oven.

2. In the frying pan in which the pork was browned, melt the remaining butter; add the shallots and garlic, and cook 2 minutes.

3. Pour in the gin and Brown Sauce, reduce the heat, and simmer, stirring, 5 minutes.

4. Stir in the cream and simmer, stirring, about 3 minutes, until the sauce has thickened slightly.

5. Spoon the sauce lightly over the pork medallions on the serving dish and sprinkle with parsley.

We like this with a Swiss Potato Torte (p. 283).

Note: Today's pork, from smaller, younger pigs, has less fat, but is often less tender than we expect. Pounding the chops with the meat mallet will tenderize them and also help speed the cooking process by opening up the fibers. Reshaping the chops by hand before cooking ensures that they will retain their original attractive loin shape.

Knockwurst, Pork Chops, and Sauerkraut

SERVES 4
HEARTY EATERS

We savored this dish in a farmers' restaurant on the lake near the village of Fuschl, not far from Salzburg.

4 tablespoons (½ stick) unsalted butter
1 tablespoon olive oil
1 large onion, chopped
1 garlic clove, minced
2-pound can of sauerkraut, thoroughly drained
Salt and freshly ground black pepper to taste
½ cup dry white wine
12 juniper berries (tied in cheesecloth)
1 teaspoon caraway seeds
2 cups beef broth, approximately
4 smoked pork chops
4 slices lean, thick-sliced bacon

2 tablespoons kirsch
4 knockwurst

1. In a flameproof casserole, heat the butter and oil and cook the onion and garlic 2 minutes, or until soft. Do not brown. Stir in the sauerkraut, sprinkling with salt and pepper. Simmer for 10 minutes, stirring occasionally. Pour in the wine; add the juniper berries and caraway seeds, stirring well. Pour in enough beef broth to barely cover the sauerkraut.
2. Cover the casserole and cook in a preheated 325° oven for 30 minutes. Add the smoked pork chops and bacon, spooning the sauerkraut over them. Cook, covered, 1 hour. Stir in the kirsch and add the knockwurst, burying them in the sauerkraut. Cook, covered, 30 minutes. Discard the juniper berries.

Serve with mashed potatoes, Purée de Pommes de Terre (p. 313).

Loin Pork Chops with Onion Sauce SERVES 4

½ cup flour
1 tablespoon salt
1 teaspoon freshly ground black pepper
¼ teaspoon dried oregano
4 loin pork chops, 1 inch thick
3 tablespoons olive oil
4 medium-sized white onions, chopped
2 garlic cloves, minced
2 cups chicken broth, heated

1. In a clean paper or plastic bag, combine the flour, salt, pepper, and oregano. Add the chops and shake until they are evenly coated with the seasoned flour.
2. To a large frying pan, over medium heat, add the olive oil and evenly brown the chops. Transfer them to a casserole that will hold them snugly in a single layer.
3. Add the onions and garlic to the frying pan the pork browned in, adding more oil if necessary, and cook until the onions are soft.

Do not brown. Add the heated broth and cook, stirring, scraping up the browned-on bits from the bottom of the pan. Simmer, stirring, until the sauce is smooth and slightly thickened. Taste for seasoning.

4. Pour the onion sauce over the chops, cover, and cook in a preheated 350° oven 45 minutes or until the chops are fork-tender. Serve with Potato-Turnip Bake (p. 353).

Palermo Pork Chops with Glazed Orange Slices   SERVES 4

We enjoyed this Sicilian specialty in Palermo, where they use their delicious, usually blood-red oranges in many unique ways.

½ cup Marsala
½ teaspoon rosemary
⅛ teaspoon cinnamon
⅛ teaspoon ground cloves
1 teaspoon salt
½ teaspoon freshly ground black pepper
2 tablespoons grated orange peel
2 garlic cloves, crushed
½ cup orange juice
4 loin pork chops, 1 inch thick
2 tablespoons olive oil
Glazed Orange Slices (see below)

1. In a bowl, combine all ingredients (except the pork chops, olive oil, and orange slices), blending well into a marinade.
2. Arrange the chops in one layer in a shallow dish. Cover with the marinade and let stand at room temperature for 2 hours. Turn several times. Remove the chops, dry with paper towels, and reserve the marinade.
3. In a flameproof casserole, heat the olive oil and brown the chops evenly.
4. Pour the reserved marinade over the chops. Bring to a boil on top of the stove. Cover and cook in a preheated 300° oven 1½

hours, or until the chops are fork-tender.

5. Serve on a hot serving platter, garnished with Glazed Orange Slices.

GLAZED ORANGE SLICES

> *3 medium-sized navel oranges, unpeeled*
> *¼ cup unsalted butter*
> *2 tablespoons light corn syrup*
> *½ cup light-brown sugar, packed*

1. Cut off the ends of the oranges; then crosswise, cut into ½-inch-thick slices.

2. In a large saucepan, combine the butter, corn syrup, and brown sugar, and simmer, stirring, over medium heat, until the sugar melts and the mixture is well blended.

3. Arrange the orange slices in the saucepan and simmer, uncovered, 3 minutes. Turn the slices over and simmer for another 3 minutes.

In Sicily, we had this dish with delicious Potatoes with Ricotta Cheese (p. 353).

Pork Chops alla Doris Limoncelli   SERVES 4

Doris Limoncelli is our sister-in-law. She cooks like a professional.

> *4 tablespoons (½ stick) unsalted butter*
> *1 tablespoon olive oil*
> *4 loin pork chops, 1 inch thick*
> *Salt and freshly ground black pepper to taste*
> *Sweet and Sour Sauce (found in jars in specialty shops or gour-*
> *   met departments of supermarkets)*

1. In a flameproof, shallow casserole, large enough to hold the chops in a single layer, heat the butter and oil. Add the chops, sprinkle with salt and pepper, and brown on both sides over medium heat. Pour off any fat.

2. Bake, uncovered, in a preheated 400° oven 20 minutes, or until

the chops are sizzling. Spoon off any juices.

3. Turn the oven down to 350°. Coat the chops with the sauce and cook 10 minutes. Coat again with sauce and bake another 10 minutes, or until cooked through and tender.

We keep this a piquant offering by serving it with Viennese Mustard Potatoes (p. 285).

Pork Chops and Sausage à la Boulangère SERVES 4

In France, when the local baker has finished his chores, he turns his oven over to his wife, who, for a small fee, cooks her neighbors' casseroles. Hence the term *à la boulangère*.

3 tablespoons butter
1 tablespoon olive oil
3 garlic cloves, peeled, mashed, but still in one piece
4 loin pork chops, ½ inch thick, pounded lightly with a meat
  mallet
Salt and freshly ground black pepper to taste
4 sweet fennel Italian sausages, or sausages of your choice
12 small white onions, root ends scored
2½ cups chicken broth
1 large celery stalk, scraped and coarsely chopped
1 bay leaf
¼ teaspoon dried marjoram
4 medium-sized potatoes, peeled and halved

1. Heat 1 tablespoon butter and the oil in a flameproof casserole, and cook the garlic until soft and golden brown. Do not brown. Remove and discard.

2. Add the remaining butter to the casserole and heat. Sprinkle the chops lightly with salt and pepper and brown them and the sausages in the pot. Remove and reserve.

3. Add the onions to the casserole and cook just until golden. Do not brown. Stir in 1 cup broth, scraping up the browned-on bits from the bottom of the pot.

4. Return the chops and sausages to the casserole with the onions. Add the celery, bay leaf, marjoram, and the remaining chicken broth. Bring to a boil on top of the stove. Cover and cook in a preheated 350° oven 30 minutes. Add the potatoes and cook 25 minutes. Remove cover, raise oven heat to 400°, and cook 15 minutes, or until the pork, potatoes, and onions are fork-tender. Discard bay leaf. Spoon some of the broth over the vegetables and meats when serving.

Jim Anelli's Porchetti

SERVES 6

Jim, a talented cook, owned a grocery store in Washington, Connecticut, where we lived for many years.

> ¼-pound piece salt pork, blanched in boiling water for 5 min-
> utes, drained, dried (rind discarded), then minced
> 1 large garlic clove, minced
> 1 tablespoon unsalted butter
> 2 tablespoons minced parsley
> 2 tablespoons grated Asiago or Parmesan cheese
> 3-pound boned pork loin, tied
> 4 slices of bacon

1. In a bowl, combine and blend into a paste the salt pork, garlic, butter, parsley, and cheese.
2. With a sharp knife, carefully cut 6 deep, narrow slits in the pork, spacing them evenly. Using your fingers, push the salt pork and garlic paste deep into the slits.
3. Place the pork in a shallow casserole, fat side up. Coat the top of the pork with any remaining paste. Lay the slices of bacon over the top and cook, uncovered, in a preheated 400° oven 10 minutes. Lower oven heat to 350° and cook 1½ hours, or until the pork is fork-tender. Do not overcook; pork should be moist-tender.
We like Porchetti with Amsterdam Mashed Potatoes with Sauerkraut (p. 315).

Carré de Porc Fumé à la Mandarin

(Smoked Loin of Pork with Orange Slices)

This special party dish of smoked loin of pork with oranges has been known to give a hostess a galloping case of ego.

> *4-pound smoked loin of pork*
> *1 onion*
> *4 cloves (studded into the onion)*
> *Bouquet garni (2 sprigs of parsley, ½ bay leaf, ¼ teaspoon thyme, and celery leaves tied in cheesecloth)*
> *2 teaspoons peppercorns*
> *1½ teaspoons salt*
> *¾ cup dark-brown sugar, packed*
> *⅛ teaspoon nutmeg*
> *4 seedless oranges, peeled (3 half-inch-thick slices cut from the center of each)*
> *1 cup fresh orange juice*
> *1 cup beef broth*
> *½ cup Triple Sec*

1. Place the pork in a pot and cover with cold water. Add the onion studded with cloves, the bouquet garni, peppercorns, and half the salt. Cover and cook over medium heat 1 hour after water starts simmering.

2. Remove the pork from the liquid and trim off most of the fat. Place the pork in a roasting pan; coat with a mixture of the brown sugar, the nutmeg, and the remaining salt.

3. Arrange the orange slices on top of the pork and pour in the orange juice, beef broth, and Triple Sec. Bring to a boil on top of the stove, cover, and cook in a preheated 450° oven 40 minutes.

4. Transfer the pork to a serving dish. Over medium-high heat, on top of the stove, reduce the liquid in the roasting pan to half and pour through a fine strainer (or cheesecloth set in a strainer).

Serve the sauce on the side with a fancy potato, such as Potato-Chestnut Puree (p. 314).

Crown Roast of Pork

SERVES 8 TO 10

Serving this unique roast ranks as a spectator sport, with favored guests gathered for the carving celebration.

STUFFING

2 cups bread crumbs

3 hot Italian sausages (the meat, not the casings), sautéed in butter 5 minutes

2 tablespoons chopped raisins

3 tablespoons grated Asiago cheese

¼ teaspoon Bell's seasoning

3 tablespoons chicken broth

1 beaten egg

CROWN ROAST

Have your butcher prepare 2 racks of pork, removing the backbones (each rack comprising 7 to 8 ribs)

Salt and freshly ground black pepper

½ teaspoon rosemary

½ teaspoon oregano

8 medium-sized white onions, root ends scored

1. In a bowl, combine and blend well all stuffing ingredients and stuff the center of the crown roast of pork. Cover with foil.

2. Place the meat in a deep roasting pan, sprinkle lightly with salt, pepper, rosemary, and oregano, and surround with the whole onions.

3. Place, uncovered, in a preheated 400° oven for 50 minutes. Lower heat to 350° and cook 1¾ hours.

Remove foil after 1 hour.

Excellent with this recipe is another dramatic offering, Spinach-Filled Baked Potatoes (p. 371).

Note: The same method can be used for a crown roast of lamb. Cooking time, however, should be reduced by half, as the lamb chops should be pink when the crown is ready to serve.

Lithuanian Pork Roast

SERVES 4 TO 6

When we lived in that lovely Connecticut village of Washington, we enjoyed and profited from our association with the local butcher, John Petrokaitis, at the Washington Market. John was generous in offering us some of his and his mother's Lithuanian recipes. They were always delicious and, even more rewarding, simple.

> *4-pound rib-end pork roast, chine bone removed*
> *6 medium-sized onions, halved*
> *1 teaspoon salt*
> *½ teaspoon freshly ground black pepper*
> *⅓ teaspoon cinnamon*

1. Place the pork in a pot just large enough to hold it snugly. (Incidentally, that's one of the secrets of effective meat cookery. Don't give any meat too much pot.) Cover with water, add 3 onions, and bring to a boil under cover. Lower heat and simmer, covered, 30 minutes.
2. Remove the pork, pat dry with paper towels, and place in a roasting pan that holds it snugly. Season with salt, pepper, and cinnamon. Surround with the remaining onions.
3. Cook, uncovered, in a preheated 325° oven 2½ hours, or until the top is crusty-brown and the pork is tender and juicy.

John serves this with his own potato cake, John Petrokaitis's Potato Kugeli (p. 298).

Mørbrad

SERVES 4 TO 6

(Pork Loin Stuffed with Apricots and Apples)

This pot-roasted, apricot-and-apple-scented tenderloin of pork is a favorite for entertaining in Denmark. We had it several times in the homes of friends in Copenhagen. The Danes often say in their gay, jesting way, "The Norwegians eat to live, the Swedes live to drink, and the Danes live to eat." We believe it. Copenhagen, where we have found many exciting dishes, is high on the list of our favorite European food cities. Their *smørrebrød,* so-called open-faced sandwiches, are widely imitated but never equaled. Neither is the following pork delight, a recipe we obtained from our Danish friend Inger-Lise Christensen.

> 6 dried apricots, halved
> 2 tablespoons port wine
> 2 pork tenderloins, 1½ pounds each (outer membranes re-
> moved, then each split almost through lengthwise but without
> separating the two halves. Spread out flat, cover with waxed
> paper, then, with a meat mallet, pound the halves, being care-
> ful not to break through the flesh. Or have your butcher do it)
> Salt and freshly ground pepper to taste
> ½ teaspoon sugar
> 2 tart green apples (we use Granny Smith), peeled, cored, and
> thinly sliced
> 5 tablespoons (slightly more than ½ stick) unsalted butter
> 4 tablespoons aquavit or brandy
> 1 cup beef broth
> 2 tablespoons flour
> 1 cup heavy cream
> 2 teaspoons currant jelly

1. In a saucepan, cover the apricots with water. Add the port wine. Bring to a boil, remove from heat, and let stand 30 minutes. Drain and dry.

2. Lay the pounded tenderloins on a flat surface. Sprinkle with salt, pepper, and the sugar. Arrange the apple slices and apricot halves, alternating, atop each flattened tenderloin, dividing them equally.

3. Carefully roll each tenderloin up, starting at the shorter end. Tie into a compact roll with cord. They will look like long sausages.

4. In a flameproof casserole that will hold both tenderloin rolls, melt 4 tablespoons butter over medium-high heat and brown the rolls evenly. Remove the pork rolls and keep warm.

5. Stir in the aquavit or brandy, mixing it with the pan juices (Beware. If the pan is too hot, the alcohol could ignite.) Re-

duce by half. Blend in the beef broth.

6. Return the pork to the casserole, cover tightly, and bring to a boil on top of the stove. Transfer to a preheated 350° oven and cook 1 hour, or until the pork is tender.

7. Transfer the cooked pork to a warm serving dish and keep hot.

8. Siphon any fat from the casserole. Strain the liquid and return it to the pot. On top of the stove, add the flour mixed with the cream to the liquid, stirring into a smooth sauce without boiling. Blend in the remaining butter and the currant jelly. Slice the pork at the table and serve with the sauce spooned over the slices. Pass any remaining sauce.

Accompany with Duchesse Potatoes (p. 290), piped into individual *couronnes*, small crowns.

Poached Pork Loin with Horseradish Applesauce   SERVES 6

4-pound pork loin, boned, with all fat removed
1 large onion, quartered
2 garlic cloves, halved
1 large carrot, scraped and quartered
2 celery stalks, scraped and quartered
4 cups chicken broth
2 cups dry white wine
1 bay leaf
2 cloves
½ teaspoon dried thyme
1 teaspoon salt
½ teaspoon freshly ground black pepper
Parsley for garnish
Horseradish Applesauce (see below)

1. Place the pork in a deep pot barely large enough to hold it and other ingredients. Surround with the vegetables and add all other ingredients (except the parsley and Horseradish Applesauce). Liquid should cover the pork nicely. Simmer over medium heat, covered, 2½ hours, or until the pork is fork-tender.

2. To serve, remove from pot and trim any fat or bone that may have been missed. Cut into slices no thicker than ⅜ inch. Overlap the slices on a serving dish and garnish with parsley.

Serve with Horseradish Applesauce and Watercress Potato Soufflé (p. 359).

HORSERADISH APPLESAUCE

> *2 cups fresh applesauce (canned may be substituted)*
> *Freshly grated horseradish, or preserved, the liquid squeezed out*

Blend applesauce with horseradish to taste.

Pork Loin en Leche   SERVES 6
(Pork Loin Poached in Milk)

We learned this recipe from the mistress of a former Spanish envoy to Cuba.

> *2 tablespoons unsalted butter*
> *2 tablespoons olive oil*
> *4-pound lean boned loin of pork, with most of the fat removed*
> *Salt and freshly ground black pepper*
> *Warm milk, enough to cover the pork, about 1 quart*
> *1 onion, quartered*
> *¼ teaspoon mace*

1. Heat the butter and oil in a flameproof casserole just large enough to hold the pork snugly. Add the pork and brown evenly over medium heat, turning with two wooden spoons and sprinkling with salt and pepper.

2. Pour off all fat accumulated in the casserole and add the milk. Add the onion. Bring to a boil on top of the stove.

3. Transfer to a preheated 325° oven and cook, covered, for 2 hours, or until the pork is fork-tender. Remove the pork and keep it warm.

4. Strain the liquid in the pot. Return to the pot and, over medium-high heat, cook it, stirring, until it thickens somewhat, being careful

not to burn it. Add the mace and taste for seasoning. Serve the pork, sliced, with the milk sauce lightly spooned over it.

Be a show-off and serve this dish with Bombay Puris (p. 288).

Pork Tenderloin with Mushroom Dill Sauce   SERVES 6

1½ pounds pork tenderloin, cut into 6 equal-sized slices
4 tablespoons unsalted butter
½ pound medium-sized, firm mushrooms, sliced
1 medium-sized onion, chopped
Salt and freshly ground black pepper to taste
½ cup dry vermouth
1 cup beef broth
1 tablespoon flour
½ cup sour cream
1 teaspoon chopped fresh dill or ⅓ teaspoon dried dill

1. If the slices of pork are thicker than ½ inch, flatten with a meat mallet to ½-inch thickness.
2. In a large frying pan, over medium heat, melt 2 tablespoons butter and cook the mushrooms 5 to 7 minutes (do not overcook, as they should be fairly firm). Transfer with a slotted spoon to a bowl and reserve. Pour off any liquid that has accumulated in the pan.
3. Over medium-high heat, melt the remaining butter in the same frying pan. Add the pork slices and cook 3 to 4 minutes on each side until browned. Add the onion and cook 3 minutes, or until soft. Do not brown. Sprinkle lightly with salt and pepper. Pour in the vermouth and half the beef broth. Cover, lower heat to medium-low, and cook 15 minutes, or until the pork is tender. Transfer the pork to a hot serving dish and keep warm.
4. Stir the flour into the pan the pork cooked in and blend well. Over medium heat, stir in the remaining beef broth and cook, stirring, until it becomes a smooth, medium-thick sauce. Taste for seasoning. Stir in the sour cream and dill. Add the mushrooms and

heat through without boiling.

Serve the mushroom sauce spooned over the pork.

Potatoes O'Brien (p. 311) hold their own with this dish.

Pork Tenderloin Slices with Prunes SERVES 4

12 large prunes
1 cup port wine mixed with 1 cup water
3 tablespoons unsalted butter
1 tablespoon olive oil
4 slices boned pork loin, ¾ inch thick, well pounded with a meat
* mallet*
Flour for dredging
Salt and freshly ground black pepper
3 ounces brandy
1 cup chicken broth
1 cup heavy cream, heated

1. Soak prunes in water for 1 hour. Drain, place in a saucepan with the wine and water, and simmer 5 minutes, or until plumped and tender. Set aside in the cooking liquid.

2. In a flameproof casserole large enough to hold the pork in one layer or just slightly overlapping, heat the butter and oil. Dredge the pork with flour and brown it evenly, seasoning with salt and pepper. Remove the pork and pour off any fat in the casserole. Return the pork to the pot and pour on the brandy. Standing back (the ignited brandy can flare up), ignite the brandy and allow it to cook off. Pour in the chicken broth, bringing it to a boil on top of the stove. Transfer to a preheated 350° oven and cook, covered, 45 minutes. Add the cream and cook, uncovered, 15 minutes, or until the pork is fork-tender.

3. Arrange the pork slices on a hot serving dish and top each with 3 prunes. Keep warm. Strain the sauce in the casserole and, if not thickened, cook over high heat until it thickens. Pour the sauce over the pork and prunes.

Serve with Dijon Potato Salad with Walnut Oil (p. 266).

Slavic Pork Roast Glazed with Applesauce   SERVES 4 TO 6

This roast is popular in most of Eastern Europe. We first encountered it in Czechoslovakia, then in Vienna, where the Viennese claimed it as their own.

> 4-pound rib-end pork roast, chine bone removed
> 1 teaspoon salt blended with ½ teaspoon freshly ground black
>   pepper
> 2 large garlic cloves, halved
> 4 whole cloves
> 1 cup applesauce

1. Rub the pork well with the salt-and-pepper blend.
2. With a sharp knife, make 8 small but rather deep slits in the meat. Alternating, insert a half garlic clove, then a clove.
3. Place the pork, fat side up, in a shallow roasting pan; cook, uncovered, in a preheated 375° oven 1½ hours.
4. Remove from the oven and evenly spread the applesauce on the pork roast. Return to the oven and cook 25 minutes. The pork should be tender and glazed a deep golden brown.
Try serving Accordion Potatoes (p. 322) with this roast.

Roast Pork Loin with Braised Red Cabbage   SERVES 6

> 4-pound center-cut pork loin
> Salt and freshly ground black pepper to taste
> 4 strips bacon, cut into 1-inch pieces
> 2 medium-sized onions, chopped
> 1 garlic clove, minced
> 1 medium-sized red cabbage, weighing 2½ to 3 pounds,
>   trimmed and shredded (do not use core)
> 1 teaspoon crushed fennel
> ½ cup dry white wine

1. Rub the pork with salt and pepper. Roast on a rack in a roasting pan, uncovered, in a preheated 350° oven for 2½ to 3 hours, or

until tender. Transfer to a hot serving dish and rest 15 minutes for easier carving.

2. While the pork is cooking, in a large frying pan over medium heat, sauté the bacon until crisp. Remove with a slotted spoon and drain on paper towels.

3. Pour off all but 3 tablespoons fat. Add the onions and garlic, and cook 2 minutes, or until soft. Do not brown. Stir in the cabbage, fennel, wine, and additional salt and pepper, stirring to mix well. Cover tightly and cook 15 minutes, or until the cabbage is tender.

4. Slice the pork. Serve with the cabbage sprinkled with bacon. It's fun to offer "Kiev" Nude Bakers with this (p. 368).

Shoulder of Pork with Peppers
SERVES 4 TO 6

This marinated pork dish, which we discovered in Portugal, is a time-proven classic. These days, an overabundance of peppers often overwhelms the meat or fish that is combined with them. In this dish the flavors assert themselves equally.

> *2 large garlic cloves, peeled and minced*
> *1½ teaspoons kosher or coarse salt*
> *½ teaspoon freshly ground black pepper*
> *2 pounds lean boneless pork shoulder, in ¼-inch-thick slices*
> *4 tablespoons olive oil*
> *2 medium-sized sweet red peppers, seeded, cored, and cut into ½-inch-wide strips*
> *2 medium-sized sweet green peppers, seeded, cored, cut into ½-inch-wide strips*
> *1 cup dry white wine*
> *½ cup chicken broth*
> *3 fresh limes, cut in 4 wedges*

1. Place the garlic in a small bowl with the salt and pepper, and work into a smooth paste with the back of a spoon.

2. Spread each pork slice with some of the paste. Place in a dish, toss together with fork and spoon, cover lightly with plastic wrap,

and refrigerate 4 hours. Remove 1 hour before cooking time.

3. In a large frying pan, heat the olive oil and evenly brown the pork slices, a few at a time. Remove the pork.

4. Add the peppers to the pork-frying pan and cook, stirring, over medium-high heat, for 5 minutes. Add the peppers to the reserved pork.

5. Pour the oil out of the frying pan and add the wine and chicken broth. Bring to a boil over high heat and cook, stirring up the browned-on bits from the bottom of the pan.

6. Add the pork and peppers to the hot liquid in the frying pan, cover tightly, reduce the heat to medium, and simmer 30 minutes, or until the pork is fork-tender.

Offer the pork and peppers on a warm serving dish, with the sauce lightly spooned over the slices and the peppers. Serve garnished with the lime wedges.

We like this zesty dish with Potatoes Mont d'Or (p. 309).

Barbecued Spareribs   SERVES 4

These spicy, tasty ribs may be the most appreciated of the pork repertoire. Here's our favorite version.

> 4 pounds fresh, meaty spareribs
> ½ cup soy sauce
> ½ cup dark-brown sugar, packed
> ¼ cup dry sherry
> 1 large garlic clove, mashed
> ¼ teaspoon ground ginger
> ½ teaspoon cinnamon
> ¼ teaspoon freshly ground black pepper

1. Leave the rib sides whole. Spread flat and remove most of the fat.

2. In a bowl, combine the remaining ingredients, blending the marinade well. Place the ribs in a shallow pan deep enough to hold

the marinade and pour the marinade over them. Let stand at room temperature 3 hours, turning frequently to keep them coated with the marinade.

3. Drain the rib pieces, arrange on a broiler pan on a rack, place in the medium-high position, and broil 40 minutes, turning often and basting with the remaining marinade.

Serve with Bakers with Sour-Cream Stuffing (p. 363).

Braised Pork Ribs Cacciatore

SERVES 4

We had this dish in Parma, where they sing the praises of pork and regard it as a nice change from chicken, which is often used in similar dishes.

> 3 tablespoons olive oil
> 4 large, very meaty ribs from the loin (sometimes called country spare ribs)
> Salt and freshly ground black pepper
> 3 medium-sized onions, chopped
> 2 garlic cloves, minced
> 2 celery stalks, scraped and chopped
> ½ teaspoon crushed red pepper flakes
> ½ teaspoon oregano
> 1-pound, 12-ounce can Italian-style tomatoes
> 2 cups dry white wine (if preferred, red can be used)

1. In a large pot, heat the olive oil and brown the ribs evenly, sprinkling them lightly with salt and pepper.

2. Remove the ribs and add the onions, garlic, celery, red pepper, and oregano, blending and stirring, cooking for 5 minutes.

3. Place the tomatoes in a bowl and break them up well with your hands. Add the tomatoes, browned ribs, and wine to the pot, blending well.

4. Cover the pot, bring to a boil on top of the stove, and cook in a preheated 300° oven 2 hours, or until the ribs are fork-tender.

We like these ribs with German Potato Dumplings #1 or #2 (p. 295 or p. 296).

Pork Hocks with Winekraut

SERVES 6

This humble dish was a favorite of one of the most elegant men we knew, Gaston Lauryssen, a Belgian, who was president of the posh Carlton House in Manhattan. Many's the night that the Lauryssens and the Scotts dined on this recipe at Lüchow's. Dumplings were recommended, but we always preferred mashed potatoes.

2 tablespoons unsalted butter
1 tablespoon olive oil
2 medium-sized white onions, minced
2 garlic cloves, minced
2 quarts sauerkraut (fresh if available), drained
1 tablespoon caraway seeds
Salt and freshly ground black pepper to taste
6 pork hocks, well scraped and scrubbed
Dry white wine, approximately 2 cups

1. In a large flameproof casserole, heat the butter and oil, and cook the onions and garlic until soft. Do not brown. Stir in the sauerkraut and caraway, blending well with the onions and garlic. Cover and cook, stirring once or twice, for 10 minutes. Sprinkle with salt and pepper.
2. Add the hocks to the pot, burying them in the sauerkraut. Pour in enough wine to cover. Bring to a boil on top of the stove. Cover and cook in a preheated 300° oven 2 hours, or until the pork is fork-tender.

Serve with Purée de Pommes de Terre (p. 313).

Note: One-inch-thick pork chops can be browned and used instead of hocks.

Roast Suckling Pig

SERVES 8 TO 10

In Spain, especially in Madrid, roast suckling pig is served daily in just about every restaurant of note. We were introduced to this succulent repast at the famous Botin—actually Antigua Casa Sobrino de Botin—in Madrid.

The owner, Antonio González, brought us this delicious offering, *cochinillo asado*, served whole in its earthenware cooking casserole, so tender that Antonio actually carved it with a plate, simply inserting the plate behind the portion he wanted to serve and pushing. With it we had roast potatoes and a pitcher of tinto Valdepeñas o Aragón, a local light red wine.

Today this tender, juicy, spectacular dish is often the centerpiece of our Thanksgiving Day feast, to the surprise (and sometimes the consternation) of guests. But what an improvement over roast turkey!

Heart and liver from the pig, simmered in salted water until
   tender, drained and finely chopped
3 tablespoons unsalted butter
3 medium-sized onions, chopped
6 cups bread crumbs
2 eggs, beaten
1 tablespoon Bell's seasoning
1 medium-sized tart green apple (we use Granny Smith),
   peeled and grated
Salt and freshly ground black pepper to taste
1 cup beef broth, approximately
10- to 12-pound suckling pig, prepared by butcher for roasting
Small wooden block, soaked in olive oil
5 tablespoons olive oil
8 to 10 medium-sized potatoes, peeled
Shiny, small red apple (we use Ida Red)

1. Place the cooked heart and liver in a large bowl.
2. In a frying pan, over medium heat, melt the butter and cook the onions 5 minutes. Do not brown.
3. To the bowl with the heart and liver, add and blend well the onion with the butter it cooked in, the bread crumbs, eggs, Bell's seasoning, and grated apple. Season with salt and pepper. Add enough beef broth to moisten, and blend again.
4. Stuff the pig with this mixture, skewering or sewing the skin closed to keep stuffing sealed and intact. Insert wooden block between the pig's jaws (keeping them open so the apple can be

inserted later when the pig is served whole), and skewer the legs, forelegs forward, hind legs in crouching position. Close eyelids, sew in closed position. Wrap ears and tail with heavy foil to prevent burning.

5. Rub the pig lavishly with the olive oil and sprinkle with salt and pepper. Place on a rack in a heavy roasting pan and cook, uncovered, in a preheated 450° oven 15 minutes. Reduce heat to 325° and cook 30 minutes per pound, until the pig is nicely browned and tender, basting every 15 minutes with pan drippings.

6. Forty minutes before the pig is cooked, add potatoes to the roasting pan. Fifteen minutes before the pig is cooked, remove the foil from ears and tail. Before serving, remove the wooden block and insert the apple.

Serve whole on a large platter, surrounded with the roast potatoes. Carve at the table. Or skip the dramatics and carve and serve in the kitchen. It's up to you.

Note: Any capable butcher worth his boning knife can obtain a suckling pig if given sufficient notice.

Ham à la King

SERVES 4

4 tablespoons (½ stick) unsalted butter
1 cup small mushrooms (about ¼ pound), sliced
½ cup chopped green pepper (no seeds or white ribs)
2 tablespoons flour
1 cup milk
½ cup light cream, or half-and-half
¼ teaspoon nutmeg
Freshly ground black pepper to taste
¾ cup grated Swiss cheese
2 cups fully cooked, smoked ham, in ½-inch cubes
2 tablespoons chopped pimiento
Salt (optional)
4 patty shells, baked according to package directions (we prefer Pepperidge Farm) or 4 croustades (see below)

1. In a frying pan, over medium heat, melt 2 tablespoons butter. Add the mushrooms and green pepper, and cook 3 minutes, or until the pepper is crisp-tender.

2. In a saucepan, over medium heat, melt the remaining butter. Add the flour, stirring and cooking into a smooth paste. Gradually add the milk and cream (or half-and-half), stirring into a smooth, medium-thick sauce. Stir in the nutmeg and black pepper. Add the cheese and stir until melted. Blend with the mushroom mixture and ham, and cook 2 minutes, or until heated through. Stir in the pimiento. Taste for seasoning, adding salt if the ham has not supplied enough.

3. Spoon the mixture into hot patty shells or croustades.

CROUSTADES   SERVES 4

4 soft, round rolls
Melted butter

1. From the top of the roll, remove the soft inside with a sharp knife, leaving just a shell.

2. With a pastry brush, paint the inside and outside of the rolls with the melted butter.

3. Place on a baking sheet and bake in a preheated 450° oven until golden brown and crisp.

Ham-Cornmeal Soufflé   SERVES 6

4 cups milk
⅔ cup white cornmeal
2 tablespoons unsalted butter
½ cup grated jalapeño Monterey Jack cheese
¼ teaspoon hot Hungarian paprika
2 teaspoons salt
6 egg yolks, beaten
1½ cups minced leftover baked ham
6 egg whites, stiffly beaten

1. Over medium heat, pour the milk into a large pot and heat just to the boiling point.

2. Stir in the cornmeal, turn heat to low, and cook, stirring, for 10 minutes. Add the butter and cheese, and cook, stirring, until the mixture is the consistency of thick mush. Cool slightly.

3. Add the paprika, salt, and egg yolks. Cook, stirring, for 1 minute. Remove from heat. Cool.

4. Blend in the ham and fold in the egg whites. Spoon into an ungreased soufflé or baking dish and bake, uncovered, in a preheated 350° oven 40 minutes, or until the top is somewhat crusty and the soufflé has risen and set.

Ground Ham and Pork Loaf with Mustard Sauce

SERVES 6 TO 8

2 tablespoons unsalted butter
2 medium-sized white onions, minced
1 garlic clove, minced
1½ pounds lean raw or cooked ham ground with 1½ pounds
  lean fresh pork
Salt and freshly ground black pepper to taste
2 large eggs, beaten
1 cup fine bread crumbs
1 cup milk
Brown sugar
1 teaspoon dry mustard
Mustard Sauce (see below)

1. Melt the butter over medium heat in a frying pan. Add the onions and garlic, and cook 3 minutes, or until soft. Do not brown.

2. In a large bowl, combine and blend well, but lightly (do not pack), the ham, pork, onions, garlic, salt, pepper, eggs, bread crumbs, and milk. Pat mixture into a buttered loaf tin. Cover loaf with a thin layer of brown sugar, then sprinkle on the dry mustard, then another thin layer of brown sugar.

3. Set in a pan of hot water (that comes halfway up the loaf tin) and bake in a preheated 350° oven 1½ hours. Pour off excess fat and let stand 10 minutes before transferring to a serving dish. Serve thickly sliced, with the Mustard Sauce.

MUSTARD SAUCE

> ½ *pint heavy cream, whipped*
> ¼ *cup Dijon mustard*
> *Pinch dry mustard*
> ½ *cup mayonnaise*

Combine and blend all ingredients into a smooth sauce.
We often serve tangy Curried Potato Salad (p. 265) with this loaf.

Ham or Pork (or Ham and Pork) Croquettes   SERVES 4 TO 6

> 4 *cups ground lean cooked pork, or ground lean cooked ham,*
>   *or 2 cups of each*
> 1 *cup mashed sweet potatoes, thoroughly dried over low heat*
>   *(be careful not to scorch)*
> 1 *cup very thick Béchamel Sauce (see below)*
> *Salt and freshly ground black pepper to taste (if ham alone is*
>   *used, you may not need salt)*
> 3 *egg yolks*
> *Flour for dredging*
> 1 *large egg, beaten (for dipping the croquettes)*
> *Fine bread crumbs for dredging*
> *Fat for deep frying*

1. In a saucepan, combine the pork, or ham, or the pork and ham, sweet potatoes, Béchamel Sauce, salt, and pepper over low heat. Cook, stirring constantly, until the mixture leaves the side of the pan. Remove from the heat and beat in the egg yolks, one at a time. Spread out on a buttered plate or baking sheet and cool for at least 2 hours.

2. When cool and firm, make cylinders, approximately 3 inches by 1 inch in diameter, moistening your hands with water to keep the mixture from sticking to them. Dredge with the flour, then dip in the beaten egg, then dredge with bread crumbs. Refrigerate for an hour or more before cooking.

3. Cook in deep fat heated to 375°, or until a 1-inch cube of bread will brown in 40 seconds. Do not crowd in the basket; cook a few at a time until they are crisply golden. They must not touch, as they could break up. Drain in the basket, then on paper towels. Keep warm in a 200° oven while cooking the remaining croquettes.

If desired, serve with a mushroom or tomato sauce.

BÉCHAMEL SAUCE

> 2 tablespoons butter
> 2 tablespoons flour
> ¾ cup milk
> ½ cup cream
> Salt and freshly ground black pepper to taste

In a saucepan, over medium heat, melt the butter. Add the flour, cooking and stirring into a smooth paste. Gradually add the milk and cream, and cook, stirring, until very thick. Season with salt and pepper.

Ham Slices Oporto

SERVES 6

(Ham with White Wine, Port, and Cream)

> 5 tablespoons unsalted butter (approximately)
> 12 medallions tender, cooked ham, cut 3 inches in diameter and
>   ½ inch thick
> ½ cup dry white wine
> ¼ cup port wine
> 3 tablespoons flour
> ½ teaspoon Dijon mustard
> 1½ cups chicken broth

Freshly ground black pepper to taste
Salt (optional)
½ cup heavy cream
2 tablespoons chopped fresh parsley

1. In a large frying pan, over medium-low heat, melt 3 tablespoons butter. Heat the ham in the pan, a few slices at a time, 1 minute on each side, just to heat through. Add more butter if needed. Stack on a hot plate and keep warm.
2. Pour the wines into the frying pan and simmer, stirring up any browned-on bits from the bottom of the pan, until the wine has reduced by half. Stir in the flour and mustard, making a smooth, thick mixture. Stir in the broth, a small amount at a time, and cook, stirring, until it becomes a smooth, thick sauce. Add pepper. Taste before adding salt, as the ham and broth may supply enough.
3. Just before serving, stir in the cream and the remaining 2 tablespoons butter. Overlap the medallions of ham in the well of a hot serving dish. Pour the sauce over and sprinkle with parsley.
For a summer menu, we like this with Chilled Mashed-Potato Salad (p. 264).

Jack Daniel's—Glazed Ham   SERVES 6

4- to 6-pound boneless "fully cooked" smoked ham half
⅓ cup light-brown sugar, packed
⅓ cup Jack Daniel's whiskey
1 tablespoon grated orange peel
⅛ teaspoon ground cloves
¼ teaspoon ground allspice
Thin orange slices for garnish
Curly endive leaves for garnish

1. Place the ham on a rack in a roasting pan. Do not add water. Roast in a preheated 325° oven, uncovered, about 20 minutes per pound, or until a meat thermometer registers 140°.
2. Before the ham is thoroughly cooked, simmer a mixture of the

brown sugar, whiskey, orange peel, cloves, and allspice over medium-low heat for 15 minutes, or until slightly thickened.

3. About 20 minutes before the ham is ready, brush the glaze over it.

4. Serve garnished with the orange slices and endive.

Try Ichabod's Baked French-Fried Slices (p. 337) with this ham.

Lake Charles Ham Jambalaya   SERVES 4 TO 6

This was prepared for us by our goose-hunting guide's mother in Lake Charles, Louisiana. Leftover ham is a valuable item in that area. The same lady later served us a delicious Ham-Cornmeal Soufflé (p. 193).

2 tablespoons unsalted butter
1 tablespoon olive oil
2 medium-sized onions, finely chopped
2 tablespoons flour
¾ pound cooked ham, cut into ½- to ¾-inch cubes
1 pound small shrimp, peeled and deveined
1 garlic clove, minced
1-pound can of tomatoes, put through blender to break up into
  a smooth consistency
2 cups tomato juice
3 cups al dente–cooked long-grain rice
2 small green peppers, finely chopped
1 teaspoon salt
¼ teaspoon cayenne pepper
½ cup grated sharp Cheddar cheese
2 tablespoons minced fresh parsley

1. In a large pot, heat the butter and oil and cook the onions 5 minutes. Do not brown. Stir in the flour, then blend in all the remaining ingredients except the cheese and parsley. Cook, stirring, for 5 minutes.

2. Butter a casserole and pour in the jambalaya. Cook, uncovered,

in a preheated 350° oven 20 minutes, or until the rice has absorbed the liquid.

Serve in large-rimmed soup bowls sprinkled with cheese and parsley.

Leftover Ham with Saupiquet Sauce · SERVES 4

One of the problems with baked ham seems to be its ubiquity—it hangs around too long. Here's a delicious solution we discovered at the elegant little Hôtel Napoléon in Nice.

4 fairly thick slices of baked ham
Saupiquet Sauce (see below)

Arrange the ham slices in an ovenproof dish and spoon the sauce evenly over each slice. Place, uncovered, in a preheated 300° oven for 15 minutes, or until the ham is heated through.

SAUPIQUET SAUCE

6 shallots, minced
½ cup red wine vinegar
6 tablespoons unsalted butter
4 tablespoons flour
1 cup beef broth, heated
½ cup dry white wine
1 cup heavy cream

1. In a frying pan or saucepan, combine the shallots and vinegar, and over medium-high heat, cook, stirring, until the liquid has cooked off and the shallots are soft. Remove shallots.

2. In the same pan, over medium heat, melt 4 tablespoons butter and slowly add the flour, stirring into a smooth light-brown paste, or roux. Slowly pour in the heated broth, stirring until the mixture thickens and remains smooth. Add the wine and the cooked shallots. Reduce the heat to medium-low and simmer, stirring, for 10 minutes.

3. Strain into a pot. Heat the cream just to the boiling point and

add to the sauce. Stir in the remaining butter to give it a finishing gloss.

Serve with Potato-Broccoli Pudding (p. 346).

Pennsylvania Dutch Ham   SERVES 6

We enjoyed this recipe in a home in Allentown, Pennsylvania. Of course, the ham was home-cured, the apples were picked from the orchard, and the butter came from the cows that literally looked over our shoulders.

> *8 tablespoons (1 stick) unsalted butter*
> *2 medium-sized onions, chopped*
> *4 medium-sized Granny Smith apples, peeled, cored, and*
> *   chopped*
> *1 teaspoon brown sugar*
> *1 tablespoon olive oil*
> *6 half-inch-thick slices bread, crusts removed*
> *6 half-inch-thick slices precooked ham, trimmed to the size of the*
> *   bread slices*

1. In a saucepan, heat 3 tablespoons butter. Add the onions and cook 2 minutes, or until soft. Do not brown. Add the apples and brown sugar, and continue cooking until the apples are soft.

2. In a frying pan, heat 3 tablespoons butter and the olive oil, and brown the bread on both sides, adding more butter if needed. Drain on paper towels.

3. Add the remaining butter to the frying pan and quickly cook the ham on both sides until golden brown.

4. On a hot serving dish, or individual plates, place a slice of ham on a slice of bread and top with the apples and onions.

Sheehans' Vermont Smoked Ham   SERVES 8 TO 10

The tastiest ham we ever had was a country-smoked ham from Vermont baked by Walter and Lynn Sheehan (Walter was director of the famous

Canterbury School in New Milford, Connecticut). Here's how they did it.

12- to 14-pound smoked uncooked ham, skin removed
1 cup light-brown sugar, packed
½ cup prepared mustard
1 cup orange juice

1. Parboil the ham, covered, simmering it gently for 1 hour.
2. In a bowl, blend the brown sugar and mustard into a spreadable paste. With a sharp knife, score the ham, evenly covering the entire surface. Spread with the brown sugar–mustard paste.
3. Place the ham on a rack in a roasting pan. Pour the orange juice over it.
4. Preheat the oven to 325°. Cover the pan and cook the ham 20 minutes per pound, basting occasionally with pan juices.
Try the ham with Vegetable-Stuffed Baked Potatoes (p. 372).
Note: The ham *must* be country-smoked, uncooked, *not* water-injected or commercially cured by the large meat packers. Harrington's in Vermont supplied the Sheehans' ham.

Potato and Ham Cakes SERVES 4

4 tablespoons (½ stick) unsalted butter
1 small white onion, minced
2 cups unseasoned mashed potatoes
1½ cups minced cooked ham
¼ teaspoon dry mustard
Freshly ground black pepper to taste
Salt (optional)
Flour for dredging
1 tablespoon olive oil

1. In a frying pan, over medium heat, melt 1 tablespoon butter and cook the onion for 1 minute, or until soft. Do not brown.
2. In a bowl, combine and blend well the potatoes, ham, onion, mustard, and pepper. Taste for seasoning and add salt if needed.

3. Form mixture into 3 × 2 × ½-inch croquettes (or size desired). Dredge lightly with flour.

4. In a large frying pan, heat the remaining butter and oil and brown the croquettes on both sides, adding more butter and oil if needed.

Scalloped Potatoes with Ham   SERVES 4 TO 6

This supper dish pleases just about everyone.

> 4 tablespoons (½ stick) unsalted butter
> 2 medium-sized white onions, chopped
> 3 tablespoons flour
> ½ teaspoon salt
> 1 teaspoon celery salt
> ½ teaspoon freshly ground black pepper
> 2 cups half-and-half
> 1 cup grated sharp cheese (New York State Cheddar works well)
> 6 medium-sized potatoes (about 2 pounds), peeled and sliced ¼ inch thick
> 2 cups cooked ham, diced (or sliced wafer-thin)

1. In a saucepan, over medium heat, melt the butter and cook the onions until soft. Do not brown. Stir in the flour, salt, celery salt, and pepper, blending thoroughly. Gradually add the half-and-half, stirring constantly until the sauce is smooth and begins to thicken. Add the cheese, blending well, and cook, stirring, until it has melted. Taste for seasoning.

2. Butter a casserole and fill it with alternating layers of potatoes, ham, and sauce. Bake, covered, in a preheated 375° oven 45 minutes. Remove cover and bake 20 minutes longer, or until the potatoes are tender and the top is golden brown.

Note: This can be varied with leftover meat, chopped or sliced thinly, and with other vegetables, such as sliced celery or chopped red or green sweet peppers. However, the above recipe is classic.

6

Veal

Boudin Blanc

Veal Loaf with Tomato Sauce

Veal Patties à la Russe

Veal Sausage

Blanquette of Veal

Émincé de Veau

Veal Marengo

Black-Olive Veal Stew with Anchovies

Scandinavian Veal Pie

Fanny Graef's Veal Stew

Veal Stew Portuguese Style

Mina Thompson's Veal with Onions, Peppers, and Mushrooms

Veal Sultana

Veal and Sausage Pie

Veal Fillets Park Imperial

Saltimbocca Romana

Fillets of Veal with Kidneys

Involtini of Veal

Hungarian Veal Medallions

Veal Cutlets with Chanterelles

Veal Cutlets in Puff Pastry

Veal Scallops Arance

Veal Piccata

Veal Chops Amandine with Wine Sauce

Veal Slices in Cheese and Cream

Veal Chops with Bacon and Shallots

Provimi Veal Chops Provençale

Veal Chops Romano

Costolette di Vitello alla Valdostana

Dora Radicchi's Braised Veal alla Perugia

Breast of Veal Contadino

Breast of Veal with Lemon Potatoes

Cima alla Genovese

Vitello Tonnato

Osso Bucho

Roast Leg of Veal

If beef is the king of red meats, veal is the queen. There is a daintiness and elegance to veal that is equaled by no other meat. Veal appeal has dominated Europe for centuries, so many of the recipes in this chapter originated there. Veal is becoming more popular in America—especially in restaurants—as a celebration food on a par with lobster. Veal is a delicate meat. It combines beautifully with herbs, spices, and light sauces, yet it always retains its own personality.

Veal has to be exactly right when purchased at the market. There are three types of veal in this country: "bob veal," from calves under one week of age, lacks color and flavor because it isn't aged; "grain-fed" veal, almost baby beef, is red and too soft; and "milk-formula-fed" veal, which is firm in texture, with an even distribution of marbling and creamy-pink color. Of the three, the best is the milk-formula-fed, and while it is scarce in the markets, one brand that consistently meets all our standards is Provimi Fancy Veal. There are, of course, a few other excellent brands of veal available, but Provimi has been the leader for over twenty years. The company consistently offers veal of such high quality that it not only equals that of Europe but in some instances surpasses it.

If the veal you buy is good enough to pass the eye and texture test, the next hurdle is proper preparation. Since veal has little interior fat (marbling), much care must be taken in simple roasting, so that the meat doesn't emerge from the oven too dry.

Probably the best way to prepare veal—as French and Italian cooks know—is to braise it. With the best braising, the veal is surrounded with the aromatic steam sent off by a combination of stock, wine, and vegetables encircling the meat, not only making it tender but also producing a delicious natural sauce.

Good examples in the recipes that follow are Blanquette, Chops with Wine Sauce, Marengo, Veal Fillets Park Imperial, Saltimbocca Romana, Piccata, the famous Osso Bucho, and some spectacular stews.

Veal

• RETAIL CUTS •
WHERE THEY COME FROM
HOW TO COOK THEM

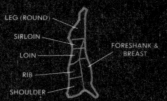

LEG (ROUND)
SIRLOIN
LOIN
RIB
SHOULDER
FORESHANK & BREAST

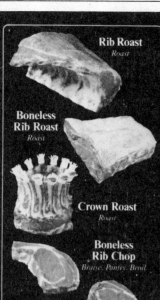

Rib Roast
Roast

Boneless Rib Roast
Roast

Crown Roast
Roast

Boneless Rib Chop
Braise, Panfry, Broil

Rib Chop
Braise, Panfry, Broil

Short Ribs
Braise, Cook in Liquid

RIB

Boneless Rump Roast
Braise, Roast

Round Steak
Braise, Panfry

Top Round Steak
Braise, Panfry

Leg Cutlet
Braise, Panfry, Broil

LEG (ROUND)

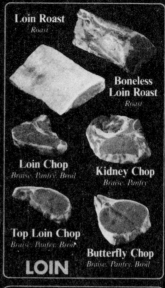

Loin Roast
Roast

Boneless Loin Roast
Roast

Loin Chop
Braise, Panfry, Broil

Kidney Chop
Braise, Panfry

Top Loin Chop
Braise, Panfry, Broil

Butterfly Chop
Braise, Panfry, Broil

LOIN

Sirloin Roast
Roast

Boneless Sirloin Roast
Roast

Sirloin Steak
Braise, Panfry, Broil

Top Sirloin Steak
Braise, Panfry, Broil

SIRLOIN

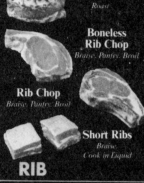

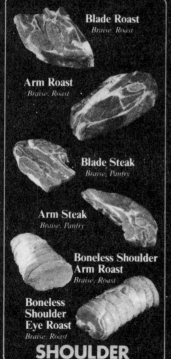

Blade Roast
Braise, Roast

Arm Roast
Braise, Roast

Blade Steak
Braise, Panfry

Arm Steak
Braise, Panfry

Boneless Shoulder Arm Roast
Braise, Roast

Boneless Shoulder Eye Roast
Braise, Roast

SHOULDER

Breast
Braise, Roast

Boneless Breast Roast
Braise, Roast

Cross Cut Shank
Braise, Cook in Liquid

Riblet
Braise, Cook in Liquid

Shank
Braise, Cook in Liquid

FORESHANK & BREAST

Veal for Stew
Braise, Cook in Liquid

Ground Veal
Panfry, Broil

Cubes for Kabobs
Braise

Cubed Steak
Braise, Panfry

OTHER CUTS

Boudin Blanc

The official translation of this dish is white pudding. We call it delicious white veal sausage. This easy version of a classic mild French veal sausage is often served with a hot potato salad (see salad section, p. 263) and a chilled white wine.

> 2½ pounds (after trimming) veal, cubed
> ¾ pound unsalted pork fatback with streaks of lean in it, cubed
> 3 tablespoons unsalted butter
> 3 medium-sized onions, minced
> ⅓ teaspoon dried thyme
> 1 bay leaf
> 2 teaspoons salt
> ½ teaspoon freshly ground black pepper
> ¼ teaspoon nutmeg
> ¼ teaspoon allspice
> 2 tablespoons minced fresh parsley
> 2 eggs, beaten
> 1 cup fine bread crumbs, soaked in 1 cup warm milk for 1 hour, with the liquid squeezed out
> 3 tablespoons heavy cream
> 1½ yards casings, approximately (optional)

1. Put the veal and fatback through the fine blade of a meat grinder and into a large bowl.
2. In a frying pan, over medium heat, melt the butter. Add the onions, thyme, and bay leaf. Cook 4 minutes, or until the onions are soft. Do not brown. Remove and discard the bay leaf.
3. Add the onions and all other ingredients (except the casings) to the meat bowl and blend well. (Your hands are good for this.) Make a small patty and cook it in butter to taste for seasoning. Then add more of the seasonings if necessary.
4. If you do not use casings, form into skinless sausage shapes in plastic wrap. If you do use casings, remove the blade from the grinder, attach the sausage funnel, and work the casings onto it.

Put sausage through the grinder (without the blade) and feed into the casings, twisting every 3 to 4 inches.

TO COOK

If in casings, prick each sausage in two or three places with the sharp point of a knife. Simmer in a small amount of hot water for 5 minutes. Drain and brown lightly in hot melted butter. If not in casings, simply brown well in hot melted butter, turning to brown evenly.

Veal Loaf with Tomato Sauce   SERVES 4 TO 6

2 tablespoons unsalted butter
1 medium-sized onion, finely chopped
½ green pepper (seeds and white ribs removed), finely chopped
1½ pounds ground veal
2 cups fresh fine bread crumbs
¼ teaspoon dried rosemary
¼ teaspoon dried tarragon
2 tablespoons minced fresh parsley
1 teaspoon salt
¼ teaspoon freshly ground black pepper
2 egg yolks
2 egg whites, stiffly beaten
Creamy Tomato Sauce (see below)

1. In a frying pan, over medium heat, melt the butter and cook the onion and green pepper until soft. Do not brown.
2. In a bowl, combine and blend well, but lightly, the onion, green pepper, veal, bread crumbs, rosemary, tarragon, parsley, salt, pepper, and egg yolks. Fold in the egg whites.
3. Butter a soufflé dish (or casserole) and spoon the mixture into it. Set in a pan of hot water, with the water coming halfway up the soufflé dish, and cook in a preheated 350° oven 1 hour, or until browned and set. Allow to set for a few minutes, then invert onto a warm rimmed serving dish (or serve right from the baking dish).

If served from the baking dish, put the sauce in a bowl at the table. If unmolded, spoon the sauce around the loaf, spooning some over lightly as you serve it.

The appeal of this loaf is heightened by Au Gratin Potatoes and Carrots (p. 322).

Note: Before inverting the loaf onto a serving dish, loosen the sides with a spatula.

CREAMY TOMATO SAUCE   MAKES ABOUT 1½ CUPS

   2 tablespoons unsalted butter
   1 large onion, finely chopped
   1 garlic clove, minced
   *4 large, ripe tomatoes, skinned, seeded, and chopped (about 2
       cups)*
   1 teaspoon sugar
   ½ teaspoon paprika
   1 tablespoon tomato paste
   Salt and freshly ground black pepper to taste
   ½ cup chopped fresh parsley
   3 tablespoons heavy cream

1. In a saucepan, over medium heat, melt the butter. Add the onion and garlic, and cook until soft. Do not brown.

2. Stir in the tomatoes, sugar, paprika, and tomato paste. Cook, uncovered, until the tomatoes are soft, much of the liquid has cooked off, and the sauce begins to thicken. Season with salt and pepper.

3. Puree in a blender. Return to the saucepan, stir in the parsley and heavy cream, and heat through.

Veal Patties à la Russe   SERVES 4 TO 6
(Russian Veal Patties)

   6 tablespoons unsalted butter
   2 tablespoons olive oil

2 medium-sized onions, chopped
1 teaspoon salt
1 cup white bread crumbs
1/8 teaspoon cayenne, or to taste
1 1/2 pounds finely ground, well-trimmed veal
2 egg yolks
Flour for dredging
1/4 cup vodka
1 cup sour cream
3/4 cup Hollandaise Sauce (see below)

1. Heat half the butter and all the oil in a frying pan. Add the onions and cook 5 minutes, or until soft. Do not brown. Add the salt and bread crumbs. Remove from heat and stir in the cayenne; mix in the veal and egg yolks, blending thoroughly but lightly. Cool. Taste for seasoning.

2. Make 4 to 6 patties, 1/2 inch thick. Refrigerate at least 2 hours.

3. Dredge the patties with flour. Melt the remaining butter in a frying pan. Add the patties, and over medium heat brown 2 or 3 minutes. Lower heat and cook 10 minutes on each side. Transfer to a hot serving dish and keep warm.

4. Pour any fat from the pan, add the vodka, and stir in the sour cream, blending well until heated through, but do not boil. Remove from heat and stir in the Hollandaise. Heat through but do not boil. Spoon over the patties.

Potatoes Savoyarde (p. 314) add panache.

HOLLANDAISE SAUCE   MAKES ABOUT 3/4 CUP

This is a very simple, foolproof method of making Hollandaise. The sauce can even be frozen, then heated over warm water.

2 egg yolks
1 tablespoon lemon juice
1/2 teaspoon salt
1/8 teaspoon cayenne
8 tablespoons (1 stick) butter, melted

1. Combine the egg yolks, lemon juice, salt, and cayenne in a blender container. Turn the blender on high, then turn off immediately.

2. Turn on high again and slowly dribble in the melted butter. Turn off blender, taste sauce for seasoning, then turn blender on high for another 2 or 3 seconds. Keep sauce warm over warm water.

Veal Sausage

SERVES 4

This simple sausage is one of our favorite veal dishes.

> *1 pound ground lean veal*
> *¼ pound ground fatback*
> *¼ cup minced broadleaf parsley*
> *½ cup minced raw spinach*
> *3 shallots, minced*
> *1 egg, beaten*
> *1 teaspoon salt*
> *½ teaspoon freshly ground black pepper*
> *½ teaspoon dried thyme*
> *2 tablespoons unsalted butter*

1. In a large bowl, combine and blend well all the ingredients, except the butter. (Your hands are good for this.)

2. Form into 4 patties. In a frying pan, over medium heat, melt the butter. Add the veal and cook until well browned on both sides. Try this sausage with Moscow Mashed-Potato Cakes (p. 375) for a quick but elegant meal.

Blanquette of Veal

SERVES 6

A popular French veal stew with vegetables in a cream sauce.

> *3 pounds veal shoulder, cut into pieces 1 inch square and ½*
> *inch thick*
> *2 medium-sized onions, peeled*
> *2 cloves (studded into the onions)*

2 medium-sized carrots, scraped, cut into 4 pieces
3 celery stalks, scraped, cut into 4 pieces (use the leaves, too)
½ teaspoon dried thyme
1 bay leaf
Chicken broth to completely cover the veal, about 5 cups
24 small fresh white mushrooms, washed, dried, and halved
18 to 24 very small white onions, whole, root ends scored
3 tablespoons unsalted butter
3 tablespoons flour
Salt and freshly ground black pepper to taste
2 egg yolks
½ cup heavy cream
Juice of ½ lemon

1. Blanch the veal in boiling water in a deep, heavy-bottomed pot for 10 minutes. Drain the veal, rinse it with warm water, and return it to the pot.

2. Add the onions with the cloves, the carrots, celery, thyme, bay leaf, and broth. Cover the pot, bring to a boil, then lower heat and simmer 1 hour, or until the veal is fork-tender.

3. With a slotted spoon, transfer the veal to a bowl. Strain the broth, discarding the vegetables and herbs, and return the broth to the pot.

4. Add the mushrooms to the pot and cook them 2 minutes. With a slotted spoon, transfer them to the veal bowl. Add the onions to the pot; cover and simmer 10 minutes, or until tender. Transfer with a slotted spoon to the bowl with the veal and mushrooms.

5. Raise heat and reduce the liquid by about one half (there should be at least 2 cups).

6. In a saucepan, over medium-low heat, melt the butter. Blend in the flour, stirring into a smooth paste. Do not brown. Gradually add the strained hot broth from the pot, stirring into a smooth, medium-thick sauce. Taste for seasoning and add salt and pepper if needed.

7. Add the veal, mushrooms, and onions to the sauce, and heat through slowly.

8. Just before serving, stir in a mixture of the egg yolks, cream, and lemon juice lightly beaten together. Cook, stirring and blending, just long enough to heat through. Do not boil, as the eggs will curdle.

We like to mix nationalities and offer German Potato Dumplings #1 or #2 (p. 295 or p. 296) with this saucy French dish.

Note: This recipe can also be prepared with lamb or pork.

Émincé de Veau SERVES 4

These veal strips with white wine are popular in Geneva.

4 tablespoons (½ stick) unsalted butter
2 tablespoons olive oil
2½ pounds veal (from the shoulder or leg), julienned (2 inches
  long, ¼ inch thick, and ½ inch wide)
3 shallots (or 1 small white onion), minced
½ cup dry white wine
1 cup heavy cream
1 tablespoon cornstarch, dissolved in 2 tablespoons water
Juice of ½ lemon
Salt and freshly ground black pepper to taste

1. In a large frying pan, heat half the butter and oil, and in a single layer, cook half the veal over high heat for 2 minutes, turning several times. With a slotted spoon, transfer the veal to a strainer over a bowl (to catch the juices). Repeat the procedure with the remaining butter, oil, and veal.

2. Cook the shallots (or onion) in the frying pan 2 minutes, or until soft. Do not brown. Stir in the wine. Bring to a simmer and reduce by one half. Add the cream and the juices in the bowl that have collected from the veal. Simmer 5 minutes. Lower heat, stir in the cornstarch mixture, stir well, and simmer 1 minute, or until thickened. Stir in the veal and lemon juice. Season with salt and pepper. Stir and simmer 2 minutes.

Serve with Swiss Potatoes Rösti (p. 312).

Veal Marengo

There's a lot of culinary chatter about how Napoleon discovered this dish in the Italian area of Marengo and then called the recipe French. So what's new? The French have been doing that for centuries.

1 cup flour
1½ teaspoons salt
½ teaspoon freshly ground black pepper
¼ teaspoon ground allspice
2½ pounds shoulder of veal, cut into 2-inch pieces
2 tablespoons unsalted butter
2 tablespoons olive oil
18 small white onions, root ends scored
2 garlic cloves, crushed
1 cup dry vermouth
1½ ounces brandy
2 large ripe tomatoes, peeled, seeded, and chopped (or 2 cups
*   drained and chopped canned tomatoes)*
12 small whole mushrooms
12 green olives, pitted
12 toast points (fried in hot oil until golden)
2 tablespoons chopped fresh parsley

1. Combine the flour, salt, pepper, and allspice in a clean paper or plastic bag and shake. Add the veal pieces and shake to evenly coat with flour. Remove the veal and shake off any excess flour.
2. In a large frying pan, heat the butter and oil. Add the veal, a few pieces at a time, and brown evenly. Transfer to a casserole.
3. Cook the onions and garlic in the frying pan (adding more oil if needed) until golden in color. Do not brown. Transfer to the casserole.
4. Add the vermouth, brandy, and tomatoes to the frying pan and simmer a minute or two, scraping up the browned-on bits from the bottom of the pan. Pour into the casserole. Cover and cook in a preheated 325° oven for 1 to 1½ hours, or until the veal is almost

tender. Add the mushrooms and olives, and cook 15 minutes longer.

Place on toast points and sprinkle with the parsley.

Potatoes Paillasson (p. 311) is an excellent accompaniment—French, of course!

Black-Olive Veal Stew with Anchovies SERVES 4 TO 6

2½ pounds boneless veal shoulder, cut into 1½-inch cubes
Flour for dredging
3 tablespoons unsalted butter
2 tablespoons olive oil
Salt and freshly ground black pepper to taste
2 small onions, minced
1 large garlic clove, minced
1 cup dry vermouth
1½ cups chicken broth
12 black Greek olives (the large plump, purplish, smooth-skinned
   ones, not the wrinkled ones), halved and pitted
8 anchovies, rinsed in cold water (to remove salt), dried and cut
   up

1. Dredge the veal with flour, shaking off any excess.
2. In a flameproof casserole, heat the butter and oil, and evenly brown the cubes, a few at a time. Season with salt and pepper. Transfer to a bowl.
3. Add the onions and garlic to the casserole and cook 5 minutes, or until soft. Do not brown. Add the vermouth and broth, and cook, stirring up the browned-on bits from the bottom of the pot. Bring to a boil on top of the stove.
4. Return the veal and any juices that have collected in the bowl to the pot. Cook in a preheated 350° oven, covered, for 1½ hours, or until the veal is tender. Add the olives and cook 5 minutes, or just long enough to heat them through. Stir in the anchovies and serve.

Serve with Potato Cheese Cakes (p. 377).

Scandinavian Veal Pie

2 pounds trimmed, boneless veal shoulder, cut into 1-inch cubes
*½ pound lean pork, cut into cubes slightly smaller than the veal
    cubes*
Flour for dredging
3 tablespoons unsalted butter
1 tablespoon olive oil
Salt and freshly ground black pepper to taste
2 medium-sized onions, finely chopped
2 cups chicken broth
2 celery stalks, scraped and cut into ½-inch squares
⅛ teaspoon dried thyme
1 deep, 10-inch pastry shell, baked (see below)
½ cup heavy cream
2 eggs, beaten
2 tablespoons unsalted butter, melted
¾ cup grated Jarlsberg cheese, or a cheese of your choice

1. Dredge the veal and pork cubes with flour.
2. In a heavy-bottomed pot, heat the butter and oil, and brown the meat evenly. Season with salt and pepper. Add more butter and oil if needed. As the pieces brown, remove with a slotted spoon and set in a bowl.
3. Add the onions to the pot and cook 3 minutes, or until soft. Do not brown.
4. Pour off any excess fat and add the broth, deglazing the pot. Return the meat to the pot. Add the celery and thyme, cover tightly, and simmer 1 to 1½ hours, or until the meat is just fork-tender. Taste for seasoning.
5. Spoon into the baked pastry shell and place in a preheated 400° oven for 10 minutes. Lower the oven heat to 325°. Remove pie from the oven and carefully pour on a mixture of the cream, eggs, melted butter, and cheese. Return to the oven and bake until the top is set, puffed, and golden, about 25 minutes.
Straw Potatoes (p. 318) add a nice touch.

2 cups sifted all-purpose flour
1½ teaspoons salt
⅓ cup lard or vegetable shortening
⅓ cup butter
⅓ cup cold water

1. In a bowl, with a pastry blender, blend the flour and salt with half the shortening and butter until the texture is that of coarse meal. Add the remaining shortening and butter, and blend until the shortening is the size of small peas. Sprinkle on the water and mix with a fork, adding just enough water to hold the dough together. When you can gather the dough into a neat ball, stop working it. Do not overwork. Seal in plastic wrap and refrigerate for an hour before rolling out.
2. Roll out the pastry and line a 10-inch pie plate with it. Line the pastry with aluminum foil and fill with dried beans (or the metal pellets that can be bought in kitchen supply stores for this purpose).
3. Bake in a preheated 425° oven for 9 minutes. Remove the foil and beans, and bake another 3 minutes. If the pastry starts to puff, prick it with the tines of a fork. Bake until golden brown.

Fanny Graef's Veal Stew   SERVES 4

1½ pounds boneless veal (leg is good), cut into 1½-inch cubes
Flour for dredging
5 tablespoons unsalted butter
1 tablespoon olive oil
Salt and freshly ground black pepper to taste
1 medium-sized onion, coarsely chopped
1 celery stalk, scraped and coarsely chopped
1½ cups beef broth
1 cup tomato juice
1 bay leaf
¼ teaspoon dried thyme

8 medium-sized mushrooms, sliced and cooked 1 minute in 2
tablespoons butter

1. Dredge the pieces of veal lightly with flour.
2. In a flameproof casserole, or deep, heavy frying pan, heat 3 tablespoons butter and the oil, and evenly brown the meat, sprinkling with salt and pepper. Remove and reserve.
3. Add the remaining butter to the pan and cook the onion and celery until soft and golden.
4. Return the meat to the pan. Add the broth, tomato juice, and herbs. Cover and simmer about 1 hour, or until the meat is tender. If the liquid cooks off, add more hot broth. Add mushrooms 10 minutes before the veal is thoroughly cooked. Taste for seasoning. Discard bay leaf before serving.

All stews benefit from being served with Purée de Pommes de Terre (p. 313).

Veal Stew Portuguese Style   SERVES 6

3 pounds veal from the shoulder, cut into 1½-inch cubes
Flour for dredging
Salt and freshly ground black pepper to taste
2 tablespoons unsalted butter
3 tablespoons olive oil
1 large red onion, coarsely chopped
2 large, ripe, firm tomatoes, peeled, seeded, and chopped
1 cup chicken broth
½ cup Madeira
½ cup dry white wine
3 medium-sized potatoes, peeled and quartered
12 large green olives, pitted and coarsely chopped
6 anchovies, drained and coarsely chopped

1. Dredge the veal with flour and sprinkle with salt and pepper.
2. In a flameproof casserole, heat the butter and oil. Add the veal and brown evenly. Add the onion and cook 5 minutes, stirring. Do

not brown. Pour off any fat remaining in the pot.

3. Add the tomatoes, broth, Madeira, and white wine. Cover, bring to a boil on top of the stove, then place in a preheated 350° oven. Cook, covered, 45 minutes, or until the veal is almost tender.

4. Add the potatoes and cook until the veal is tender and the potatoes are cooked, about 25 minutes.

5. Stir in the olives and anchovies. Simmer on top of the stove just long enough to heat them. Taste for seasoning.

Mina Thompson's Veal with Onions, Peppers, and Mushrooms

SERVES 4 TO 6

From Maria's younger sister, the best cook in the family.

3 tablespoons olive oil
2 medium-large white onions, thinly sliced
2 green peppers (seeded, white ribs removed and discarded), cut into 1½ × ½-inch strips
1 pound small, firm fresh mushrooms, halved
2 pounds veal rump, cut into 1-inch cubes
Salt and freshly ground black pepper to taste
1-pound, 12-ounce can Italian tomatoes, drained
1 tablespoon chopped fresh basil, or 1 teaspoon dried
3 tablespoons chopped parsley

1. In a heavy-bottomed, large, deep frying pan or flameproof casserole, heat the olive oil and cook the onions and peppers just until they are crisp-tender. Do not brown. Add the mushrooms and cook 1 minute, stirring. Remove the vegetables with a slotted spoon and set aside.

2. In the same pan, evenly brown the veal, adding more oil if needed. Sprinkle with salt and pepper.

3. Pour the tomatoes into a bowl and break them up (your hands are good for this). Add them to the pan with the veal. Stir in the basil. Simmer, over low heat, covered, for 45 minutes, or until the

veal is nearly tender. Return the reserved vegetables to the pan and cook over low heat until the vegetables and veal are tender. If, after adding the vegetables to the pan, there is too much liquid, cook, uncovered, to reduce liquid. Taste for seasoning. Sprinkle with parsley.

Potatoes Chantilly (p. 304) add a deliciously classic touch.

Veal Sultana
SERVES 4

(Veal Stew with White Raisins)

> *2 pounds boneless veal shoulder, trimmed and cut into 1½-inch*
>   *cubes*
> *Flour for dredging*
> *4 tablespoons (½ stick) unsalted butter*
> *2 tablespoons olive oil*
> *Salt and freshly ground black pepper*
> *3 ounces dry sherry*
> *½ pound medium-sized, firm mushrooms, sliced*
> *2 tablespoons tomato paste*
> *2 cups chicken broth, approximately*
> *1 small bay leaf*
> *¼ teaspoon dried marjoram*
> *¾ cup white raisins, plumped in brandy and drained*
> *1 cup sour cream*

1. Dredge the veal cubes lightly with flour.

2. In a flameproof casserole, heat 2 tablespoons butter and the oil. Evenly brown the veal, sprinkling it with salt and pepper.

3. Stir in the sherry, shake the pot to distribute it, and cook 1 minute. With a slotted spoon, transfer the veal to a bowl and keep warm.

4. Add the remaining butter to the pot and cook the mushrooms 2 minutes. Transfer with a slotted spoon to a bowl (not the one the veal is in). Stir in the tomato paste, blending well with the fat. Pour in and blend well 1½ cups chicken broth. Return the veal to

the casserole; add the bay leaf and marjoram. Bring to a boil on top of the stove.

5. Transfer to a preheated 375° oven and cook, covered, 1 hour (if the sauce gets too thick, add a small amount of hot broth). Turn the oven down to 325°, add the raisins, and cook ½ hour, or until the veal is tender. Remove from the oven. Discard the bay leaf. Stir in the mushrooms and sour cream, blending well, and heat on top of the stove just to a simmer. Taste for seasoning.

Serve with Spanish Parsley Potatoes (p. 284).

Veal and Sausage Pie   SERVES 4 TO 6

2 pounds veal for stew, cut into 1-inch cubes
Flour for dredging
3 tablespoons unsalted butter
1 tablespoon olive oil
Salt and freshly ground black pepper to taste
3 cups chicken broth
¼ teaspoon dried tarragon
2 tablespoons chopped fresh parsley
1 bay leaf
1 onion
2 cloves (studded in the onion)
*½ pound sausage meat, broken up, cooked, and drained
    through a strainer*
*½ pound small mushrooms, quartered and cooked in 2 table-
    spoons butter 2 minutes*
Pastry for a 1-crust, 10-inch pie (p. 73)
1 egg beaten with 1 tablespoon water (optional)

1. Dredge the veal with the flour.
2. In a heavy-bottomed pot, heat the butter and oil. Add the veal and brown evenly, adding more butter and oil if needed. Season with salt and pepper.
3. Pour off any excess fat. Add the broth, tarragon, parsley, bay leaf, and the onion with the cloves to the pot. Stir, scraping up the

browned-on bits from the bottom. Lower heat and simmer, covered, for 1 hour, or until the veal is fork-tender. Transfer the veal with a slotted spoon to a bowl and keep warm. Discard the onion, cloves, and bay leaf. Taste sauce for seasoning. If the sauce needs thickening, stir in 1 tablespoon flour kneaded with 1 tablespoon butter, and simmer until somewhat thickened.

4. Layer the bottom of a 10-inch pie plate or baking dish (deep enough for the contents to come within a quarter inch of the rim) with the sausage meat. Spoon the mushrooms evenly over the sausage and the veal over the mushrooms. Spoon on the sauce.

5. Roll out the pastry to ⅛-inch thickness. Moisten the edge of the pastry that touches the baking dish, cover the pie, and seal firmly to the rim of the dish. Cut three slits in the pastry to allow steam to escape. Brush lightly with the egg and water mixture and bake in a preheated 450° oven 10 minutes. Lower heat to 400° and bake 20 minutes, or until the top is golden brown and the pie is steaming.

Veal Fillets Park Imperial

SERVES 4

(Veal Fillets with Tomatoes)

> *2 tablespoons olive oil*
> *2 medium-sized onions, chopped*
> *2 garlic cloves, minced*
> *3 firm, ripe tomatoes, peeled, seeded, and cut into ½-inch-thick slices*
> *Salt and freshly ground black pepper to taste*
> *1 teaspoon chopped fresh thyme leaves, or ⅓ teaspoon dried*
> *1 teaspoon chopped fresh basil, or ⅓ teaspoon dried*
> *8 tablespoons (1 stick) unsalted butter*
> *2 pounds veal from the leg, cut into 2-inch squares, ¼ inch thick*
> *¾ cup Madeira*
> *½ cup Brown Sauce (see below)*
> *½ cup grated Swiss cheese*
> *2 tablespoons chopped fresh parsley*

1. Heat the oil in a heavy-bottomed saucepan. Add the onions and cook 5 minutes. Do not brown. Add the garlic and cook 2 minutes. Add the tomatoes, salt, pepper, thyme, and basil. Cook 10 minutes. Line a baking dish with the tomato mixture.

2. In a heavy-bottomed frying pan, melt half the butter over medium-high heat. Add the veal and cook rapidly, turning the pieces often, so each will become golden; about 5 minutes should be enough. Arrange the veal fillets on top of the tomato mixture in the baking dish, slightly overlapping if necessary.

3. Pour off any fat in the frying pan; add the Madeira and the Brown Sauce. Cook, stirring, 4 minutes, scraping up the browned-on bits from the bottom of the pan. Remove from the heat and add the remaining butter in small lumps, stirring slowly. Taste sauce for seasoning. Pour over the veal and sprinkle with the cheese and parsley.

4. Transfer to a preheated 400° oven and cook, uncovered, for 15 minutes, or until the veal is tender. If the top starts to get too brown before the veal is tender, cover loosely with aluminum foil. Simple Snow Potatoes (p. 318) go well with this dish.

BROWN SAUCE   MAKES ABOUT 1 CUP

> *2 tablespoons unsalted butter*
> *1 tablespoon chopped onion*
> *1 tablespoon chopped celery leaves*
> *1 tablespoon chopped carrot*
> *1 bay leaf*
> *2 tablespoons flour*
> *1 cup beef broth*
> *Salt and freshly ground black pepper to taste*

1. In a saucepan, over medium-low heat, melt the butter. Add the onion, celery leaves, carrot, and bay leaf, and cook until the vegetables begin to get brown, stirring.

2. Sprinkle in the flour and cook, blending well. Gradually add the beef broth and cook, stirring constantly, until the sauce thickens. Season with salt and pepper, and strain through a fine sieve.

Saltimbocca Romana SERVES 6

These prosciutto and mozzarella slices sandwiched between pieces of veal cooked in wine are so good that, as the Romans say, they "jump in the mouth," which is what Saltimbocca means.

> *12 slices veal from the rump, cut 4 inches long, 2 inches wide, and slightly thicker than ¼ inch*
> *6 thin slices of prosciutto, cut slightly smaller than the pounded veal (see below)*
> *6 fresh sage leaves*
> *6 thin slices of mozzarella, cut the same size as the prosciutto*
> *Flour seasoned with freshly ground black pepper, and very lightly with salt (the ham will supply salt)*
> *6 tablespoons unsalted butter*
> *1½ cups dry white wine*

1. Pound the veal between sheets of wax paper with a meat mallet, making it slightly thinner.
2. Spread the veal out on a large work surface. On 6 of the pieces, place a slice of prosciutto, then a sage leaf, and finally a slice of mozzarella. Top with another slice of veal and seal with toothpicks, or by pounding the edges together.
3. Carefully dredge the veal with the seasoned flour.
4. In a large frying pan (you may need two, so all the veal is cooked at one time), melt the butter over medium-high heat and evenly brown the veal on both sides (adding more butter if needed).
5. Lower heat, pour in the wine, and simmer, uncovered, for 10 minutes, or until the veal is just tender. At this point most of the wine will have evaporated and the juices in the pan will have simmered into a tasty sauce. Spoon the sauce over the veal just before serving.

Serve with Leftover-Potato Pancakes New England Style (p. 376).
Note: If two frying pans are used, divide the butter and wine, adding more of each if needed.

Fillets of Veal with Kidneys

4 tablespoons (½ stick) unsalted butter
1 tablespoon olive oil
4 fillets of veal, each 1 inch thick
Flour for dredging
Salt and freshly ground black pepper to taste
2 veal kidneys, trimmed and cut into 1-inch-thick slices
½ cup beef broth
½ cup dry white wine
4 large mushroom caps, cooked in butter until brown but still
  somewhat firm (kept warm)

1. Heat 2 tablespoons butter and the olive oil in a frying pan. Dredge the fillets very lightly in flour. Add them to the pan and brown evenly. Lower heat, cover, and cook 20 minutes, or until tender, turning 2 or 3 times. Season. Transfer to a hot serving dish and keep warm.
2. Add the remaining butter to the frying pan and cook the kidney slices until they are brown on the outside and slightly pink inside (overcooking will toughen them). Season with salt and pepper. Remove from the pan and keep warm.
3. Pour the beef broth and wine into the frying pan, stirring and scraping up the browned-on bits from the bottom of the pan. Cook, stirring, to reduce by one-third.
Arrange the kidney slices on the veal fillets. Top with a mushroom cap and spoon the sauce over each serving.
Try Champagne Potatoes (p. 331) with the fillets.

Involtini of Veal

(Veal Bundles)

12 slices veal, cut from the leg, in 3-inch squares, ½ inch thick
Salt and freshly ground black pepper

4 thin slices of prosciutto, or good boiled ham, minced
2 tablespoons raisins, plumped in Marsala, drained and chopped
Marsala (for plumping raisins)
2 tablespoons soft, unsalted butter
1 garlic clove, minced
4 tablespoons minced parsley
6 tablespoons fine bread crumbs
6 tablespoons freshly grated Asiago or Parmesan cheese
1 teaspoon finely grated lemon rind (do not use the white part)
1 egg, beaten
2 tablespoons cream
1/4 teaspoon nutmeg
Flour for dredging
3 tablespoons unsalted butter
2 tablespoons olive oil
1-pound can Italian tomatoes, put through food mill
1/2 cup beef broth
2 packages frozen tiny peas, defrosted but not cooked

1. With a meat mallet flatten the veal slices as thin as possible without perforating them. Cut into squares, trimming excess meat, and mince the meat you cut off.

2. Lay out all the veal squares on a large work area. Lightly sprinkle each with salt and pepper.

3. In a bowl, combine and blend well the minced veal (from the trimmings), ham, raisins, soft butter, garlic, 2 tablespoons parsley, bread crumbs, cheese, lemon rind, egg, cream, and nutmeg. Divide into 12 equal portions and spread on each veal square. Roll up the veal, tie with string, or skewer with toothpicks (it is easier to brown them if they are tied), and dust them very lightly with flour.

4. In a frying pan large enough to hold the rolls in one layer, heat the butter and oil. Add the rolls and brown evenly. Pour any fat from the pan. Pour in the tomatoes and broth. Cover the pan and simmer, turning occasionally, for 30 minutes, or until tender. If the liquid cooks off, add a small amount of hot broth or water. Take

the veal rolls from the cooking pan and remove strings (or tooth-picks). Put into a 250° oven to keep warm.

5. Add the peas to the sauce and simmer until tender, about 3 minutes. Taste sauce for seasoning. Place the veal rolls on a hot serving dish; cover with the peas and sauce. Sprinkle with the remaining parsley.

Serve with Spicy Pakistani Potatoes (p. 282).

Hungarian Veal Medallions   SERVES 4

Medallions of veal are 1-inch-thick slices, 3 inches in diameter, cut from the loin or fillet and trimmed.

6 tablespoons unsalted butter
1 tablespoon olive oil
4 veal medallions, each about 6 ounces
2 medium-sized onions, finely chopped
Salt to taste
1 tablespoon Hungarian paprika
½ cup heavy cream
1 cup Velouté Sauce (see below)
⅛ teaspoon cayenne pepper, or to taste

1. In a heavy-bottomed saucepan, heat 4 tablespoons butter and the olive oil. Cook the medallions 3 minutes on each side.

2. Add the onions, sprinkle with salt, and cook over low heat 20 minutes, or until the veal is tender, turning it occasionally. Sprinkle on the paprika and cook 3 minutes. Transfer to a hot serving dish and keep warm.

3. Pour any fat from the pan, add the cream and Velouté Sauce. Simmer, stirring, 5 minutes, scraping up any browned-on bits from the bottom of the pan. Strain through a fine sieve, pushing the onions through with a wooden spoon. Add the cayenne and the remaining butter. Bring to simmer. Do not boil. Spoon over the medallions of veal.

Excellent with Potato Zucchini Pancakes (p. 378).

> 2 tablespoons unsalted butter
> 2 tablespoons flour
> 1 cup rich chicken stock
> Salt and freshly ground black pepper to taste

In a saucepan, over medium heat, melt the butter. Add the flour, stirring into a smooth paste. Gradually add the stock and stir into a smooth, medium-thick sauce. Season with salt and pepper.

Veal Cutlets with Chanterelles   SERVES 4

Try to buy fresh chanterelles, but if you can't find them, the dried variety are available in specialty food shops.

> 4 veal cutlets, about 6 to 8 ounces each
> Salt and freshly ground black pepper to taste
> 5 tablespoons unsalted butter
> 4 shallots, minced
> 2 ounces dried chanterelles, soaked in 1 cup hot water for 30
>   minutes, well drained, and chopped, or ⅔ pound fresh
>   chanterelles, chopped
> ¾ cup beef broth
> 2 tablespoons minced chives

1. Pound the cutlets to ¼-inch thickness, lightly seasoning with salt and pepper.
2. In a large frying pan, over medium-high heat, melt 3 tablespoons butter and evenly brown the cutlets, turning several times, cooking about 8 minutes. Place the cutlets on a heated serving dish and keep warm.
3. In a small frying pan, melt the remaining butter and cook the shallots 3 minutes. Add the mushrooms and cook 2 minutes, stirring. Remove from heat.
4. Pour the beef broth into the frying pan used for the veal and

cook over medium-high heat, stirring until the broth is reduced by half.

5. Spoon the sauce lightly over the veal cutlets, top with a little of the mushroom-shallot mixture, and sprinkle with the chives.

We like to offer Potatoes Parma (p. 349) with this elegant veal.

Veal Cutlets in Puff Pastry   SERVES 6

5 tablespoons unsalted butter
1 tablespoon olive oil
6 medallions veal loin, 3 inches in diameter, ½ inch thick
Salt and freshly ground black pepper to taste
1 medium-sized onion, finely chopped
6 medium-sized mushrooms, chopped
⅛ teaspoon oregano
⅓ cup Madeira
6 frozen patty shells (we use Pepperidge Farm), defrosted (do not bake)
6 thin slices cooked ham, 3 inches in diameter
1 egg, beaten with 1 tablespoon water (optional)

1. In a large frying pan, heat 4 tablespoons butter and the oil. Add the veal and brown evenly on both sides. Sprinkle with salt and pepper. Cover, lower heat, and simmer 15 minutes, or until tender, turning at least once. Transfer the veal to a dish to cool.

2. Melt the remaining butter in the frying pan over medium heat and cook the onion until soft. Do not brown. Add the mushrooms and cook 3 minutes. Season with salt and pepper. Add the oregano and Madeira, and over high heat, cook just until the liquid has evaporated. Cool.

3. Roll out the defrosted patty-shell pastry into 7-inch squares. Place a slice of ham in the center. Spread equal amounts of the onion and mushroom mixture on the ham and place a veal medallion on top. Moisten the edges of the pastry, fold envelope fashion, and seal well. Arrange, separated, seam side down, on a baking sheet. Brush tops with the egg-water mixture and bake in

a preheated 400° oven 20 minutes, or until puffed and golden brown.

We pair these pastries with abundant little Pommes de Terre Noisette (p. 299).

Veal Scallops Arance

SERVES 4

(Veal with Orange Juice and Marsala)

*1½ pounds veal scallops, cut ⅜ of an inch thick, carefully
   pounded with a meat mallet to a ¼-inch thickness*
Salt and freshly ground black pepper to taste
Flour for dredging
2 tablespoons unsalted butter
2 tablespoons olive oil
½ cup dry Marsala
½ cup strained fresh orange juice
3 tablespoons soft unsalted butter
*1 tablespoon chopped fresh sage (dry will not do), or
   2 tablespoons chopped fresh parsley*

1. Sprinkle the veal with salt and pepper and dredge lightly with flour.

2. In a large frying pan, heat 2 tablespoons butter and the oil and brown the scallops on both sides. Brown a few at a time; do not crowd them. Add more oil if needed. Transfer to a bowl.

3. Pour off all but 1 tablespoon fat from the pan (if the veal absorbed all the fat, add 1 tablespoon oil). Stir in the Marsala and half the orange juice, and simmer, scraping up the browned-on bits from the bottom of the pan. Return the scallops to the pan with any liquid that has accumulated in the bowl. Cover and simmer 10 minutes, basting with the liquid from time to time.

4. Transfer the scallops to a hot serving dish. Keep warm. Add the remaining orange juice to the pan and cook quickly, 2 to 3 minutes, or until the sauce thickens. Taste for seasoning. Stir in the soft butter and spoon over the scallops. Sprinkle with fresh sage or parsley. Serve with Quick Potato Cake with Skins (p. 356).

Veal Piccata

(Veal Scallops with a Piquant Sauce)

This recipe remains one of our favorite veal dishes, and one of the gems of the Italian repertoire.

> *4 veal scallops, each weighing about 6 ounces*
> *Flour for dredging*
> *Salt and freshly ground black pepper to taste*
> *2 tablespoons olive oil*
> *3 tablespoons unsalted butter*
> *⅓ cup dry white wine*
> *⅓ cup chicken broth*
> *Juice of one lemon (freshly squeezed)*

1. Between pieces of wax paper, pound each piece of veal with a meat mallet until wafer-thin. Do not pound so hard, however, that the meat is perforated or shredded; each piece should be intact. Dredge lightly with flour and season with salt and pepper.
2. Heat the oil in a frying pan. Brown the scallops evenly. Transfer to a warm dish and keep warm.
3. Pour any fat from the pan. Add the butter, wine, broth, and lemon juice. Simmer, stirring, over medium-high heat for 5 minutes. Add the scallops, spooning sauce over them, and serve piping hot. Potatoes Lorette (p. 307) make this a feast to remember.

Veal Chops Amandine with Wine Sauce

> *4 loin veal chops, cut 1 inch thick*
> *Flour for dredging*
> *Salt and freshly ground black pepper to taste*
> *6 tablespoons unsalted butter*
> *½ cup dry white wine*
> *Chicken broth (optional)*
> *4 half-inch-thick slices of white bread, cut to fit the chops, fried*
> *   in butter (not the butter listed above) until golden and crisp on*
> *   both sides, drained on paper towels and kept warm*

½ cup dry sherry
3 tablespoons slivered almonds, toasted

1. Lightly dredge the chops with flour and sprinkle with salt and pepper.
2. In a large frying pan, heat 4 tablespoons butter. Add the chops and brown on both sides, adding more butter if needed.
3. Pour in the white wine, cover, lower heat, and simmer 15 minutes or until the veal is tender. If the wine cooks off before the chops are tender, add spoonfuls of hot broth or water.
4. Arrange the slices of bread on a hot serving dish, place a chop on each, and keep warm.
5. Add 2 tablespoons butter and the sherry to the pan. Simmer 1 minute, stirring up the browned-on bits from the bottom of the pan.
6. Spoon the sauce over the chops and sprinkle with almonds. Serve with Potatoes and Spinach Cochin Style (p. 276).

Veal Slices in Cheese and Cream   SERVES 6

Our ongoing theory, that simple food is always the best, which has survived despite all the weird combinations that the food establishment is desperately experimenting with today, was never more clearly exemplified than on one excursion we took, trying to reach the North Pole. This was on the Norwegian ketch *Havella*, with a five-man crew, which included a talented chef who showed us how simply veal can be treated and still emerge as a superlative dish.

4 tablespoons (½ stick) unsalted butter
1 tablespoon olive oil
6 slices of veal from the rump, pounded ¼ inch thick, each
    weighing about 6 ounces
Salt and freshly ground black pepper to taste
4 medium-sized white onions, chopped
¼ cup chicken broth
1½ cups sour cream
½ cup grated gjetost cheese (or a sharp cheese of your choice)

1. In a large frying pan (or use two), heat the butter and oil. Add the veal to the pan and brown on both sides, sprinkling with salt and pepper. Remove and keep warm. Add the onions to the frying pan and cook 3 minutes, or until soft. Do not brown. Remove with a slotted spoon and keep warm. Pour off any fat from the pan. Add the broth to the pan and cook, stirring, to scrape up the browned-on bits from the bottom. Return the veal and onions to the pan and cook, over medium-low heat, covered, about 15 minutes, or until the veal is tender, turning occasionally. Remove the veal from the pan and keep warm.

2. Stir the sour cream into the pan, add the cheese, and cook over low heat, stirring, until the cheese has melted. Do not boil. Return the veal to the pan to heat through in the sauce.

Serve with sauce spooned over each slice.

This veal was accompanied by Steamed Potatoes with Caraway Seeds (p. 357), a Norwegian recipe we obtained from the *Havella* chef.

Veal Chops with Bacon and Shallots   SERVES 4

2 tablespoons unsalted butter
4 slices bacon, chopped
4 loin veal chops, 1 inch thick
Flour for dredging
Salt and freshly ground black pepper to taste
24 shallots (or very small white onions), peeled, root ends scored
1 cup rich chicken stock
1 cup dry white wine
1 cup heavy cream

1. In a frying pan, heat the butter. Add the bacon and cook, stirring, until golden brown and fat is rendered. With a slotted spoon, remove the bacon and drain on paper towels. Reserve.

2. Lightly dredge the chops with flour and sprinkle with salt and pepper. Over medium-high heat, brown the chops on both sides

in the bacon-butter fat. Transfer to a baking dish just large enough to hold them in one layer.

3. Add the shallots (or onions) to the frying pan and cook over medium-high heat until golden and crisp-tender. Do not brown. With a slotted spoon, remove and drain on paper towels. Reserve.

4. Pour off all fat left in the frying pan. Add the stock and wine, and cook, scraping up the browned-on bits from the bottom. Cook until the liquid has been reduced by one-half. Stir in the cream, and over medium-low heat, simmer until slightly thickened.

5. Return the bacon and shallots to the frying pan and mix with the sauce. Spoon the bacon, shallots, and cream sauce over and around the chops. Cover with a lid or aluminum foil and bake in a preheated 350° oven 45 minutes, or until tender. Taste sauce for seasoning.

These chops deserve the classic treatment; serve with Pommes de Terre Soufflées (p. 301).

Provimi Veal Chops Provençale
SERVES 4
(Veal Chops with Vegetables and Wine)

2 carrots, scraped and diced
2 turnips, scraped and diced
1 tablespoon unsalted butter
1 medium-sized onion, finely chopped
4 loin veal chops, 1 inch thick
Flour for dredging
3 tablespoons olive oil
Salt and freshly ground black pepper to taste
½ cup dry vermouth, or Madeira

1. Cook the carrots and turnips in a small amount of boiling, lightly salted water until crisp-tender. Drain well and reserve.

2. In a frying pan, over medium heat, melt the butter and cook the onion until soft. Do not brown. Remove and set aside with the other vegetables.

3. Lightly dredge the chops with the flour.

4. Add the oil to the frying pan, and over medium heat, brown the chops evenly. Sprinkle with salt and pepper. Lower heat, cover, and cook about 12 minutes on each side, or until tender, turning occasionally to cook evenly. Transfer to a warm serving dish and keep warm.

5. Add the wine to the frying pan, stirring to scrape up the browned-on bits from the bottom of the pan, and over medium heat reduce by one-third. Add the vegetables, mix well, and heat through. Spoon over the chops and serve.

Serve with a reliable favorite, French Fries (p. 293).

Veal Chops Romano   SERVES 4

These veal chops are breaded and baked with potatoes, as they prepare them in Rome's Trastevere.

> 6 tablespoons olive oil
> 2 garlic cloves, peeled, crushed
> 4 tablespoons chopped broadleaf parsley
> 1½ teaspoons salt
> ½ teaspoon freshly ground black pepper
> 4 loin veal chops, ¾ inch thick
> Fine bread crumbs for dredging
> 2 teaspoons paprika
> 4 medium-sized potatoes, quartered lengthwise

1. Combine and blend well in a shallow bowl the oil, garlic, parsley, salt, and pepper. Add the chops. Turn to coat them well. Marinate 4 hours or longer, turning them several times.

2. Remove the chops from the marinade (saving the marinade), allowing most of it to drip off. Dredge them with bread crumbs and arrange them in a shallow baking dish large enough to hold them and the potatoes snugly (but not too snugly) in a single layer. Sprinkle the chops with paprika.

3. Toss the potato quarters in the marinade, coating them evenly. Arrange the potatoes around and in between the chops. Bake in a

preheated 400° oven 20 minutes. Lower the heat to 350°, turn the potatoes, and cook 20 minutes, or until the veal and potatoes are tender.

Note: For a taste variation, ¼ teaspoon rosemary can be added to the marinade.

Costolette di Vitello alla Valdostana
(Veal Chops with Truffles)

SERVES 4

This is a popular veal chop dish in Italy's Piedmont area, especially in Valle d'Aosta, for which it is named. It calls for white truffles, but you can use tiny, firm fresh mushrooms lightly sautéed in butter instead. The truffles cost more than the veal!

> *4 loin veal chops, 1 inch thick*
> *4 ounces Fontina cheese, thinly sliced*
> *4 small white truffles (if fresh aren't available, used canned or,*
>   *as suggested above, use several small mushrooms)*
> *Salt and freshly ground black pepper to taste*
> *Flour for dredging*
> *1 egg, beaten in a shallow dish (for dipping the chops)*
> *Bread crumbs for dredging*
> *5 tablespoons unsalted butter*
> *1 tablespoon olive oil*

1. With a sharp knife, cut the chop back horizontally, three-quarters of the way through, making a pocket, with both parts still attached to the bone.
2. Stuff the pocket with thin slices of Fontina cheese and white truffles (or mushrooms). Sprinkle with salt and pepper, and press the pocket closed, lightly beating the edges so that they are properly sealed.
3. Dredge the stuffed chops with flour. Dip into the beaten egg to completely coat, then dredge well with the bread crumbs.
4. In a large frying pan, over medium heat, heat the butter and oil and cook the chops for 30 minutes, turning occasionally, until

golden brown and tender. Add more butter if necessary.
Serve with Potato Zucchini Pancakes (p. 378).

Dora Radicchi's Braised Veal alla Perugia   SERVES 6

On one visit to Rome, Dora was our cook (a great one) and housekeeper.
This unique veal dish is braised in milk.

2 tablespoons unsalted butter
2 tablespoons olive oil
3-pound boned roast of veal, tied
Salt and freshly ground black pepper to taste
½ cup dry white wine
1 medium-sized carrot, scraped and quartered
1 large celery stalk, scraped and quartered
1 large onion, quartered
1 bay leaf
½ teaspoon dried thyme
1½ pints of milk, approximately, at room temperature
* (enough to just cover the veal)*
Chopped parsley

1. In a flameproof casserole, just large enough to snugly hold the veal, heat the butter and oil. Evenly brown the veal, sprinkling with salt and pepper.
2. Remove the veal, add the wine, carrot, celery, onion, bay leaf, and thyme, and simmer 3 minutes.
3. Return the veal to the casserole and barely cover with the milk. Heat on top of the stove to a simmer, cover, and cook in a preheated 325° oven 1½ to 2 hours, or until the veal is tender.
4. Transfer the veal to a hot serving dish. Remove cords. Strain the liquid in the casserole, pushing the vegetables through the strainer. If the sauce is too thin, cook over medium heat until it reduces to about 1 cup. Taste for seasoning. Slice veal and serve with a spoonful of sauce over each slice. Sprinkle with parsley. Serve with Baked Parmesan Potato Fingers (p. 326).

Breast of Veal Contadino

(Veal Stew with Tomatoes, Mushrooms, and Peas)

3 tablespoons unsalted butter

2 tablespoons olive oil

2 pounds boneless breast (or shoulder) of veal, cut into 1½-inch cubes

Salt and freshly ground black pepper to taste

1 medium-sized onion, finely chopped

1 celery stalk, scraped and finely chopped

4 medium-sized, ripe, firm tomatoes, peeled, seeded, and coarsely chopped

4 fresh basil leaves, chopped, or ¼ teaspoon dried basil

Enough beef broth to barely cover the veal

2 cups fresh hulled peas, undercooked, or 1 package frozen peas, defrosted but not cooked

6 large, firm mushrooms, quartered and cooked in 1 tablespoon butter for 1 minute

2 tablespoons chopped broadleaf parsley

1. In a flameproof casserole, heat the butter and oil. Add the veal and brown evenly, sprinkling with salt and pepper. With a slotted spoon, transfer to a bowl. If any fat remains in the pot, pour off all but 1 tablespoon. If the veal has absorbed all the fat, add 1 tablespoon butter. Add the onion and celery, and cook 1 minute. Do not brown.

2. Return the veal and any juices that have accumulated in the bowl to the pot; add the tomatoes, basil, and broth. Cover, bring to a boil on top of the stove. Transfer to a preheated 300° oven for 1 hour, or until the veal is fork-tender. Taste for seasoning.

3. About 10 minutes before the veal is cooked, add the peas and mushrooms with the butter in which they cooked. Serve sprinkled with parsley.

This dish deserves Duchesse Potatoes Galettes (p. 290).

Breast of Veal with Lemon Potatoes SERVES 6

2 tablespoons unsalted butter
1 medium-sized onion, chopped
½ pound lean ground chuck of beef
½ pound fresh mushrooms, chopped
1 ten-ounce package frozen chopped spinach, thawed
  and squeezed dry
1 egg, beaten
½ cup grated Monterey Jack cheese
½ teaspoon basil
Salt and freshly ground black pepper to taste
1 breast of veal (about 4 pounds), boned
1 cup beef broth
2 medium-sized onions, cut into chunks
6 medium-sized potatoes (about 2 pounds), unpeeled and cut
  into chunks
1 teaspoon dried thyme
1 teaspoon grated lemon rind
1 teaspoon paprika
Lemon slices

1. In a frying pan, melt the butter and cook the onion and beef 10 minutes, then transfer to a bowl.

2. In the same pan, cook the mushrooms until they have exuded their moisture. Remove with a slotted spoon and add to the bowl with the meat. Cook the spinach 5 minutes, remove with a slotted spoon, and add to the meat bowl, also blending in the egg, cheese, basil, salt, and pepper. Mix well.

3. Lay the veal flat, sprinkle with salt and pepper, and spread the seasoned meat stuffing on the center third of the veal. Fold over both ends of the veal breast and tie into a compact shape with cord. Place in a roasting pan, add the broth, cover the pan, and cook in a preheated 325° oven 1½ hours. Baste occasionally.

4. Place the onion and potato chunks in a bowl and toss well with thyme, lemon rind, and paprika. Add the seasoned onions and

potatoes to the veal roasting pan, stirring to coat with the veal drippings.

5. Cook, uncovered, 45 minutes, or until the veal and potatoes are tender, stirring the potatoes and onions occasionally.

Serve garnished with lemon slices.

Cima alla Genovese
SERVES 6

(Breast of Veal Stuffed with Pork, Prosciutto, Sweetbreads, and Spinach)

"Cima" is a unique specialty of Genoa. We order it any time we are in that city—or anywhere in Italy where we can get it.

½ pound lean ground pork
¼ pound prosciutto, minced
1 calf's sweetbread, trimmed, blanched 5 minutes, chopped
4 slices white bread, soaked in milk and squeezed dry
2 tablespoons grated Parmesan cheese
½ cup cooked, chopped spinach, squeezed dry
1 tablespoon minced pistachios
2½ teaspoons salt
½ teaspoon freshly ground black pepper
⅛ teaspoon nutmeg
2 eggs, beaten
4-pound breast of veal, boned and trimmed
Water
1 large carrot, scraped and quartered
1 large onion, coarsely chopped
2 garlic cloves
1 bay leaf

1. In a large bowl, combine pork, prosciutto, sweetbread, bread, cheese, spinach, pistachios, 1½ teaspoons salt, pepper, nutmeg, and the eggs. Blend well.

2. Spread open the breast of veal, skin side down, and arrange the pork mixture evenly over it. Fold the veal over carefully, skewering or sewing it to keep it in a compact roll that will retain the

filling. Tie it with cord in several places to keep its shape.

3. Place the veal roll in a pot just large enough to hold it. Cover with water; add the remaining salt, the carrot, onion, garlic, and bay leaf.

4. Cover the pot, bring to a boil on top of the stove, then place in a preheated 325° oven for 1½ hours, or until the veal is fork-tender.

5. After cooking, the Genovese place a weight on top of the veal, flattening it somewhat. Remove the cords, skewers, or thread before slicing. This dish can be served hot or cold; many Italians like it cold as a special summer dish.

We like it hot with Vernon Jarratt's Ciapotta (p. 275).

Vitello Tonnato   SERVES 6
(Cold Veal with Tuna Sauce)

> *3 anchovy fillets*
> *3-pound solid piece of veal from the leg, tied in several places*
> *2 cups chicken broth*
> *2 cups dry white wine*
> *1 carrot, scraped and sliced*
> *1 large onion, sliced*
> *2 garlic cloves, crushed*
> *2 celery stalks, scraped and sliced*
> *1 bay leaf*
> *½ teaspoon dried thyme*
> *Grated rind of 1 lemon (none of the white part)*
> *Tuna Sauce (see below)*

1. Cut the anchovy fillets into halves. Make 6 incisions in the veal and insert a half into each.

2. Place the veal in a deep pot that it will just fit in snugly. Pour in the chicken broth and wine. Add the carrot, onion, garlic, celery, bay leaf, thyme, and lemon rind. If the meat is not covered with

liquid, add just enough water to barely cover it.

3. Bring to a boil, then simmer, covered, over medium heat, about 1½ hours, or until tender, skimming the top when necessary. Remove from heat and allow the veal to cool in the liquid. As the veal cools, make the Tuna Sauce.

TO ASSEMBLE AND SERVE

When the veal has thoroughly cooled, remove from the liquid. Trim it and cut into thin, uniform slices. Arrange them on a large serving dish (with raised edges, if possible), slightly overlapping if necessary. Coat the slices with the Tuna Sauce. Cover with plastic wrap and refrigerate overnight. Before serving, garnish with capers, cornichons, parsley, quartered hard-boiled eggs, and black Greek olives (the plump, purplish ones, not the wrinkled ones), or anything else that you find attractive and appropriate.

Note: If the serving dish does not have raised edges, set several toothpicks upright in the veal to keep the plastic from coming in contact with the sauce.

For the perfect summer meal, we like this with Potato-Stuffed Tomatoes (p. 271).

TUNA SAUCE   MAKES ABOUT 2½ CUPS

1½ cups mayonnaise
3½-ounce can "solid" tuna, drained
3 anchovy fillets, drained, rinsed, and dried
2 tablespoons lemon juice
¼ cup (approximately) of the liquid that the veal poached in, strained
Salt and pepper to taste

In a blender container, combine the mayonnaise, tuna, anchovy fillets, lemon juice, and ¼ cup of the poaching liquid. Blend for 30 seconds into a smooth sauce. If the sauce seems too thick, add small amounts of the liquid to make a sauce the consistency of heavy cream. Season with salt and pepper.

Osso Bucho

SERVES 4

(Braised Veal Shanks)

This unique and famous dish even had a special utensil created for it—a long narrow spoon that slips into the center of the bone to scoop out the marrow. In their colorful way, the Italians call this marrow spoon *agente delle tasse*—"the tax collector."

> *4 meaty, 3-inch pieces of veal shank, with marrow, cut from*
> *   the center part of the shank*
> *Flour for dredging*
> *Salt and freshly ground black pepper to taste*
> *5 tablespoons olive oil*
> *⅛ teaspoon dried rosemary*
> *2 garlic cloves, minced*
> *2 medium-sized onions, chopped*
> *2 small carrots, scraped and chopped*
> *1 celery stalk, scraped and chopped*
> *1 cup dry white wine*
> *1 cup chicken broth*
> *Gremolata (see below)*

1. Tie the shanks with cord to keep the meat on the bone as it cooks. Dredge the shanks with flour and sprinkle with salt and pepper.
2. In a flameproof casserole, heat the oil and brown the shanks evenly. Remove the shanks.
3. Add the rosemary, garlic, onions, carrots, and celery to the casserole and cook over medium heat, stirring up the browned-on bits from the bottom of the pot. Stir in the wine and broth. Bring to a boil.
4. Add the browned shanks, standing them in an upright position, with the marrow showing on top. This position keeps the marrow intact so it can be spooned out later by the diners. Spoon some of the sautéed vegetables on top of the shanks.
5. Transfer to a preheated 325° oven and cook, covered, for 1½

hours, or until the shanks are tender.

Serve each shank with a spoonful of the Gremolata sprinkled on top and the vegetable sauce beside the shanks. Serve with long narrow (or marrow) spoons to extract the marrow.

As a change from rice, we like Shoestring Potatoes and Vermicelli (p. 357) with this dish.

GREMOLATA

> 1 large garlic clove, minced
> 2 tablespoons minced parsley
> 1 tablespoon grated lemon rind

Combine all ingredients and blend well with a fork.

Roast Leg of Veal   SERVES 6

> ½ teaspoon dried sage
> 1 teaspoon salt
> ½ teaspoon freshly ground black pepper
> 1 boned leg of veal weighing 4 pounds after boning, tied
> 2 tablespoons unsalted butter
> 2 tablespoons olive oil
> 1 large carrot, scraped and sliced
> 1 large onion, sliced
> 1 bay leaf
> ½ cup dry white wine
> 3 thin slices fatback, or salt pork

1. Combine the sage, salt, and pepper, and rub the veal with it.
2. Heat the butter and oil in a flameproof casserole, just large enough to hold the roast snugly, and brown the veal evenly.
3. Distribute the carrot and onion around the veal. Add the bay leaf. Pour in the wine. Lay the strips of fatback or salt pork over the veal. Cover the casserole with aluminum foil, then its lid. Cook in a preheated 300° oven 1½ to 2 hours, or until the veal is tender,

basting frequently with the juices from the pan. The juices should run yellow when the veal is pricked with a fork. If the liquid in the pan cooks off before the veal is tender, add a small amount of hot broth or water.

4. To serve, transfer the veal to a hot serving dish and remove the trussing cord. While keeping the veal warm, siphon the fat from the casserole. Mash the vegetables against the side of the pan and stir up with the juices in the pan. Taste for seasoning and strain into a bowl to serve with the sliced veal.

Try Château Potatoes (p. 290) with the veal.

7

Variety Meats

Calf's Brains Contadina
Veal Kidneys Marsala
Broiled Herbed Lamb Kidneys
Veal Kidneys with Parsley
Danish Beef Liver with Watercress Sauce
Calf's Liver in Sour Cream
Calf's Liver Veneziana
Soufflé of Calf's Liver
Sweetbreads with Peas and Onions
Sweetbreads Florentine
Sweetbread, Oyster, and Ham Pie
Trippa alla Romana

The French prize *abats de boucherie*. They're fond of saying that this is food that is appreciated mostly by the poor and the sophisticated. It is certainly true that in this country it is mainly the sophisticated who like them. But the poor couldn't afford them.

For want of a better name, we call them "variety meats," by which we mean calf's liver and brains, kidneys, sweetbreads, and tripe.

Just as many of us avoid rabbit because of Peter Rabbit and the Easter Bunny, too many of us shun variety meats. This is unfortunate, for these are delicate and delicious offerings and an asset to any menu.

If you're not convinced, try Broiled Herbed Lamb Kidneys, Trippa alla Romana, Soufflé of Calf's Liver, or Sweetbreads with Peas and Onions.

Calf's Brains Contadina   SERVES 6
(Calf's Brains with Green Olives and Capers)

3 veal brains soaked in cold water 2 hours
1 tablespoon vinegar
1 onion, quartered
1 bay leaf
1 carrot, quartered
Salt and freshly ground black pepper to taste
18 small, green pimiento-stuffed olives, quartered
2 tablespoons capers, rinsed in water and drained
1 cup fine bread crumbs
1 teaspoon dried oregano
2 tablespoons olive oil
2 tablespoons chopped fresh broadleaf parsley

1. Drain the brains and trim the membrane and veins. Soak again in cold water with 1 tablespoon vinegar for 1 hour.
2. Simmer in boiling water with the onion, bay leaf, and carrot 15 minutes. Drain and cool in cold water. Drain, dry, and cut into ½-inch-thick slices.
3. Arrange the brains in a single layer in a buttered, shallow baking

dish. Sprinkle with salt and pepper. Sprinkle with the olives and capers, and then a mixture of the bread crumbs, oregano, and olive oil.

4. Bake in a preheated 350° oven 15 minutes, or until the top is golden. Sprinkle with parsley and serve with Czechoslovakian Potato Pudding (p. 336).

Veal Kidneys Marsala SERVES 4

4 tablespoons (½ stick) unsalted butter
2 tablespoons olive oil
4 veal kidneys (remove membrane, fat and tough inner part, and discard), cut into large bite-sized pieces (the meat will shrink as it cooks)
Salt and freshly ground black pepper to taste
2 medium-sized onions, thinly sliced
1 garlic clove, minced
6 medium-sized, firm mushrooms, cut into ¼-inch-thick slices
1 cup Marsala
½ cup heavy cream
1 teaspoon Dijon mustard
2 tablespoons chopped fresh parsley

1. In a large frying pan, heat half the butter and all the oil. Add the kidneys, sprinkle with salt and pepper, and brown evenly. Do not overcook, as they will toughen; the pieces should be slightly pink inside. Transfer with a slotted spoon to a warm bowl.
2. Add the onions and garlic to the frying pan, adding more butter (in addition to the above 4 tablespoons) if needed. Cook 2 minutes, or until the onions are soft and golden. Do not brown. Add the mushrooms and cook 1 minute.
3. Return the kidneys to the pan and cook with the onions and mushrooms just long enough to heat through. Transfer to a hot serving dish and keep warm.
4. Pour the Marsala into the frying pan. Raise heat and simmer until the wine has reduced by one-half. Stir in the remaining butter,

the cream, and the mustard. Heat through, taste for seasoning, and pour over the kidneys. Sprinkle with parsley.

Serve with Norma Jean Maxwell's Buttered Bakers (p. 369).

Broiled Herbed Lamb Kidneys

SERVES 6

18 lamb kidneys
¾ cup chopped fresh parsley
1½ teaspoons chopped fresh tarragon, or ½ teaspoon dried
1 small onion, minced
1 cup soft butter
1 tablespoon Worcestershire sauce
Salt and freshly ground black pepper to taste
1 cup dry sherry

1. Remove outside membrane from the kidneys and slit down the center lengthwise, but do not cut through. Cut out the white, hard core in the center.
2. Make a paste of the parsley, tarragon, onion, butter, Worcestershire sauce, salt, and pepper.
3. Arrange the kidneys, spread out, cut side up, on a rack that has a drip pan underneath. Divide the paste evenly and spread over the kidneys. Sprinkle with the sherry. Broil 5 minutes.
4. Turn the kidneys over, spoon the drippings from the pan on top of them, and broil another 5 minutes. The kidneys should be slightly pink inside. If cooked more, they will toughen.

Serve on a hot plate with the drippings spooned over them and Snow Potatoes (p. 318) on the side.

Veal Kidneys with Parsley

SERVES 4

Here is a quick, simple dish from our Roman friend Vernon Jarratt.

4 veal kidneys
3 tablespoons unsalted butter
Salt and freshly ground black pepper to taste

Juice of ½ lemon, freshly squeezed
3 tablespoons minced fresh broadleaf parsley

1. Wash kidneys, remove any fat, and peel off covering membrane. Dry. Cut into ⅓-inch-thick slices and remove the fatty nugget in the center.
2. In a large frying pan, over medium-high heat, melt the butter. Cook the kidneys 5 minutes, turning several times. Do not over-cook. The centers should be slightly pink.
3. Sprinkle with salt, pepper, and lemon juice. Cook 2 minutes.
4. Sprinkle in the parsley, stir, and serve.
Serve with Vernon Jarratt's Ciapotta (p. 275).

Danish Beef Liver with Watercress Sauce   SERVES 4

Beef liver seems to remain largely unappreciated in this country. What a pity, since it's a delicious and inexpensive treasure house of protein, iron, and vitamins. Here's a celebrated version we discovered in Copenhagen.

4 slices of beef liver, cut slightly less than ½ inch thick, trimmed
½ cup flour, seasoned with 1 teaspoon salt
2 small eggs, beaten
Bread crumbs for dredging
6 tablespoons unsalted butter
3 large scallions, white part only, minced
1½ cups beef broth
Juice of 1 lemon
½ cup chopped, fresh watercress leaves (no stems)

1. Dredge the liver slices with the seasoned flour, shaking off excess.
2. Dip into the beaten eggs, then dredge lightly with bread crumbs.
3. In a large frying pan, over medium heat, melt 4 tablespoons butter and cook the liver until golden brown on both sides but quite pink inside. (Do not overcook, or it will toughen; 1½ minutes on each side should do it.) Remove from pan and keep warm.

4. Pour off any fat remaining in the pan, and over medium heat, melt the remaining butter. Add the scallions and cook 3 minutes. Stir in the beef broth, lemon juice, and watercress, simmering and stirring for 6 minutes, or until the liquid has reduced by half and the sauce thickened.

5. Taste for seasoning, and spoon the watercress sauce over the liver slices.

Serve with Shirley Capp's au Gratin Potatoes (p. 329).

Calf's Liver in Sour Cream

SERVES 6

8 tablespoons (1 stick) unsalted butter
1 tablespoon olive oil
1 large white onion, chopped
1 small green pepper (seeds and white ribs removed and discarded), cut into thin strips, parboiled 2 minutes, thoroughly drained
2 garlic cloves, minced
6 half-inch-thick slices of liver, trimmed, cut into ½-inch-wide strips
Salt and freshly ground black pepper to taste
Flour for dredging
½ cup dry vermouth
¾ cup sour cream

1. In a large, heavy-bottomed saucepan, or a large deep frying pan, heat half the butter and oil. Add the onion, pepper, and garlic, and cook 3 minutes, or until soft and slightly golden. Do not brown. Transfer with a slotted spoon to a bowl and keep warm. Pour any liquid or fat from the pan.

2. Season the liver strips with salt and pepper and dredge them lightly with flour. Add the remaining butter and oil to the pan, and over medium heat, brown the liver strips, turning several times, about 2 minutes. The liver will be pink on the inside. If desired well-done, cook 3 to 4 minutes, but overcooking will toughen it.

Transfer the liver with a slotted spoon to the bowl with the vegetables. Keep warm.

3. Pour any fat from the pan. Add the vermouth and deglaze the pan, scraping up any browned-on bits from the bottom. Reduce the wine by half. Blend in the sour cream. Return the liver and vegetables to the pan. Gently stir and heat just to a simmer.

We like Potatoes à la Camembert (p. 370) with this dish.

Calf's Liver Veneziana

SERVES 6

(Calf's Liver with White Vinegar)

> 6 half-inch-thick slices calf's liver, trimmed, cut into 2-inch-long
>   narrow strips
> Flour for dredging
> Salt and freshly ground black pepper
> 4 tablespoons (½ stick) unsalted butter
> 1 tablespoon olive oil
> 2 medium-sized onions, sliced
> ⅔ cup white vinegar
> Lemon wedges

1. Lightly dredge the liver strips with flour and sprinkle with salt and pepper.

2. In a large frying pan (or use two frying pans), heat the butter and oil. Add the strips of liver and cook quickly to evenly brown, about 2 or 3 minutes, turning the strips often. Do not overcook, as the liver will toughen. The strips should be pink inside. Transfer to a hot serving dish and keep warm (a 200° oven is good for this).

3. Add the onions to the pan, lower heat to medium, and cook until soft and slightly golden. Do not brown. Remove with a slotted spoon and layer them over the liver strips.

4. Add the vinegar to the pan, raise heat, and reduce it by half. Spoon the vinegar over the onions and garnish with the lemon wedges.

We like crisp buttery Potatoes Anna—Pommes Anna—with this simple but elegant dish (p. 302).

Soufflé of Calf's Liver

Here's another elegant dish from Antoine Gilly, who often considered variety meats first when planning a meal. This makes an impressive luncheon, served with a tomato sauce of your choice.

8 tablespoons (1 stick) unsalted butter

¼ cup flour

6 chopped shallots, cooked in 2 tablespoons butter just until they start to soften

¾ cup light cream, or half-and-half

¾ pound calf's liver, trimmed, put through the fine blade of a food chopper

2 ounces cognac

3 egg yolks

1½ teaspoons chopped fresh basil

1½ teaspoons chopped fresh tarragon

Salt and white pepper to taste

4 egg whites, stiffly beaten

1 tablespoon chopped parsley

1. In a heavy-bottomed saucepan, over medium heat, melt 6 tablespoons butter. Stir in the flour and shallots, blend and simmer, stirring, for 3 minutes; do not brown. Gradually stir in the cream and cook, stirring, until it thickens.

2. Add the liver, blending well, and cook 2 minutes. Stir in the cognac. Remove from heat, cool slightly, and, one at a time, beat in the egg yolks. Stir in the basil, tarragon, salt, and pepper, blending well. Fold in the beaten egg whites and parsley.

3. Butter an 8-inch soufflé mold with the remaining butter and pour in the liver mixture. Set in a pan containing 2 inches of boiling water, and place in a preheated 400° oven for 35 minutes, or until the soufflé rises, is set, and is nicely browned. The soufflé should be served as soon as it emerges from the oven.

Here's another Gilly favorite: Hashed Brown Potatoes with Vinegar (p. 297).

Sweetbreads with Peas and Onions SERVES 6

3 pairs sweetbreads, soaked in cold water 2 hours
1 tablespoon lemon juice
1 bay leaf
1 onion, quartered
¼ pound salt pork, cut into ½-inch cubes
Flour for dredging
Salt and freshly ground black pepper to taste
¼ cup dry sherry
1 heart Boston lettuce, well washed and shredded
24 very small white onions, root ends scored, browned in butter
1 pound new green peas (about 1 cup shelled)
½ teaspoon sugar
1 cup chicken broth
3 tablespoons unsalted butter, at room temperature

1. Drain and rinse the sweetbreads and gently remove as much as possible of the membrane that encases them. Cook in simmering water to cover with the lemon juice, the bay leaf, and the quartered onion 15 minutes. Drain and cool in cold water. Remove any other remaining membranes. Cut the sweetbreads into halves lengthwise, then in half crosswise.

2. Blanch the salt pork 2 minutes in boiling water. Rinse under running water and dry. In a flameproof casserole, over medium-high heat, cook the salt pork until golden and crisp. Remove with a slotted spoon, drain on paper towels, and set aside.

3. Pour all but 3 tablespoons fat from the casserole. Lightly dredge the sweetbreads with flour. Brown in the hot fat, over medium heat, turning, 2 minutes. Sprinkle on the salt and pepper. Pour on the sherry and cook 1 minute.

4. Add all other ingredients except the butter. Cover, bring to a simmer on top of the stove, and transfer to a preheated 400° oven for 20 minutes. Remove cover and cook 10 minutes longer. Taste for seasoning.

5. Just before serving, stir in the butter and the reserved salt-pork cubes.

Serve with Potatoes Roquefort (p. 370).

Sweetbreads Florentine   SERVES 6

It is best to prepare the spinach and Mornay Sauce before cooking the sweetbreads.

3 pairs sweetbreads, soaked in cold water 2 hours
1 tablespoon lemon juice
1 bay leaf
1 onion, quartered
4 tablespoons (½ stick) unsalted butter
1 tablespoon olive oil
Salt and freshly ground black pepper to taste
Chopped Spinach (see below)
2 cups Mornay Sauce (see below)
3 tablespoons grated Gruyère cheese
3 tablespoons fine bread crumbs
3 tablespoons melted butter

1. Drain and rinse the sweetbreads and gently remove as much as possible of the membrane that encases them. Cook in simmering water to cover with the lemon juice, bay leaf, and quartered onion 15 minutes. Drain and cool in cold water and remove any remaining membrane, being careful not to separate the lobes. Cut the sweetbreads into ⅓-inch-thick slices.

2. In a large frying pan over medium-high heat, warm the butter and oil. Add the sweetbread slices and cook on both sides until just golden. Sprinkle with salt and pepper.

3. Arrange the spinach on the bottom of a large, shallow, buttered baking dish and cover with the slices of sweetbreads, overlapping if necessary. Spoon the Mornay Sauce over the sweetbreads (the sweetbreads should be just nicely coated). Sprinkle on the grated

cheese and the bread crumbs, and drizzle on the butter.

4. Transfer to a preheated 450° oven for 15 minutes, or until the top is golden.

Excellent with Jerry's Low-Calorie Mock French Fries (p. 339).

CHOPPED SPINACH

2 ten-ounce packages fresh spinach, well washed and trimmed,
   or 2 ten-ounce packages frozen chopped spinach
3 tablespoons unsalted butter
¼ teaspoon nutmeg
Salt and freshly ground black pepper to taste

1. If frozen spinach is used, just defrost, squeeze out water, and heat slightly with the butter, nutmeg, salt, and pepper. If fresh spinach is used (this is better), bring a large saucepan of water to a boil. Add the spinach, pushing it down into the water with a fork. Bring the water to a boil, cook 2 minutes, and immediately drain the spinach.

2. Cool slightly and squeeze all liquid from it (your hands are good for this). Finely chop the spinach and heat with the butter, nutmeg, salt, and pepper, just long enough to melt the butter.

MORNAY SAUCE   MAKES 2 CUPS

3 tablespoons unsalted butter
3 tablespoons flour
2 cups milk
1 cup grated Gruyère cheese
Salt and freshly ground black pepper to taste

1. In a saucepan, over medium heat, melt the butter. Add the flour and cook, stirring, till it forms a smooth, thick paste. Gradually add the milk and stir, cooking into a smooth, medium-thick sauce.

2. Add the cheese and cook, stirring, just until the cheese has melted. Taste for seasoning and add salt and pepper (the cheese may supply enough salt).

Sweetbread, Oyster, and Ham Pie

SERVES 4

2 pairs sweetbreads, soaked in water 2 hours
1 tablespoon lemon juice
1 onion, quartered
1 small celery stalk, sliced
⅛ teaspoon dried thyme
½ cup dry white wine
¼ cup flour
½ teaspoon hot Hungarian paprika
4 tablespoons (½ stick) unsalted butter
1 cup heavy cream
⅛ teaspoon nutmeg
2 ounces dry sherry
1 pint of oysters, with their liquor
1 cup cooked ham in ½-inch cubes
Salt to taste
Cream Cheese Pastry with Herbs (see below)
1 egg beaten with 1 tablespoon water (optional)

1. Drain and rinse the sweetbreads and remove as much of the membrane that encases them as possible. In a saucepan, combine the sweetbreads, lemon juice, onion, celery, thyme, wine, and enough water to cover. Bring to a boil, lower heat, and simmer 5 minutes. Drain, straining and reserving ¾ cup of the liquid.

2. Cool the sweetbreads in cold water and remove any membrane remaining. Cut sweetbreads into large cubes. Coat the cubes well with a mixture of the flour and paprika.

3. In a large frying pan, heat the butter. Add the sweetbreads and cook, turning them until they are evenly golden in color. Add the reserved liquid, cream, nutmeg, and sherry, and simmer, stirring gently, until the sauce is smooth and thick.

4. Heat the oysters in their liquor just until the edges curl. Drain and add them and the ham to the frying pan with the sweetbreads, blending. Taste and add salt if necessary. Spoon into a baking dish large enough to allow the contents to come just slightly below the

rim of the dish. Sauce should barely cover sweetbreads, oysters, and ham.

5. Roll out the pastry to a ¼-inch thickness (or slightly thinner). Cut into ½-inch-wide strips the width of the pie dish and arrange these over the pie, lattice-fashion, moistening the edges, sealing them to the rim of the dish, and trimming the ends. Cut small leaves (about 1 inch in diameter) from the remaining pastry, moisten bottoms with water, and arrange, pressing down over the rim of the dish and the ends of the lattice strips to produce an even border of leaves (or you can cut the extra pastry into long strips and cover the ends of the lattice strips and the rim of the dish with them to give the pie a neat, finished look). Brush with the egg yolk–water mixture.

6. Bake in a preheated 400° oven 15 minutes, or until nicely browned.

Idaho Potatoes Arrabbiata (p. 339) make this a menu to remember.

CREAM CHEESE PASTRY WITH HERBS

> *2 cups sifted all-purpose flour*
> *½ teaspoon salt*
> *⅛ teaspoon freshly ground black pepper*
> *1 teaspoon minced fresh parsley*
> *1 teaspoon minced fresh dill*
> *8 tablespoons (1 stick) butter*
> *3 ounces cream cheese*
> *3 tablespoons water, approximately*

1. Stir together the flour, salt, and pepper in a bowl. With a fork, stir the parsley and dill into the flour mixture.

2. Add the butter and cream cheese, and with a pastry blender, cut into small particles.

3. Mixing with a fork, sprinkle on just enough water to hold the dough together. Form into a ball. Seal tightly in plastic wrap and refrigerate for at least 1 hour before rolling out.

Trippa alla Romana

(Veal Tripe with Tomatoes and Peas)

Veal tripe is a delicacy that deserves popularity. If a taste for sushi and Cajun cuisine can be acquired, a passion for classic tripe can be developed as well.

3 pounds fresh white veal honeycomb tripe
2 tablespoons chopped salt pork
3 tablespoons olive oil
1 large lemon, cut into 1-inch slices
1-pound, 12-ounce can Italian-style tomatoes, put through a
*   blender or food processor to break up and evenly blend the*
*   tomatoes*
½ teaspoon dried oregano
2 bay leaves
Salt and freshly ground black pepper to taste
¼ teaspoon crushed red pepper
4 tablespoons fresh peas, partially cooked

1. Wash tripe well in four changes of fresh cold water.
2. Place in a pot, cover with 4 quarts water, and simmer over medium heat for 3 hours, or until the tripe is tender. Pour off the water twice during the cooking and replace with fresh hot water. When the tripe is tender, drain well and cut into ½- by 2-inch pieces.
3. In a deep heavy saucepan, sauté the salt pork in the olive oil until crisp.
4. Add the lemon slices, tomatoes, oregano, bay leaves, salt, black pepper, red pepper, and the sliced tripe.
5. Simmer over medium heat, uncovered, stirring occasionally, for 30 minutes, or until the sauce has thickened and the watery consistency has vanished.
6. Stir in the peas and simmer 10 minutes. Remove and discard the lemon slices and bay leaves. Serve the tripe in its sauce.

We like this with another Roman dish, Shoestring Potatoes and Vermicelli (p. 357).

PART TWO

POTATOES

Americans eat four times more potatoes than any other vegetable. The potato appears on menus more often than any other single food. Every year, Americans buy $2 billion worth of fresh and $2.5 billion of processed potatoes, a crop that is grown in every state. Per capita, we eat 122 pounds each year. Our total potato consumption is 30 billion pounds a year, 2 billion of which are French fries. We bake, hash, mash, mince, cream, fry, steam, boil, and roast potatoes. We add them to soups and chowders; combine them with cheese, butter, and milk as a main dish; and make croquettes, patties, and even pies out of them.

Perhaps one of the reasons the potato has maintained its popularity in these calorie-conscious times is that, ounce for ounce, it is one of the most healthful foods around—low-fat, high-carbohydrate, low-sodium, mineral-rich, and relatively low in calories. The Agricultural Research Service of the U.S. Department of Agriculture declared: "A diet of whole milk and potatoes would supply almost all of the food necessary for the maintenance of the human body."

In the chapters ahead are potato recipes to match any meat and please any appetite, from the finicky and fussy to the lusty: a challenge only the potato can meet.

8

Potato Salads

Chilled Mashed-Potato Salad
Curried Potato Salad
Dijon Potato Salad with Walnut Oil
Hot German Potato Salad with Bacon
Hot Potato Salad with Balsamic Vinegar
Persian Red Potato Salad with Yogurt Dressing
Red Potato Salad
Potato-Broccoli Salad
Potato-Cucumber Salad with Sour Cream and Dill Dressing
Potato-Stuffed Tomatoes
Potato Salad à la Lisbon

For many of us potato salads mean picnic fare. But potato salads can be as varied and innovative as the imagination of the person who prepares them. The potato salad is full of surprises. Most countries have their own versions, including India's curried salad, France's Dijon salad with walnut oil, Germany's hot potato salad with bacon. And how many of us have tried a Chilled Mashed-Potato Salad?

Chilled Mashed-Potato Salad   SERVES 4 TO 6

> 6 medium-sized potatoes (about 2 pounds)
> Salt and freshly ground black pepper to taste
> 3 tablespoons butter
> 3 tablespoons light cream
> 3 hard-boiled eggs, sliced
> ⅓ cup minced scallions (white part only)
> ½ cup minced celery, including some of the light-green leaves
> 1 cup tiny peas, cooked until tender-crisp
> Double Boiler Salad Dressing (see below)
> 12 large stuffed green olives, halved

1. Cook the potatoes in their skins in boiling water until just tender (do not overcook). Drain and dry over heat in the pan. Peel the potatoes and put through a potato ricer into a bowl. Season with salt and pepper. Add the butter and cream, and blend well. Cool to room temperature.
2. Chop 1½ cooked eggs and stir them, the scallions, the celery, and the peas into the potatoes. Add small amounts of salad dressing until desired consistency is reached. Avoid making mixture too moist. Mound into a serving dish and chill.
3. Before serving, garnish with the remaining egg slices and the olives.

DOUBLE BOILER SALAD DRESSING   MAKES ABOUT 1 CUP

> 2 teaspoons sugar
> 1½ teaspoons flour

1 teaspoon dry mustard
½ teaspoon salt
1 egg, beaten
⅓ cup cider vinegar
½ cup sour cream

1. In the top of a double boiler, over hot water, blend all the dry ingredients. Add the egg and mix well. Add the vinegar, a little at a time, then the sour cream, beating well so the mixture is smooth.
2. Cook over the simmering water, stirring, until the dressing is thick and smooth. Refrigerate.
This cold dressing is also excellent on crisp lettuce salads as well as on cold vegetables.

Curried Potato Salad

SERVES 4

5 medium-sized new potatoes (slightly under 2 pounds)
2 tablespoons butter
1 tablespoon olive oil
4 large scallions (all of the white part and some of the light-green
*   stems), chopped*
2 teaspoons curry powder
½ teaspoon ground allspice
¹⁄₁₆ teaspoon hot crushed red pepper flakes, or to taste (optional)
2 tablespoons chopped fresh parsley
1 cup sour cream
¼ cup white raisins, chopped
1 teaspoon salt

1. Cook the potatoes in their skins in boiling water until just tender. Do not overcook. Drain and dry over heat. Peel and dice them. Set aside.
2. In a large frying pan, heat the butter and oil and cook the scallions 1 minute, stirring. Add the curry powder, allspice, and potatoes, tossing well but gently. Add the red pepper flakes, parsley,

and sour cream blended with the raisins and salt, and mix well. Taste for seasoning. Transfer to a bowl.

3. Chill slightly. Just before serving, toss again and spoon into a serving bowl.

Dijon Potato Salad with Walnut Oil SERVES 6

With its unusual, delicate flavor, walnut oil is worth its somewhat expensive price. It is available in gourmet and specialty shops.

7 medium-sized new potatoes (slightly over 2 pounds)
½ cup walnut oil
2 garlic cloves, peeled and crushed
Salt and freshly ground black pepper to taste
¼ teaspoon sugar
2 tablespoons tarragon vinegar
1 tablespoon chopped chives
1 tablespoon chopped chervil
1 bunch watercress, cleaned, blemished parts discarded

1. Cook the potatoes in their skins in boiling water until just tender. Do not overcook. Drain and dry over heat in the pan. Peel the potatoes, or rub the skins off, and slice.

2. In a large bowl, mix all the ingredients except the potatoes and watercress. Add the potatoes, and with a wooden spoon and fork gently toss without breaking up the slices. Remove and discard the garlic. Taste for seasoning, adding more of any of the seasonings you desire.

Arrange the watercress on a serving dish. Spoon the potatoes onto the bed of watercress and serve at room temperature.

Hot German Potato Salad with Bacon SERVES 6

This dish has become a classic. It is so tasty that the Germans serve it with one of their many sausages as a meal. We like it with that mild veal sausage, Weisswurst.

7 medium-sized new potatoes (slightly over 2 pounds)
8 slices lean bacon, diced
1 medium-sized onion, finely chopped
2 tablespoons white vinegar
½ cup chicken broth
Salt and freshly ground black pepper to taste
½ teaspoon caraway seeds
2 tablespoons chopped parsley
4 radishes, sliced

1. Cook the potatoes in their skins in boiling water until just tender. Do not overcook. Drain and dry over heat in the pan. Peel and cut into ¼-inch-thick slices. Set aside and keep hot.
2. In a frying pan, over medium heat, cook the bacon until golden. Pour off all but 3 tablespoons fat. Add the onion and cook until soft and transparent. Do not brown. Add the vinegar, broth, salt, pepper, and caraway seeds. Simmer, stirring, for 1 minute.
3. Pour the bacon and onion mixture over the hot potatoes, mixing well but carefully. Taste for seasoning. Just before serving, sprinkle with parsley and garnish with the radish slices.

Hot Potato Salad with Balsamic Vinegar   SERVES 4 TO 6

6 medium-sized new potatoes (about 2 pounds)
2 garlic cloves, peeled
¼ cup fresh broadleaf parsley leaves
6 tablespoons olive oil
Salt and freshly ground black pepper to taste
2 tablespoons balsamic vinegar

1. Cook the potatoes in their skins in boiling water until just tender. Do not overcook. Drain and dry over heat in the pan. Peel and cut into small bite-sized cubes while still hot. Set aside and keep hot.
2. Place the garlic, parsley, and 2 tablespoons oil in a blender container or processor bowl and blend or process into a paste. Gradually blend in the remaining olive oil, salt, pepper, and bal-

samic vinegar. Add to the hot potatoes and mix well but carefully. Taste for seasoning. Serve warm.

Persian Red Potato Salad with Yogurt Dressing

SERVES 4 TO 6

12 small new red potatoes
6 small, tender carrots, scraped and shredded
1 small red onion, coarsely chopped
1 cup cooked small lima beans, or fava beans
Yogurt Dressing (see below)
Tender, crisp romaine lettuce leaves
1 ripe, firm avocado
2 tablespoons fresh lemon juice
Several large radishes, sliced

1. Cook the potatoes in their skins in boiling water until just tender. Do not overcook. Drain and dry over heat in the pan. Peel the potatoes and cut into bite-sized pieces. Cool slightly.
2. Add the carrots, onion, beans, and salad dressing to the potatoes, and mix well but gently. Taste for seasoning, adding more of any of the salad-dressing ingredients desired.
3. Line a salad bowl with the lettuce leaves and spoon in the salad. Just before serving, cut the avocado into strips lengthwise, mix with the lemon juice, and drain. Garnish the salad with the avocado and radish slices.

YOGURT DRESSING

MAKES ABOUT ⅔ CUP

⅓ cup olive oil
3 tablespoons yogurt
2 tablespoons tarragon vinegar
Pinch turmeric
Salt and freshly ground black pepper to taste

Combine all ingredients and blend well.

Red Potato Salad

14 small red potatoes in their skins (about 2 pounds)
3 cups chicken broth
¼ cup Chablis
1 tablespoon white wine vinegar
½ cup olive oil
1 garlic clove, minced
Salt and freshly ground black pepper to taste
2 tablespoons chopped fresh dill

1. Place the potatoes in a pan, pour in the chicken broth, cover and simmer over medium-low heat until the potatoes are tender.
2. Drain potatoes, cool just long enough to handle, and peel.
3. Slice them into a bowl while they are still warm. Pour on a mixture of the Chablis, vinegar, olive oil, garlic, salt, and pepper (amount depends on your taste) and mix well but gently. Taste for seasoning. Transfer to a serving bowl and sprinkle with dill.

Potato-Broccoli Salad

7 medium-sized new potatoes (slightly more than 2 pounds)
1 pound crisp, dark-green broccoli with tightly closed buds
5 tablespoons olive oil
3 tablespoons fresh lemon juice
1 two-ounce can anchovy fillets, drained
Freshly ground black pepper to taste
Salt (optional—anchovies may supply enough salt)

1. Cook the potatoes in their skins in boiling water until just tender. Do not overcook. Drain and dry over heat. Peel.
2. Peel the broccoli stems (if stems are very thick, divide by cutting from the floweret end to bottom of stem to make several ½-inch-thick stems). Cook the stems and flowerets in boiling water until crisp-tender (better underdone than overdone).

3. In a saucepan, over medium temperature, heat the oil, lemon juice, and anchovies, breaking up the fillets.

4. Cut the potatoes and broccoli into bite-sized cubes. Place in a bowl, pour the hot olive oil, lemon juice, and anchovy sauce over them. Sprinkle with pepper. Mix carefully but well. Taste, adding salt if necessary.

This can be served hot or cold. If served hot, keep the potatoes and broccoli warm to mix with the hot sauce. To serve cold, marinate in the sauce in the refrigerator. Remove from the refrigerator an hour before serving. The salad should not be too cold.

Potato-Cucumber Salad with Sour Cream and Dill Dressing

SERVES 6

7 medium-sized new potatoes (slightly over 2 pounds)
1 to 1½ cups Sour Cream and Dill Dressing (see below)
2 medium-sized, firm cucumbers, peeled, cut in half lengthwise
  (seeds removed and discarded), cut into ¼-inch-thick slices
Center leaves of Boston or romaine lettuce to line salad bowl
2 tablespoons chopped fresh dill

1. Cook the potatoes in their skins in boiling water until just tender. Do not overcook. Drain and dry over heat. Peel and slice while still warm.

2. In a large bowl, mix the warm potato slices with ½ cup of the dressing. Refrigerate 1 hour.

3. Add the cucumbers and ½ cup of the remaining dressing to the potatoes and blend well. Taste, adding more dressing if desired.

4. Line a salad bowl with the lettuce leaves, spoon in the potato-cucumber mixture, and sprinkle with dill. Serve chilled but not too cold.

SOUR CREAM AND DILL DRESSING   MAKES ABOUT 1½ CUPS

1½ cups sour cream
¼ cup chopped fresh dill

1 teaspoon minced onion
1/4 teaspoon sugar
1/4 teaspoon ground cumin
Salt to taste

Combine and blend well.

Potato-Stuffed Tomatoes

SERVES 6

This is an unusual and refreshing summer salad.

6 large, firm, ripe tomatoes
Salt and freshly ground black pepper to taste
4 medium-sized new potatoes (slightly more than a pound)
2 scallions (white part only), minced
1 cup Fontina cheese (or a cheese of your choice), in 1/2-inch
　cubes
1/2 cup mayonnaise
Pinch of cayenne
1/4 teaspoon grated lemon rind
1 tablespoon chopped fresh basil
Watercress, washed, bruised parts discarded

1. Cut a slice from the stem end of the tomatoes. Remove the seeds and the center pulp (leaving the pulp around the sides and bottom, as a substantial shell). Sprinkle the insides lightly with salt and pepper and invert to drain for 1 hour.
2. Cook the potatoes in their skins in boiling water until just tender. Do not overcook. Drain and dry over heat in the pan. Peel and dice. Cool.
3. In a bowl, combine and blend well the potatoes, scallions, cheese, and a mixture of the mayonnaise, cayenne, and lemon rind. Taste for seasoning.
4. Mound the potato salad in the tomato shells and dot with the basil. Serve on a bed of watercress.

Potato Salad à la Lisbon

SERVES 6 TO 8

7 medium-sized new potatoes (slightly more than 2 pounds)
¼ cup Madeira
2 tablespoons dry white wine
1 sweet Bermuda onion, sliced and separated into rings
½ cup Gruyère cheese slivers
3 small, tender celery hearts, finely sliced (about 2 cups)
1 tablespoon chopped fresh oregano, or 1 teaspoon dried
¼ cup chopped fresh mushrooms
1 cup Vinaigrette Sauce (see below)

1. Cook the potatoes in their skins in boiling water until just tender. Do not overcook. Drain and dry over heat. While they are still quite warm, peel and cut into ¼-inch-thick slices. Put the potatoes into a bowl and sprinkle with the Madeira and white wine, tossing gently. Marinate for 30 minutes. Pour off any excess wine in the bottom of the bowl.

2. Add to the potato bowl the onion rings, cheese, celery, oregano, and mushrooms. Add the Vinaigrette Sauce (amount depends upon your taste) and toss carefully but well.

VINAIGRETTE SAUCE

MAKES ABOUT 1 CUP

3 tablespoons wine vinegar
¾ cup olive oil
½ cup chopped fresh parsley
1 tablespoon capers, drained and chopped
½ teaspoon dry mustard
Salt and freshly ground black pepper to taste

Combine and blend.

9

Potato Specialties

Athenian Potato Soufflé
Vernon Jarratt's Ciapotta
Potato Balls Amandine
Potatoes and Spinach Cochin Style
Potatoes with Three Cheeses
Potato-Parsnip Custard
Red Potatoes with Quick Hollandaise Sauce
Potato Ragout
Spanish Garlic Potatoes
Stuffed Potato "Chops"
Spicy Pakistani Potatoes
Swiss Potato Balls
Swiss Potato Torte
Spanish Parsley Potatoes
Viennese Mustard Potatoes

The dictionary definition of special—"surpassing what is common or usual, exceptional"—could be the definition of the versatile potato itself. To accompany red meat, how about a soufflé, a torte, a custard, a ragout, potatoes Pakistani style, or a potato "chop"?

Athenian Potato Soufflé
SERVES 4 TO 6

4 large potatoes (about 2 pounds)
4 tablespoons (½ stick) unsalted butter
2 tablespoons yogurt
2 tablespoons heavy cream
½ cup finely crumbled feta cheese
Salt and freshly ground black pepper to taste
1 medium-sized white onion, minced
3 tablespoons minced broadleaf parsley
3 large egg yolks, beaten
½ teaspoon paprika
½ teaspoon cumin
3 egg whites, stiffly beaten
3 medium-sized ripe, firm tomatoes, peeled, seeded, and cut into
* 6 half-inch-thick slices (from the center), allowed to drain in a*
* large strainer for an hour to eliminate excess liquid*

1. Cook the potatoes in their skins in boiling water until tender. Drain and dry over heat in the pan. Peel the potatoes and put them through a ricer into a bowl. Beat in the butter, yogurt, cream, cheese, salt, pepper, onion, parsley, egg yolks, paprika, and cumin. Fold in the egg whites. Spoon the mixture into a buttered soufflé or baking dish.

2. Arrange the tomato slices in a border around the edge of the dish on top of the potato mixture, overlapping if necessary. Sprinkle with salt and pepper.

3. Bake, uncovered, in a preheated 350° oven for 40 minutes, or until well puffed and set.

Vernon Jarratt's Ciapotta

SERVES 4

(An Italian Potato, Tomato, and Onion Casserole)

This dish comes from our friend, the owner of Rome's famous George's restaurant. Mr. Jarratt remarks that this is a good dish if you and your guests are late in getting to the table, for it can be kept hot in a 250-degree oven without any loss of flavor. We serve it with broiled fat sausages and a glass of ale.

> 5 medium-sized potatoes (slightly less than 2 pounds), peeled and cut into ¼-inch-thick slices
> 4 tablespoons (½ stick) unsalted butter
> Salt and freshly ground black pepper to taste
> 4 medium-sized ripe, firm tomatoes, peeled and cut into ¼-inch-thick slices
> 4 medium-sized white onions, thinly sliced and separated into rings

1. Layer the bottom of a greased casserole with potato slices, dot with butter, and season with salt and pepper. Cover with a layer of tomatoes, then one of onion rings, dotting with butter and seasoning with salt and pepper. Continue the layering, buttering, and seasoning, ending with buttered potatoes.

2. Bake, uncovered, in a preheated 375° oven 45 minutes, or until the potatoes are tender.

Potato Balls Amandine

SERVES 6

(Potato and Mushroom Balls Coated with Almonds)

> 2 medium-sized firm mushrooms, chopped
> 1 tablespoon unsalted butter
> 3 cups Duchesse Potatoes (p. 290)
> 2 eggs, beaten
> 1½ cups finely chopped almonds, toasted until golden (this can be done on top of the stove over medium-low heat, carefully watched, stirring constantly)
> Vegetable oil for deep frying

1. Over medium-high heat, in a frying pan, cook the mushrooms in the butter 2 minutes, or until all the liquid has been exuded. Remove with a slotted spoon.

2. Combine the potatoes and mushrooms and blend well.

3. Form mixture into balls about 1 inch in diameter (or slightly larger or smaller if desired). Roll them in the beaten eggs and coat with the almonds.

4. Heat the oil to 375°. With a slotted spoon, lower the balls into the hot oil, a few at a time (do not crowd), and cook until golden brown. Drain on paper towels. Keep those that are finished in a 200° oven until all are cooked.

Potatoes and Spinach Cochin Style   SERVES 4 TO 6

These spicy boiled potatoes, served with spinach and yogurt, are popular in the Cochin area of India, where we first tasted them.

6 medium-sized potatoes (about 2 pounds)

2 ten-ounce packages of fresh spinach, or 2 ten-ounce packages frozen, chopped spinach, defrosted but not cooked

2 tablespoons vegetable oil

2 medium-sized onions, chopped

1 teaspoon grated fresh ginger

Crushed hot red pepper flakes to taste (1/8 teaspoon should be sufficient)

1/8 teaspoon cinnamon

1/4 teaspoon ground cardamom

Salt to taste

2 tablespoons water

1 cup yogurt

1 teaspoon chopped fresh mint

2 tablespoons fresh lime juice

1. Cook the potatoes in their skins in boiling water until tender but still slightly firm. Drain and dry over heat in the pan. Peel and cut into small bite-sized pieces. Set aside.

2. If fresh spinach is used, cook each package separately. Remove tough stems and blemished parts. Bring 4 quarts water to a boil. Add 1 package spinach, pushing the leaves down into the water with a large fork. When water comes to a boil again, cook the spinach 1 minute, then remove it with a fork and drain. Using the same water, cook the second package of spinach the same way. Thoroughly drain, or squeeze with your hands to remove all liquid, then chop the spinach. Set aside.

3. In a large saucepan, over medium temperature, heat the oil. Add the onions and ginger, and cook 3 minutes, or until the onion is soft. Do not brown. Stir in the pepper flakes, cinnamon, cardamom, and potatoes. Sprinkle with salt and add 2 tablespoons water and 2 tablespoons yogurt. Cook 5 minutes, turning.

4. Stir in the chopped spinach and cook 2 minutes, or until the spinach is heated through. Stir in the remaining yogurt, mint, and lime juice, blending well. Heat thoroughly and serve.

Potatoes with Three Cheeses SERVES 4 TO 6

6 medium-sized potatoes (about 2 pounds)
4 tablespoons (½ stick) soft, unsalted butter
¼ pound mozzarella, shredded
¼ pound Gouda cheese, shredded
Freshly ground black pepper to taste
Salt (optional—the cheese may supply enough)
⅓ cup grated Asiago or Parmesan cheese
⅓ cup fine bread crumbs
2 tablespoons melted butter

1. Cook the potatoes in their skins in boiling water until tender. Do not overcook. Drain and dry over heat in the pan.

2. While the potatoes are still warm, peel and cube them. In a large bowl, combine the potatoes, soft butter, mozzarella, Gouda, and a generous grinding of black pepper. Mix well, taste, and add salt if needed.

3. Spoon the potato mixture into a lightly buttered, large, shallow baking dish. Sprinkle the top with a mixture of the grated cheese and bread crumbs. Dribble the melted butter over the top and bake, uncovered, in a preheated 450° oven 10 minutes, or until heated through and golden on top.

Potato-Parsnip Custard

SERVES 4

3 large potatoes (about 1½ pounds), peeled and quartered
1 pound parsnips, scraped and quartered
3 eggs
1½ cups hot milk
2 tablespoons melted unsalted butter
2 tablespoons grated onion
Salt and freshly ground black pepper to taste

1. Cook the potatoes and parsnips separately in boiling salted water until tender. Drain and dry over heat in the pan. Mash well and mix together. Cool slightly.
2. In a large bowl, beat the eggs. Stir in the potato and parsnip mash, the milk, butter, onion, salt, and pepper. Pour into a shallow baking dish. Set in a pan of hot water (the water coming halfway up the sides of the baking dish) and bake in a preheated 350° oven 30 minutes, or until set. Do not overcook.

Red Potatoes with Quick Hollandaise Sauce

SERVES 6

18 to 24 small red new potatoes
½ teaspoon white pepper and salt to taste
4 tablespoons (½ stick) unsalted butter, melted
6 tablespoons minced parsley
Hollandaise Sauce (see below)

1. Cook the potatoes in boiling water in their skins until tender. Drain and dry over heat in the pan.

2. Remove a band of skin from the center third of the potatoes, leaving skin on both ends. Season with the pepper and salt. Dip in the butter and roll in the parsley.

3. Serve with Hollandaise Sauce spooned on top of the potatoes.

QUICK HOLLANDAISE SAUCE   MAKES ABOUT ⅔ CUP

> *3 large egg yolks*
> *2 tablespoons fresh lemon juice*
> *½ teaspoon salt*
> *Dash of cayenne (¹⁄₁₆ of a teaspoon), or to taste*
> *8 tablespoons (1 stick) unsalted butter, melted but not hot*

1. Combine the egg yolks, lemon juice, salt, and cayenne in a blender container. Run on high for a few seconds, then switch it off.

2. Turn the blender on high again, and slowly pour in the melted butter. Taste for seasoning, then blend on high for another second or two.

Potato Ragout   SERVES 4 TO 6

This tasty potato stew comes in several versions in France. We like it with veal or pork chops.

> *8 slices bacon, cut crosswise into ¼-inch pieces*
> *3 medium-sized white onions, coarsely chopped*
> *5 medium-sized potatoes (slightly less than 2 pounds), peeled*
>   *and cut into 1-inch cubes*
> *1 garlic clove, minced*
> *¼ teaspoon oregano*
> *¾ cup beef broth*
> *1 tablespoon cider vinegar*
> *Salt and freshly ground black pepper to taste*

1. In a saucepan large enough to hold all ingredients, over medium heat, cook the bacon until golden. Pour off all but 3 tablespoons fat. Add the onions to the saucepan and cook for 2 minutes, or

until soft. Do not brown. Stir in the potatoes, garlic, and oregano, and cook 1 minute, stirring.

2. Add the broth, vinegar, salt, and pepper. Cover and simmer 15 minutes, or until the potatoes are tender and the liquid absorbed. Taste for seasoning.

If the potatoes become tender before the liquid is absorbed, remove the cover, raise the heat, and cook it off quickly, but do not burn. If potatoes are not yet tender and liquid has been absorbed, add a small amount of hot broth (or water).

Spanish Garlic Potatoes   SERVES 4 TO 6

2 tablespoons olive oil
2 tablespoons unsalted butter
3 garlic cloves, minced
3 large potatoes (about 1½ pounds), peeled and cut into
  ¼-inch-thick slices
1 tablespoon chopped fresh chives
½ teaspoon savory
1 cup baby lima beans, fresh or frozen (if frozen, defrost but do
  not cook)
Salt and freshly ground black pepper to taste
¾ cup hot chicken broth
3 tablespoons finely chopped broadleaf parsley

1. In a large flameproof baking dish or casserole that will accommodate the potatoes in one overlapping layer, heat the oil and butter and cook the garlic about 1 minute. Do not brown. Arrange the potatoes overlapping in one layer over the garlic. Sprinkle with the chives and savory.

2. Distribute the limas over the potatoes, sprinkle with the salt and pepper, and pour the broth around the edge of the vegetables.

3. Cover tightly and bake in a preheated 325° oven 30 minutes, or until the potatoes and beans are tender.

Serve sprinkled with parsley.

Stuffed Potato "Chops"

SERVES 6

These "chops" go beautifully with a beef fillet.

8 medium-sized potatoes (slightly less than 3 pounds)
9 tablespoons butter (a stick, plus 1 tablespoon)
Salt and freshly ground black pepper to taste
½ teaspoon nutmeg
1 whole egg and 1 egg yolk, beaten together
4 shallots, chopped
4 chicken livers, coarsely chopped
3 medium-sized fresh mushrooms, chopped
½ teaspoon crushed leaf sage
2 tablespoons Marsala
2 teaspoons flour
1 tablespoon olive oil
Flour for dredging
2 eggs, beaten, for dipping the "chops"
Fine bread crumbs for dredging

1. Peel and cook the potatoes in boiling salted water until tender. Drain and dry thoroughly over heat in the pan. Mash or rice in a large bowl with 4 tablespoons butter, salt, pepper, and nutmeg. Blend well. Cool slightly. Beat in the egg and egg yolk. Cool thoroughly.

2. In a frying pan, heat 2 tablespoons butter. Add the shallots and cook 2 minutes, or until soft. Do not brown. Stir in the livers, mushrooms, and sage, and cook until the livers are brown on the outside but slightly pink inside. Stir in the Marsala, flour, salt, and pepper. Turn up the heat and cook quickly, stirring, until the liquid has evaporated. Set aside and cool.

3. Lightly flour your hands and make 12 chop-shaped patties from the potato mixture, about ½ inch thick, and lay them on a lightly floured board or wax paper. Divide the liver stuffing into 6 portions, put one in the center of six of the "chops," and flatten them a bit. Top each with a second chop and press the edges together to seal in the stuffing. Refrigerate 2 or 3 hours.

4. When ready to cook, heat the remaining butter and the oil in a frying pan large enough to accommodate all the chops (or use two frying pans, or cook in two batches). Dredge the stuffed chops lightly with flour, dip in the beaten egg, then dredge with bread crumbs and evenly brown on both sides, adding more butter and oil to the pan if needed.

Spicy Pakistani Potatoes

SERVES 4 TO 6

6 medium-sized potatoes (about 2 pounds)
1 tablespoon olive oil
½ teaspoon mustard seeds
1 small, hot green chili, seeded and finely chopped
1 small white onion, finely chopped
Salt to taste
½ teaspoon turmeric
¼ teaspoon ground coriander
¼ teaspoon cumin
¼ teaspoon black pepper
¼ teaspoon cardamom
*Pinch (approximately ¹⁄₁₆ teaspoon) each of cinnamon, ground
    cloves, nutmeg, and chili powder*
3 tablespoons fresh lime juice
2 tablespoons chopped fresh mint or parsley

1. Cook the potatoes in their skins in boiling water until tender. Drain and dry over heat in the pan. Peel and put through a ricer. Set aside.
2. In a saucepan, heat the oil. Stir in the mustard seeds, then the chili and onion, and cook 2 minutes, or until the onion is soft. Do not brown. Add the salt and spices, mixing well. Stir in the lime juice, then the potatoes, blending well. Taste for seasoning. Serve sprinkled with the mint or parsley.

Pass a bowl of curds or yogurt at the table, as the Pakistanis do, to cool this a bit.

Swiss Potato Balls

5 medium-sized potatoes (slightly under 2 pounds)
4 tablespoons (½ stick) soft unsalted butter
2 large eggs, each egg beaten separately (1 in a shallow dish for dipping the balls)
½ teaspoon ground mace
Salt and freshly ground black pepper to taste
¼ pound Gruyère cheese, cut into ½-inch cubes
Flour for dredging
Fine bread crumbs for dredging
Vegetable oil for deep frying

1. Cook the potatoes in their skins in boiling water until tender. Drain and dry over heat in the pan. Peel and, while still hot, put through a potato ricer into a bowl and blend in the butter. Cool slightly and add the beaten egg, the mace, salt, and pepper, blending well.
2. Shape into Ping-Pong–size balls, or smaller if desired. Push a cube of cheese into the center and reshape the ball to completely encase the cheese.
3. Roll the balls in flour, then dip into the beaten egg in the shallow dish. Coat well with bread crumbs and deep-fry, without crowding, until golden. Drain on paper towels and keep warm in a 200° oven until all are cooked.

Swiss Potato Torte

Here is a simple but dramatic potato torte that we first tasted with roast veal in Geneva, Switzerland.

2 cups shredded Swiss cheese
4 tablespoons (½ stick) hard unsalted butter, cut into tiny pieces
1½ teaspoons salt
½ teaspoon freshly ground black pepper
¼ teaspoon dried marjoram
6 medium-sized potatoes (about 2 pounds), peeled

1. In a bowl, combine and blend well with a fork the cheese, butter, salt, pepper, and marjoram, and refrigerate.

2. Thinly slice the potatoes and, if they are not to be cooked soon, set them in a bowl of cold water to prevent discoloring, but drain and dry them well on a kitchen towel before arranging in the baking dish.

3. Butter a 2-quart casserole or other baking dish. Place a layer of sliced potatoes in the dish and sprinkle lightly with the cheese mixture. Do not overlap the potatoes. The purpose is to arrange as many layers as possible. Repeat layers, ending with a sprinkling of the cheese mixture.

4. Bake, covered, in a preheated 400° oven for 1¼ hours or until the potatoes are tender.

5. Remove from the oven and let stand 10 minutes. With a spatula gently loosen the potatoes from the bottom and sides of the dish. Place a serving dish, larger than the baking dish, over and invert the potatoes onto it. Cut into wedges at the table.

Spanish Parsley Potatoes   SERVES 4 TO 6

3 tablespoons unsalted butter
1 tablespoon olive oil
1 medium-sized onion, chopped
1 medium-sized carrot, scraped and chopped
1 small green pepper, seeded, cored, and chopped
6 medium-sized potatoes (about 2 pounds), peeled and cut into ½-inch cubes
Salt and freshly ground black pepper to taste
⅛ teaspoon powdered saffron
¼ teaspoon dried oregano
1 small bay leaf
¾ cup chopped fresh broadleaf parsley
1 cup chicken broth
½ cup dry white wine

1. In a large frying pan or saucepan, over medium heat, heat the butter and oil. Add the onion, carrot, and green pepper, and cook 2 minutes, or until the onion is soft. Do not brown. Add the potatoes, salt, pepper, saffron, oregano, bay leaf, and parsley, and cook 2 minutes, stirring.

2. Mix the broth and wine together, and pour in enough of the mixture to not quite cover the potatoes. Cover the pan, lower the heat, and simmer 15 minutes (shaking the pan occasionally), or until the potatoes are almost tender but still slightly firm. If the liquid cooks off before the potatoes are tender, add a small amount of hot broth.

3. Remove the cover and the bay leaf, raise the heat, and cook off any excess liquid.

Viennese Mustard Potatoes
SERVES 4 TO 6

6 medium-sized potatoes (about 2 pounds)
6 tablespoons (¾ stick) unsalted butter
2 medium-sized white onions, chopped
3 tablespoons flour
2 cups chicken broth
Salt and freshly ground black pepper to taste
¼ cup Dijon mustard
¼ cup fine bread crumbs

1. Cook the potatoes in their skins in boiling water until tender. Drain and dry over heat in the pan. Peel and cut into ½-inch-thick slices.

2. In a saucepan, over medium heat, melt 3 tablespoons butter and cook the onions until soft. Do not brown. Stir in the flour, mixing well. Add the broth, a small amount at a time, stirring constantly. Season with salt and pepper. Bring to a simmer and cook, stirring, until slightly thickened. Add the mustard, blending well. Taste for seasoning.

3. Butter a large, shallow baking dish and arrange the potato slices,

overlapping, in a single layer. Pour the sauce evenly over the potatoes, sprinkle with the bread crumbs, and dot with the remaining butter.

4. Bake, uncovered, in a preheated 375° oven for 15 minutes, or until the sauce is bubbling and the potatoes are heated through.

10

Classic Potato Dishes

Bombay Puris
Berrichonne Potatoes
Château Potatoes
Duchesse Potatoes
Franconia Potatoes
French Creamed Potatoes
French Fries
German Potato Dumplings #1
German Potato Dumplings #2
Gnocchi
Hashed Brown Potatoes with Vinegar
John Petrokaitis's Potato Kugeli
Polish Potato Dumplings
Polish Potato Puffs
Pommes de Terre Cocotte,
à la Parisienne, and Noisette
Pommes de Terre Marguerite
Pommes de Terre Soufflées
Potatoes Anna
Potatoes à la Boulangère
Potatoes Dauphine
Potatoes Chantilly
Potatoes Dauphinoise

Potatoes Delmonico
Potato Fritters
Potatoes Lorette
Potatoes Lyonnaise
Potatoes à la Maître d'Hôtel
Potatoes Mont d'Or
Potatoes Macaire
Potatoes Nanette
Potatoes O'Brien
Potatoes Paillasson
Potatoes Rösti
Purée de Pommes de Terre
Potatoes Savoyarde
Potato-Chestnut Puree
Amsterdam Mashed Potatoes
with Sauerkraut
Potato-Cauliflower Puree
Mashed Potatoes with Scallions
Mashed Potatoes au Gratin
Rissolé Potatoes
Snow Potatoes
Straw or Matchstick Potatoes

The word "classic" in reference to food means "of the highest rank." Classic red meats call for classic potato dishes, such as Château, Duchesse, cocotte, à la Parisienne, noisette, dumplings, kugeli, puffs, gnocchi, hashed browns, Delmonico, and even French fries.

Bombay Puris

MAKES ABOUT 30

On our trips to India, we confess that one of the consistent visions that flashed before our eyes (as we jetted that 10,000 miles) was not the Taj Mahal but the golden, crisp, hot puffed potatoes called puris or pooris. An Indian classic, puris are as ubiquitous in that subcontinent as French fries are here in the States.

2 large Idaho baking potatoes (about 1 pound)
3 tablespoons melted butter
1 large white onion, minced
2 cups all-purpose flour
2/3 cup whole wheat flour
1/3 teaspoon freshly ground black pepper
1 1/2 teaspoons salt
1/3 teaspoon cardamom
1 teaspoon cumin
Yogurt
Vegetable oil for frying

1. Cook the potatoes in their skins in boiling water until tender. Drain and dry over heat in the pan. Peel and mash without adding liquid or seasoning.
2. In a large bowl, combine the potatoes, butter, and onion, and blend well. Stir in the flours sifted with the pepper, salt, cardamom, and cumin. Add small equal amounts of yogurt and water, working the mixture with your hands into a pliable dough. (You can use only water, but the yogurt makes the puris crisper.) When the dough

is pliable and elastic, cover with a damp kitchen towel and let it set in the bowl for 40 minutes.

3. On a lightly floured pastry board, with a lightly floured rolling pin, roll the dough into a ¼-inch-thick sheet. With a cookie cutter, cut into circles, 2½ inches in diameter. Deep-fry the puri circles, a few at a time, in oil heated to 360°, completely immersing them and gently pressing them down in the oil with a spatula. This helps puff them up. When puffed and golden, remove with a slotted spoon and drain on paper towels. Unlike ours, these glorified potato chips are served hot.

Berrichonne Potatoes
(Sautéed Potato Balls with Bacon and Onion)

SERVES 4 TO 6

> 6 medium-sized potatoes (about 2 pounds), peeled and cut into
>   balls with a melon scoop
> 5 tablespoons unsalted butter
> Salt to taste
> 4 slices bacon
> 2 medium-sized onions, chopped
> ⅛ teaspoon dried tarragon
> ⅛ teaspoon dried thyme
> ⅛ teaspoon dried chervil
> 1 tablespoon chopped fresh parsley

1. Cook the potato balls in boiling salted water for 6 minutes. Drain and dry in the pan over heat, shaking pan as they dry.
2. In a large frying pan, melt the butter over medium-high heat and cook the potatoes until they are golden, shaking the pan often so they do not stick. When tender, salt lightly.
3. In another frying pan, cook the bacon until crisp. Drain, dice, and reserve. Discard all but 2 tablespoons bacon fat. Add the onions to the pan and cook until soft. Do not brown.
4. Serve the potatoes on a warm serving dish, sprinkled with the onion, bacon, and herbs.

Château Potatoes

6 medium-sized Idaho baking potatoes (about 2 pounds)
1 teaspoon salt
8 tablespoons (1 stick) unsalted butter, melted

1. Peel the potatoes and quarter them. Trim the sharp edges so they look like small eggs. In a saucepan, cover the potatoes with cold water, add the salt, and bring to a boil. Remove and drain; then dry in the pan over heat.
2. In a single layer, arrange the potatoes in a shallow, buttered baking dish and dribble melted butter over them. Bake in a preheated 400° oven 15 minutes, turn, then cook another 15 minutes, or until tender and browned. Sprinkle lightly with salt.

Duchesse Potatoes
(Mashed Potato Mounds)

4 large potatoes (about 2 pounds)
1½ teaspoons salt
¼ teaspoon nutmeg
4 tablespoons (½ stick) soft, unsalted butter
1 whole egg and 2 egg yolks, beaten together
Glaze (see below)

1. Cook the potatoes in their skins in boiling water to cover until tender. Drain and dry over heat, then peel.
2. Put the potatoes through a potato ricer into a bowl. Add the salt, nutmeg, and butter. Beat until smooth.
3. Add the egg mixture to the potatoes and beat until smooth and fluffy.
4. Form into mounds of any shape or size (or pipe through a pastry bag) onto a buttered baking sheet and brush with glaze. Brown lightly in a preheated 425° oven, or place under the broiler until lightly browned.

PIPING DUCHESSE POTATOES INTO VARIOUS SHAPES

Experienced cooks pipe Duchesse Potatoes as a decorative border around various meat dishes. They also use the pastry bag and tube (we use a 14-inch bag with a large metal tube to fit) to form the potatoes into interesting and appealing shapes. After they have shaped the potatoes, they brush them with a glaze and bake them, uncovered, in a preheated 425° oven for 15 minutes, or until they are golden and the edges slightly brown. First, the glaze.

GLAZE

> *1 egg*
> *½ teaspoon salt*
> *1½ teaspoons olive oil*

In a bowl, combine all ingredients and blend thoroughly.

The French have names for the shapes: *petites pyramides*, which are mounded to form tiny pyramids; *rosettes doigts*, which are fingers about 3 inches long; *longues*, which look like 3-inch pieces of rope, achieved by twisting the piping nozzle as you squeeze the potato through it; *couronnes*, resembling small crowns, made by holding the bag and tube vertically and swirling the little rings directly onto a baking sheet. *Petits pains*, which look like small potato boats, are shaped by making a depression with the thumb; *galettes*, also hand-shaped, are round, flat cakes, usually with a pattern on top, a crisscross made with the blade of a table knife.

Working with a pastry bag and tube is fun-cooking, and you certainly do not have to stay with the classic shapes. The technique isn't difficult; a few trial runs will not only make you an expert but encourage you to serve potatoes with interesting and imaginative shapes.

Here is an abbreviated version of the piping system: Spoon the Duchesse Potatoes into the bag (amount depends upon the number of potato shapes you wish to make), packing the potatoes as close to the tube as possible so that you will not have to exert too much pressure to send them through in a controlled stream. Twist the empty portion of the bag and hold it in place with your left hand. Cradle the bag in your right hand, resting your index finger on the top of the tube. The right hand squeezes the bag and guides the stream of potatoes from the tube.

All the shapes should be piped directly onto a lightly floured baking sheet.

Franconia Potatoes

SERVES 6

(Browned Potatoes)

Like many of the classics, this dish is simplicity itself. It is served exclusively with roast meats.

> *6 medium-sized potatoes (about 2 pounds)*
> *Roast beef, pork, veal, or lamb*
> *Salt and freshly ground black pepper to taste*

1. Cook the potatoes in their skins in boiling water for 12 minutes. Drain and dry over heat in the pan. Peel the potatoes and cut into halves.

2. About 45 minutes before the roast is ready, circle it with the potatoes. At least three times during the final cooking of the meat, turn the potatoes and baste them well with the pan drippings. Season with salt and pepper.

If your roast is ready before the potatoes are, remove it and keep warm. The potatoes will be tender in a short time.

French Creamed Potatoes

SERVES 4 TO 6

This is a simple but delicious French classic. The French heavy cream, *crème fraîche*, is almost twice as heavy as our heavy cream, due to the fact that it is aged and slightly fermented. We can almost duplicate it by adding buttermilk to heavy cream as directed below.

2 teaspoons buttermilk
2 cups heavy cream
4 large potatoes (about 2 pounds)
1½ teaspoons salt
⅛ teaspoon mace

1. In a saucepan, combine and blend the buttermilk and cream. Heat until warm over low heat. Remove from heat and let stand until it thickens.
2. Cook the potatoes in their skins in boiling water until tender but still firm. Drain and dry over heat in the pan. Peel and cut into ¼-inch-thick slices. Sprinkle with salt and mace. Arrange in layers in a shallow baking dish or casserole. Heat the cream mixture and pour over the potatoes.
3. Cook, uncovered, in a preheated 300° oven, just until the potatoes have absorbed most of the cream.

Note: Watch carefully so the cream isn't absorbed too quickly and the potatoes don't become too brown. If necessary, cover lightly with foil. The French add more warm *crème fraîche* just before serving, but we like the potatoes just as they come out of the oven.

French Fries   SERVES 4

One of the tastiest of all potatoes, and one of the most popular, this is most certainly a classic. Created by the French many years ago, this supposedly simple dish has several vociferous schools of procedure: they should be thin and crisp; no, they should be thick and mealy; better still, a midway French Fry, not thin, not thick, crisp on the outside, mealy inside. Two things are certain: they shouldn't be soggy, and they should be piping hot and lightly salted. Various utensils exist to help produce perfect French Fries: cutters that quickly chop a batch into the proper size and mini-fryers, which save on time and oil.

We like French Fries thin, crisp, but still slightly mealy. Some believe that the potatoes should first be soaked in water. This method probably came into popularity some years ago when potatoes were stored for long periods and placing them in water soaked out the excess sugar that develops from overlong storage. Soaking is no longer necessary, nor does it aid in producing crisp fries. Use only the center parts of the potato. Firm, unblemished Idahos are best.

> *Crisco or other vegetable oil for deep frying*
> *4 large Idaho potatoes, peeled, cut (from the center) into*
> *   3-inch-long by ⅜-inch-thick strips, rinsed under cold water,*
> *   and dried thoroughly on kitchen or paper towels*
> *Salt*

1. Heat the fat to 365° and cook the thoroughly dried potatoes a layer at a time, without crowding in the fryer, for 15 to 20 minutes, or until tender and golden brown. Drain on paper towels. While cooking remaining potatoes, keep the cooked potatoes warm in a 200° oven.

2. Season with salt just before serving.

Note: If desired, potatoes can be cut somewhat thinner (¼ inch thick) or thicker (½ inch) and cooked a shorter time for the thinner and longer for the thicker.

DOUBLE FRYING

Double frying produces crispier potatoes.

1. Place 2 inches of oil in your fryer (or enough to come up to the oil line). Preheat 7 minutes (if you have a temperature control, it should be on medium or 325°) with the fry basket in for the last 3 minutes. A cold basket will quickly lower the temperature of the oil and disrupt timing. Lift the basket, place in the amount of potatoes that can be comfortably cooked at one time (about 1½ cups is right for each frying). Cook for 3 minutes. This will seal the potatoes. Drain on paper towels. Take the fryer off heat, or turn off. Cool the potatoes 20 minutes.

2. If you have a temperature control, set to 375°; if not, raise to

high, and heat the oil 10 minutes. Preheat the basket for a couple of minutes. Place the potatoes in the basket and cook a second time for 4 minutes, or until browned as desired. Immediately drain well on paper towels and serve, or keep warm in a 200° oven until all are cooked. Salt just before serving.

Potatoes may be held as long as 3 hours after first cooking.

German Potato Dumplings #1 SERVES 4 TO 6

German potato dumplings are classic in both versions — using cooked potatoes (this recipe) or using raw potatoes (see the following recipe). With any variety of potato dumpling, always cook one first to taste and see if your mixture is correct.

4 large Idaho baking potatoes (about 2 pounds)
¾ cup flour, approximately
2 eggs, beaten
1½ teaspoons salt
Croutons (optional)

1. Cook the potatoes in their skins in boiling water until tender; drain and dry over heat in the pan. Peel and rice. Set aside to cool.
2. In a bowl, combine and blend well the cooled potatoes, flour, eggs, and salt. Knead with your hands until you have a smooth, elastic dough. If the dough is too soft and moist, add more flour, a small amount at a time, until the consistency is right. Shape the dumplings into the size you desire (about 1¼ inches in diameter is a good size). Lower them with a slotted spoon into simmering salted water and cook 10 to 12 minutes. Do not crowd in the pot. Remove with the slotted spoon and drain well.

If you use croutons, mold the dumplings around the croutons before cooking. One crouton for small dumplings, 2 or 3 for larger ones. After cooking, using two forks, split the dumplings and serve them hot, drenched with melted butter and sprinkled with browned bread crumbs. Or serve with dishes such as stews with the sauce from the stew spooned over them.

German Potato Dumplings #2   SERVES 6

*4 large Idaho baking potatoes (about 2 pounds), peeled and
    grated raw into a bowl of cold water*
*2 large Idaho baking potatoes (about 1 pound), cooked in boil-
    ing water in their skins, drained, dried over heat, peeled, riced*
1 whole egg and 1 egg yolk, beaten together
1½ teaspoons salt
Flour
*15 (depending upon number of dumplings made) croutons,
    toasted*

1. Drain the grated potatoes thoroughly; then place in a kitchen
towel and wring out all moisture.
2. In a bowl, combine the dry raw potatoes, the riced potatoes,
the egg and egg yolk, and salt. With your hands, knead until you
have a smooth mass resembling dough. If too moist, add small
amounts of flour until you can work it into a non-sticky dough.
Form into small balls, pressing 1 crouton into the center of each
dumpling, then re-forming it around the crouton.
3. With a slotted spoon, lower dumplings into a large pot of simmering salted water and cook about 15 minutes. Cook a test dumpling first to test seasoning. Do not crowd dumplings in the pot of
water. Remove with a slotted spoon and drain well.
Serve the dumplings with hot melted butter sprinkled on top or
with the sauce from a stew.

Gnocchi   SERVES 8

These small Italian potato dumplings are nearly always served with melted
butter and cheese.

4 large potatoes (about 2 pounds)
Salt (1 teaspoon, plus 3 tablespoons)
1 whole egg and 2 egg yolks
1½ to 2 cups flour
6 quarts water

1 cup melted butter
1½ cups grated Asiago or Parmesan cheese

1. Cook the potatoes in their skins in boiling water until just tender. Do not overcook. Drain and dry over heat in the pan. Peel and put the potatoes through a potato ricer onto a lightly floured pastry board.
2. When the potatoes have cooled, make a well in the center. Add 1 teaspoon salt, the egg and egg yolks, and mix thoroughly. Work in 1½ cups flour, kneading into a dough. Add additional flour to make a firm, smooth dough that does not stick to your fingers.
3. Divide the dough into 6 parts and roll each into a long cylinder about ½ inch in diameter. Cut into 1-inch pieces. Gently press the center of each with your thumb. Do not allow them to touch each other.
4. Heat the water in a large pot to a simmer and add the 3 tablespoons salt. Cook the dumplings, a few at a time, in the simmering water about 5 minutes. They are ready when they rise to the surface. Remove with a slotted spoon, drain well, and arrange in a shallow baking dish so that they do not touch each other.
5. Spoon on some of the butter and sprinkle on some of the cheese. Place in a preheated 400° oven for 15 minutes, or until heated through. Serve with the remaining butter and cheese at the table.

Hashed Brown Potatoes with Vinegar   SERVES 6

The addition of vinegar in this recipe aids in browning and improves the flavor.

6 tablespoons unsalted butter
1 tablespoon white vinegar
6 medium-sized potatoes (about 2 pounds), peeled and cut into
  ¼-inch dice
Salt and freshly ground black pepper to taste

1. In a large frying pan, melt the butter over medium heat. Stir in

the vinegar. Add the potatoes and sprinkle with salt and pepper.

2. Cook, turning with a spatula, until the potatoes are the desired degree of crustiness and tenderness. Taste for seasoning.

We like ours very crusty and brown. Some prefer them more moist; it's all in the turning and timing.

John Petrokaitis's Potato Kugeli SERVES 6

6 medium-sized (about 2 pounds) Idaho potatoes
3 eggs, beaten
½ pound bacon, minced, sautéed until crisp, and drained on paper towels
1 medium-sized onion, minced
1 five-ounce can evaporated milk
Salt and freshly ground black pepper to taste

1. Peel and grate the potatoes into a bowl. Add the eggs, bacon, onion, milk, salt, and pepper, blending well.

2. Spoon into a casserole and bake, uncovered, in a preheated 350° oven 40 minutes, or until golden brown.

3. Test like a cake. If a toothpick or thin knife blade emerges clean, the kugeli is done.

Polish Potato Dumplings SERVES 4

3 medium-sized (about 1 pound) Idaho potatoes, peeled, cooked in boiling salted water until tender, dried over heat, and put through a potato ricer
1 egg, beaten
⅓ cup flour
2 tablespoons fine bread crumbs
1½ teaspoons salt
¼ teaspoon freshly ground black pepper
1 tablespoon minced parsley

1. In a large bowl, beat the potatoes and egg together. Then beat

in the flour, bread crumbs, salt, pepper, and parsley.

2. With lightly floured hands, shape into 1-inch balls.

3. Drop the dumplings atop the Perrys' Pork Stew (p. 165), cover, and simmer 15 minutes, or until a toothpick inserted comes out clean.

Note: These can be cooked on any type of stew.

Polish Potato Puffs SERVES 6

The Poles serve these with a mixture of sugar and sour cream.

> *7 medium-sized potatoes (slightly more than 2 pounds)*
> *2 tablespoons unsalted butter*
> *4 egg yolks*
> *1/8 teaspoon nutmeg*
> *4 tablespoons sour cream*
> *1 teaspoon sugar*
> *Salt to taste*
> *4 egg whites, stiffly beaten*
> *Vegetable oil for deep frying*

1. Cook the potatoes in their skins in boiling water until tender. Drain, dry over heat in the pan, cool slightly, and peel. Put the potatoes through a ricer into a bowl. Thoroughly blend in the butter, egg yolks (one at a time), nutmeg, sour cream, sugar, and salt. Fold in the egg whites.

2. Heat the oil in a deep fryer to 335°, or until a 1-inch bread cube browns in 40 seconds. Drop in spoonfuls of the potato mixture, a few at a time (they should not be crowded). They are cooked when they float to the surface and are puffed and evenly browned. Drain on paper towels.

Pommes de Terre Cocotte, à la Parisienne, and Noisette

These little potatoes are almost a duplicate of another classic, Rissolé, so check that recipe for amounts and procedure (p. 317). The difference is that Rissolé are boiled before browning in butter and Cocotte are sautéed raw in butter until golden. Traditionally, they are also shaped like olives and are sometimes referred to as "olive potatoes."

À la Parisienne are a perfect small ball shape (as are Rissolé). They are sautéed raw in butter and sprinkled with chopped parsley before serving. Sometimes the French sauté them in beef drippings.

Noisette are very small potato balls, the size of hazelnuts. They are also sautéed raw in butter, with much shaking of the pan.

The French insist that all three of these classics must be sautéed in "clarified" butter. Fine. But we do them in butter, period, and they are excellent—golden, soft, and delicious.

Note: We use a melon scoop to form these potatoes, and then, if necessary, a sharp knife to trim them into the size and shape desired.

Pommes de Terre Marguerite
(Baked Mashed Potatoes with Mushrooms)

SERVES 4

> 5 medium-sized potatoes (slightly less than 2 pounds), peeled and quartered
> 1 teaspoon salt
> 1 garlic clove, peeled and halved
> 5 tablespoons unsalted butter
> ¼ pound small firm mushrooms, sliced
> 1 egg yolk
> ¼ cup medium cream, or half-and-half
> 2 tablespoons chopped fresh parsley
> Paprika

1. In a saucepan, over medium heat, in 1 inch of water, cook the potatoes, tightly covered, with the salt and garlic until tender.
2. Meanwhile, in a frying pan, heat 2 tablespoons butter. Add the mushrooms and cook 1 minute over high heat. Set aside.
3. When the potatoes are tender, drain, discard the garlic, and dry the potatoes over heat in the pan. Put through a ricer and beat with an electric beater until fluffy. Beat in the remaining butter, the egg yolk, and the cream. Remove the mushrooms with a slotted

spoon and add them and the parsley to the potatoes. Mix well. Taste for seasoning.

4. Spoon into a buttered, shallow baking-serving dish. Bake in a preheated 375° oven 15 minutes, to heat through. Sprinkle lightly with paprika.

Note: This may be prepared early in the day, then warmed in a preheated 375° oven for 45 minutes, or until thoroughly heated.

Pommes de Terre Soufflées

Some of us may not consider this classic worth the effort or the gamble, for both are involved, as are patience, luck, and exactly the right potatoes, sliced precisely and cooked in hot oil at a specific temperature. But these potato "balloons" are real show-stoppers and will make your dinner a memorable one.

Suggestions: First, do not attempt this dish for the first time when you are expecting guests. Second, it helps to have two deep fryers (the mini-fryers work well if not overloaded) with temperature controls, or two deep saucepans and a deep-frying thermometer.

6 medium-sized, perfect, solid Idaho potatoes (about 2 pounds)
Vegetable oil for deep frying
Salt

1. Peel potatoes and cut them into rectangular lengthwise slices (there are excellent, inexpensive potato slicers on the market), 3 × 1½ × ⅛ inches. Trim the corners to look like a "flat football," as one chef put it. Place in ice water until chilled, then drain and dry very well on a cloth towel.

2. Heat the oil (enough to completely submerge several slices so they will not touch while cooking) to 285° in one fryer and to 400° in the other. The heat should be medium and constant in the first, high in the second fryer. Fry the slices in the lower heat for 3 minutes; then, with a slotted spoon, transfer to paper towels to drain and cool 5 minutes.

3. Place the cooked, cooled slices in the very hot oil. If all is working well, they will almost immediately puff into balloons. The extreme heat will have caused instant expansion, but the brown skins will not burst or even crack. As soon as they are brown, a matter of seconds, lift the slices out with a slotted spoon, or better still, take the wire cooking basket out and drain the potatoes on paper towels. Sprinkle with salt and serve immediately.

Note: The first cooking stage can be done hours ahead. Also, if the potato balloons collapse after the second cooking, as they are draining on paper towels, don't despair. Try cooking them again very briefly in the 400° oil just before serving. Usually they repuff.

Potatoes Anna   SERVES 6

Pommes Anna, thinly sliced potatoes baked with much melted butter and seasoned with pepper, is one of France's favorite dishes.

7 medium-sized potatoes (slightly more than 2 pounds), peeled,
*   cut into ⅛-inch-thick slices, and set in cold water for ½ hour*
12 tablespoons unsalted butter (1½ sticks), melted
Salt and freshly ground black pepper to taste

1. Drain and dry the potatoes with a kitchen towel.
2. Butter generously a deep glass or Pyrex casserole, 8 inches in diameter. Line the bottom with a circular layer of overlapping potato slices; do the same on the sides, forming a shell. Then layer remaining slices (they need not be so carefully arranged), spooning a little melted butter over each layer. Lightly salt and pepper the layers. The potatoes in the center will protrude above the slices arranged along the sides of the casserole, but will settle as they cook.
3. Bake, uncovered, in a preheated 400° oven 1¼ hours, or until the potatoes are tender and the slices lining the dish are very brown. (You will be able to see this through the glass dish.) Remove from the oven and let set for 10 minutes. Loosen the sides with a spatula and invert onto a hot serving dish. You will have a golden cake.

Potatoes à la Boulangère

(Potatoes and Onions Baked in Broth)

> *6 medium-sized potatoes (about 2 pounds)*
> *6 medium-sized onions*
> *Salt and freshly ground black pepper to taste*
> *½ teaspoon dried thyme*
> *1 cup hot beef broth*

1. Peel the potatoes and cut into ½-inch-thick slices. Peel the onions and cut into ¼-inch-thick slices.
2. Butter a baking dish and layer the potatoes and onions, sprinkling the thyme on the first layer of potatoes and sprinkling each layer of potatoes and onions with salt and pepper. The last layer should be potatoes. Use less salt if the broth is salty.
3. Heat the broth to a boil and pour around the edges of the vegetables. Cover and bake in a preheated 400° oven 20 minutes. Uncover and cook until the liquid has been absorbed, the potatoes are tender, and the top layer is golden.

Potatoes Dauphine

(Deep-Fried Puff Pastry and Mashed Potato Balls)

> *6 tablespoons unsalted butter*
> *1 cup water*
> *1½ teaspoons salt*
> *1¼ cups sifted all-purpose flour*
> *4 large eggs*
> *4 cups mashed potatoes, seasoned with salt and ½ teaspoon*
> *   mace*
> *Vegetable oil for deep frying*

1. In a deep saucepan, over medium heat, combine the butter, water, and salt. Bring to a boil and quickly stir in all the flour. Reduce the heat to low and cook, stirring, for 2 minutes, or until

the contents of the pan form a ball, pulling away from the side of the pan.

2. Transfer the paste to a bowl and cool for 15 minutes. Beat in the eggs, one at a time. (This is what the French call *pâte à choux*, a paste which is also used for cream puffs, éclairs, and profiteroles.) Add the mashed potatoes to the paste, blending well.

3. Heat the oil in a deep fryer and drop in the potato mixture, a tablespoonful at a time. Do not crowd the balls in the fryer. Cook until they are golden and drain well on paper towels. Keep warm in a 200° oven while the rest are cooking. Sprinkle with salt just before serving.

Potatoes Chantilly
(Mashed Potatoes with Cheese and Cream)

SERVES 4

> *½ cup heavy cream, stiffly whipped*
> *1 teaspoon salt*
> *⅓ cup grated Emmentaler cheese*
> *2½ cups mashed potatoes*

1. Blend the whipped cream, salt, and cheese.
2. Evenly mound the mashed potatoes in a baking dish, masking them with the whipped-cream mixture.
3. Bake, uncovered, in a preheated 400° oven until the cheese melts and the potato mound is golden brown.

Potatoes Dauphinoise
(Potato, Cheese, and Milk Casserole)

SERVES 4 TO 6

> *6 medium-sized potatoes (about 2 pounds)*
> *5 tablespoons butter*
> *1 garlic clove, peeled and crushed*
> *Salt and freshly ground black pepper to taste*
> *1 cup grated Gruyère cheese*

⅛ teaspoon nutmeg
1½ cups milk

1. Peel the potatoes and cut into ⅛-inch-thick slices. Soak in a bowl of cold water 1 hour.
2. Butter a shallow baking dish, using 2 tablespoons butter. Rub the buttered dish with the garlic clove.
3. Drain and dry the potatoes with a towel. Arrange half the potato slices in one layer, overlapping if necessary, on the bottom of the dish. Sprinkle with salt and pepper and half the cheese. Place the remaining slices on top of the first layer and sprinkle with salt and pepper.
4. Combine the nutmeg and milk and heat to a simmer. Pour the milk over the potatoes. Sprinkle with the remaining cheese and dot with the remaining butter.
5. Bake in a preheated 400° oven 45 minutes, or until the potatoes are tender, the milk absorbed, and the top golden. If the top starts to brown before the potatoes are cooked, cover loosely with aluminum foil.

Potatoes Delmonico   SERVES 6
(Potato, Egg, and Cheese Casserole)

6 medium-sized potatoes (about 2 pounds)
6 tablespoons unsalted butter
3 tablespoons flour
2 cups hot cream
Salt to taste
4 hard-boiled eggs, cut into ¼-inch-thick slices
5 tablespoons grated sharp Cheddar cheese
½ cup bread crumbs

1. Cook the potatoes in their skins in boiling water until just tender. Do not overcook. Drain and dry over heat in the pan. Peel the potatoes and cut into ¼-inch-thick slices.
2. In a saucepan, over medium heat, melt 4 tablespoons butter.

Add the flour and cook, stirring, into a smooth paste. Blend in the cream, stirring into a smooth, medium-thick sauce. Add the salt.

3. Butter a baking dish and alternate layers of potato slices and egg slices (bottom and top layers should be potatoes), masking each with the cream sauce and sprinkling with cheese, using all of the sauce and cheese. Sprinkle bread crumbs on top and dot with the remaining butter.

4. Bake, uncovered, in a preheated 350° oven 30 minutes, or until bubbling and browned.

Potato Fritters   SERVES 4

The French claim to have developed this classic fritter, and we don't doubt it. After they were pushed by Parmentier (who first ate them in a German prisoner-of-war camp) into an appreciation of potatoes, the French have indeed created marvelous dishes with them.

> 4 medium-sized potatoes (slightly over 1 pound), coarsely grated
>   and squeezed in a kitchen towel to dry
> 5 tablespoons flour
> 1½ teaspoons salt
> ½ teaspoon freshly ground black pepper
> 2 large eggs, lightly beaten
> 2 tablespoons vegetable oil
> Vegetable oil for frying

1. In a bowl, combine and blend well the potatoes, flour, salt, and pepper. Stir in the eggs and the 2 tablespoons vegetable oil, mixing thoroughly.

2. In a frying pan, heat ½ inch of oil. It is hot enough when a small amount of the mixture dropped into it instantly sizzles. Drop heaping teaspoonfuls of the mixture into the hot oil. Do not crowd. Taste one of the first fritters for seasoning. Stir mixture each time before dropping into the oil. When the bottoms of the fritters are crisply golden, turn and brown the other side. Drain on paper towels and serve immediately.

Note: This can be converted into another recipe by grating the potatoes more finely, then forming the fritters into small balls, deep-frying them, and draining them on paper towels.

Potatoes Lorette
(Deep-Fried Cheese Potato Balls)

SERVES 6

This classic is usually made with the addition of *pâte à choux* puff paste (see Potatoes Dauphine, p. 303). This version is simpler, and we think it's just as good.

> 6 medium-sized potatoes (about 2 pounds)
> 4 tablespoons (½ stick) unsalted butter
> ⅛ teaspoon nutmeg
> 1½ teaspoons salt
> ½ teaspoon freshly ground black pepper
> 1 cup grated Gruyère cheese
> 2 egg yolks
> 2 egg whites, stiffly beaten
> Vegetable oil for frying

1. Cook the potatoes in boiling water in their skins until tender. Drain and dry over heat in the pan. Cool slightly, peel, and rice them into a large bowl.
2. Beat the butter, nutmeg, salt, pepper, cheese, and the egg yolks, one yolk at a time, into the potatoes. Fold in the beaten whites.
3. In a deep frying pan or fryer, heat ¾ inch oil until a bread cube browns quickly. Using 2 teaspoons, scoop out a heaping spoonful of the mixture with one, and with the other push it off the filled spoon into the hot fat. Do not crowd in the pan. Cook until golden. Drain well on paper towels. Taste one of the first potato balls for seasoning. The cooked potatoes can be kept warm in a 200° oven while the rest are cooking, but serve as soon as all are cooked.
Note: Fat can spatter when the mixture is dropped into the hot oil, so caution is advised.

Potatoes Lyonnaise

SERVES 4 TO 6

(Potatoes and Onions Sautéed in Butter)

This dish can be prepared with either raw potato slices or potatoes slightly cooked in boiling water in their skins, and then peeled and sliced. Both are excellent and simple. We prefer working with the raw potatoes.

5 tablespoons unsalted butter
5 medium-sized potatoes (slightly less than 2 pounds), peeled and thinly sliced
Salt and freshly ground black pepper to taste
3 medium-sized white onions, thinly sliced

1. In a heavy-bottomed saucepan or heavy, deep frying pan, over low heat, melt 3 tablespoons butter and add the potatoes. Sprinkle with salt and pepper, and cook, covered, for 15 minutes, shaking the pot several times.
2. In another pan, heat the remaining butter and cook the onions for 2 minutes. Do not brown. Add the onions and the butter they cooked in to the potato pot, tossing them together. Cover and cook 10 minutes, or until the potatoes are tender. Taste for seasoning.

Potatoes à la Maître d'Hôtel

SERVES 6

(Potatoes in Broth and Cream)

6 medium-sized potatoes (about 2 pounds), peeled and halved
4 tablespoons (½ stick) unsalted butter
¼ teaspoon nutmeg
¹⁄₁₆ teaspoon cayenne, or to taste
Salt to taste
½ cup beef broth
About 2 cups hot cream
2 tablespoons finely chopped fresh parsley, chives, tarragon, thyme, or basil, or a combination of fresh herbs

1. Cook the potatoes 10 minutes in boiling salted water. Drain and

dry over heat in the pan. Cool slightly and cut into ¼-inch-thick slices.

2. Over medium heat, in a large frying pan, melt the butter. Add the potatoes, nutmeg, cayenne, salt, beef broth, and enough of the cream to just cover the potatoes. Bring to a boil, lower heat, cover and simmer 15 minutes, or until the potatoes are almost tender. Remove cover and cook until the sauce thickens. Taste for seasoning.

Transfer to a hot serving dish and sprinkle with the fresh herbs.

Potatoes Mont d'Or   SERVES 4 TO 6
(Potatoes Mashed with Eggs)

Some of the classics have slight variations, almost the same techniques but different cheeses and different methods of presentation.

> 5 medium-sized baking potatoes (slightly less than 2 pounds),
>   peeled and quartered
> Salt and freshly ground black pepper to taste
> ⅛ teaspoon mace
> 2 egg yolks
> ½ cup warm heavy cream
> 2 egg whites, stiffly beaten
> ½ cup grated Swiss cheese, Gruyère, or Gouda

1. Cook the potatoes in a small amount of boiling water until tender. Drain, dry over heat in the pan, then rice them into a bowl. With a whisk or beater, whip in the salt, pepper, mace, egg yolks, one yolk at a time, then the cream. Fold in the egg whites.

2. Butter an au gratin dish and spoon in the potato mixture, smoothing the top, cake-fashion. Sprinkle on the cheese.

3. Bake, uncovered, in a preheated 350° over 25 minutes, or until the cheese has melted and the top is golden. Place under the broiler for a minute or two until crusty brown, but watch carefully.

Potatoes Macaire

SERVES 6 TO 8

(Potato Patties Browned in Butter)

7 medium-sized Idaho potatoes (slightly more than 2 pounds)
7 tablespoons butter
Salt and freshly ground black pepper to taste

1. Bake the potatoes in a 400° oven 1 hour, or until tender.
2. Cut into halves, scoop out the pulp, and chop coarsely. Mix in 5 tablespoons butter and season to taste.
3. Form into 6 to 8 cakes or patties. In a large frying pan, over medium heat, melt the remaining butter and brown the cakes evenly on both sides. The outsides should be brown and crisp; the insides soft and mealy.

Potatoes Nanette

SERVES 6

(Baked Herbed Potato Slices)

5 tablespoons butter
2 tablespoons olive oil
6 medium-sized potatoes (about 2 pounds), peeled and cut into
   ¼-inch-thick slices
Salt and freshly ground black pepper to taste
1 tablespoon finely chopped fresh chives
2 tablespoons finely chopped fresh broadleaf parsley
¾ cup chicken broth

1. In a large frying pan, heat half the butter and oil. Cook the potatoes, 1 layer at a time. Sprinkle with salt and pepper, and cook until golden, turning, but do not cook until the potatoes are soft. Add more butter and oil as needed.
2. Arrange the potato slices, overlapping, in a shallow baking dish, sprinkle with the chives and parsley, and moisten with the chicken broth. Bake, uncovered, in a preheated 375° oven for 20 minutes, or until the potatoes are tender and the liquid absorbed.

Potatoes O'Brien

SERVES 4 TO 6

This dish, diced potatoes with peppers and onion, was once an Irish favorite in Dublin. Now it is world-famous.

2 tablespoons unsalted butter
1 small onion, finely chopped
1 small green pepper (seeds and white ribs removed and discarded), chopped
1 four-ounce can pimientos, drained and cut into strips
Vegetable oil
6 medium-sized potatoes (about 2 pounds), peeled and diced
Salt and freshly ground black pepper to taste

1. In a frying pan, over medium heat, melt the butter. Add the onion and green pepper, and cook until soft. Do not brown. Stir in the pimiento and set aside.
2. In a large frying pan, heat ½ inch of oil. Add the diced potatoes and cook until golden and tender, turning occasionally. Remove with a slotted spoon and drain on paper towels. Pour all oil from the pan.
3. Return the potatoes to the pan and sprinkle with salt and pepper. Add the onion and green pepper mixture and toss together over high heat for 1 minute, or until heated through. Taste for seasoning. Serve immediately.

Potatoes Paillasson

SERVES 4

(Julienne Potatoes Sautéed in Butter)

Rinsing these potatoes is very important. If they're not rinsed properly they will stick and be too glutinous.

5 medium-sized potatoes (slightly less than 2 pounds), peeled and cut julienne style
8 tablespoons (1 stick) butter
Salt to taste

1. Carefully rinse the potatoes in two changes of cold water. Wrap in a kitchen towel and squeeze very dry.

2. Using a heavy omelet or frying pan with a cover, over medium heat, melt 4 tablespoons butter. Add the potatoes and season with salt. Lower heat and cook, covered, 20 minutes, or until the bottom is crisply golden. Shake pan occasionally to help prevent sticking.

3. Flip the potatoes over. This is done by placing a plate larger than the pan over the top of the pan and inverting it so the potatoes fall out onto it, golden side up. If necessary, loosen potatoes with a spatula before turning out.

4. Before returning the potatoes to the pan, melt the remaining butter in the pan, then slide the potatoes back, golden side up. Cover and, over low heat, cook for another 15 minutes, or until golden on the bottom.

Potatoes Rösti   SERVES 6
(A Crisp Potato Cake in the Swiss Style)

6 medium-sized potatoes (about 2 pounds)
12 tablespoons unsalted butter (1½ sticks)
Salt and freshly ground black pepper to taste

1. Cook the potatoes in their skins in boiling water for 15 minutes. Cool. Peel and grate the potatoes on the medium blade of a hand grater (so they become thin strips ½ × 1½ inches).

2. Cook each grated potato separately, or make one large rösti. If you cook them separately, melt 2 tablespoons butter in a 6-inch frying pan over medium heat. Add the potato and mix it well with the butter, then season with salt and pepper. Lower heat and cook about 10 minutes, or until the bottom is golden. Shake the pan from time to time, so the potato doesn't stick. Place a plate larger than the frying pan over the pan and invert the pan so the potato cake falls out onto the plate, golden side up. Slide the potato back into the pan and brown the other side. Hold the cooked potatoes in a warm oven until all are cooked.

To make one large rösti, use a large frying pan and proceed as above, using all the potatoes and 8 tablespoons butter.

Purée de Pommes de Terre

SERVES 4 TO 6

(Mashed Potatoes)

Everyone prepares mashed potatoes his own way, but the French seem to make the best. We'll never forget one experience in Paris in the Berkeley Hotel, which has a small elegant restaurant. As we sometimes do in Europe, we decided to make luncheon rather substantial and late and skip dinner. So we ordered loin lamb chops, new peas cooked with lettuce, and mashed potatoes, Pommes Purée. It seemed mere minutes later that two waiters wheeled in a table. The thick lamb chops were in a chafing dish; the drained, boiled potatoes were in a copper pot. One waiter dried the potatoes in the pot over the flame of another chafing dish, then warmed cream over the same flame, while the second waiter mashed the potatoes in the copper pot, adding salt, butter, and grated nutmeg. When the first waiter had the cream slightly scalded, he took over, gradually adding the cream and vigorously whipping the potatoes until they resembled whipped cream. They were the best we have ever had, perhaps because of the respect shown the potato—and the showmanship.

We prefer to boil the potatoes in their skins to retain the nutrients, but the French don't, at least not in this recipe, which we asked for and promptly received.

> 5 medium-sized potatoes (slightly less than 2 pounds)
> 1½ teaspoons salt
> 5 tablespoons unsalted butter
> ½ cup medium cream, approximately, or half-and-half, heated
> ⅛ teaspoon nutmeg

1. Peel and cut each potato into 3 pieces. Place in a pan, cover with cold water, and add the salt. Bring to a boil; then simmer for 25 minutes, or until the potatoes are tender. Drain, and dry them in the pan over heat. Do not scorch.

2. Transfer to a bowl and mash with a potato masher, or put them through a ricer. Add the butter, whipping it in vigorously. Gradually add the cream, which has been heated almost to the scalding point, whipping as you add it. Add the nutmeg and whip until the potatoes are creamy, fluffy, and light.

Potatoes Savoyarde
(Potato Cheese Casserole)

Follow the recipe for Potatoes Dauphinoise (p. 304), substituting chicken broth for the milk. Use less salt, as the chicken broth may supply enough, but taste for seasoning and adjust accordingly.

Potato-Chestnut Puree   SERVES 6 TO 8

1 pound chestnuts
3 cups beef broth
3 garlic cloves, unpeeled
3 cups freshly cooked mashed potatoes
6 tablespoons soft unsalted butter
½ to ¾ cup heavy cream
Salt to taste
⅛ teaspoon mace
4 shallots, finely chopped

1. Slash the chestnuts in one or two places and roast them on a cookie sheet in a preheated 425° oven 8 minutes, or until the hulls crack. When cool enough to handle, peel off the outer shell and the inner layer of skin. In a saucepan simmer the chestnuts, broth, and garlic, covered, for 25 minutes, or until the chestnuts are tender and easily pierced with a fork. Drain, discard the garlic, and push them through a sieve, or puree them in a food processor or blender (don't overprocess, as they could become gummy).
2. Transfer the chestnut puree to a saucepan large enough to hold

all ingredients. Beat in the potatoes, 5 tablespoons butter, ½ cup cream, salt, and mace. Add more cream if the mixture seems too heavy. Taste for seasoning.

3. In a frying pan, over medium heat, cook the shallots in the remaining butter until soft. Do not brown. Cook the puree over low heat, stirring, until heated through. Blend in the shallots and serve immediately.

Amsterdam Mashed Potatoes with Sauerkraut   SERVES 6

This is a favorite all over Holland, but we understand that it originated in Amsterdam. It seems an unusual pairing, but it's delicious, especially with roast pork.

6 medium-sized potatoes (about 2 pounds), peeled and halved
1½ teaspoons salt
5 tablespoons unsalted butter
½ cup heavy cream, approximately
1 medium-sized onion, minced
1-pound can sauerkraut, well drained
1 cup water
Salt and freshly ground black pepper to taste

1. Cook the potatoes in boiling water until tender with the 1½ teaspoons salt added. Drain well, return to heat, and dry well, being careful not to burn. Put the potatoes through a ricer into a bowl. Beat in 3 tablespoons butter and enough of the cream to make the potatoes creamy and fluffy.

2. In a saucepan, over medium heat, melt the remaining butter and cook the onion until soft. Do not brown. Blend in the sauerkraut and water. Cover and simmer 35 minutes, stirring occasionally so the sauerkraut doesn't burn, adding small amounts of water if necessary. When all the water has cooked off and the sauerkraut is tender, blend it well with the mashed potatoes. Season with salt and pepper, and serve the potato-kraut very hot.

Potato-Cauliflower Puree

SERVES 6 TO 8

6 large potatoes (about 3 pounds)
1 medium-sized, firm white head of cauliflower, broken up into flowerets
6 tablespoons soft unsalted butter
Salt and freshly ground black pepper to taste
1/2 teaspoon mace
3/4 cup heavy cream, approximately
2 tablespoons chopped fresh parsley

1. Cook the potatoes in their skins in boiling water until tender. Drain and dry over heat in the pan.
2. Drop the cauliflower into a pan of boiling salted water and cook until tender, about 10 minutes. Drain and dry thoroughly in the pan over heat, being careful not to burn it.
3. Peel the potatoes and put them and the cauliflower through a potato ricer into a large warmed bowl. With an electric beater, beat in the butter, salt, pepper, mace, and enough of the cream to make a light but firm creamy mixture. It should not be too thin. Cook, stirring, over medium-low heat just long enough to heat through. Taste for seasoning.
Serve sprinkled with parsley.

Mashed Potatoes with Scallions

SERVES 4 TO 6

6 medium-sized potatoes (about 2 pounds), peeled
1 cup minced scallions (use some of the green ends)
6 tablespoons soft unsalted butter
1/4 teaspoon nutmeg
Salt and freshly ground black pepper to taste
3/4 cup cream, approximately, heated

1. Cook the potatoes in boiling salted water until tender. Drain and dry over heat in the pan.
2. In a frying pan cook the scallions over medium heat in 1 table-

spoon butter for 1 minute, or until soft. Do not brown.

3. Put the potatoes through a ricer into a large bowl. Mix in the remaining butter, scallions, nutmeg, salt and pepper, and enough cream to make the mixture light but not soupy. Whip well.

Mashed Potatoes au Gratin   SERVES 6

7 medium-sized potatoes (slightly over 2 pounds), peeled and
*   quartered*
6 tablespoons unsalted butter
Salt and freshly ground black pepper to taste
½ cup heavy cream, approximately
½ cup grated Asiago or Parmesan cheese
½ cup fine bread crumbs

1. Cook the potatoes in boiling salted water until tender. Do not overcook. Drain and dry over heat in the pan.

2. Put through a potato ricer into a bowl. Add the butter, salt, and pepper, and blend well. Gradually blend in the cream until you have the desired consistency. The mixture should not be too thin.

3. Spoon the potatoes into a shallow baking dish. Sprinkle evenly with a mixture of the cheese and bread crumbs. Bake in a preheated 400° oven until heated through and golden on top. Or, if the potatoes are very hot, place under a broiler until golden on top.

Rissolé Potatoes   SERVES 4

This French classic—small potato balls sautéed in butter—is one of our favorites.

5 medium-sized potatoes (slightly less than 2 pounds), peeled
*   and cut into small balls with a melon scoop*
5 tablespoons unsalted butter
1½ teaspoons salt

1. Cook the potatoes in boiling salted water for 7 minutes. Drain and dry well.

2. In a large frying pan, over medium-high heat, melt the butter, add the potatoes, and cook until they are an even golden-brown color, shaking the pan frequently so they don't stick. Season with salt and serve immediately.

Snow Potatoes

SERVES 4

5 medium-sized Idaho potatoes (slightly less than 2 pounds),
    peeled and each cut into 8 pieces
5 tablespoons butter
1½ teaspoons salt
Boiling water
Soft butter
Freshly ground black pepper to taste

1. In a deep, heavy-bottomed saucepan, place the potatoes, the 5 tablespoons butter, and the salt, and add boiling water to the depth of a quarter-inch. Cover tightly; cook over medium heat for 3 minutes. Remove cover and cook until all the water has evaporated and the potatoes are tender. (If the potatoes are not tender after the water has evaporated, add a small amount of boiling water and continue cooking until it cooks off.)

2. Put the potatoes through a ricer and serve immediately with a dollop of soft butter on top and a grating or two of black pepper.

Straw or Matchstick Potatoes

SERVES 4

4 medium-sized potatoes (slightly more than 1 pound), peeled
    and cut into long, thin sticks (about the size of a wooden
    matchstick)
Vegetable oil for deep frying
Salt

1. Soak the potato sticks in cold water for 1 hour. Drain and dry very well with a cloth towel.

2. Heat the oil in a deep fryer and cook the potatoes, a handful at a time in order not to crowd them, for about 4 minutes, or until they are golden brown. Drain on paper towels and keep those that are cooked warm in a 225° oven while the others are cooking.

3. When all have been cooked, sprinkle with salt and serve immediately.

11

Potato Partners

Accordion Potatoes
Au Gratin Potatoes and Carrots
Austrian Paprika Potatoes
Aunt Edie's Roasted Potatoes
Bacon-Flavored Roast Potatoes
Baked Potato Piroshki
Baked Parmesan Potato Fingers
Belgian Potatoes
Bogota Potatoes with Tomato-Cheese Sauce
Burgundian Potato-Leek Pie
Shirley Capp's au Gratin Potatoes
Shirley Capp's Potatoes, Beans, and Bacon
Caramelized Potatoes
Champagne Potatoes
Copenhagen Sugared Potatoes
Cottage Fried Potatoes
Creamed Potatoes with Fresh Peas
Creamed Potatoes au Gratin
Curried Potatoes and Peas
Fried Potatoes au Gratin
Czechoslovakian Potato Pudding
Antoine Gilly's Grandmother's Potatoes
Ichabod's Baked French-Fried Slices
Inca Spicy Potatoes with Cheese and Tomato
Idaho Potatoes Arrabbiata
Jerry's Low-Calorie Mock French Fries
Lemon Dill Potatoes

Lleela's Madras Potato, Onion, and Tomato Mix
Lleela's Potatoes with Yogurt
Paprika Creamed Potatoes
Polish Potatoes for Game Dishes
Peruvian Potatoes
Pommes de Terre Amandine
Potatoes with Anchovy Butter and Spinach
Potato-Carrot Pudding
Potato-Broccoli Pudding
Potato Cones with Mushroom Sauce
Potato Croquettes Stuffed with Salami and Cheese
Potatoes Parma
Potatoes Frigo
Potato and Leek Casserole
Potato Pudding for Roast Beef
Potatoes with Pizzaiola Sauce
Potatoes with Ricotta Cheese
Potato-Turnip Bake
Potatoes with Salt Pork
Sticky Potatoes
Saged Potatoes
Quick Potato Cake with Skins
Steamed Potatoes with Caraway Seeds
Shoestring Potatoes and Vermicelli
Swedish Anchovy Potatoes
Tiny New Potatoes alla Ralph Guidetti
Watercress Potato Soufflé
Wyoming Camp Potatoes

Accordion Potatoes

4 large, long Idaho baking potatoes (about 2 pounds), peeled
4 tablespoons (½ stick) soft unsalted butter
1 tablespoon olive oil
Salt and freshly ground black pepper to taste

1. Cut a thin slice from the bottom of each potato, lengthwise, so it will sit up and not roll over. One at a time, run a metal skewer a bit more than halfway down, lengthwise, through the potato. Using a sharp knife, cut straight down to the skewer, every ⅛ inch, so that you have about twenty or thirty deep gashes in the potato. Remove the skewer and rub the potato with a mixture of the butter and oil. (The remaining potatoes should be kept in cold water until you are ready to slice them, but dry each thoroughly before slicing.)
2. Set in a shallow pan and bake in a preheated 375° oven 40 minutes, or until the potatoes are golden and tender, at which time they will have opened up like accordions. Season with salt and pepper and serve immediately while still crisp.

Au Gratin Potatoes and Carrots

4 medium-sized carrots, scraped and cut into ¼-inch-thick slices
½ cup water
4 tablespoons (½ stick) unsalted butter
1 small onion, chopped
⅛ teaspoon dried thyme
1 teaspoon sugar
7 medium-sized potatoes (slightly over 2 pounds), peeled and
  cut into ⅛-inch-thick slices
Salt and freshly ground black pepper to taste
1 cup grated Swiss cheese (reserve ⅓ cup for the top)
1¾ cups medium cream, or half-and-half, heated to a simmer

1. In a saucepan, combine the carrots, water, 2 tablespoons butter, onion, thyme, and sugar. Simmer, covered, over medium heat for

10 minutes. If the liquid has not cooked off, remove the cover, raise the heat, and quickly cook it off, being careful that the carrots do not burn.

2. Butter a shallow baking dish. Arrange a layer of potato slices on the bottom; sprinkle lightly with salt, pepper, and cheese. Top with a skimpy layer of carrots, and continue making layers until all the potatoes, carrots, and ⅔ cup cheese are used, ending with a layer of potatoes.

3. Pour on the hot cream and sprinkle on the reserved ⅓ cup cheese. Dot with the remaining butter and bake in a preheated 325° oven 45 minutes, or until the potatoes are cooked, most of the cream is absorbed, and the top is golden. If the top begins to brown before the potatoes are tender, cover loosely with foil.

Austrian Paprika Potatoes

SERVES 6

6 medium-sized potatoes (about 2 pounds)
2 tablespoons unsalted butter
1 tablespoon olive oil
2 garlic cloves, minced
2 small green peppers, seeded, cored, and chopped
1 tablespoon Hungarian paprika
2 small, ripe tomatoes, peeled, seeded, and chopped
Salt and freshly ground black pepper to taste
½ teaspoon crushed caraway seeds
1 cup chicken broth

1. Cook the potatoes in their skins in boiling water until tender. Drain and dry over heat in the pan, then peel.

2. In a deep saucepan, heat the butter and oil, and cook the garlic 2 minutes, over medium heat. Do not brown. Add the peppers and cook 4 minutes. Stir in the paprika, blending well. Add the tomatoes, salt, pepper, caraway seeds, and chicken broth. Cover and simmer 15 minutes.

3. Cut the potatoes into ¼-inch-thick slices and add them to the saucepan with the sauce. Simmer, uncovered, for 5 minutes, or

until the potatoes are heated through, spooning sauce over them as they heat. Taste for seasoning.

Aunt Edie's Roasted Potatoes
SERVES 4 TO 6
From Barbara M. Valbona

> 4 medium-sized Idaho baking potatoes (slightly over 1 pound),
>   unpeeled
> 2 garlic cloves, minced
> 3 tablespoons vegetable oil
> Salt and freshly ground black pepper to taste
> 1½ teaspoons dried oregano
> 1 tablespoon Hungarian paprika

1. Scrub the potatoes, dry them, and cut them into eighths lengthwise.
2. Place in a large, shallow baking dish that will hold them in a single layer. Sprinkle with the remaining ingredients. With your hands, roll in *all* ingredients until the potatoes are thoroughly coated.
3. Bake in a preheated 400° oven 1 hour, or until the potatoes can be pierced easily with a fork.

Bacon-Flavored Roast Potatoes
SERVES 4 TO 6

> 4 large Idaho baking potatoes (about 2 pounds), cut lengthwise
>   into eighths, soaked for 1 hour in ice water, drained and
>   dried well between paper towels
> 1½ cups melted bacon fat (butter can be used, but bacon fat
>   is better)
> Salt (optional)

1. Dip the potatoes in the bacon fat and arrange in a large, shallow baking dish in a single layer without touching.
2. Cook, uncovered, in a preheated 400° oven 35 minutes, or until delicately browned and fork-tender. Turn occasionally for even

browning. Taste for seasoning and sprinkle on salt just before serving. The bacon fat may supply enough salt.

Baked Potato Piroshki
MAKES ABOUT 20

FILLING

> 3 cups mashed potatoes
> 1 egg, beaten
> Salt and freshly ground black pepper to taste
> 2 tablespoons butter
> 4 scallions (using part of the green ends along with all of the
>   white part), finely chopped
> 2 hard-boiled eggs, finely chopped

1. In a bowl, combine and mix well the potatoes, beaten egg, salt, and pepper. Set aside.
2. In a frying pan, over medium heat, melt the butter and cook the scallions 2 minutes, or until soft. Do not brown.
3. Add the scallions and hard-boiled eggs to the potato mixture and blend well. Taste for seasoning.

PASTRY

> 2 cups flour
> 1½ teaspoons salt
> ⅓ cup unsalted butter
> ⅓ cup Crisco or lard
> ½ cup grated sharp Cheddar cheese
> ⅓ cup cold water
> 1 egg yolk mixed with ¼ cup milk

1. In a bowl, combine and mix with a pastry blender the flour, salt, butter, Crisco, and cheese. Add the water and mix thoroughly with a fork. Divide and roll into 2 balls. Seal in plastic wrap and refrigerate until ready to roll out, taking the dough out of the refrigerator a half hour before using.
2. Roll dough out as thinly as possible on a floured board. Cut

into 3-inch (or larger, depending on your choice) circles. Place a tablespoonful of the filling just off center on each circle, moisten the edges with water, fold over and press the edges together with the tines of a fork or a pastry cutter. Prick top with a fork. Brush with the egg yolk and milk mixture. Place on a baking sheet and bake in a preheated 350° oven 20 minutes, or until golden brown.

Baked Parmesan Potato Fingers   SERVES 4

3 large potatoes (about 1½ pounds)
6 tablespoons olive oil
¼ teaspoon fresh garlic that has been put through a garlic press
⅔ cup grated Parmesan cheese
Salt to taste

1. Wash potatoes well. Cut, unpeeled, into strips slightly more than ½ inch thick. Set in a bowl of ice water for an hour. Drain and thoroughly dry.
2. In a bowl, toss the potatoes with a mixture of the olive oil and garlic until the fingers are coated.
3. Arrange in a single layer in a shallow baking dish. The fingers should not touch. Bake in a preheated 450° oven 15 minutes. Turn; bake another 15 minutes, or until the potatoes are tender and golden brown.
3. Remove from the oven, sprinkle with the cheese, and shake the dish to distribute the cheese evenly. Sprinkle with salt and serve immediately.

Belgian Potatoes   SERVES 6

5 tablespoons unsalted butter
6 medium-sized potatoes (about 2 pounds), peeled and
    quartered
¼ cup dry white wine
1 medium-sized onion, minced

Salt and freshly ground black pepper to taste
2 tablespoons chopped fresh parsley

1. In a heavy frying pan, melt the butter over medium heat. Add the potatoes, wine, onion, salt, and pepper.
2. Cover tightly and cook over low heat 45 minutes, or until the potatoes are fork-tender. Shake the pan from time to time. If the liquid should cook off before the potatoes are done, add a small amount of hot water. Sprinkle with parsley before serving.

Bogota Potatoes with Tomato-Cheese Sauce   SERVES 4 TO 6

6 medium-sized (about 2 pounds) potatoes, peeled
2 tablespoons butter
1 medium-sized onion, minced
4 large, ripe, firm tomatoes, peeled, seeded, and finely chopped
Salt to taste
¼ teaspoon (or to taste) cayenne
½ teaspoon turmeric
½ teaspoon ground cumin
¼ cup heavy cream
1 cup grated Edam or Gouda cheese (or a cheese of your
*   choice)*
1 tablespoon minced fresh coriander or parsley

1. Cook the potatoes in boiling salted water until tender. Drain and dry over heat in the pan.
2. While the potatoes are cooking, prepare the sauce. In a large frying pan, over medium heat, melt the butter. Add the onion and cook 2 minutes, or until soft. Do not brown. Stir in the tomatoes, salt, cayenne, turmeric, and cumin, cooking until the sauce is smooth and thick. Stir in the cream and cheese, and simmer, stirring, until the cheese has melted.
3. Cut the hot potatoes into thick slices and arrange them, slightly overlapping, on a large hot serving dish. Pour the sauce over them and sprinkle with the coriander or parsley.

Burgundian Potato-Leek Pie

This is especially good with perfectly cooked pink fillets of beef or a leg of lamb.

Pastry for a double-crust 10-inch pie (see below)

6 medium-sized potatoes (about 2 pounds), peeled and thinly sliced

4 medium-sized (about ¾ inch in diameter) leeks, using the white part and some of the light-green part, thoroughly washed and cut into ¼-inch-thick slices

7 tablespoons unsalted butter

2 garlic cloves, minced

Salt and freshly ground black pepper to taste

¼ teaspoon ground mace

⅔ cup heavy cream, at room temperature

1 small egg, beaten

1 teaspoon chopped fresh parsley

1. Make the pastry and refrigerate.

2. Place the potatoes in a saucepan, cover with water, and bring to a boil. Carefully stir the potatoes and cook 2 minutes, or until they can be pierced with a fork. Do not overcook. Remove before the slices begin to break up, and drain thoroughly. Cool slightly.

3. In the same saucepan, cook the leeks in 3 tablespoons butter for 5 minutes, or until soft. Do not brown. Drain, saving the butter they cooked in.

4. Divide the dough into two parts, one slightly larger than the other. Roll out the larger on a floured board and line the sides and bottom of a 10-inch pie plate, overhanging slightly. Arrange a layer of potato slices on the bottom and sprinkle with some garlic. Arrange a few slices of leeks on top. Sprinkle with salt, pepper, and mace, and dot with butter. Repeat layers until the potatoes, leeks, seasoning, and butter are used up. Spoon on the butter the leeks cooked in. Pour on ⅓ cup cream. Roll out the remaining dough. Moisten the edge of the bottom dough. Cover with the top dough and press, sealing the edge, and flute. Prick in several places with

a fork and cut a ½-inch hole in the center.

5. Bake in a preheated 400° oven 30 minutes, or until the top is golden. With a small funnel inserted into the opening in the center of the crust, slowly pour in a mixture of the egg, beaten with ⅓ cup cream and the parsley. Bake another 10 minutes. If the top starts to get too brown, cover lightly with aluminum foil and continue baking.

PASTRY

⅔ cup lard, or vegetable shortening (Crisco)
⅓ cup unsalted butter
3 cups flour sifted into a bowl, with 2 teaspoons salt
6 tablespoons water, approximately

With a pastry blender, blend half the shortening and butter with the flour until it has the consistency of coarse meal. Add remaining shortening and butter, and work until it has the consistency of tiny peas. Add just enough water to hold the mixture together, mixing with a fork. Seal in plastic wrap and refrigerate.

Shirley Capp's au Gratin Potatoes SERVES 4

Our friend is a noted cook in the Wingdale, New York, area.
The texture of the potatoes determines how much sauce is needed. If the potatoes are sticky, add more.

4 medium-sized (slightly over 1 pound) potatoes
1 tablespoon butter
1 tablespoon flour
1 cup milk
¼ pound very sharp Cheddar cheese, grated
Salt to taste
⅛ teaspoon cayenne, or to taste
Cream (optional)
⅓ cup bread crumbs

1. Peel the potatoes and cook in boiling salted water until tender

but not too soft. Drain, dry over heat in the pan, and cool. Mince the potatoes and place in a shallow buttered baking dish in a smooth layer.

2. In a saucepan, over medium heat, melt the butter, stir in the flour, blending until smooth, then gradually add the milk, stirring until it is smooth. Add three-quarters of the cheese and season with salt and cayenne, stirring and simmering into a smooth sauce.

3. Pour the sauce over the potatoes and mix in. If too thick, add a small amount of cream. Sprinkle with the remaining cheese and the bread crumbs, and bake in a preheated 375° oven 35 minutes, or until brown and bubbly.

Shirley Capp's Potatoes, Beans, and Bacon   SERVES 4 TO 6

You must have your own garden or know a specialty greengrocer for this recipe; you must use new potatoes, small as walnuts, and baby green beans, twice the thickness of matchsticks.

6 slices bacon
24 tiny new potatoes
1 pound baby green beans
Salt and freshly ground black pepper to taste

1. In a large frying pan or saucepan, cook the bacon over medium heat until crisp. Drain on paper towels and break into ¼-inch pieces. Set aside.

2. Wash the potatoes well, leaving most of the moisture on them. Place the potatoes in the pan with the bacon fat, cover, and cook for 7 minutes.

3. Rinse the green beans, leaving most of the moisture on them, and add them to the pan. Cover and cook over medium heat until potatoes and beans are tender and the beans still slightly crisp. If there is not enough moisture to cook them until tender, add small amounts of hot water.

4. Before serving, stir in the bacon and cook, covered, for 2 minutes. Taste for seasoning, then add salt and pepper. Serve with a slotted spoon.

Caramelized Potatoes

SERVES 4

8 small potatoes (about 1½ pounds), not too small but smaller
  than medium-sized potatoes
1 cup rich beef broth
¼ cup dark-brown sugar, loosely packed

1. Cook the potatoes in their skins in boiling water until tender. Drain and dry over heat in the pan, then peel.
2. Pour the broth into a saucepan and bring to a boil. Reduce heat so the broth barely simmers. Add the sugar, stirring until it has dissolved. Cook, stirring, until the liquid becomes thick and syrupy.
3. Add the potatoes to the syrupy beef broth, turning them until they are evenly coated. Serve them whole and hot from the saucepan with roasted meat.

Note: Most of us associate caramelizing potatoes with sweet potatoes (which aren't potatoes at all), coating them in a marmalade or sugared fruit sauce. Yet, caramelized potatoes are one of the delicacies of the table, excellent with all kinds of roast meats, especially with gigot, the tender leg of spring lamb cooked in the French fashion so that it slices pink. We like to surround the leg of lamb with these shiny golden beauties.

Champagne Potatoes

SERVES 4

5 medium-sized potatoes (slightly under 2 pounds), peeled and
  thinly sliced
2 medium-sized white onions, peeled and thinly sliced
Salt and freshly ground black pepper to taste
5 tablespoons unsalted butter
½ cup champagne
½ cup heavy cream
¼ cup bread crumbs
¼ cup grated Asiago or Parmesan cheese

1. Butter a 9-inch pie plate or shallow baking dish. Arrange a layer

of half the potatoes and onions, interlacing them. Season lightly with salt and pepper, and dot with 2 tablespoons butter. Arrange a second layer with the remaining potatoes and onions and pour a mixture of the champagne and cream over it. Sprinkle with salt and pepper, then with the bread crumbs and the cheese. Dot with the remaining butter.

2. Bake, uncovered, in a preheated 350° oven 45 minutes, or until the potatoes are tender and the top is golden. If the top starts browning before the potatoes are cooked, cover loosely with aluminum foil.

Copenhagen Sugared Potatoes   SERVES 4

16 small new potatoes (about 1½ pounds)
1½ tablespoons sugar
4 tablespoons (½ stick) unsalted butter
2 tablespoons warm water
¼ teaspoon salt (optional)
2 tablespoons minced parsley

1. Cook the potatoes in their skins in boiling water until tender. Drain and dry over heat in the pan, then peel.
2. Over medium heat, in a saucepan, lightly brown the sugar. Add the butter and water, blending well.
3. Add the potatoes, turning them to coat evenly, cooking and turning until they are sugar-browned. Taste for seasoning.
4. Sprinkle with the parsley.

Cottage Fried Potatoes   SERVES 4 TO 6

4 large Idaho potatoes (about 2 pounds)
4 tablespoons (½ stick) unsalted butter
1 tablespoon olive oil
Salt and freshly ground black pepper to taste

1. Cook the potatoes in their skins in boiling water until barely tender (they should be undercooked). Drain and dry over heat in the pan. Peel and cut into ½-inch-thick slices.

2. Heat the butter and oil in a large frying pan (you may have to have two fryings and more butter and oil) and, in single layers, brown the potatoes evenly, making them as crusty as you like. Shake the pan occasionally as they brown.

3. Season with salt and pepper.

Note: The potato slices should be crisp and brown on both sides, and soft and mealy inside.

Creamed Potatoes with Fresh Peas   SERVES 4

4 medium-sized potatoes (slightly over a pound)
1 pound young, fresh peas, shelled (about 1 cup, shelled) or 1
   cup frozen tiny peas
1 cup heavy cream
½ cup milk
Salt and freshly ground black pepper to taste
⅛ teaspoon mace
¼ teaspoon sugar

1. Cook the potatoes in their skins in boiling water until barely tender (do not overcook, as they will cook more later), drain and dry over heat in the pot. Peel and cut into ¼-inch-thick slices.

2. Cook the peas in boiling salted water until just about tender, and drain thoroughly. If using frozen peas, cook according to package directions, but undercook slightly.

3. In a rather large saucepan, combine the potatoes, cream, and milk. Bring to a boil, then reduce to a simmer. Season with salt, pepper, and mace. Sprinkle in the sugar and stir carefully, being careful not to break up the potatoes. Simmer 6 minutes.

4. Add the peas while the potatoes and sauce are still simmering. Cook 1 minute. Taste for seasoning.

Creamed Potatoes au Gratin

SERVES 4 TO 6

6 medium-sized potatoes (about 2 pounds)
Salt and freshly ground black pepper
1½ to 2 cups heavy cream, heated
⅔ cup grated Asiago or Parmesan cheese
¼ cup fine bread crumbs
3 tablespoons unsalted butter

1. Cook the potatoes in boiling water in their skins until just tender. Do not overcook. Drain and dry over heat in the pan. Peel and cut into ¼-inch-thick slices.

2. Arrange the potato slices in overlapping layers in a buttered, shallow baking dish. Sprinkle each layer lightly with salt and pepper.

3. Pour enough of the heavy cream over the potatoes to barely cover the top. Sprinkle the top with a mixture of the cheese and bread crumbs, and dot with butter.

4. Bake in a 400° oven until most of the cream has been absorbed and the top is golden.

Curried Potatoes and Peas

SERVES 6

6 medium-sized potatoes (about 2 pounds)
2 tablespoons olive oil
1 medium-sized onion, finely chopped
1 teaspoon curry powder, or to taste
1 teaspoon grated fresh ginger
½ cup tomato puree blended with ¼ cup water
10-ounce package frozen tiny peas, defrosted
Salt to taste
1 cup yogurt

1. Cook the potatoes in their skins in boiling water until tender. Drain and dry over heat in the pan. Peel and cut into small bite-sized pieces. Set aside.

2. In a large saucepan, heat the oil and cook the onion for 1 minute, or until soft. Do not brown. Stir in the curry powder and ginger. Cook 1 minute. Stir in the tomato puree and water mixture and simmer, uncovered, until it starts to thicken. Add the peas and simmer until the peas are tender-crisp. Add the potatoes, salt, and yogurt, and cook until heated through. Do not boil.

Fried Potatoes au Gratin

SERVES 6

6 tablespoons unsalted butter, or more
2 tablespoons olive oil, or more
6 medium-sized potatoes (about 2 pounds), peeled and cut into
   ¼-inch-thick slices
Salt and freshly ground black pepper to taste
1½ cups medium-thick Cream Sauce (see below)
2 tablespoons tomato puree
2 medium-sized, ripe, firm tomatoes, peeled, seeded, chopped,
   and drained in a sieve for ½ hour
¼ cup fine bread crumbs
¼ cup grated Asiago or Parmesan cheese

1. In a large frying pan, heat 2 tablespoons butter and 1 tablespoon olive oil. Fry the potatoes, one layer at a time, until tender and golden on both sides. Add more butter and oil as needed. Drain on paper towels.
2. Arrange the potato slices in two or three layers in a large, shallow baking dish and sprinkle each layer with salt and pepper.
3. Combine the Cream Sauce with the tomato puree and the drained tomatoes, and spoon over the top layer of potatoes. Sprinkle with the bread crumbs, then with the cheese. Dot with any remaining butter (if all the butter has been used to fry the potatoes, dot with 2 tablespoons butter).
4. Bake in a preheated 400° oven 25 minutes, or until the top is golden brown.

CREAM SAUCE   MAKES 1½ CUPS

3 tablespoons unsalted butter
3 tablespoons flour
1 cup milk
½ cup cream
Salt and freshly ground black pepper to taste
¼ teaspoon nutmeg

1. In a saucepan, over medium heat, melt the butter. Stir in the flour and cook, stirring, into a smooth paste.
2. Gradually add the milk and cook, stirring, until the sauce thickens. Add the cream, salt, pepper, and nutmeg, and cook into a medium-thick sauce.

Czechoslovakian Potato Pudding   SERVES 4 TO 6

4 large potatoes (about 2 pounds), peeled and coarsely grated
2 medium-sized white onions, finely grated
2 whole eggs, beaten with 1 egg yolk
2 tablespoons minced parsley
1½ teaspoons salt
½ teaspoon freshly ground black pepper
3 tablespoons unsalted butter, melted
1 tablespoon olive oil

1. Generously butter an 8-inch baking dish.
2. Place the grated potatoes in a sieve or strainer for 5 minutes to drain.
3. In a large bowl, combine and blend well the potatoes, onion, eggs with the egg yolk, parsley, salt, and pepper. Spoon the mixture into the baking dish and smooth the top. Drizzle a mixture of the melted butter and olive oil over the top.
4. Bake, uncovered, in a preheated 400° oven 1 hour, or until set and top is crusty and golden.

Antoine Gilly's Grandmother's Potatoes

1½-inch cube fatback, diced
2 medium-sized onions, sliced
1 garlic clove, peeled
½ cup tomato sauce (commercial or homemade)
⅓ cup dry white wine
2 sprigs parsley
1 bay leaf
⅛ teaspoon thyme
Salt and freshly ground black pepper to taste
5 medium-sized new red potatoes (less than 2 pounds), peeled
and cut into 1-inch cubes
3 ounces boiled ham, diced
1 tablespoon chopped fresh parsley

1. In a flameproof casserole, over medium-high heat, cook the fatback for 5 minutes. Add the onion and garlic, and cook until soft. Do not brown.
2. Stir in the tomato sauce and wine, then add the parsley sprigs, bay leaf, thyme, salt, and pepper. Bring to a boil and stir in the potatoes and ham, keeping on the boil. Cover and cook in a pre-heated 350° oven 35 minutes, or until the potatoes are tender.
3. Taste for seasoning. Discard the garlic, parsley sprigs, and bay leaf. Sprinkle with chopped parsley.

Ichabod's Baked French-Fried Slices

This dish, a specialty of Ichabod's Restaurant in Canton, Connecticut, is so delicious that some people go there just for the potatoes.

4 medium-sized Idaho baking potatoes (slightly more than 1
pound), scrubbed
Vegetable oil for deep frying
Salt and freshly ground black pepper to taste

1. Partially bake the potatoes in a preheated 400° oven about 25 to 30 minutes. They should still be firm, not soft.

2. In a large frying pan, over medium heat, heat 2 inches of oil until a cube of bread sizzles when dropped into it and quickly browns. Keep the oil at that heat.

3. Cut the unpeeled potatoes into ⅓-inch-thick slices. Fry the slices just until they crust and are golden. Drain on paper towels, season with salt and pepper, and serve immediately.

Inca Spicy Potatoes with Cheese and Tomato   SERVES 4 TO 6

Peru's Incas were the first to cultivate potatoes. Of the many imaginative ways they prepare them, this is one of our favorites.

6 medium-sized potatoes (about 2 pounds)
2 tablespoons unsalted butter
1 tablespoon olive oil
8 scallions (use all the white part and part of the green part), cut into ½-inch-thick pieces
3 ripe tomatoes, peeled, seeded, and chopped
½ teaspoon ground cumin
½ teaspoon ground coriander
1 teaspoon salt
¼ teaspoon freshly ground black pepper
1 cup grated Swiss cheese (Peruvians use queso blanco [white cheese], but any mild white cheese will do)

1. Cook the potatoes in their skins in boiling water until tender. Drain and dry over heat in the pan. Set aside and keep warm.

2. In a saucepan, heat the butter and oil over medium heat and cook the scallions 3 minutes. Do not brown. Stir in the tomatoes, cumin, coriander, salt, and pepper, and simmer 10 minutes, un-covered, or until the sauce thickens slightly. Taste for seasoning.

3. Add the cheese, stirring until it has melted.

4. Peel the warm potatoes and quarter them. Spoon the spicy tomato-cheese sauce (it should be very hot) over the potatoes.

Idaho Potatoes Arrabbiata

SERVES 4

(Spicy Potatoes Sautéed in Butter and Olive Oil)

In Italian, *arrabbiata* means "raging," which gives you an idea of how hot this dish is. If you want it less hot, reduce the amount of red pepper.

> *3 tablespoons unsalted butter*
> *3 tablespoons olive oil*
> *2 garlic cloves, minced*
> *4 medium-sized Idaho potatoes (slightly over 1 pound), peeled*
>   *and thinly sliced*
> *½ teaspoon oregano*
> *1 teaspoon crushed red pepper*
> *Salt to taste*

1. In a large frying pan, heat the butter and oil and cook the garlic for 1 minute.
2. Add the potatoes, oregano, and red pepper. Cook 5 minutes, then turn the potatoes. Cover and cook 5 minutes. Remove the cover and sprinkle with salt. Cook 10 minutes, turning the potatoes so they brown evenly. They should not be too crusty brown, but should be tender and mealy. If necessary, add more butter and oil.

Jerry's Low-Calorie Mock French Fries

SERVES 4 TO 6

Jerry, the brother-in-law of a chef friend in Wingdale, New York, prides himself, justifiably, on his potato cookery. Here's an easy dish with practically no calories: a baked potato that looks and tastes French-fried.

> *3 large Idaho baking potatoes (about 1½ pounds), scrubbed*
> *2 egg whites, beaten until frothy*
> *Salt to taste*

1. Cut each potato lengthwise into 8 pieces, then dry with a paper towel.
2. Dip the potato slices in the egg white to coat lightly. Place on a lightly oiled baking sheet, not touching, and sprinkle with salt.

3. Bake in a preheated 425° oven 40 minutes, or until golden-crisp and tender. Serve right from the oven.

Lemon Dill Potatoes

SERVES 6

24 very small new potatoes (about 2½ pounds)
3 tablespoons unsalted butter
3 tablespoons flour
½ cup milk
1 cup medium cream, or half-and-half
2 tablespoons fresh strained lemon juice
Salt and freshly ground black pepper to taste
2 tablespoons chopped fresh dill

1. Cook the potatoes in their skins in boiling water until tender; drain and dry over heat in the pan. Keep warm.
2. Make the sauce while the potatoes are cooking. In a saucepan, over medium heat, melt the butter. Add the flour and cook, stirring, into a smooth paste. Gradually add the milk and cream, stirring constantly, until the sauce is smooth and thick. Stir in the lemon juice, salt, and pepper.
3. Peel the potatoes while they are still warm. Pour the hot sauce over them; sprinkle with dill.

Lleela's Madras Potato, Onion, and Tomato Mix

SERVES 4 TO 6

3 tablespoons vegetable oil
2 medium-sized onions, chopped
1 garlic clove, chopped
6 medium-sized potatoes (about 2 pounds), peeled and cut
  into bite-sized cubes
3 medium-sized ripe, firm tomatoes, peeled, seeded, and
  chopped
Salt to taste

⅛ teaspoon (or to taste) crushed red pepper
½ teaspoon ground coriander
¼ teaspoon turmeric
1 teaspoon mustard seeds
2 tablespoons chopped fresh coriander leaves or parsley

1. In a large saucepan, heat 2 tablespoons oil. Add the onion and garlic, and cook 3 minutes, or until soft. Do not brown.
2. Add the potatoes, tomatoes, salt, red pepper, ground coriander, and turmeric. Simmer, covered, about 20 minutes, or until the potatoes are tender and the sauce has thickened. If the potatoes become tender before the sauce thickens, remove the cover, raise the heat, and cook off excess liquid, being careful that the sauce doesn't burn.
3. In a small frying pan, heat the remaining oil. Add the mustard seeds and cook until they pop. Stir them into the potato pan. Taste for seasoning.
4. Serve sprinkled with the fresh coriander or parsley.

Lleela's Potatoes with Yogurt   SERVES 4 TO 6

16 to 24 very small new potatoes (about 2 pounds)
2 tablespoons vegetable oil
3 tablespoons finely chopped green pepper
1 large garlic clove, minced
½ teaspoon turmeric
½ teaspoon ground cumin
¼ teaspoon mace
Salt to taste
1 cup yogurt
1 tablespoon currants, cooked in oil until puffed and golden
2 tablespoons coarsely chopped cashew nuts, cooked in oil until golden and crisp
2 tablespoons chopped fresh coriander or parsley

1. Cook the potatoes in their skins in boiling water until tender;

drain and dry over heat in the pan. Keep warm.

2. In a large saucepan, heat the oil and cook the pepper and garlic 1 minute. Stir in the turmeric, cumin, and mace. Cook 1 minute, stirring.

3. Peel the potatoes and stir them into the saucepan. Add the salt and cook 5 minutes, or until the potatoes are heated through.

4. Stir in the yogurt and heat 2 or 3 minutes, blending well. Do not boil. Taste for seasoning.

5. Just before serving, stir in the currants, cashews, and coriander or parsley.

Paprika Creamed Potatoes   SERVES 4 TO 6

6 tablespoons unsalted butter

1 tablespoon olive oil

6 medium-sized potatoes (about 2 pounds), peeled and cut into
  ¾-inch cubes

Salt to taste

2 scallions (use all the white part and the light-green part), finely
  chopped

1 cup sour cream

¼ cup heavy cream

1 teaspoon Hungarian paprika

1. In a large frying pan, heat the butter and oil. Add the potatoes, sprinkle on salt, and cook, covered, for 20 minutes, or until tender and golden. As the potatoes cook, shake the pan often to prevent them from sticking.

2. Stir in the scallions and cook 1 minute.

3. Add the sour cream mixed with the heavy cream and paprika, and blend well, but carefully, coating the potatoes. Heat through without boiling and serve.

Polish Potatoes for Game Dishes

SERVES 4

As the name indicates, the Poles use this unique preparation with duck, venison, rabbit, and other kinds of game. We also serve these potatoes with roast veal.

4 medium-sized baking potatoes (about 1⅓ pounds)
4 tablespoons (½ stick) unsalted butter
6 anchovies, drained, dried, and chopped
1 tablespoon chopped broadleaf parsley
1 tablespoon chopped fresh dill
1 generous tablespoon capers, rinsed, dried, and chopped
¼ teaspoon freshly ground black pepper
½ cup beef broth
Salt to taste (anchovies may supply enough salt)

1. Cook the potatoes in their skins in boiling water until they are just slightly undercooked. Drain, dry over heat in the pan, peel, and cut into slices slightly thicker than ¼ inch.
2. In a large frying pan, over medium heat, melt the butter and add the potatoes. Cook, turning with a spatula, until they are tender and golden.
3. In a bowl, combine and blend well the anchovies, parsley, dill, capers, pepper, and beef broth. Stir mixture into the potatoes, being careful not to break up the slices. Cook 2 minutes to heat through.
4. Taste for seasoning, adding salt if needed, and serve hot.

Peruvian Potatoes

SERVES 6 TO 8

6 large potatoes (about 3 pounds)
1 cup olive oil
2 medium-sized white onions, minced
Salt and freshly ground black pepper to taste
⅛ teaspoon cayenne, or to taste
½ cup fresh lime juice

1. Cook the potatoes in their skins in boiling water until tender. Drain, dry over heat in the pan, then peel. Put them through a potato ricer into a bowl and puree with an electric beater (do not use a food processor, as it can make them gummy).

2. In another bowl, combine and blend well the oil, onions, salt, pepper, cayenne, and lime juice. Beat this sauce, a tablespoonful at a time, into the potato puree, until the consistency and flavor are right for your taste. Serve at room temperature.

Pommes de Terre Amandine
(Potato Croquettes with Almonds)

SERVES 4

5 medium-sized potatoes (slightly less than 2 pounds)
3 eggs
3 tablespoons soft unsalted butter
¼ teaspoon dried tarragon
Salt and freshly ground black pepper to taste
Flour for dredging
1 cup fine bread crumbs
1 cup finely ground almonds
Vegetable oil for deep frying

1. Peel the potatoes and cook them in boiling salted water until tender. Drain and dry over heat in the pot, then mash or put through a ricer.

2. In a bowl, lightly beat 1 whole egg and 1 egg yolk (save the white). Add the potatoes, butter, tarragon, salt, and pepper, and blend well.

3. Shape the mixture into croquettes (as large or small as you like). Refrigerate for 2 hours.

4. In a shallow bowl, beat the remaining eggs with the reserved egg white. Dredge the croquettes with the flour. Dip them into the beaten egg, then dredge with a mixture of the bread crumbs and almonds.

5. Deep-fry in 375° oil about 5 minutes, or until golden brown.

Do not crowd while frying. Cook three or four at a time, draining them on paper towels, and keep warm in a 200° oven while the rest are cooking.

Potatoes with Anchovy Butter and Spinach SERVES 4 TO 6

2 ten-ounce packages of fresh spinach or 2 ten-ounce packages of frozen leaf spinach (if frozen, precook only until the leaves separate)
4 medium-sized potatoes (slightly more than 1 pound)
6 anchovy fillets, drained and mashed
4 tablespoons (½ stick) unsalted butter
Freshly ground black pepper to taste
1 cup grated Gruyère cheese
3 tablespoons fine bread crumbs
2 tablespoons unsalted butter

1. If fresh spinach is used, cook each package separately. First remove tough stems and any bruised parts. Bring 4 quarts of water to a boil. Add one package of the spinach, pushing it down into the water with a large fork. When the water returns to the boil, cook the spinach for 1 minute, then remove with a fork and drain well. Using the same water, cook the remaining package of spinach the same way and drain thoroughly. Set aside.

2. Cook the potatoes in their skins in boiling water until tender. Drain and dry over heat in the pan. Peel and cut into ¼-inch-thick slices. Arrange half the potato slices on the bottom of a buttered, shallow baking dish. Dot with half the anchovies blended into half the butter. Sprinkle with pepper. Arrange half the spinach over the potatoes and sprinkle with half the cheese. Repeat, ending with cheese. Sprinkle the bread crumbs over the top layer of cheese and dot with the butter. Bake in a preheated 400° oven for 15 minutes, or until heated through and golden brown on top.

Note: The leafy part of Swiss chard can be substituted for the spinach, but it should be precooked a few minutes longer.

Potato-Carrot Pudding

SERVES 6

4 medium-sized carrots, scraped and grated
1 cup milk
5 medium-sized potatoes (slightly less than 2 pounds), peeled
  and grated
⅓ cup fine cracker crumbs
1½ teaspoons salt
¼ teaspoon cayenne
5 tablespoons soft unsalted butter
3 egg yolks, beaten
3 egg whites, stiffly beaten

1. Simmer the carrots in the milk for 10 minutes.
2. In a bowl, mix and blend well the carrots, the milk they cooked in, the potatoes, cracker crumbs, salt, cayenne, and butter. Blend in the egg yolks and fold in the egg whites.
3. Pour into a buttered 1½-quart baking dish and bake in a pre-heated 375° oven 45 minutes, or until set and golden on top.
Note: As you grate the potatoes, put them in a bowl of cold water to prevent discoloring. Drain them well before mixing with other ingredients.

Potato-Broccoli Pudding

SERVES 4

3 medium-sized potatoes (about 1 pound)
1 bunch of broccoli (about 1½ pounds)
2 tablespoons butter
1½ cups chopped scallions, or 2 medium-sized white onions,
  chopped
2 eggs
1 tablespoon fresh lemon juice
Salt and freshly ground black pepper to taste
1 cup grated sharp Cheddar cheese, or a cheese of your choice

1. Cook the potatoes in boiling water in their skins until tender.

Drain and dry over heat in the pan. Peel and put them through a potato ricer. Set aside.

2. Separate the broccoli; peel the stalks and cut into quarters or halves. Cook the flowerets and stalks, covered, in a small amount of boiling salted water until tender-crisp (more crisp than tender). Drain well and set aside.

3. Melt the butter in a frying pan over medium heat. Add the scallions (or onions) and cook until soft. Do not brown. Set aside.

4. Place the eggs, lemon juice, salt, and pepper and ½ cup of the cheese in a blender container or food processor bowl and blend (or process) for 10 seconds. Add the broccoli, potatoes, and scallions and process or blend for 15 seconds, or until the broccoli is finely chopped but not pureed. Taste for seasoning.

5. Pour into a buttered baking dish. Sprinkle the remaining cheese on top. Bake in a preheated 350° oven 30 minutes, or until just set and golden on top. Do not overcook.

Potato Cones with Mushroom Sauce   SERVES 4 TO 6

6 medium-sized potatoes (about 2 pounds)
5 tablespoons unsalted butter
2 egg yolks, beaten
Salt and freshly ground black pepper to taste
¼ teaspoon nutmeg
½ cup fine bread crumbs
Paprika
½ pound firm mushrooms, thinly sliced
1 teaspoon cornstarch mixed with 1 tablespoon water
1 cup heavy cream
1 tablespoon finely chopped fresh parsley
1 teaspoon fresh lemon juice

1. Peel the potatoes and cook them in boiling salted water until tender. Drain and dry over heat in the pot; then mash or rice them

in a bowl. Combine and blend well the potatoes, 2 tablespoons butter, the egg yolks, salt, pepper, and nutmeg. Cool.

2. Make cone-shaped mounds (about ⅓ cup of the mixture for each), shaping them with your hands or using a pastry bag, and place them on a buttered baking sheet. Sprinkle with the bread crumbs and paprika. Bake in a preheated 400° oven 15 minutes, or until golden. While the cones are baking, make the sauce.

3. In a frying pan or saucepan, over medium-high heat, melt the remaining butter. Add the mushrooms and cook 3 minutes. Remove with a slotted spoon and set aside. Mix the cornstarch and water mixture with the cream. Stir it into the pan the mushrooms cooked in, mixing well.

4. Return the mushrooms to the pan; add the parsley, lemon juice, salt, and pepper. Simmer just long enough for the sauce to thicken. Serve the cones on top of the sauce, with additional sauce on the side.

Potato Croquettes Stuffed with Salami and Cheese

SERVES 4 TO 6

4 large potatoes (about 2 pounds)
6 tablespoons soft unsalted butter
¼ cup grated Asiago or Parmesan cheese
Salt and freshly ground black pepper to taste
2 egg yolks, beaten
1 cup Gruyère cheese, cut into ¼-inch cubes
½ cup finely chopped salami
2 tablespoons minced parsley
Flour for dredging
2 eggs, beaten in a shallow bowl
Fine bread crumbs for dredging
Vegetable oil for deep frying

1. Peel and cook the potatoes in boiling salted water until just tender. Drain and dry over heat in the pan. Rice and return to the

pan to dry further, being careful not to burn them. Cool slightly. Stir in the butter, grated cheese, salt, pepper, and egg yolks.

2. Blend well the Gruyère cheese, salami, and parsley.

3. Spoon out mounds (about ⅓ cup) of the potato mixture onto a board. Place a mound in your hand, flatten it, and push a portion of the salami mixture in the center. Then enclose it with the potato mixture. Continue until you have used all the potatoes and the filling.

4. Dredge the croquettes with flour; dip in the beaten eggs and dredge with bread crumbs. Refrigerate 1 hour.

5. Deep-fry a few at a time in 375° vegetable oil until golden brown. Drain on paper towels.

Potatoes Parma
SERVES 4 TO 6

(Potato Fingers with Cheese and Spices)

> *5 medium-sized potatoes (slightly under 2 pounds), peeled and*
> * quartered*
> *7 tablespoons (slightly under 1 stick) unsalted butter*
> *Salt and freshly ground black pepper to taste*
> *¼ teaspoon nutmeg*
> *1 tablespoon minced fresh chives*
> *½ cup grated Asiago or Parmesan cheese*
> *1 whole egg, beaten*
> *Flour for dusting*
> *2 eggs, beaten (for dipping)*
> *Fine bread crumbs for dredging*
> *1 tablespoon olive oil*

1. Cook the potatoes in boiling salted water until tender. Drain and dry thoroughly over heat in the pan. Put the potatoes through a potato ricer back into the same pan. Place on low heat to further dry out, being careful not to burn. Remove from heat and beat in 4 tablespoons butter, the salt, pepper, nutmeg, chives, cheese, then the whole egg. Cool slightly.

2. When the mixture is cool enough to handle, form cylinders 2 to 3 inches long and 1 inch in diameter (oiling the palms of the hands makes this job easier). Dust the cylinders lightly with flour, dip into the beaten eggs, and roll in bread crumbs.

3. Heat the remaining butter and the oil in a large frying pan. Brown the cylinders evenly without crowding them. Add more butter and oil if needed. Keep the cylinders warm in a 200° oven while the rest are browning.

Note: You can also arrange the cylinders in a shallow, buttered baking dish, not touching, and brown them in a preheated 400° oven, turning once to brown evenly.

Potatoes Frigo   SERVES 4

We call these tasty potatoes "Frigo" in honor of David Frigo and his superb cheese shop on 46 Summer Street in Torrington, Connecticut, where we get two important ingredients, Gorgonzola and Asiago cheeses (among other choice items). The Frigo family virtually invented Asiago in Italy's Vicenza. Today, they age this cheese for three years until it is golden, hard, nutty, and, in our opinion, superior to Parmesan as a grating cheese.

4 medium-sized Idaho baking potatoes (slightly over 1 pound)
4 tablespoons (½ stick) unsalted butter
½ cup cream
⅓ cup crumbled Gorgonzola cheese
⅓ cup grated Asiago cheese

1. Cook the potatoes in their skins in boiling water until just tender (do not overcook, as they will cook more later). Drain and dry in the pan over heat. Peel and cut into ½-inch-thick cubes.

2. In a shallow, flameproof casserole, over medium heat, melt the butter and stir in the potatoes and cream. Sprinkle with the cheeses.

3. Bake, uncovered, in a preheated 350° oven 15 minutes, or until the cheeses have melted and the potatoes are heated through.

Note: Salt and pepper are not needed; the cheeses add the seasoning authority. But add them, if you like.

Potato and Leek Casserole

SERVES 4

*4 medium-sized potatoes (slightly more than 1 pound), peeled
 and cut into ¼-inch-thick slices*
1½ cups light cream, or half-and-half
1 teaspoon salt
*3 large leeks (white part only), thoroughly washed and thinly
 sliced*
Salt and freshly ground black pepper to taste
⅓ cup fine bread crumbs
3 tablespoons unsalted butter

1. Combine the potatoes, cream, and 1 teaspoon salt in a sauce-pan. Over low heat, simmer, covered, for 10 minutes, or until the potatoes are almost tender, just partially cooked. Shake the pan occasionally to keep the potatoes and cream from scorching. Drain.
2. Lightly butter a casserole and arrange layers of the potatoes and leeks, lightly seasoning each layer with salt and pepper and ending with a layer of potatoes. Sprinkle with bread crumbs and dot with the butter.
3. Bake, uncovered, in a preheated 375° oven 25 minutes, or until the potatoes and leeks are tender and the top is golden. If the top starts to color before the potatoes are cooked, cover lightly with aluminum foil.

Potato Pudding for Roast Beef

SERVES 4 TO 6

You must first roast the beef for this recipe.

7 medium-sized Idaho potatoes (slightly more than 2 pounds)
⅓ cup hot cream
¼ cup of the pan drippings from the roast beef
2 tablespoons melted, unsalted butter
¼ teaspoon thyme
Salt and freshly ground black pepper to taste
2 eggs, beaten (reserve 2 tablespoonfuls)
Cayenne

1. Cook the potatoes in their skins in boiling water until tender. Drain and dry over heat in the pan. Peel and mash or rice them in a bowl.

2. With a wire whisk or electric beater, beat in the cream, pan drippings, butter, thyme, salt, and pepper. Add the eggs (reserving the 2 tablespoonfuls) and whip them in.

3. Lightly butter a cake pan of sufficient size. Spoon in the potatoes, smoothing the surface, cake-fashion, without packing down. Brush on the 2 tablespoons beaten egg and sprinkle lightly with cayenne.

4. Cook, uncovered, in a preheated 425° oven 15 minutes, or until browned.

Potatoes with Pizzaiola Sauce   SERVES 6

6 medium-sized potatoes (about 2 pounds)
3 tablespoons olive oil
1 garlic clove, chopped
1 small onion, chopped
1 tablespoon chopped fresh oregano or 1 teaspoon dried oregano
1 tablespoon chopped fresh basil or 1 teaspoon dried basil
6 large, ripe tomatoes, peeled, seeded, and chopped or a 1-pound, 12-ounce can of Italian tomatoes broken up (with your hands)
⅛ teaspoon crushed red pepper
¼ cup dry red wine
Salt to taste
6 tablespoons unsalted butter, approximately
2 tablespoons chopped broadleaf parsley

1. Cook the potatoes in their skins in boiling water until just tender; drain and dry thoroughly over heat in the pot. Do not overcook. Peel and cut into ½-inch-thick slices.

2. In a large, deep frying pan, heat 2 tablespoons oil and cook the garlic and onion until soft. Do not brown. Stir in the oregano, basil, tomatoes, red pepper, wine, and salt. Simmer, uncovered, for 15

minutes, or until the sauce thickens. Taste for seasoning.

3. While the sauce cooks, in a frying pan, heat 3 tablespoons butter and the remaining oil, and quickly brown the potato slices, a layer at a time, on both sides. Add more butter, as needed.

4. As the potatoes brown, transfer them to the tomato-sauce pan. When all have been browned and added, mix them gently, but well, with the sauce. Simmer 2 minutes. Serve on a hot serving dish with parsley sprinkled on top.

Potatoes with Ricotta Cheese SERVES 4 TO 6

6 medium-sized potatoes (about 2 pounds)
4 tablespoons (½ stick) unsalted butter
Salt and freshly ground black pepper to taste
2 cups ricotta (drained)
1 egg yolk, beaten
¼ cup heavy cream
1 teaspoon sugar
¼ teaspoon cinnamon
1 cup julienne-cut cooked ham
2 tablespoons chopped parsley

1. Cook the potatoes in their skins in boiling water until tender. Drain and dry over heat in the pot. Peel and cut into ½-inch cubes.

2. In a large bowl, mix the potatoes while still warm with the butter, salt, and pepper. Blend in the ricotta mixed with the egg yolk, cream, sugar, and cinnamon. Fold in the ham and parsley.

3. Spoon into a buttered, shallow baking dish and bake in a preheated 400° oven 20 minutes, or until heated through.

Potato-Turnip Bake SERVES 4

Such is the personality of the potato that it can even hold its own with the authoritative turnip. We like this dish with a roast loin of pork.

5 medium-sized potatoes (slightly less than 2 pounds), peeled
   and thinly sliced
3 small turnips, scraped and thinly sliced
6 tablespoons unsalted butter
Salt and freshly ground black pepper to taste
1 cup grated Asiago or Parmesan cheese
¼ teaspoon mace
1 cup chicken broth

1. Butter a casserole or baking dish. Arrange alternating layers of potato and turnip slices until half of them have been used, dotting each layer with butter and seasoning with salt and pepper. Evenly sprinkle on half the cheese; then season with the mace.
2. Continue layering, ending with potato. Sprinkle with the remaining cheese and dot with butter. Pour the chicken broth around the edge of the vegetables.
3. Bake, covered, in a preheated 375° oven 30 minutes, or until the vegetables are nearly tender. Remove cover and continue cooking until tender and all the liquid has been absorbed.

Potatoes with Salt Pork   SERVES 4 TO 6

¼ pound salt pork, cut into ¼-inch cubes
1 medium-sized onion, coarsely chopped
6 medium-sized potatoes (about 2 pounds), peeled and cut into
   ½-inch cubes
1 tablespoon flour
⅛ teaspoon dried tarragon
Salt and freshly ground black pepper to taste
1 cup chicken broth
2 tablespoons chopped fresh parsley

1. In a large frying pan, over medium heat, cook the salt pork 5 minutes, or until it is transparent. Pour off all but 3 tablespoons fat (if the salt pork does not render that amount, add butter).

2. Add the onion and cook for 3 minutes, or until soft. Do not brown.

3. Add the potatoes; sprinkle them with flour, tarragon, salt, and pepper, and cook, stirring, 3 minutes.

4. Pour in the broth. Cover and cook over low heat for 20 minutes, or until the potatoes are tender. If the sauce becomes too thick before the potatoes are tender, add a small amount of hot broth (or water). Sprinkle with parsley before serving.

Sticky Potatoes SERVES 4

4 medium-sized potatoes (slightly more than 1 pound)
2 tablespoons unsalted butter
Salt and freshly ground black pepper to taste
1½ tablespoons flour
1½ cups milk, heated
2 tablespoons chopped broadleaf parsley

1. Cook the potatoes in their skins in boiling water until tender. Drain and dry in the pan over heat. Peel and cut into small cubes.

2. In a deep saucepan, melt the butter and add the potatoes, stirring them into the butter. Season with salt and pepper. Sprinkle the flour over the potatoes, and over low heat, gradually add the milk, stirring all the time, cooking until the milk has been absorbed and the potatoes are "sticky" moist. Taste for seasoning.

3. Stir in the parsley and serve very hot.

This is excellent with your favorite chopped beef dish.

Saged Potatoes SERVES 6

The Italians, probably the first to take the potato seriously, bring their unique imagination and flavoring techniques into play with the *patata*. They serve these potatoes with tender young roast lamb, delicately scented with rosemary. So do we.

6 medium-sized potatoes (about 2 pounds), peeled and cut into
   wedges
4 tablespoons (½ stick) unsalted butter
1 tablespoon olive oil
1½ teaspoons finely crumbled dried leaf sage
1 cup grated Parmesan cheese
Salt to taste
⅛ teaspoon crushed red pepper, or to taste

1. Cook the potatoes in boiling salted water until tender but still somewhat firm (what the Italians call *al dente*). Drain; dry thoroughly over heat in the pot, and keep warm.
2. In a large frying pan, heat the butter and oil; stir in the sage and heat until the butter is light brown.
3. Add the potatoes and sprinkle in the cheese, salt, and red pepper, turning the potatoes several times until they are well coated.

Quick Potato Cake with Skins

SERVES 4 TO 6

6 medium-sized Idaho baking potatoes (about 2 pounds),
   scrubbed
3 small white onions, grated
1½ teaspoons salt
½ teaspoon freshly ground black pepper
About 6 tablespoons vegetable oil for frying

1. Grate the unpeeled potatoes and squeeze dry in a kitchen towel.
2. In a bowl, combine and mix well the potatoes, onions, salt, and pepper.
3. In a large frying pan, heat enough oil to cover the bottom of the pan well. Spread the potato mixture, evenly forming one large cake, about ½ inch thick. Cover and cook until the bottom is brown and crisp (lift with a spatula to check on the progress). Place a plate, larger than the frying pan, over the top of the pan and turn the cake out onto the plate, brown side up. Add more oil to cover the bottom of the pan and, when it is hot, slide the cake back into

the frying pan (brown side up). If the cake breaks up a bit, reshape it with the spatula. Cook until the bottom is brown and crisp.
Note: As you grate the potatoes, put them in a bowl of cold water to prevent discoloring. Drain well, then dry in a towel.

Steamed Potatoes with Caraway Seeds SERVES 6

24 to 36 tiny new potatoes
6 tablespoons unsalted butter
1 small onion, minced
2 tablespoons caraway seeds, crushed
Salt and freshly ground black pepper to taste
Paprika

1. Cook the potatoes in a steamer until tender but firm. Set aside.
2. Over medium heat, in a frying pan, melt 2 tablespoons butter. Add the onion and cook until soft. Do not brown. Stir in the potatoes, caraway seeds, salt, pepper, and the remaining butter.
3. Sprinkle lightly with paprika and cook, turning, until the potatoes are slightly golden.

Shoestring Potatoes and Vermicelli SERVES 6

This may seem like an unlikely combination, but we've enjoyed it several times in Rome. The potatoes are crisp in contrast to the pasta. The result is delicious.

4 medium-sized potatoes (slightly over 1 pound), peeled and
*   julienned*
Vegetable oil for deep frying
6 ounces vermicelli, broken into 2-inch lengths
8 tablespoons (1 stick) butter, cut into small pieces
1 cup grated Asiago or Parmesan cheese
Freshly ground black pepper to taste
Salt to taste

1. Deep-fry the potatoes, a few at a time, in the vegetable oil until golden crisp. Drain on paper towels and keep cooked potatoes warm in a 250° oven while the others are being cooked and while the pasta is cooking.

2. Cook the pasta in a deep pot of boiling salted water until it is *al dente*, slightly chewy. Drain and toss with the butter, cheese, and a generous grinding of pepper.

3. Sprinkle the potatoes lightly with salt, add them to the pasta, and toss gently but thoroughly. Serve immediately.

Swedish Anchovy Potatoes
SERVES 6 TO 8

8 medium-sized potatoes (slightly under 3 pounds), peeled and cut into long, narrow strips
4 medium-sized white onions, thinly sliced
2 two-ounce cans flat anchovy fillets, drained, rinsed, and dried
Freshly ground black pepper to taste
1½ cups medium cream, or half-and-half
2 tablespoons unsalted butter

1. Lightly butter a large, shallow baking dish and arrange a layer of potato strips on the bottom, and then a layer of onions. Arrange half the anchovies over the onions and sprinkle with pepper. Repeat, ending with a layer of potatoes. Pour in 1 cup cream and dot with butter.

2. Bake, uncovered, in a preheated 375° oven 40 minutes. Add the remaining cream and cook 10 minutes longer, or until the casserole bubbles, the potatoes are tender, and most of the cream has been absorbed.

Tiny New Potatoes alla Ralph Guidetti
SERVES 4

Ralph Guidetti, a friend, was chef and owner of Guidetti's, a well-known and respected restaurant in Wingdale, New York.

24 new potatoes, not larger than walnuts, washed but not dried,
  with some moisture left on them
4 tablespoons olive oil
5 garlic cloves, peeled (do not cut up)
Salt and freshly ground black pepper to taste
2 tablespoons chopped broadleaf parsley

1. In a large frying pan, over low heat, cook the wet potatoes, tightly covered, for 10 minutes, shaking the pan often to keep the potatoes from sticking (their moisture should help, but shake anyway).
2. Add the olive oil and garlic to the pan, then sprinkle with salt and pepper. Cover again and cook over low heat for another 20 minutes, shaking the pan frequently, until the potatoes are tender. Sprinkle with parsley.

These are a delight, golden-skinned and soft inside.

Watercress Potato Soufflé SERVES 4

Watercress gives a delicate yet peppery authority to this dish.

2½ cups mashed potatoes
½ cup yogurt
1 cup grated Asiago or Parmesan cheese
¼ cup chopped watercress (no stems)
Salt to taste
3 egg yolks, beaten
3 egg whites, stiffly beaten

1. In a bowl, combine and blend well the potatoes, yogurt, cheese, watercress, salt, and egg yolks. Whip into a smooth, light mixture. Fold in the egg whites.
2. Turn into a lightly buttered 1½-quart casserole. Bake, uncovered, in a preheated 375° oven 40 minutes, or until puffed, golden, and set.

Wyoming Camp Potatoes

5 slices bacon
5 medium-sized potatoes, peeled and cut into ¼-inch-thick slices
2 medium-sized white onions, cut into ¼-inch-thick slices
1-pound can stewed tomatoes, chopped
Salt and freshly ground black pepper to taste
½ teaspoon sugar
1 teaspoon prepared mustard

1. In a frying pan, over medium heat, cook the bacon until crisp. Remove, drain, and break into small pieces and reserve.
2. Add the potatoes and onions to the pan with the bacon fat and cook 10 minutes, turning frequently with a spatula. Pour or spoon off any fat left in the pan.
3. Add the tomatoes, salt, pepper, sugar, and mustard. Simmer 20 minutes, or until the sauce is thickish and the potatoes are tender. Taste for seasoning. Sprinkle the bacon pieces over the top and serve very hot.

12

Baked Potatoes and Potato Pancakes

Baked New Potatoes
Baked Potatoes with Avocado Sauce
Baked Potatoes with Madras Spicy Yogurt Topping
Bakers with Sour-Cream Stuffing
Bakers with Red Caviar and Sour Cream
Basil-Baked New Potatoes en Papillote
French-Country-Style Stuffed Baked Potatoes
Garlicky Stuffed Bakers
Antoine Gilly's Stuffed Baked Potatoes
B. J. Guidetti's Stand-Up "Kiev" Nude Bakers
Hash-Stuffed Bakers
Norma Jean Maxwell's Buttered Bakers
Pigs in a Poke
Potatoes à la Camembert
Potatoes Roquefort
Spinach-Filled Baked Potatoes
Vegetable-Stuffed Baked Potatoes
Potato Pancakes
German Sour-Cream Pancakes
Moscow Mashed-Potato Cakes
Green Mashed-Potato Pancakes
Leftover-Potato Pancakes New England Style
State of Maine Potato Pancakes
Potato Cheese Cakes
Potato Zucchini Pancakes

Don't trust anyone who doesn't like baked potatoes or potato pancakes. But don't make the mistake of thinking that there's anything dull or boring about these two favorites. With such recipes as Potatoes Roquefort, Vegetable-Stuffed Baked Potatoes, Baked Potatoes with Avocado Sauce, or Bakers with Red Caviar and Sour Cream, Potatoes en Papillote, German Sour-Cream Pancakes, and Green Mashed-Potato Pancakes, nothing could be further from the truth.

Baked New Potatoes

SERVES 6

24 small (but not tiny) new potatoes (about 2 pounds), scrubbed, dried, and rubbed with olive oil
Salt to taste

Cut the potatoes in half and sprinkle with salt. Bake in a shallow dish, cut side down, in a single layer, in a preheated 450° oven 30 minutes, or until the potatoes are tender and browned.

Baked Potatoes with Avocado Sauce

SERVES 6

6 medium-sized Idaho baking potatoes (about 2 pounds), scrubbed and pricked
2 tablespoons lemon juice
1 small ripe avocado, peeled, pitted, and diced (do this at the last minute)
12 tablespoons (1½ sticks) soft unsalted butter
⅓ teaspoon minced garlic
Salt to taste

1. Bake the potatoes in a preheated 400° oven 1 hour, or until tender.
2. Just before the potatoes are ready, prepare the sauce. Place the lemon juice, avocado, butter, and garlic in an electric blender con-

tainer and blend into a puree. Spoon into a bowl and whip into a smooth sauce. Taste for seasoning, adding salt if necessary.

3. Spoon the sauce over piping hot, split baked potatoes.

Baked Potatoes with Madras Spicy Yogurt Topping

SERVES 6

*6 medium-sized Idaho baking potatoes (about 2 pounds),
    scrubbed and pricked*
1 tablespoon olive oil
½ teaspoon mustard seeds
¼ teaspoon curry powder
2 tablespoons chick-pea flour
¼ teaspoon cayenne
½ teaspoon ground cumin
1 garlic clove, minced
½ teaspoon ground ginger
Salt to taste
1 cup yogurt

1. Bake the potatoes in a preheated 400° oven until tender, about 45 minutes.
2. In a frying pan, heat the oil. Add the mustard seeds and curry, and cook, stirring, until the mustard seeds pop. Lower heat and stir in the flour, cayenne, cumin, garlic, ginger, and salt, blending well. Stir in the yogurt over low heat, blending well. Heat to a simmer, stirring to heat through. Do not boil.
3. Split the hot potatoes and spoon on the yogurt topping.

Bakers with Sour-Cream Stuffing

SERVES 4

The baked potato-sour cream combination is a favorite of just about everyone. But here it is not simply a matter of dolloping sour cream on top of a baked potato.

*3 large Idaho baking potatoes (about 1½ pounds), scrubbed and
  pricked*
5 tablespoons soft unsalted butter
Salt to taste
2 egg yolks
½ cup sour cream

1. Rub the potatoes with oil and bake in a preheated 400° oven until easily pierced with a fork, about 45 minutes.
2. Cut the potatoes into halves, lengthwise, and carefully scoop out the pulp, reserving the four best shells. Rice the pulp into a bowl and, while the potatoes are still hot, whip in 3 tablespoons butter and the salt. Beat in the egg yolks and sour cream, whipping into a smooth puree. Taste for seasoning.
3. Heap the mixture into the reserved shells and place on a baking sheet. Dot with the remaining butter and place under the broiler until golden brown.

Bakers with Red Caviar and Sour Cream   SERVES 4

Few of us can afford the classic gray caviar from the sturgeon, but red fish roe (from salmon) is very tasty and almost affordable.

*4 medium-sized Idaho baking potatoes (slightly more than 1
  pound), scrubbed and pricked*
1 cup sour cream
1 scallion (white part and a little of the light green), minced
Salt and freshly ground black pepper to taste
4 heaping teaspoons red caviar

1. Bake the potatoes in a preheated 400° oven 45 minutes, or until easily pierced with a fork.
2. In a bowl, combine and blend well the sour cream, scallion, salt, and pepper.
3. Split the hot potatoes in half lengthwise. Spoon on the sour-cream mixture and top with a spoonful of caviar.

Basil-Baked New Potatoes en Papillote

SERVES 6

36 very small new potatoes (about 2 to 2½ pounds)
1½ teaspoons salt
4 tablespoons (½ stick) unsalted butter, melted
4 fresh basil leaves, chopped

1. Place the potatoes on a large sheet of heavy aluminum foil. Sprinkle with salt and spoon the butter over them. Place the basil leaves between the potatoes. Wrap the foil tightly around the potatoes (with the seam side up), completely encasing them.
2. Set on a baking sheet and bake in a preheated 400° oven for 30 minutes, or until the potatoes are tender. When opening the foil, beware of the steam that will pour out.
Note: To test potatoes, pinch foil with a pot holder.

French-Country-Style Stuffed Baked Potatoes

SERVES 6

4 large Idaho baking potatoes (about 2 pounds), scrubbed
*   and pricked*
1 cup grated Gruyère cheese
¼ cup heavy cream
4 tablespoons (½ stick) unsalted butter
½ cup minced cooked ham
Salt and freshly ground black pepper to taste

1. Bake the potatoes in a preheated 400° oven for 45 minutes, or until tender.
2. Cut the potatoes in half lengthwise and spoon out the pulp without damaging the shells. Reserve the six best shells.
3. Rice the pulp into a bowl. Add and blend well ½ cup of the cheese, the cream, 2 tablespoons butter, the ham, salt, and pepper. If necessary, add more cream to obtain the consistency you desire.
4. Spoon the mixture in equal portions into the six potato half shells and place on a baking sheet. Sprinkle on the remaining cheese and dot with the remaining butter.

5. Bake in a preheated 400° oven 10 minutes, or until heated through; then place under the broiler until crusty and golden brown. Serve one filled potato half shell for each guest, along with a nice, fat, pink fillet of beef.

Garlicky Stuffed Bakers   SERVES 4

Sophisticated cooks have discovered that large amounts of garlic do not overwhelm. Instead they impart a slightly sweet, very memorable flavor.

2 large Idaho baking potatoes (about 2 pounds), scrubbed
   and pricked
10 garlic cloves, unpeeled
4 tablespoons (½ stick) unsalted butter
1½ tablespoons flour
1 cup light cream, or half-and-half
Salt and freshly ground black pepper to taste
2 tablespoons heavy cream
1 teaspoon chopped chives

1. Bake the potatoes in a preheated 400° oven 45 minutes, or until easily pierced with a fork.
2. While the potatoes are cooking, in a small saucepan, cover the garlic with boiling water and cook for 3 minutes. Drain the garlic, cool slightly, and peel.
3. In another saucepan, melt 2 tablespoons butter over medium-low heat, add the garlic, and cook, covered, 6 minutes, or until golden and tender. Do not brown. With a slotted spoon, remove the garlic and reserve. Stir the flour into the butter the garlic cooked in (if the butter has been absorbed by the garlic, add a tablespoon of butter, in addition to the amount listed in the ingredients), stirring into a smooth paste. Gradually add the light cream, stirring into a smooth, thickish sauce. Season with salt and pepper.
4. Combine the sauce and garlic in a blender container, blending thoroughly.

5. Split the baked potatoes in half lengthwise and remove the pulp, keeping the four half shells intact. Rice the pulp into a bowl and whip in the remaining butter and the heavy cream. Add enough of the garlic sauce to give the consistency you desire. Taste for seasoning. Stir in the chives.

6. Spoon equal amounts into the shells. Bake in a preheated 400° oven 10 minutes, or until heated through. Brown under the broiler if desired.

Serve any remaining sauce at the table.

Antoine Gilly's Stuffed Baked Potatoes   SERVES 4

4 large Idaho baking potatoes (about 2 pounds)
1 tablespoon chopped fresh chives
1 teaspoon chopped fresh tarragon
Salt and freshly ground black pepper to taste
⅛ teaspoon nutmeg
2 tablespoons shallots, minced and cooked in 2 tablespoons butter 2 minutes, or until soft and transparent (do not brown)
¼ cup heavy cream
1 small package Liederkranz cheese (about 3 ounces)
2 tablespoons fine bread crumbs

1. Wrap the potatoes in aluminum foil and bake in a preheated 400° oven 1 hour, or until tender.

2. Remove the potatoes from the oven and, laying them lengthwise, cut off and save the tops. Remove the pulp with a spoon and place the empty potato shells on a baking sheet.

3. Rice the potato pulp into a bowl. Add and blend well, one at a time, all the other ingredients (except the bread crumbs), to make a smooth puree. Taste for seasoning.

4. Fill the potato shells with the puree and sprinkle with the bread crumbs. Bake in a preheated 450° oven 5 minutes, or until heated through and golden on top.

5. Replace tops and serve.

B. J. Guidetti's Stand-Up "Kiev" Nude Bakers SERVES 4

4 large Idaho baking potatoes (about 2 pounds), peeled
8 tablespoons (1 stick) unsalted butter, half hard, half soft
Salt and freshly ground black pepper to taste

1. Stand the potatoes vertically and cut a small slice off the bottom of each so the potatoes stand solidly upright. With a vegetable corer, scoop a nickel-sized cavity in the center of each potato. Push as much as possible of the hard butter into each cavity. Rub the outside of the potatoes well with the soft butter. Sprinkle with salt and pepper.
2. Stand upright, so the butter won't run out, on a baking sheet, and bake in a preheated 375° oven 40 minutes, or until the potatoes are tender and golden-crisp on the outside.
Note: The cavity in the center should not run all the way through the potato.

Hash-Stuffed Bakers SERVES 4

4 medium-sized long Idaho baking potatoes (slightly more than 1
  pound), scrubbed and pricked
1 cup chopped, cooked meat (leftover beef is ideal)
¼ cup minced celery (scrape celery before mincing)
2 scallions (white part only), minced
Salt and freshly ground black pepper to taste
1 tablespoon finely chopped parsley
3 tablespoons beef broth
1 teaspoon bottled meat sauce
8 tablespoons grated Asiago cheese

1. Bake the potatoes in a preheated 400° oven about 45 minutes, or until easily pierced with a fork.
2. Cut a thin slice off the top of the potato, lengthwise. Scoop out the pulp, reserving the four larger shells, and rice it into a bowl. Add the meat, celery, scallions, salt, pepper, parsley, beef broth,

and bottled meat sauce, blending thoroughly. Taste for seasoning.
3. Heap the mixture into the large potato shells, sprinkle with the cheese, and bake in a preheated 400° oven until heated through and golden on top.

Norma Jean Maxwell's Buttered Bakers   SERVES 4

4 large Idaho baking potatoes (about 2 pounds), scrubbed,
  dried, and pierced in several places with the sharp point
  of a knife
8 tablespoons (1 stick) soft unsalted butter
Salt and freshly ground black pepper to taste

1. Rub the skin of the potatoes well with the butter, using all of it. Sprinkle with salt and pepper.
2. Cook on a baking sheet in a preheated 375° oven for 1 hour, or until the potatoes are soft to the squeeze.
Eat the entire potato, skin and all.

Pigs in a Poke   SERVES 4

This recipe is from a friend, Bruno Valbona, president of Waring and a Connecticut epicure of note.

4 large Idaho baking potatoes (about 2 pounds), scrubbed
1 package Brown 'n Serve sausage
Salt and freshly ground black pepper to taste

1. With a vegetable corer, make two holes through each potato the narrow way. Stuff these holes full of sausage meat. Sprinkle on salt and pepper and wrap the stuffed potatoes in aluminum foil (shiny side in).
2. Bake in a preheated 375° oven 45 minutes, or until done. Serve immediately from the oven.

Potatoes à la Camembert

Appropriately enough, we first tried this dish in the village of Camembert, Normandy, where Marie Harel is said to have invented this cheese in 1791. People in that area like the cheese best when it's twenty-one days old—that's when it first comes out of the curing room—and use it with just about everything but ice cream. It's outrageously delicious with baked potatoes.

> 4 medium-sized Idaho baking potatoes (slightly more than 1
>   pound), scrubbed and pricked
> 4 tablespoons Camembert cheese

1. Bake the potatoes in a preheated 400° oven for 45 minutes, or until tender.
2. Cut the potatoes in half lengthwise. With a fork, mash the potatoes right in the skins, being careful not to perforate the skins. Press 1 tablespoon Camembert into one half of each potato; replace the other half potato, pressing together, sandwiching the cheese between the halves. Wrap well in foil and bake in the preheated 400° oven 10 minutes, or until thoroughly heated.

Potatoes Roquefort

> 6 large Idaho baking potatoes (about 3 pounds), scrubbed and
>   pricked
> ½ cup crumbled Roquefort cheese, firmly packed
> ½ cup heavy cream, approximately
> 2 small scallions, minced
> Salt and freshly ground black pepper to taste
> ½ cup fine bread crumbs
> ½ garlic clove, minced
> 3 tablespoons melted butter

1. Bake the potatoes in a preheated 400° oven for 45 minutes, or until easily pierced with a fork.
2. Cut off the tops of the potatoes lengthwise and scoop out the

pulp, reserving the large bottom shells. Put the pulp through a potato ricer into a bowl. Beat in the cheese and enough cream to make the potatoes light and fluffy. Mix in the scallions, salt, and pepper.

3. Spoon the mixture back into the shells, mounding it. Sprinkle a mixture of the bread crumbs, garlic, and butter over the top and bake in a preheated 350° oven 20 minutes, or until crusty-brown.

Spinach-Filled Baked Potatoes   SERVES 6

These potatoes can be prepared ahead, but if they are placed in the oven cold, they will take longer to heat.

> 6 medium-sized long Idaho baking potatoes (about 2 pounds),
>   scrubbed and pricked
> 6 tablespoons soft unsalted butter
> Salt and freshly ground black pepper to taste
> 1 teaspoon dried dill
> 10-ounce package fresh spinach, slightly undercooked, well
>   drained, chopped, or 10-ounce package frozen, chopped spin-
>   ach, cooked half the time suggested on package
> 3 tablespoons chopped shallots, cooked in 2 tablespoons butter
>   until soft (do not brown)
> 6 tablespoons grated sharp Cheddar cheese

1. Bake the potatoes in a preheated 400° oven until easily pierced with a fork, about 45 minutes.

2. Cut the tops off the potatoes, lengthwise. Carefully scoop out the pulp, leaving the larger bottom shells intact. Put the pulp through a ricer into a bowl and blend thoroughly with the butter, salt, pepper, and dill.

3. Squeeze all the liquid from the spinach and add spinach and shallots to the potato mixture, blending well. Taste for seasoning.

4. Heap the mixture in the shells, set on a baking sheet, and bake, uncovered, in a preheated 400° oven 20 minutes, or until heated

through. Remove from the oven and sprinkle 1 tablespoon of the cheese on top of each potato. Place under the broiler until the cheese has melted and the top is golden.

Vegetable-Stuffed Baked Potatoes SERVES 4

Here is a potato-vegetable course in one serving.

4 medium-sized, long Idaho baking potatoes (slightly more than
    1 pound), scrubbed and pricked
1 cup Creamy Cheese Sauce (see below)
½ cup chopped cooked carrots
½ cup cooked baby lima beans
¼ cup chopped, cooked sweet red pepper
Salt to taste
¼ cup bread crumbs
2 tablespoons unsalted butter

1. Bake the potatoes in a preheated 400° oven 45 minutes, or until easily pierced with a fork.
2. Cut the potatoes in half lengthwise. Carefully scoop out the pulp, reserving the four best shells, and rice the pulp into a bowl. Stir in half the sauce and all the cooked vegetables. Season with salt and blend well.
3. Mound the mixture in the potato shells. Spoon on the remaining sauce. Sprinkle with bread crumbs, dot with the butter, and place on a baking sheet. Cook in a preheated 400° oven until heated through and golden on top.

CREAMY CHEESE SAUCE MAKES ABOUT 1 CUP

2 tablespoons unsalted butter
2 tablespoons flour
1 cup light cream, or half-and-half
1 tablespoon dry sherry

¹/₃ cup grated Gruyère cheese
Salt and freshly ground black pepper to taste

In a saucepan, over medium heat, melt the butter and add the flour, stirring into a smooth paste. Gradually blend in the cream, stirring into a medium-thick, smooth sauce. Add the sherry and cheese, and stir until the cheese has melted. Season with salt and pepper.

Potato Pancakes

Serving potato pancakes with any meal always causes comment, but many of us do not cook them because we consider them complicated. Actually, they are simplicity itself. Here are some tips that will ensure success.

Peel the potaoes last, after you have prepared everything else. Once peeled, potatoes will darken if they are exposed to the air for any length of time. One sure way to avoid this is to peel and then grate the potatoes into a bowl of cold water. But always make certain they are well drained, then squeezed dry, preferably in a kitchen towel.

In a bowl, lightly beat the eggs or yolks that will be used; then add the flour, salt, pepper, and any other ingredients, such as onion. Also, beat the egg whites (if they are beaten separately) and heat the oil or other fat in a griddle or frying pan. In short, do everything you can in advance, so when the potatoes are grated they can quickly be beaten into the other ingredients and cooked immediately.

Potato pancakes are like pasta and soufflés; they should be cooked and served immediately. The guests wait for the pancakes, not vice versa. We like to conscript a willing guest who wants to learn pancake technique or who knows it. He stays with the frying pan turning out pancakes while we deliver them piping hot and crisp to the table. True, the pancakes can be kept warm in a low oven until the whole batch is cooked, and they will be quite good. But there is no substitute for serving them straight from the pan.

BASIC POTATO PANCAKE RECIPE

We suggest this recipe be used as a test run to get the swing of the thing. If you like it, then increase amounts accordingly for more pancakes. This will produce 4 three-inch pancakes.

> *2 cups raw Idaho potatoes, grated on next to the finest side of a four-sided hand grater*
> *2 eggs, beaten*
> *1 tablespoon all-purpose flour*
> *1 teaspoon salt*
> *1 tablespoon grated onion*
> *Vegetable oil for frying*

1. Grate potatoes last, after all other ingredients are ready. Place grated potatoes in a kitchen towel and squeeze moisture out.
2. In a bowl, mix potatoes, eggs, flour, salt, and onion, blending well.
3. Shape into pancakes ¼ inch thick, patting firmly into shape.
4. In a frying pan, over medium heat, warm about 3 tablespoons oil. (This is not deep-frying, so do not use too much oil.) Raise heat slightly until oil sizzles.
5. Cook pancakes until brown and crisp on both sides. Drain on paper towels, and keep warm in a preheated 250° oven, or better yet, serve immediately.

German Sour-Cream Pancakes   SERVES 8

> *2 eggs, lightly beaten*
> *3 tablespoons flour*
> *1½ teaspoons salt*
> *⅓ cup sour cream*
> *8 medium-sized Idaho baking potatoes (slightly less than 3 pounds), peeled, grated, and squeezed dry in a kitchen towel*
> *6 tablespoons olive oil*

1. In a large bowl combine and beat well the eggs, flour, salt, and sour cream. Add the potatoes and blend well.

2. Using two frying pans, heat 3 tablespoons oil in each. Spread half the potato mixture in each and, with a spatula, shape into ½-inch-thick cakes. Cook until golden brown on the bottom (shake the pan to prevent from sticking, or if it does stick, loosen with a spatula). Cut each cake into quarters, turn, and brown on the other side.

Moscow Mashed-Potato Cakes   SERVES 4 TO 6

6 medium-sized potatoes (about 2 pounds)
6 tablespoons butter
2 egg yolks
Salt and freshly ground black pepper to taste
1 small white onion, finely chopped
6 medium-sized, fresh, firm mushrooms, finely chopped
1 teaspoon flour
2 whole eggs, beaten
Fine bread crumbs for dredging

1. Peel the potatoes and cook them in boiling salted water until tender. Drain and dry over heat in the pan.
2. Mash the potatoes while still warm or put through a ricer into a bowl. Beat in 2 tablespoons butter, the egg yolks, salt, and pepper. Cool and shape into flat 3- or 4-inch cakes.
3. In a frying pan, over medium heat, melt 2 tablespoons butter. Add the onion and cook for 1 minute, or until soft. Do not brown. Raise the heat to medium-high. Add the mushrooms to the frying pan. Sprinkle with the flour, salt, and pepper, and cook quickly, stirring, to allow moisture to exude, without overcooking the mushrooms. Transfer with a slotted spoon to a bowl.
4. Place a spoonful of the mushroom filling off center on each potato cake; fold over. Press the edges together. Brush with the beaten egg and dust with the bread crumbs.
5. Melt the remaining butter in a frying pan, over medium heat, and cook the cakes until golden brown on both sides, being careful when turning to keep the cakes intact. Add more butter if needed.

Green Mashed-Potato Pancakes SERVES 4

4 medium-sized potatoes (slightly more than 1 pound)
Salt and freshly ground black pepper to taste
3 tablespoons heavy cream
1 egg, lightly beaten
2 tablespoons finely chopped fresh chives
3 tablespoons finely chopped fresh parsley
3 tablespoons unsalted butter
1 tablespoon olive oil

1. Peel the potatoes and cook in boiling salted water until tender. Drain and dry over heat in the pot. Put the potatoes through a potato ricer into a bowl. Add and blend thoroughly the salt, pepper, cream, egg, chives, and parsley.
2. Shape the mixture into four cakes (or more, depending on the size you prefer). Heat the butter and oil in a large frying pan and cook until the cakes are golden brown on both sides.

Leftover-Potato Pancakes New England Style SERVES 4 TO 6

½ cup bread crumbs
½ cup light cream, or half-and-half
3 cups leftover (or fresh) mashed potatoes
1 small onion, grated
1 egg yolk and 1 whole egg, lightly beaten
1 teaspoon salt
½ teaspoon freshly ground black pepper
⅛ teaspoon nutmeg
⅛ teaspoon dried thyme
3 tablespoons bacon drippings (or use butter, but bacon fat is
  better), approximately

1. Combine the bread crumbs and cream in a large bowl and let stand for 1 hour.
2. Add the potatoes, onion, egg yolk and egg, salt, pepper, nutmeg,

and thyme to the bread-crumb bowl and blend well.

3. In a large frying pan, heat the bacon fat, drop in 1 heaping tablespoonful of the potato mixture for each cake, and flatten with a spatula. Cook over medium-high heat until the bottom is brown and crisp. Turn and repeat the process. Add more fat as needed.

State of Maine Potato Pancakes

SERVES 4

2 egg yolks
1½ cups milk
1 teaspoon salt
1½ cups sifted flour
1 tablespoon melted unsalted butter
3 medium-sized potatoes (about 1 pound), peeled, grated, and
squeezed dry in a kitchen towel
2 egg whites, stiffly beaten

1. In a large bowl, combine and beat together the egg yolks, milk, and salt. Gradually beat in the flour; then blend in the melted butter and potatoes. Fold in the egg whites.

2. Drop the potato batter by the tablespoonful onto a hot greased griddle. Cook until golden brown on each side.

Potato Cheese Cakes

SERVES 4

⅓ cup sour cream
½ cup grated sharp Cheddar cheese
2 tablespoons melted butter
1 teaspoon salt
½ teaspoon freshly ground black pepper
5 medium-sized baking potatoes (slightly less than 2 pounds),
peeled, grated, and squeezed dry in a kitchen towel
Olive oil for frying
Additional melted butter

1. In a large bowl, combine the sour cream, cheese, 2 tablespoons melted butter, salt, and pepper, and blend well.

2. Add the potatoes to the bowl with the sour-cream mixture and blend well.

3. In a large frying pan (one that can go under a broiler), over medium-low heat, warm 3 tablespoons oil. Add the potato mixture, 1 heaping tablespoonful at a time, and press into cakes with a spatula. Cook until golden brown and crisp underneath. Do not turn cakes. Sprinkle them lightly with melted butter and place under a broiler until they are golden brown and crisp on top.

If necessary, use more than one frying pan, or hold those that are cooked in a 200° oven until all are ready; then place all of them on a baking sheet, sprinkle with melted butter, and put under the broiler.

Potato Zucchini Pancakes
SERVES 4 TO 6

5 medium-sized baking potatoes (slightly under 2 pounds),
    peeled and grated into a bowl of cold water
2 medium-sized zucchini, grated
1 small white onion, grated
3 tablespoons flour
1/2 teaspoon baking powder
1 1/2 teaspoons salt
1/2 teaspoon freshly ground black pepper
3 eggs, lightly beaten in a large bowl
Vegetable oil

1. Drain the potatoes well and place them, the zucchini, and the onion in a kitchen towel and squeeze to remove as much moisture from the vegetables as possible.

2. Add the vegetables and the flour combined with the baking powder, salt, and pepper to the egg bowl, mixing well.

3. Lightly oil a pancake griddle or frying pan. Spoon a heaping tablespoon for each pancake onto the thoroughly heated griddle or pan. Press into cake shape with a spatula, and cook on both sides until crisp and golden brown.

I N D E X

Abbacchio alla Romana, 144
Abbacchio Chianti Style, 120
Abruzzi Potato and Sausage Pie, 157
Accordion Potatoes, 322
Alsatian Soup, 26
American Country Sausage, 152
Amsterdam Mashed Potatoes with Sauerkraut, 315
Andalusian Steak, Braised, 95
Antoine Gilly's Filets Mignon, 97
Antoine Gilly, Fillet of Beef Haché, 52
Antoine Gilly's Grandmother's Potatoes, 337
Antoine Gilly's Stuffed Baked Potatoes, 367
APPETIZERS
   Canadian Bacon and Onion Quiche, 12
   Chopped Beef, Ricotta, and Mozzarella Cannelloni, 8
   Edward T. Thompson's Watercress Sausage, 13
   Greek Lamb Tidbits, 14
   Ham and Asparagus Crêpes, 10
   Ham Logs, 6
   Ham-Stuffed Mushrooms, 16
   Hungarian Goulash Crêpes, 11
   Kielbasa Snap-Ups, 14
   Lamb-Stuffed Mushrooms, 16
   Meatballs with Herbs, 17
   Meatballs and Peas Cannelloni, 6
   Onions Stuffed with Lamb and Mushrooms, 15
   Pâté of Baby Beef Veal, 19
   Pâté of Veal, 20
   Salami and Black Olive Crostata, 22
   Sweet and Sour Lamb Meatballs, 18
Appetizer Ham Logs, 6
Applesauce, Horseradish, 183
Arabian Lamb Shanks, 140
Armenian Shish Kebab, 123
Asia Minor Tongue and Potato Salad, 133
Asparagus and Ham Crêpes, 10
Athenian Lamb with Chestnuts, 119
Athenian Potato Soufflé, 274
Au Gratin Potatoes and Carrots, 322
Aunt Edie's Roasted Potatoes (from Barbara M. Valbona), 324
Austrian Paprika Potatoes, 323

Bacon-Flavored Roast Potatoes, 324
Bacon and Onion Quiche, 12
Baked Bananas, 122
Baked Lamb Chops with Mushrooms and Sour Cream, 136
Baked Mashed Potatoes with Mushrooms, 300

Baked New Potatoes, 362
Baked Parmesan Potato Fingers, 326
Baked Potato Piroshki, 325
Baked Potatoes with Avocado Sauce, 362
Baked Potatoes with Madras Spicy Yogurt Topping, 363
Bakers with Red Caviar and Sour Cream, 364
Bakers with Sour Cream Stuffing, 363
Balsamic Vinegar Sauce for Beef Brisket, 76
Bananas, Baked, 122
Barbara and Richard Perry's Pork Stew, 165
Barbecued Spareribs, 188
Barley, Beef, and Mushroom Soup, 28
Basil-Baked New Potatoes en Papillote, 365
Batter for Crêpes or Canelloni, 7
Béchamel Sauce, 196
BEEF
   Birds, Portuguese, 100
   Boiled, with Horseradish Walnut Sauce, 79
   Boiled, Miroton of, 69
   Bourguignonne, 58
   Braised in Beer, Belgian Style, 64
   with Braised Celery Hearts, 59
   Braised Rump of, Florentine, 83
   Brisket, with Balsamic Vinegar Sauce and Vegetables, 75
   en Daube, 60
   Deviled Short Ribs of, Gilly, 89
   Fillet of, Haché, Antoine Gilly, 52
   Fillet of, Michelangelo, Rick Canali's, 96
   Fillet, with Olives Tuscany, 93
   Fillets of, Pan-Broiled, 99
   Hung with a String, 78
   and Italian Sausage Patties, 48
   Liver, Baby, Paté of, 19
   Liver, Danish, with Watercress Sauce, 249
   à la Mode, 77
   Rib of, Caterer's, 82
   Roll, Foggia, Katherine Spadaccino's, 54
   Rolled, Stuffed, 80
   Round, Roast of, Coffee Braised, 82
   Rump Roast, with Creamy Caper Sauce, 88
   Salad, Cold, 66
   Short Ribs of, with Caper Lemon Sauce, 70
   Soufflé, 62
   (or Oxtail) Soup, 27
   Steak, Plaka, 63
   Stock, 29
   Stroganoff in Patty Shells, 65
   Stuffed, Rolled, 80
Beef, Barley, and Mushroom Soup, 28
Beefsteak Pommarola, 94
Beet Potato Soup, 34

Belgian Potatoes, 326
Belgian Style Beef, Braised in Beer, 64
Berrichonne Potatoes, 289
Bigos, 163
B. J. Guidetti's Stand-Up "Kiev" Nude Bakers, 368
Black Olive and Salami Crostata, 23
Black-Olive Veal Stew with Anchovies, 214
Blanquette of Veal, 210
Blue Cheese–Stuffed Burgers, 48
Boeuf à la Ficello, 78
Bogota Potatoes with Tomato-Cheese Sauce, 327
Boiled Beef with Horseradish Walnut Sauce, 79
Boiled Beef, Miroton of, 69
Boiled Dinner, French, 87
Bombay Puris, 288
Bordelaise Sauce, 69
Borscht, 30
Boudin Blanc, 206
Braciola, 80
Braised Andalusian Steak, 95
Braised Beef in Beer, Belgian Style, 64
Braised Celery, 60
Braised Lamb Shanks, Étienne Merle, 141
Braised Pork Ribs Cacciatora, 189
Braised Rump of Beef Florentine, 83
Braised Veal alla Perugia, Dora Radicchi's, 236
Braised Veal Shanks, 242
Breast of Veal Contadino, 237
Breast of Veal with Lemon Potatoes, 238
Breast of Veal Stuffed with Pork, Prosciutto, Sweetbreads, and Spinach, 239
Brisket Beef with Balsamic Vinegar Sauce and Vegetables, 75
Brisket of Corned Beef, Glazed, 84
Brisket Corned Beef with Herbed Vegetables, 85
Broccoli-Potato Pudding, 346
Broccoli-Potato Salad, 269
Broiled Dijon Pork Chops, 168
Broiled Herbed Lamb Kidneys, 248
Broth, Scotch, 40
Brown Sauce (for Beef Soufflé), 62
Brown Sauce (for Veal Fillets with Tomatoes), 222
Browned Potatoes, 292
Burgers, Blue Cheese–Stuffed, 48
Burgundian Potato-Leek Pie, 328

Cabbage, Stuffed, Eastern European, 113
Calf's Brains Contadina, 246
Calf's Brains with Green Olives and Capers, 246
Calf's Liver Soufflé, 252
Calf's Liver in Sour Cream, 250
Calf's Liver Veneziana, 251

Calf's Liver with White Vinegar, 251
Canali Sauce (for Fillet of Beef Michelangelo), 97
Candeur Steak, 102
Canelloni, Basic Batter for, 7
Canelloni, Chopped Beef, Ricotta, and Mozzarella, 8
Caper Lemon Sauce, 70
Caper Sauce, Creamy, 89
Caramelized Potatoes, 331
Carbonnades à la Flamande, 64
Carré de Porc Fumé à la Mandarin, 178
Carrot-Potato Pudding, 346
Carrots and Potatoes au Gratin, 322
Caterer's Rib of Beef, 82
Cauliflower Potato Puree, 316
Celery, Braised, 60
Champagne Potatoes, 331
Château Potatoes, 290
Cheese and Potato Soup, 36
Cheese and Tomato, Inca Spicy Potatoes with, 338
Chestnut Potato Puree, 314
Chile con Carne, First-Alert, 49
Chilled Mashed Potato Salad, 264
Chilled Potato Beet Soup, 34
Chopped Spinach, 255
Chorizo, 154
Chowder, Corn Potato, 37
Ciapotta, Vernon Jarratt's, 275
Cima alla Genovese, 239
Clams and Pork, Portuguese, 167
Coffee-Braised Round Roast of Beef, 83
Cold Veal with Tuna Sauce, 240
Copenhagen Sugared Potatoes, 332
Corn Potato Chowder, 37
Corned Beef Brisket with Herbed Vegetables, 85
Corned Beef, Glazed Brisket of, 84
Corned Beef Hash, 66
Costolette di Vitello alla Valdostana, 235
Cottage Fried Potatoes, 332
Couscous, Lamb with, 128
Cream Cheese Pastry with Herbs, 257
Cream Sauce for Fried au Gratin Potatoes, 336
Creamed Potatoes with Fresh Peas, 333
Creamed Potatoes au Gratin, 334
Creamy Caper Sauce, 89
Creamy Cheese Sauce, for Vegetable-Stuffed Baked Potatoes, 372
Creamy Tomato Sauce, 208
Crêpes, Basic Batter for, 7
Crisp Potato Cake, Swiss Style, 312
Crisp Puffed Potatoes, Indian Style, 288
Croustades, 193
Croutons, 33
Crown Roast of Pork, 179

Cucumber Potato Salad with Sour Cream and Dill Dressing, 270
Curried Potato Salad, 265
Curried Potatoes and Peas, 334
Curried Steak, 67
Curry of Lamb with Baked Bananas, 121
Curry Powder, 122
Czechoslovakian Potato Pudding, 336

Danish Beef Liver with Watercress Sauce, 249
Deep-Fried Cheese Potato Balls, 307
Deep-Fried Puff Pastry and Mashed Potato Balls, 303
Deviled Short Ribs of Beef, Gilly, 89
Diable, Sauce à la, 90
Diane, Steak, 105
Dijon Pork Chops, Broiled, 168
Dijon Potato Salad with Walnut Oil, 266
Dora Radicchi's Braised Veal alla Perugia, 236
Double Boiler Salad Dressing, 264
Double Racks of Lamb, 142
Duchesse Potatoes, 290
  Piping into Various Shapes, 291–2
  Glaze for, 291
  Shapes for: petites; pyramides; rosettes; longues; doigts; couronnes; petits pains; galettes, 291
Dutch Meat and Potato Soup, 31

Eastern European Stuffed Cabbage, 113
Edward T. Thompson's Watercress Sausage, 13
Émincé de Filet de Boeuf Sauce Bordelaise, 68
Émincé de Veau, 212
Étienne Merle's Braised Lamb Shanks, 141
Étienne Merle's Jarret d'Agneau Braisée, 141
Étienne Merle's Rack of Lamb, Persillé, 142

Fanny Graef's Veal Stew, 216
Fillet Mignon Marquis de Sade, see Filets Mignon, Antoine Gilly's
Filets Mignon, Antoine Gilly's, 97
Filet à la Antoine Gilly, 86
Fillets of Beef, Pan-Broiled, 99
Fillets of Veal with Kidneys, 224
First-Alert Chili con Carne, 49
Florentine Braised Rump of Beef, 83
Florette Sauce, 53
Four Spices, 22
Franconia Potatoes, 292
French Boiled Dinner, 87
French-Country-Style Stuffed Baked Potatoes, 365
French Fries, 293
  double frying of, 294
Fresh Tomato Sauce (for Steak), 94
Fricadelles Flamande, 155

Fried Potatoes au Gratin, 335
Fritters, Potato, 306

Garlic Potatoes, Spanish, 280
Garlicky Stuffed Bakers, 367
George Herz's Bacon-Pork Sausage, 156
German Caraway Meat Eggs, 50
German Lentil Soup, 32
German Potato Dumplings #1, 295
German Potato Dumplings #2, 296
German Potato Salad with Bacon, Hot, 266
German Sour-Cream Pancakes, 374
Gigot Roti Boulangère, 145
Glaze for Duchesse Potatoes, 291
Glazed Brisket of Corned Beef, 84
Glazed Lamb Roast, Lemon-Zested, 146
Glazed Orange Slices, 175
Gnocchi, 296
Golden Soup, Vernon Jarratt's, 42
Greek Lamb Sausages without Casings, 110
Greek Lamb Tidbits, 14
Greek Lemon Sauce, 116
Green Beans, Bacon, and Potatoes, Shirley Capp's, 330
Green Mashed-Potato Pancakes, 376
Gremolata for Osso Bucho, 243
Ground Ham and Pork Loaf with Mustard Sauce, 194

HAM
  and Asparagus Crêpes, 10
  Cornmeal Soufflé, 193
  Jack Daniel's–Glazed, 197
  Jambalaya, Lake Charles, 198
  à la King, 192
  Leek and Succotash Soup with Croutons, 33
  Leftover, and Saupiquet Sauce, 199
  Logs, Appetizer, 6
  Pennsylvania Dutch, 200
  or Pork Croquettes (or Ham and Pork), 195
  and Pork Loaf with Mustard Sauce, 194
  and Potato Cakes, 201
  with Scalloped Potatoes, 202
  Slices, Oporto, 196
  Smoked, Sheehans' Vermont, 200
  Sweetbread, and Oyster Pie, 256
  with White Wine, Port, and Cream, 196
Hamburger Steaks, 51
Hash, Corned Beef, 66
Hash-Stuffed Bakers, 368
Hashed Brown Potatoes with Vinegar, 297
Helen Renné's Pork Chops Mahón, 169
Herb Butter, 100
Herbed Pork Chops, 169
Herbed Potato Slices, 310
Hollandaise Sauce, 209
Hollandaise Sauce, Quick, 279
Horseradish Applesauce, 183

Horseradish Sauce, Hot, 88
Horseradish Sauce with Walnuts, 79
Hot German Potato Salad with Bacon, 266
Hot Horseradish Sauce (for Pot-au-Feu), 88
Hot Pot, Lancashire, 129
Hot Potato Salad with Balsamic Vinegar, 267
Hungarian Goulash Crêpes, 11
Hungarian Lamb and Pork, 124
Hungarian Lamb Soup, 34
Hungarian Lamb Stew, 125
Hungarian Veal Medallions, 226

Ichabod's Baked French-Fried Slices, 337
Idaho Potatoes Arrabbiata, 339
Inca Spicy Potatoes with Cheese and Tomato, 338
Involtini of Veal, 224
Irish Sausage and Potato Coddle, 157
Irish Stew, 126
Italian Fennel Pork Sausage, 158
Italian Potato Dumplings, 296
Italian Potato, Tomato, and Onion Casserole, 275
Italian Sausage and Beef Patties, 48
Italian Sausage Loaf, 159
Italian Sausage alla Pizzaiola, 159

Jack Daniel's–Glazed Ham, 197
Jambalaya Ham, Lake Charles, 198
Jerry's Low-Calorie Mock French Fries, 339
Jim Anelli's Porchetti, 177
John Petrokaitis's Potato Kugeli, 298
Julienne Potatoes Sautéed in Butter, 311

Katherine Spadaccino's Foggia Beef Roll, 54
Kibbeh, 112
Kidneys, Lamb, Broiled Herbed, 248
Kidney and Steak Pie with Oysters, 72
Kidneys with Veal Fillets, 224
Kidneys, Veal, Marsala, 247
Kidneys, Veal, with Parsley, 248
Kielbasa Snap-Ups, 14
Knockwurst, Pork Chops, and Sauerkraut, 172

Lake Charles Ham Jambalaya, 198
LAMB
    Athenian, with Chestnuts, 119
    Boneless Pieces, with Tarragon, 137
    Chops, Baked, with Mushrooms and Sour
        Cream, 136
    Chops in Tomato Sauce, 135
    with Couscous, 128
    Cubes with Okra, 128
    Curry, with Baked Bananas, 121
    Double Racks of, 142
    and Lamb-Kidney Pie, 126
    Leg of, Greek Style, 147
    Leg of, Parsleyed, Madeline Altman's, 148

LAMB (continued)
    Loaf, with Apple Slices, 114
    Navarin of, 132
    Paprikash, 131
    Patties, Pakistani, 118
    and Pork, Hungarian, 124
    Rack of, Persillé, of Étienne Merle, 142
    Roast, Glazed, Lemon-Zested, 146
    Roast Leg of, Boulangère, 145
    Roman Style, 144
    Sausages, Greek, without Casings, 110
    Sausage with Greek Lemon Sauce, 115
    Shanks with Acorn Squash, 144
    Shanks, Arabian, 140
    Shanks, Braised, Étienne Merle, 141
    Shanks in Red Wine, 139
    Soup, Hungarian, 34
    Steak with Grapes, 138
    Steak Véronique, 138
    Stew, Hungarian, 125
    Stew, Piraeus, 130
    Stuffed Leg of, Cooked with Port Wine, 149
Lancashire Hot Pot, 129
Leek, Ham, and Succotash Soup with Crou-
    tons, 33
Leek and Potato Casserole, 351
Leek-Potato Pie, Burgundian, 328
Leftover Ham with Saupiquet Sauce, 199
Leftover-Potato Pancakes, New England Style, 376
Leg of Lamb, Greek Style, 147
Leg of Lamb, Parsleyed, Madeline Altman's, 148
Leg of Lamb, Stuffed, Cooked with Port Wine, 149
Lemon Cream Sauce, 54
Lemon Dill Potatoes, 340
Lemon Potatoes, with Breast of Veal, 238
Lemon-Zested Glazed Lamb Roast, 146
Lentil Soup, German, 32
Lithuanian Pork Roast, 180
Liver, Calf's, Soufflé of, 252
Liver, Calf's, in Sour Cream, 250
Liver, Calf's, Veneziana, 251
Liver, Calf's, with White Vinegar, 251
Liver, Danish Beef, with Watercress Sauce, 249
Lleela's Madras Potato, Onion, and Tomato
    Mix, 340
Lleela's Potatoes with Yogurt, 341
Low-Calorie Mock French Fries, Jerry's, 339

Madeline Altman's Parsleyed Leg of Lamb, 148
Marrow Sauce, see Bordelaise Sauce
Mashed Baked Potatoes with Mushrooms, 300
Mashed Potato Mounds, see Duchesse
    Potatoes

Mashed Potato Salad, Chilled, 264
Mashed Potatoes, 313
Mashed Potatoes Amsterdam, with Sauerkraut, 315
Mashed Potato Balls and Deep-Fried Puff Pastry, 303
Mashed Potatoes with Cheese and Cream, 304
Mashed Potatoes with Eggs, 309
Mashed Potatoes au Gratin, 317
Mashed Potatoes with Scallions, 316
Matchstick, or Straw, Potatoes, 318
Meat Eggs, German Caraway, 50
Meat Loaf à la Turca, 116
Meat Loaf, Turkish, 116
Meat Patties, with Lemon Cream Sauce, 53
Meat and Potato Soup, Dutch, 31
Meatballs with Herbs, 17
Meatballs and Peas Cannelloni, 9
Meatballs, Pork, 39
Meatballs, Pork, with Vegetables, 155
Meatballs, Swedish, 56
Meatballs, Sweet and Sour Lamb, 18
Meatballs, Turkish, 57
Mina Thompson's Veal and Onions, Peppers, and Mushrooms, 218
Minute Steaks with Herb Butter, 99
Miroton of Boiled Beef, 69
Mørbrad, 180
Mornay Sauce, for Sweetbreads Florentine, 255
Moscow Mashed-Potato Cakes, 375
Moussaka with Zucchini, 117
Mozzarella, Ricotta, and Chopped Beef Canelloni, 8
Mushroom, Beef, and Barley Soup, 28
Mushrooms, Lamb-Stuffed, 16
Mushrooms, Onions Stuffed with Lamb and, 15
Mushroom and Potato Balls Coated with Almonds, 275
Mustard Potatoes, Viennese, 285
Mustard Sauce, for Ground Ham and Pork Loaf, 195
Mustard Sauce, for Rib of Beef, 82

Navarin of Lamb, 132
Noisettes d'Agneau à l'Estragon, 137
Norma Jean Maxwell's Buttered Bakers, 369

Olives, Black, and Salami Crostata, 23
Onion and Bacon Quiche, 12
Onion, Tomato, and Potato Casserole, Italian, 275
Onion, Tomato, and Potato Mix, Madras, Lleela's, 340
Onions Stuffed with Lamb and Mushrooms, 15
Orange Slices, Glazed, 175
Osso Bucho, 242

Oven Stew, 76
Oxtail (or Beef) Soup, 27
Oyster, Sweetbread, and Ham Pie, 256
Oysters, Steak and Kidney Pie with, 72

Pakistani Lamb Patties, 118
Pakistani Spicy Potatoes, 282
Palermo Pork Chops with Glazed Orange Slices, 174
Paprika Creamed Potatoes, 342
Paprikash Lamb, 131
Parmentier Soup, 35
Parsnip-Potato Custard, 278
Pasta and Sausage Soup, 39
Pastry, Cream Cheese, with Herbs, 257
Pastry for Potato-Leek Pie, 329
Pastry, Rich Salty, for Pork and Apple Pie, 167
Pastry Shell, for Scandinavian Veal Pie, 216
Pastry, for Steak and Kidney Pie, 73
Paté of Baby Beef Liver, 19
Paté of Veal, 20
Patties, Beef and Italian Sausage, 48
Patties, Meat, with Lemon Cream Sauce, 53
Peas, Fresh, with Creamed Potatoes, 333
Peas and Curried Potatoes, 334
Peas and Meatballs Canelloni, 9
Pennsylvania Dutch Ham, 200
Peppers, Pork-Stuffed, 161
Persian Red Potato Salad with Yogurt Dressing, 268
Peruvian Potatoes, 343
PIE
    Abruzzi Sausage and Potato, 157
    Burgundian Potato-Leek, 328
    Lamb and Lamb-Kidney, 126
    Pork and Apple, 166
    Sausage and Veal, 220
    Scandinavian Veal, 215
    Shepherd's, 134
    Steak and Kidney, with Oysters, 72
    Sweetbread, Oyster, and Ham, 256
Pig, Roast Suckling, 190
Pigs in a Poke, 369
Piraeus Lamb Stew, 130
Pizzaiola, Italian Sausage alla, 159
Plaka Beef Stew, 63
Poached Pork Loin with Horseradish Applesauce, 182
Polish Hunter's Stew, 163
Polish Potato Dumplings, 298
Polish Potato Puffs, 299
Polish Potatoes for Game Dishes, 343
Pommarola Beefsteak, 94
Pommes de Terre Amandine, 344
Pommes de Terre Marguerite, 300
Pommes de Terre Soufflées, 301
Porchetti, Jim Anelli's, 177

PORK
and Apple Pie, 166
Chops Dijon, Broiled, 168
Chops alla Doris Limoncelli, 175
Chops, Herbed, 169
Chops, Knockwurst, and Sauerkraut, 172
Chops, Loin, with Onion Sauce, 173
Chops, Mahón, Helen Renné's, 169
Chops, Palermo, with Glazed Orange Slices, 174
Chops and Sausage à la Boulangère, 176
Chops, Stuffed Loin, 170
Chops, with Winekraut, 190
and Clams, Portuguese, 167
(or Ham, or Pork and Ham) Croquettes, 195
Crown Roast of, 179
and Ham Loaf, with Mustard Sauce, 194
Hocks with Winekraut, 190
and Lamb, Hungarian, 124
Loin en Leche, 183
Loin, Poached, with Horseradish Apple-sauce, 182
Loin, Poached in Milk, 183
Loin Slices with Prunes, 185
Meatball and Swiss Chard Soup, 38
Meatballs, 39
Meatballs with Vegetables, 155
Medallions Jagd-Schloss Fuschl, 171
Ribs, Braised Cacciatore, 189
Roast, Glazed, with Applesauce, Slavic, 186
Roast, Lithuanian, 180
Roast Loin with Braised Red Cabbage, 186
Sausage, Italian Fennel, 158
Shoulder of, with Peppers, 187
Smoked Loin of, with Orange Slices, 178
Stew, Barbara and Richard Perry's, 165
Stuffed Peppers, 161
Tenderloin with Mushroom Dill Sauce, 184
Tenderloin Stuffed with Apricots and Apples, 180
Porkburgers, 150
Portuguese Beef Birds, 100
Portuguese Pork and Clams, 167
Portuguese Veal Birds, 100
POTATO (See also POTATOES)
Baked, Piroshki, 325
"Balloons," 301
Balls, Amandine, 275
Balls with Bacon and Onion, Sautéed, 289
Balls, Mashed, and Deep-Fried Puff Pastry, 303
Balls Sautéed in Butter, 317
Balls, Swiss, 283
Beet Soup, Chilled, 34
Blankets, Sausages in, 162
Broccoli Pudding, 346
Broccoli Salad, 269

POTATO (continued)
Cake, Crisp, Swiss Style, 312
Cake, with Skins, Quick, 356
Carrot Pudding, 346
Cauliflower Puree, 316
Cheese Balls, Deep-Fried, 307
Cheese Cakes, 377
Cheese Casserole, 314
Cheese, and Milk Casserole, 304
and Cheese Soup, 36
Chestnut Puree, 314
"Chops," Stuffed, 281
Coddle and Irish Sausage, 157
Cones, with Mushroom Sauce, 347
Corn Chowder, 37
Croquettes with Almonds, 344
Croquettes, Stuffed with Salami and Cheese, 348
Cucumber Salad, with Sour Cream and Dill Dressing, 270
Dumplings #1, German, 295
Dumplings #2, German, 296
Dumplings, Italian, 296
Dumplings, Polish, 298
Egg, and Cheese Casserole, 305
Fingers, Baked Parmesan, 326
Fingers, with Cheese and Spices, 349
Fritters, 306
and Ham Cakes, 201
Kugeli, John Petrokaitis's, 298
and Leek Casserole, 351
Leek Pie, Burgundian, 328
and Meat Soup, Dutch, 31
and Mushroom Balls Coated with Almonds, 275
Onion, and Tomato Mix, Lleela's Madras, 340
Pancakes, see POTATO PANCAKES
Parsnip Custard, 278
Patties Browned in Butter, 310
Pudding for Roast Reef, 351
Pudding, Czechoslovakian, 336
Puffs, Polish, 299
Ragoût, 279
Salad, Curried, 265
Salad, Dijon, with Walnut Oil, 266
Salad, Hot with Balsamic Vinegar, 267
Salad, Hot German, with Bacon, 266
Salad à la Lisbon, 272
Salad, Mashed, Chilled, 264
Salad, Persian, Red, with Yogurt Dressing, 268
Salad, Red, 269
and Sausage Pie, Abruzzi, 157
Slices, Herbed, 310
Soufflé, Athenian, 274
Stuffed Tomatoes, 271
Tomato and Onion Casserole, Italian, 275

POTATO (*continued*)
  and Tongue Salad, Asia Minor, 133
  Turnip Bake, 353
  Watercress Soufflé, 359
POTATO PANCAKES, 373
  Basic Recipe for, 374
  Cheese, 377
  German Sour-Cream, 374
  Green Mashed-Potato, 376
  Leftover-Potato, New England Style, 376
  Moscow Mashed, 375
  State of Maine, 377
  Zucchini, 378
POTATOES
  Accordion, 322
  Amsterdam, Mashed with Sauerkraut, 315
  with Anchovy Butter and Spinach, 345
  Anna, 302
  Antoine Gilly's Grandmother's, 337
  Antoine Gilly's Stuffed Baked, 367
  Austrian Paprika, 323
  Bacon-Flavored Roast, 324
  Baked, with Avocado Sauce, 362
  Baked, with Madras Spicy Yogurt Topping, 363
  Baked, Mashed, with Mushrooms, 300
  Baked, with Red Caviar and Sour Cream, 364
  Baked, with Sour-Cream Stuffing, 363
  Baked, Stuffed, French-Country-Style, 365
  Basil-Baked New, en Papillote, 365
  Beans, and Bacon, Shirley Capp's, 330
  Belgian, 326
  Berrichonne, 289
  B. J. Guidetti's Stand-Up "Kiev" Nude Bakers, 368
  Bogota, with Tomato-Cheese Sauce, 327
  à la Boulangère, 303
  in Broth and Cream, 308
  Browned, 292
  à la Camembert, 370
  and Carrots au Gratin, 322
  Caramelized, 331
  Champagne, 331
  Chantilly, 304
  Château, 290
  Copenhagen Sugared, 332
  Cottage Fried, 332
  Creamed, with Fresh Peas, 333
  Crisp, Puffed, Indian Style, 288
  Curried, and Peas, 334
  Dauphine, 303
  Dauphinoise, 304
  Delmonico, 305
  Franconia, 292
  French-Fried, 293
  Frigo, 350
  Garlicky Stuffed Bakers, 366

POTATOES (*continued*)
  au Gratin, Creamed, 334
  au Gratin, Fried, 335
  Hash-Stuffed Bakers, 358
  Hashed Brown, with Vinegar, 297
  Ichabod's Baked French-Fried Slices, 337
  Inca Spicy with Cheese and Tomato, 338
  Jerry's Low-Calorie Mock French Fries, 339
  Julienne, Sautéed in Butter, 311
  Lemon, with Breast of Veal, 238
  Lemon Dill, 340
  Lorette, 307
  Lyonnaise, 308
  Macaire, 310
  à la Maître d'Hôtel, 308
  Mashed, 313
  Mashed, with Cheese and Cream, 304
  Mashed, with Eggs, 309
  Mashed, with Scallions, 316
  Matchstick or Straw, 318
  Mont d'Or, 304
  Nanette, 310
  New, Baked, 362
  Norma Jean Maxwell's Buttered Bakers, 369
  O'Brien, 311
  and Onions, Baked in Broth, 303
  and Onions Sautéed in Butter, 308
  Paillasson, 311
  Paprika Creamed, 342
  Parma, 349
  with Peppers and Onion, 311
  Peruvian, 343
  Pigs in a Poke, 369
  with Pizzaiola Sauce, 352
  Polish, for Game Dishes, 343
  Red, with Quick Hollandaise Sauce, 278
  and Ricotta Cheese, 353
  Rissolé, 317
  Roasted, Aunt Edie's, 324
  Roquefort, 370
  Rösti, 312
  Saged, 355
  with Salt Pork, 354
  Savoyarde, 314
  Scalloped, with Ham, 202
  Shirley Capp's au Gratin, 329
  Shoestring and Vermicelli, 357
  Snow, 318
  Spanish Garlic, 280
  Spanish Parsley, 284
  Spicy Pakistani, 282
  Spicy, Sautéed in Butter and Olive Oil, 339
  and Spinach, Cochin Style, 276
  Spinach-Filled Baked, 371
  Steamed, with Caraway Seeds, 357
  Sticky, 355
  Swedish Anchovy, 358
  with Three Cheeses, 277

POTATOES (*continued*)
  Tiny New, alla Ralph Guidetti, 358
  Vegetable-Stuffed Baked, 372
  Wyoming Camp, 360
  with Yogurt, Lleela's, 341
Pot-au-Feu, 87
Provimi Veal Chops Provençale, 233
Pudding, Czechoslovakian Potato, 336
Pudding, Potato, for Roast Beef, 351
Pudding, Potato-Broccoli, 346
Pudding, Potato-Carrot, 346
Purée de Pommes de Terre, 313

Quatre Épicés, 22
Quiche, Canadian Bacon and Onion, 12
Quick Hollandaise Sauce, 279
Quick Potato Cake with Skins, 356

Racks of Lamb, Double, 142
Red Potato Salad, 264
Red Potato Salad, Persian, with Yogurt Dress-
  ing, 268
Red Potatoes with Quick Hollandaise Sauce,
  278
Rib of Beef, Caterer's, 83
Rib, Royal Standing, 90
Rick Canali's Fillet of Beef Michelangelo, 96
Ricotta, Chopped Beef, and Mozzarella Canel-
  loni, 8
Rissolé Potatoes, 311
Roast Leg of Veal, 243
Rossini Tournedos, 107
Round Roast of Beef, Coffee-Braised, 83
Royal Standing Rib, 90
Rump of Beef Florentine, Braised, 83
Rump Beef Roast with Creamy Caper Sauce,
  88
Rump Steaks Cooked in Beer, 101
Rumstecks Carbonnade à la Flamande, 101
Russian Veal Patties, 208

Saged Potatoes, 355
Salad, Asia Minor Tongue and Potato, 133
Salad, Cold Beef, 66
Salad Dressing, Double Boiler, 264
Salad Dressing, Sour Cream and Dill, 270
Salad Dressing for Tongue and Potato Salad,
  134
Salad Dressing, Yogurt, 268
Salami and Black Olive Crostata, 23
Salami and Cheese-Stuffed Potato Croquettes,
  348
Saltimbocca Romana, 223
SAUCES
  Balsamic Vinegar, for Beef Brisket, 76
  Béchamel, 196
  Bordelaise, 69

SAUCES (*continued*)
  Brown, 222
  Brown, for Beef Soufflé, 62
  Canali, 97
  Caper Lemon, 70
  Cream, 336
  Creamy Caper, 89
  Creamy Cheese, 372
  Creamy Tomato, 208
  à la Diable, 90
  Florette, 53
  Fresh Tomato, 94
  Greek Lemon, 116
  Hollandaise, 209
  Horseradish with Walnuts, 79
  Hot Horseradish, 88
  Lemon Cream, 54
  Lemon, Greek, 116
  Mornay, 255
  Mustard, 82, 195
  Quick Hollandaise, 279
  #1 for Sauerbraten, 92
  #2 for Sauerbraten, 92
  Saupiquet, 194
  Tuna, 241
  Velouté, 227
  Vinaigrette, 272
Sauerbraten, 91
Sauerkraut, Amsterdam, Mashed Potatoes with,
  315
Saupiquet Sauce, 199
SAUSAGE(S)
  American Country, 152
  Bacon-Pork, George Herz's, 156
  Greek Lamb, without Casings, 110
  Irish, and Potato Coddle, 157
  Italian, and Beef Patties, 48
  Italian Fennel Pork, 158
  Italian alla Pizzaiola, 159
  Lamb, with Greek Lemon Sauce, 115
  Loaf, Italian, 159
  and Pasta Soup, 39
  Pigs in a Poke, 369
  and Pork Chops à la Boulangère, 176
  in Potato Blankets, 162
  and Potato Pie, Abruzzi, 157
  in Red Wine, Burgundy Style, 164
  Spanish Spicy, 154
  Veal, 210
  and Veal Pie, 220
  White Veal, 206
Sautéed Potato Balls with Bacon and Onion,
  289
Scandinavian Veal Pie, 215
Scotch Broth, 40
Sheehans' Vermont Smoked Ham, 200
Shepherd's Pie, 134
Shirley Capp's au Gratin Potatoes, 329

Shirley Capp's Potatoes, Beans, and Bacon, 330
Shish Kebab, Armenian, 123
Shoestring Potatoes and Vermicelli, 357
Short Ribs of Beef with Caper Lemon Sauce, 70
Short Ribs of Beef Deviled, Gilly, 89
Shoulder of Pork with Peppers, 187
Sirloin with Cider, 71
Sirloin Steak Lyonnaise, 104
Sirloin Steak with Onions, 104
Slavic Pork Roast Glazed with Applesauce, 186
Smoked Ham, Sheehans' Vermont, 200
Smoked Loin of Pork with Orange Slices, 178
Snow Potatoes, 318
Soufflé, Athenian Potato, 274
Soufflé, Beef, 62
Soufflé of Calf's Liver, 252
SOUPS
  Alsatian, 26
  Beef (or Oxtail), 27
  Beef, Barley, and Mushroom, 28
  Beef Stock, 29
  Borscht, 30
  Chilled Potato Beet, 34
  Dutch Meat and Potato, 31
  German Lentil, 32
  Ham, Leek, and Succotash with Croutons, 33
  Hungarian Lamb, 34
  Parmentier, 35
  Pork Meatball and Swiss Chard, 38
  Potato and Cheese, 36
  Potato Corn Chowder, 37
  Sausage and Pasta, 39
  Scotch Broth, 40
  Veal Ragout, 41
  Vernon Jarratt's Golden, 42
  Vichyssoise, 42
  White Stock, 43
Sour Cream and Dill Dressing, 270
Spanish Garlic Potatoes, 280
Spanish Parsley Potatoes, 284
Spanish Spicy Sausage, 154
Spareribs, Barbecued, 188
Spicy Pakistani Potatoes, 282
Spicy Potatoes with Cheese and Tomato, Inca, 338
Spicy Potatoes, Sautéed in Butter and Olive Oil, 339
Spinach, Chopped, 255
Spinach-Filled Baked Potatoes, 371
Spinach with Potatoes and Anchovy Butter, 345
Spinach and Potatoes, Cochin Style, 276
State of Maine Potato Pancakes, 377

STEAK
  Andalusian, Braised, 95
  Candeur, 102
  with Crushed Peppercorns, 105
  Curried, 67
  Diane, 105
  with Fresh Tomato Sauce, 94
  and Kidney Pie with Oysters, 72
  Minute, with Herb Butter, 99
  au Poivre, 105
  with Red Wine Butter Sauce, 103
  Rump, Cooked in Beer, 101
  Sirloin with Cider, 71
  Sirloin Lyonnaise, 104
  Sirloin with Onions, 104
  Strip, with Gorgonzola "Sauce," 106
  Strips, with Sour Cream, 74
  Teriyaki, 92
Steamed Potatoes with Caraway Seeds, 357
STEW
  Black Olive Veal with Anchovies, 214
  Fanny Graef's Veal, 216
  Irish, 126
  Lamb, Hungarian, 125
  Oven, 76
  Piraeus Lamb, 130
  Polish Hunter's, 163
  Veal, Portuguese Style, 217
  Veal, with Tomatoes, Mushrooms, and Peas, 237
  Veal, with White Raisins, 219
Sticky Potatoes, 355
Stock, Beef, 29
Stock, White, 43
Straw or Matchstick Potatoes, 311
Strip Steak with Gorgonzola "Sauce," 106
Stroganoff Beef in Patty Shells, 65
Stuffed Leg of Lamb Cooked with Port Wine, 149
Stuffed Loin Pork Chops, 170
Stuffed Potato "Chops," 281
Stuffed Rolled Beef, 80
Stuffing for Crown Roast of Pork, 179
Succotash, Leek, and Ham Soup with Croutons, 33
Swedish Anchovy Potatoes, 358
Swedish Meatballs, 56
Sweet and Sour Lamb Meatballs, 18
Sweetbread, Oyster, and Ham Pie, 256
Sweetbreads Florentine, 254
Sweetbreads with Peas and Onions, 253
Swiss Chard, 38
Swiss Chard and Pork Meatball Soup, 38
Swiss Potato Balls, 283
Swiss Potato Torte, 283

Tenderloin Tips with Marrow Sauce, 68
Teriyaki Steak, 92

Tiny New Potatoes alla Ralph Guidetti, 358
Tomato, Onion, and Potato Casserole, Italian, 275
Tomato, Onion, and Potato Mix, Lleela's Madras, 340
Tomato Sauce, Creamy, 208
Tomato Sauce, Fresh, for Steak, 94
Tomato Sauce, Lamb Chops in, 135
Tomatoes, Potato-Stuffed, 271
Tongue and Potato Salad, Asia Minor, 133
Tournedos Rossini, 107
Tripe, Veal, with Tomatoes and Peas, 258
Trippa alla Romana, 258
Tuna Sauce for Cold Veal, 241
Turkish Meatballs, 57
Turkish Meat Loaf, 116
Turnip-Potato Bake, 353

VEAL
  Birds, Portuguese, 100
  Blanquette of, 210
  Breast of, with Lemon Potatoes, 238
  Breast of, Stuffed, with Pork, Prosciutto, Sweetbreads, and Spinach, 239
  Bundles, 224
  Chops Amandine, with Wine Sauce, 230
  Chops, with Bacon and Shallots, 232
  Chops, Provençale, Provimi, 233
  Chops, Romano, 234
  Chops, with Truffles or Mushrooms, 235
  Chops, with Vegetables and Wine, 233
  Cold, with Tuna Sauce, 240
  Cutlets with Chanterelles, 227
  Cutlets in Puff Pastry, 228
  Fillets, with Kidneys, 224
  Fillets, Park Imperial, 221
  Fillets, with Tomatoes, 221
  Involtini of, 224
  Kidneys, Marsala, 247
  Kidneys with Parsley, 248
  Loaf, with Tomato Sauce, 207
  Marengo, 213
  Medallions, Hungarian, 226
  with Onions, Peppers, and Mushrooms, Mina Thompson's, 218
  with Orange Juice and Marsala, 229
  Patties à la Russe, 208
  alla Perugia, Braised, Dora Radicchi's, 236
  Piccata, 230
  Pie, Scandinavian, 215

VEAL (continued)
  with Prosciutto and Mozzarella, 223
  Ragout Soup, 41
  Roast Leg of, 243
  Sausage, 210
  and Sausage Pie, 220
  Sausage, White, 206
  Scallops, Arance, 229
  Scallops with a Piquant Sauce, 230
  Shanks, Braised, 242
  Slices, in Cheese and Cream, 231
  Stew, with Anchovies, Black-Olive, 214
  Stew, Fanny Graef's, 216
  Stew, Portuguese Style, 217
  Stew, with Tomatoes, Mushrooms, and Peas, 237
  Stew, with White Raisins, 219
  Strips, with White Wine, 212
  Sultana, 219
  Tripe with Tomatoes and Peas, 258
Vegetables for Beef Brisket, 76
Vegetables, Herbed, with Brisket Corned Beef, 85
Vegetable-Stuffed Baked Potatoes, 372
Velouté Sauce, for Hungarian Veal Medallions, 227
Vermicelli and Shoestring Potatoes, 357
Vermont Smoked Ham, Sheehans', 280
Vernon Jarratt's Ciapotta, 275
Vernon Jarratt's Golden Soup, 42
Véronique Lamb Steak, 138
Vichyssoise, 42
Viennese Mustard Potatoes, 285
Vinaigrette Sauce, 272
Vinegar Sauce, Balsamic, for Beef Brisket, 76
Vitello Tonnato, 240

Watercress Potato Soufflé, 259
Watercress Sausage, Edward T. Thompson's, 13
White Pudding, 206
White Stock, 43
White Veal Sausage, 206
Wyoming Camp Potatoes, 360

Yogurt Salad Dressing, 268

Zucchini, Moussaka with, 117
Zucchini Potato Pancakes, 378